Denise C. Lewis

INTERGENERATIONAL AMBIVALENCES: NEW PERSPECTIVES ON PARENT-CHILD RELATIONS IN LATER LIFE

CONTEMPORARY PERSPECTIVES IN FAMILY RESEARCH

Series Editor: Felix M. Berardo

Recent Volumes:

2. CONCEPTUALIZING AND UNCOVERING INTERGENERATIONAL AMBIVALENCE

Kurt Lüscher

INTRODUCTION: NEW PERSPECTIVES ON AN OLD THEME

Intergenerational relations imply dealing with ambivalences. This thesis is what the contributions to this volume have in common. Yet, critics may claim that it is not a new insight. Among them are those who recall that some of the greatest sagas in Greek mythology depicted what we now refer to as ambivalence. Others may argue that the experience of ambivalence pervades everyday life. Adult children, for example, feel ambivalent about placing their elderly father or mother in a nursing home. Parents have mixed feelings about their child's living with a partner without an intention to marry and have children. A son's or a daughter's "coming out" as gay or lesbian is fraught with ambivalence on both sides.

Taking up ideas laid out by Lüscher and Pillemer (1998), Walker (2002) has initiated a debate in the *Journal of Marriage and Family*. Among the participants in favor of advancing the ambivalence perspective and research, Connidis and McMullin (2002a, b) make a strong case for a structural approach in a sociological and feminist perspective. Curran (2002) suggests further enriching this line of thought by bringing in fundamental economic considerations. Bengtson, Giarusso, Mabry and Silverstein (2002), long-term advocates of solidarity as a key tool for

Intergenerational Ambivalences: New Perspectives on Parent-Child Relations in Later Life
Contemporary Perspectives in Family Research, Volume 4, 23–62
© 2004 Published by Elsevier Ltd.
ISSN: 1530-3535/doi:10.1016/S1530-3535(03)04002-0

the study of intergenerational relations, argue that their multi-dimensional model of intergenerational relationships already covers, at least partially, what is meant by "ambivalence." The question then is: What can we gain by using this concept in contemporary theory and research? This basic issue leads to several sets of questions, around which I have chosen to organize this chapter.

I begin with the terminological issues. What does the term ambivalence *mean*? Is ambivalence just another word for conflict? Does it carry a negative connotation – in the sense of being undesirable? What are the different contexts in which the concept is useful and how are they interrelated? I would like to outline these terminological issues not only because conceptual clarification is always useful, but also, more importantly, because a closer look at the word as used in daily life and in different disciplines can be a source of productive/important insights.

Thus, although it may seem somewhat unfamiliar to research-oriented readers, I find it useful to begin by exploring briefly the origins and history of the term "ambivalence," and I will attempt to make a convincing case for the merits of this approach. Knowledge of the concept's history provides background for a broad view of its meanings as a cultural topic, as well as for selecting dimensions of ambivalence that are relevant for research. At the same time, we begin to set the stage for future interdisciplinary work. Also of interest is the odd fact that for several hundreds or even thousands of years, ambivalence has been a genuine human experience, yet the word itself was not coined until 1910. What does this say about its relevance in present times, often labeled as "postmodern?" In fact, the concept indeed plays a prominent role in postmodernist writings, as shown below.

I would even maintain that the challenge of ambivalence lies in its ambiguities. Donald N. Levine's stimulating book, *The Flight from Ambiguity* (1985), provides a solid basis for contending that insight into the ambiguity of a concept is what powers the development of new ideas. But in order for this driving force truly to function and advance our knowledge, we need guidelines for the formulation of specific hypotheses and for the development of research instruments.

This necessity leads to a set of questions about conceptualization: Could there be a more than accidental connection between the deeper meanings of the words "generation" and "ambivalence?" Do we have reasons to assume that intergenerational relations are especially prone to create or induce ambivalences, or to be permeated with them? Looking carefully into these questions soon reveals that the major issue about thinking in terms of ambivalence is not its "newness" as such, but rather the fruitfulness it displays by including all aspects of relationships and building bridges between disciplines.

Seeing its different meanings in different contexts and different disciplines provokes the question of what is common to the different notions of ambivalence

CONTEMPORARY PERSPECTIVES IN FAMILY RESEARCH
VOLUME 4

INTERGENERATIONAL AMBIVALENCES: NEW PERSPECTIVES ON PARENT-CHILD RELATIONS IN LATER LIFE

EDITED BY

KARL PILLEMER
Cornell University, Ithaca, NY, USA

KURT LÜSCHER
University of Konstanz, Germany

2004

ELSEVIER
JAI

Amsterdam – Boston – Heidelberg – London – New York – Oxford – Paris
San Diego – San Francisco – Singapore – Sydney – Tokyo

ELSEVIER Ltd
The Boulevard, Langford Lane
Kidlington, Oxford OX5 1GB, UK

Notice
No responsibility is assumed by the Publisher for any injury and/or damage to persons or property as a matter of products liability, negligence or otherwise, or from any use or operation of any methods, products, instructions or ideas contained in the material herein. Because of rapid advances in the medical sciences, in particular, independent verification of diagnoses and drug dosages should be made.

First edition 2004

A catalogue record from the British Library has been applied for.

ISBN: 0-7623-0801-X
ISSN: 1530-3535 (Series)

⊗ The paper used in this publication meets the requirements of ANSI/NISO Z39.48-1992 (Permanence of Paper).
Printed in The Netherlands.

CONTENTS

vi

LIST OF CONTRIBUTORS

Pauline Boss	Department of Family Social Science, University of Minnesota, USA
Bertram J. Cohler	The Committee on Human Development, Chicago, USA
Frank Fincham	Department of Psychology, University of Buffalo, USA
Karen L. Fingerman	Purdue University, Child Development & Family Studies, USA
Elizabeth Hay	Human Development and Family Studies, The Pennsylvania State University, USA
Lori Kaplan	Rush Alzheimer's Center, Chicago, USA
David M. Klein	Department of Sociology, University of Notre Dame, USA
Frieder R. Lang	Martin Luther University, Halle-Wittenberg, Germany
Frank Lettke	Universität Konstanz, Fachbereich Geschichte und Soziologie, Germany
Dagmar Lorenz-Meyer	Centre for Gender Studies, Department of Social Work, Faculty of Philosophy, Charles University, Czech Republic
Kurt Lüscher	Universität Konstanz, Fachbereich Geschichte und Soziologie, Germany
Gregory R. Maio	School of Psychology, Cardiff University, Cardiff, UK
Francesca Giorgia Paleari	Catholic University, Milan, Italy

PREFACE

This fourth volume of our series on Contemporary Perspectives in Family Research addresses timely and pressing issues concerning intergenerational relations among adults within families. As our guest editors note, there has been a dramatic rise in research interest in this area, spurred in part by large scale demographic trends. Prominent among these are world-wide increases in longevity, which in turn have noticeably extended the shared lifetimes of generations. This rise in living multi-generational families and their member interactions have led to renewed discussions and debates regarding norms of filial responsibility and a resurging interest in changing patterns of kin assistance, among several other issues treated in this volume.

Contributors to the present volume represent the efforts of a network of scholars with a history of interdisciplinary collaboration. They seek to bring greater understanding of intergenerational relations by exploring conceptual approaches that help integrate the accumulating research findings on various dimensions of ambivalence in different contexts. Drawing on a variety of social scientific theories, this group of international scholars define and adopt a framework that posits ambivalence as a key organizing concept for studying and comprehending multi-generational ties. Indeed, as the chapters in this volume demonstrate, intergenerational ambivalence can be a particularly fruitful paradigm for grasping the complex intricacies of parent-child relations, especially those which occur among families in later life.

Academic gerontologists as well as practitioners should find this innovative approach particularly useful in understanding issues related to family and aging. Moreover, they will find that each chapter also raises a number of questions or further exploration by future investigators. The answers to those questions have not only theoretical but applied and policy implications as well. In a very real sense, then, the contributors have laid out a heuristic blueprint for the years ahead. For that alone, they are to be congratulated.

Felix M. Berardo
Series Editor

1. INTRODUCTION: AMBIVALENCE IN PARENT-CHILD RELATIONS IN LATER LIFE

Karl Pillemer and Kurt Lüscher

> Long before the term was coined, [the] experience of ambivalence – of being pulled in psychologically opposed directions – had of course been endlessly noted . . . . It could scarcely be otherwise. No observer of the human condition could long fail to note the gross facts of mingled feelings, mingled beliefs, and mingled actions. He had only to look inward at his own psyche or outward at the behavior of others.
>
> Robert Merton and Elinor Barber

Interest in intergenerational relations among adults has grown dramatically in recent years. Indeed, the amount of empirical work on this topic has made it one of the more vigorous research areas in contemporary social science. This interest corresponds to new demographic realities: increases in the life span have greatly lengthened the shared lifetimes of generations, and many adult children can look forward to continued relationships with their parents until well into the children's middle age. Although concerns about the weakening of intergenerational ties are frequently expressed, the evidence demonstrates the continued importance and influence of these linkages (Lüscher, 1997; Pillemer & Suitor, 1998) even after the parents' deaths (Shmotkin, 1999).

Against this background, it is not surprising that considerable effort has been spent on describing the demographic structure of parent-child relations in later life and the amount and type of contact, interaction, and exchanges between the generations. Indeed, the literature contains an abundance of empirical insights, based on large-scale surveys and longitudinal studies, as well as hundreds of small-scale interview and case studies. Some observers, however, have expressed

Intergenerational Ambivalences: New Perspectives on Parent-Child Relations in Later Life
Contemporary Perspectives in Family Research, Volume 4, 1–19
© 2004 Published by Elsevier Ltd.
ISSN: 1530-3535/doi:10.1016/S1530-3535(03)04001-9

the concern that the development of new conceptual approaches to integrate the host of findings has not kept up with empirical productivity. Indeed, the field has been aptly characterized as "data-rich and theory-poor."

The relative paucity of conceptual work has led to a variety of apparent "paradoxes of family and aging" (Bengtson, Rosenthal & Burton, 1995; Rosenmayr, 1992, 1998). Without renewed development of conceptual frameworks in the field, which are sensitive to the ambiguities in scientific work (Levine, 1985), it is difficult to interpret seemingly contradictory findings. Further, a lack of new theoretical approaches can lead to stagnation in the field. Awareness of this situation has prompted sociologists and psychologists to search for models that capture the complexity of relationships between older parents and adult children, as they are played out under contemporary social conditions (Blieszner, Usita & Mancini, 1996; Connidis, 2001; Fingerman, 2001a, b; Lye, 1996).

Over the past several years, an innovative framework for understanding parent-child relationships in later life has emerged from work in several disciplines in the United States and Europe. This framework draws on sociological, psychological, and anthropological theory and research that highlight *ambivalence* as a key organizing concept for the study of intergenerational relations. This perspective appears to be a promising approach to the study of families in later life, and interest in it has been growing (Connidis & McMullin, 2002; Curran, 2002; Daatland & Herlofson, 2001).

The present volume is the result of the joint activity of an organized international group of scholars concerned with intergenerational ambivalence. The book's goal is to provide both conceptual and methodological background for the study of intergenerational ambivalence, as well as to offer a number of empirical examples inspired by this concept.

BACKGROUND OF THE VOLUME

Every book has its unique history. Our own interest in intergenerational ambivalence developed in discussions during Karl Pillemer's sabbatical in 1996 at the University of Konstanz Research Center on Society and the Family. Despite using different methods, samples, and research frameworks, both of us had come up with findings about intergenerational relations that could not be interpreted easily within existing theoretical frameworks. Kurt Lüscher's study of family reorganization after older parents' divorce pointed toward complex tensions between interpersonal closeness and distance, and between a desire to preserve traditional family forms and to strike out in new directions (Lüscher & Pajung-Bilger, 1998). Similarly, Lüscher's work on family rhetoric (Lüscher, 2000) and on contemporary families (Lüscher, 1998) suggested the limitations of existing frameworks in these areas. Karl Pillemer's research on elder mistreatment had revealed the paradoxical circumstance that extreme conflict and a high degree of solidarity coexist in abusive families (Pillemer & Suitor, 1992; Pillemer & Wolf, 1998; Wolf & Pillemer, 1997) and his studies of parent-child relationships had pointed to the prevalence of interpersonal conflict and unmet expectations (Pillemer & Suitor, 1998; Suitor & Pillemer, 1988, 1996) as well as their negative impact on parental well-being (Pillemer & Suitor, 1991).

To better encompass the family complexity these findings implied, we collaborated on a qualitative study of within-family differences in parent-child relations in later life, interviewing elderly parents in depth about each of their adult children. In the course of that study, we became increasingly aware of the simultaneous presence of positive and negative assessments of each individual relationship. We also noted a marked contrast between the global assessments of relationships provided by conventional closed-ended questions, and the complex interplay of intimacy and upset that was evident in narrative responses. To provide a simple example, a parent's choice of the answer category "somewhat close" on a measure of the parent-child relationship might actually reflect: feelings of attachment based on early childhood experience, greater estrangement in adulthood, worry about the child's marital choice, desire for more contact, and a feeling of being taken advantage of by requests for financial assistance.

We became increasingly persuaded that our findings (and those of a number of other scholars) did not fit easily into existing paradigms and frameworks. In particular, we noted that qualitative studies of parent-adult child relations often identified mixed feelings as common occurrences. To give only a few examples, immigrant Jewish parents were found both to promote occupational mobility and to deeply regret the lack of contact with children which resulted from moves (Myerhoff, 1980); caregiving children found themselves caught between conflicting norms of reciprocity and intergenerational solidarity (George, 1986); and mothers and adult daughters struggled with competing desires for autonomy and dependency (Cohler & Grunebaum, 1981). Although such studies are based on in-depth analysis of a small number of cases, it seemed likely that larger-scale survey research would also uncover ambivalence around these and similar issues. Over time, we became convinced that ambivalence provides a highly useful conceptual framework within which to develop empirical studies and to interpret research findings regarding parent-child relations in later life.

With funding from the Transcoop Program of the Alexander von Humboldt Foundation, it was possible to create the infrastructure for a network of scholars interested in ambivalence in parent-child relations. Many of the ideas that are developed in the chapters in this volume were discussed and refined in two international conferences on intergenerational ambivalence. An important task has been the development of both theoretical ideas and empirical measurement strategies. What unites the authors in the present volume is their central interest in applying ambivalence – and closely related concepts such as contradictions, dilemmas, paradox, and ambiguity – to the field of intergenerational relations. The overall goal of this volume is to explore the promise of the ambivalence perspective to improve understanding of parent-child relations in later life in various contexts and domains.

AMBIVALENCE: A NEGLECTED TOPIC IN INTERGENERATIONAL FAMILY RESEARCH

It may seem surprising to some readers that researchers on the aging family have not pursued the topic of ambivalence. This fact is indeed extraordinary, given the apparent universality of the experience of positive and negative feelings in parent-child relations. Literature (von Matt, 1995), theater (from *King Lear* to *Death of a Salesman*), and film have portrayed parent-child relationships as a complex web of positive and negative emotions and thoughts. A vast body of self-help literature also highlights mixed feelings toward parents (and especially mothers), and suggests ways children can resolve them (cf. Cleese & Bates, 2001; Cohen & Cohen, 1997; Secunda, 1991).

The almost proverbial aspect of parent-child ambivalence is evident throughout popular culture. Many prime-time television shows now include an elderly parent whose involvement in the family life of an adult child is a source of both support and stress (and of course comic relief). Comic strips also portray the mingled experience of affection and irritation experienced by parents and offspring, as indicated by the line *Cathy* creator Cathy Guisewaite provided for her character: "The story of a mother's life: Trapped between a scream and a hug." The humorist Erma Bombeck, whose writing career was in part based on portraying family life as joyous and disappointing in equal measure, made the point succinctly: "No mother is all good or all bad, all laughing or all serious, all loving or all angry. Ambivalence rushes through their veins."

Despite this history of acknowledgement and acceptance of ambivalence, until very recently the concept of ambivalence has never been employed explicitly and systematically in research on intergenerational relations in later life. Prior to work published in the late 1990s (Lüscher & Pillemer, 1998), no empirical study had directly addressed this issue. (Indeed, a review of publication databases in the social sciences in 1997 did not uncover a single published empirical article in English on parent-adult child relations that employed the term "ambivalence" as a keyword.)

Thus, it was clear that social scientists were not considering a phenomenon – ambivalence – that lies at the heart of contemporary relations between older parents and their adult children.

MOVING BEYOND DUALISTIC APPROACHES

Why has the study of ambivalence in intergenerational relations not been pursued? It is likely that efforts to create new models for understanding intergenerational relations are hindered by a deeply ingrained tendency toward what one might call *historically* dualistic thinking regarding the aging process in general, and the family life of older persons in particular. In his groundbreaking cultural history of aging in America, Cole (1992) sums up this predominant theme as follows: "Since the early nineteenth century, American culture has characteristically oscillated between attraction to a 'good' old age ... and repulsion from a 'bad' old age" (p. 237). To advance knowledge and understanding of aging, Cole asserts, requires "a new and integrated appreciation of aging that transcends our historical tendency to split old age into positive and negative poles."

either or notions of age

Such dualistic thinking pervades not just analyses of aging, but also of family life throughout the life course. As the historian Harvey Graff (1995) has noted, views of adolescents reflect this duality:

> The young may be well-adjusted or maladjusted, conformist or rebellious, and so on. These conceptions allow for little diversity among either the young themselves or the ways in which they grow, the lines they follow in their transitions through childhood, adolescence, and youth to maturity. Regardless, powerful expectations, theories, laws, and policies are constructed around them, sometimes with high human and social costs (p. 17).

It has been noted that the tendency to vacillate between positive and negative assessments of the family in later life has found its way into policy discussions (Filipp & Mayer, 1999). As Lüscher (2000) has pointed out, public "family rhetoric" (including political statements and media portrayals) typically points toward either an idealization of the family or its imminent deconstruction. Thus, researchers must overcome a burden of "either/or" tendencies in thinking both about the aging process and about family life.

There is compelling evidence of dualistic thinking in the study of intergenerational relations in later life. A long research tradition has demonstrated deeply rooted patterns of enduring intergenerational contact, intimate emotional ties, and mutual assistance in contemporary society (Litwak, 1965; Shanas et al., 1968; Sussman, 1959). Since the early 1970s, Bengtson and colleagues have conducted a very productive and influential research program on the structure, determinants, and consequences of what they have termed "intergenerational solidarity" (cf. Bengtson, 2001; Bengtson & Harootyan, 1994; Roberts, Richards & Bengtson, 1991; Silverstein & Bengtson, 1997). Research in this dominant tradition has emphasized shared values across generations, normative obligations to provide help, and enduring ties between parents and children. Other researchers have employed the solidarity perspective in the United States (cf. Rossi & Rossi, 1990), as well as in Europe (Attias-Donfut, 1995; Kohli & Künemund, 2000).

However, another research tradition exists that appears to be at variance with the solidarity perspective. It would not be accurate to say that there is a clearly defined "conflict" perspective that is an alternative to the solidarity framework. However, several streams of research have pointed consistently to structural conflicts between the generations (Cohler, 1983; Connidis & McMullin, 2002; Finch & Mason, 1993; Foner, 1984; Sprey, 1991) that are manifested in difficult or distant interpersonal relationships. Researchers with this orientation have focused on intergenerational family problems such as isolation from kin, caregiver stress, troubled relationships, interpersonal conflict, and abuse (Lüscher & Pillemer, 1998).

Thus, as Marshall and colleagues (1993) have succinctly put it, "the substantive preoccupations in gerontology over the past 30 years point to a love-hate relationship with the family" (p. 47). The state of the field of parent-child relations in later life could be characterized as having a dominant theme – intergenerational solidarity – and an array of minor motifs, all of which point to family problems, alienation, and weakened ties. It is a premise of the present volume that this "love-hate relationship" is impossible to resolve, for one fundamental reason.

Specifically, we would argue that the vacillation in gerontology between a focus on conflict, abuse, and neglect on one hand, and reports of support and intimacy on the other, are not two sides of an academic argument that will eventually be resolved in favor of one side or the other. In contrast, we propose that societies, and the individuals within them, are characteristically ambivalent about relationships between parents and children in adulthood. That is, rather than being formed on a basis of solidarity, or being under imminent threat of conflict or dissolution, the social dynamics of intergenerational relations among adults revolve around sociological and psychological *contradictions or dilemmas* and their management in day-to-day family life.

Scholars from a variety of orientations have recently begun to support this view, arguing that to understand the quality of parent-child relations, studies must begin to incorporate *both* positive and negative elements in a single study. For example, Fingerman (1998) posits that both loyalty and upset can characterize the parent-adult child relationship. Blieszner, Usita and Mancini (1996) suggest that research should move beyond the focus on "nurturant and affectionate" aspects of parent-child interaction to take into consideration both the beneficial and the undesirable aspects of these relationships (see also Boss, 2000; Henwood & Coughlin, 1993). Similarly, Clarke et al. (1999) and Bengtson et al. (2002) argue that studies should address the balance between solidarity and conflict in intergenerational relations.

The ambivalence perspective takes this range of evidence into account by its focus on deeply ingrained contradictions in family life, and attempts to approach them in a systematic, empirical way. That is, the concept of ambivalence provides legitimacy for studying dilemmas and contradictions in late-life families; indeed, it moves them into the foreground and suggests that they should be the primary topic of study. The research goal becomes not one of establishing the extent and correlates of solidarity on the one hand or conflict on the other. Instead, the aim is to examine the interplay of solidarity and conflict in families and the way in which this interplay is accomodated and managed. Further, the approach points to the need for new methods and measures that are appropriate for the study of ambivalence.

DIMENSIONS OF INTERGENERATIONAL AMBIVALENCE

Based on these arguments, the contributions in the present volume explore ambivalence as an orientation for social science research on intergenerational relations. It is the premise of this book that ambivalence, although not reaching the status of a formal theory, is a highly useful "general orientation" (Aldous, 1990) to the subject of intergenerational relationships. In Blumer's (1969) terms, ambivalence can serve as a "sensitizing concept" to guide research. As such, the ambivalence perspective can orient researchers in their empirical investigations and suggest the types of variables that studies should consider. Further, ambivalence can serve as a research construct to guide specific studies. Under these circumstances, it is not surprising that the contributors to this volume have somewhat different understandings of the concept of ambivalence. Over time, the perspective is likely to become more clearly articulated and the field of study more integrated. An approach to elucidating the theoretical background and implications of the ambivalence concept appears in Chapter 2 of this volume.

The available literature suggests that one can distinguish two interconnected dimensions of ambivalence that are highly relevant to the study of intergenerational relations: sociological ambivalence, which is evident in social structural positions, and psychological ambivalence, which is experienced on the individual level. We believe that both of these dimensions are important to the study of parent-child relations in adulthood. Based on this premise, we have organized this volume around contributions that examine one or both of two dimensions: (a) contradictions at the level of social structure, evidenced in institutional resources and requirements, such as statuses, roles, and norms; and (b) contradictions at the subjective level, in terms of cognitions, emotions, and motivations. These contradictions or dilemmas are interpreted as not being reconcilable, at least temporarily, with one another. Further, we suggest the use of ambivalence as a neutral term for the analysis of intergenerational relations. That is, ambivalences are to be seen as a fact of social life and should not be assumed a priori to be negative or pathological.

not negative [handwritten margin note]

SOCIOLOGICAL AMBIVALENCE

Several lines of theorizing and research support the notion of sociological ambivalence. Sociological ambivalence was given its first formulation in an article by Merton and Barber (1963) and in Coser's (1966) expansion of their argument. In Merton and Barber's view, sociological ambivalence focuses on "incompatible normative expectations of attitudes, beliefs, and behavior" (pp. 94–95). These incompatible expectations may be assigned to or incorporated into a particular status (or set of statuses) within a society or even within a single role of a single status. In this way, "the core-case of sociological ambivalence puts contradictory demands upon the occupants of a status in a particular relation" (p. 96).

incompatible expectations [handwritten margin note]

Sociological ambivalence in this perspective refers to "opposing normative tendencies in the social definition of a role" (p. 99). Thus, as Coser notes, sociological ambivalence is "built into the structure of statuses and roles" (p. 175). This perspective encourages social scientists to examine social roles not only in terms of their dominant attributes (which, we would note, has been the case in the study of intergenerational relations), but rather as a dynamic organization of norms and counter-norms that in combination produce ambivalence. Ambivalence results when these norms require contradictory attitudes and actions.

Support for the notion of sociological ambivalence comes from studies of family history, which characteristically have pointed to core societal dilemmas that affect family life. A recurring theme in historical research is the structural conflict between parents' control of resources on the one hand, and social norms that fostered children's desire for freedom from parental authority on the other. For example, in a study of father-son relations in ancient Greece, Strauss (1993) found that the position of fathers in Athens toward their adult sons was one of structural ambivalence regarding inheritance and dependency of children. Studies of European family history show intense contradictions between respect for the elderly and conflict over property relationships (Stearns, 1986). Similarly, colonial American history shows the pattern of children's desire for independence on one hand, and parental control of property on the other (Demos, 1986; Graff, 1995; Mintz & Kellogg, 1988). In sum, the preponderance of family historical research shows that intergenerational relations are characterized by both conflict *and* cohesion (Ehmer, 2000; Foner, 1986). Plakans's contribution to this volume uses a historical approach to intergenerational ambivalence (Chapter 3).

In social science, feminist scholarship has highlighted sociological ambivalence in family life. Feminist theory challenges the assumption that a harmony of interests exists among all members of a family. Thus, feminist scholars' treatment of a variety of issues, from reproductive control to household division of labor and parenthood, have alerted us to fundamental (and not entirely resolvable) conflicts within contemporary families (Thorne, 1992). Ferree (1990) notes that the feminist approach to the family involves a critique of the concept of solidarity, by which is meant "the conventional conceptualization of 'the family' as a unitary whole" (p. 867). When the notion of an undifferentiated "family interest" and the conventional view of family unity are challenged, internal contradictions can take center stage. Research evidence of ambivalence comes from the feminist literature on household labor (DeVault, 1991; Thorne, 1992) and on women's caregiving activities (Abel & Nelson, 1990). Connidis and McMullin (2002) merge critical and feminist theory in proposing a social structural approach to intergenerational ambivalence. Thus, feminist research suggests that sociological ambivalence permeates family relations, particularly for women. The contribution to this volume by Lorenz-Meyer represents work in this tradition.

Although not explicitly using the term "ambivalence," other contemporary theorists have also pointed to structural dilemmas that create ambivalence. For example, James Coleman's (1990) approach emphasized a distinction between the family and "corporate actors," such as businesses, voluntary associations, labor unions, and the state. Coleman proposes that structural incompatibilities exist between the new corporate actors in the modern world and the family. In his view, the demands of the family are strongly counterbalanced throughout the life course by the demands of corporate actors, especially as expressed in the pressures of the job market. The individual, as a member of a family, is called upon to act responsibly on behalf of economically or physically dependent members at certain points in the life course. However, the person who responds to the family's demands is also embedded in, and affected by, the pressures of corporate actors. When corporate actors make their most serious demands (for example, the need to move away from a frail parent in order to be employed by such an organization), it is likely that intergenerational ambivalence will be heightened. This dilemma has been emphasized in research on conflicts between work and family throughout the life course (cf. Moen, 2003; Pillemer & Moen, 2000).

PSYCHOLOGICAL AMBIVALENCE

Moving from the sociological level, ambivalence also has been used to describe the psychological experience of individuals. Within recent sociological thought, ambivalence on the individual level has received some attention in the literature on the sociology of emotions. A detailed discussion is offered by Weigert (1991), who expands the definition of the term to "the experience of contradictory emotions toward the same object" (p. 21). According to Weigert, ambivalence also can be observed in individual motivations, that is, "simultaneous attraction to and repulsion from pursuing a particular line of action" (p. 19). In everyday speech, the term has this connotation of holding two contradictory emotions, motivations, or values at the same time.

Two bodies of literature on intergenerational relations focus on psychological ambivalence. First, the clinical psychological and psychiatric literature on parent-child relations has portrayed this relationship as ambivalent. For Bleuler (1911), who originated the term, Freud (1913), and later psychoanalysts (see Eidelberg, 1968; Otscheret, 1988; Rycroft, 1973), both normal and pathological individuals are described as experiencing simultaneous feelings of love and hate toward parents throughout the life course. Erikson's (1994) epigenetic theory of psychosocial development has ambivalence at its core. Conflicts between two countervailing tendencies (for example, autonomy vs. shame in children) lead to the next stage of development, and are shaped by relations between parents and children. Contemporary clinical accounts also portray intergenerational relationships as generators of ambivalent feelings (Parker, 1995; Rubin, 2000; Sincoff, 1990). The chapters in this volume by Boss and Kaplan, by Cohler, and by Segal demonstrate insights gained by merging clinical and empirical research perspectives.

Second, recent developments in social psychology suggest that studying ambivalence in intergenerational relations will be fruitful. Specifically, a rapidly growing field within empirical social psychology is the study of *ambivalent attitudes*. In studying attitudes in a wide variety of domains (for example, race relations), these researchers have reacted to a traditional view, which held that attitudes should be conceived of as bipolar (Bell, Esses, & Maio, 1996; Priester & Petty, 1996). This theory and research holds instead that attitudes typically contain both positive and negative components at the same time – that is, they are ambivalent (Jonas, Diehl & Broemer, 1997). Therefore, it becomes a key scientific task to separate the positive and negative aspects of attitudes, and to explore whether such positive and negative evaluations are sometimes positively related to one another. In the field of intergenerational relations, it is possible (and even likely) that an attribute such as parental concern or children's drive for greater independence would elicit both positive and negative emotions and evaluations. Chapters in this volume by Pillemer and by Maio and colleagues employ insights raised by this social psychological line of research.

In sum, several bodies of literature suggest that ambivalence can be a key concept in understanding family relationships in later life and can significantly advance our understanding of this issue. To date, however, ambivalence has not been employed as a general approach to the study of intergenerational relationships. This volume addresses on a fundamental level the questions: Why focus on ambivalence in the study of parent-child relations in later life? How can employing ambivalence as an organizing concept for research advance scientific knowledge about parent-child relations? Ultimately, the issue is an empirical one. What does the research show about the dynamics of actual intergenerational relationships among adults? Do they reflect fundamental ambivalences, and if so, what are the causes and consequences of such ambivalences? This volume's goal is to shed light on these and related issues.

OVERVIEW OF CONTRIBUTIONS

This book is divided into four major sections. Part I provides a broad conceptual overview of intergenerational ambivalence and includes an analysis of historical evidence of ambivalence in parent-child relations. Part II begins with an overview of measurement issues of importance to research on intergenerational ambivalence and includes three empirical chapters that assess the extent and the correlates of ambivalent attitudes and feelings in parent-child relationships. Part III examines ambivalence in the specific context of providing care to dependent family members. Part IV extends the intergenerational ambivalence perspective to young adults and middle-aged parents.

Kurt Lüscher opens Part I with a discussion of the historical and contemporary context of the current interest in intergenerational ambivalence. He provides a focused review of the origins of the term in psychiatry and psychoanalysis and its later uses in family therapy and in sociological and psychological theory and research, as well as in other disciplines. Possible definitions of ambivalence are discussed and an operational definition is described and justified. Lüscher then provides a schematic model of intergenerational ambivalence. This model incorporates an institutional dimension and a personal dimension. It encourages investigators to examine different strategies for dealing with ambivalences, depending on whether the behaviors and actions are closer to one or the other pole on both dimensions.

The chapter by Andrejs Plakans assesses historical research, drawn for the most part from European social history, in which operative customs and individual and family interests generated ambivalent generational relationships that required "solutions" for the survival or well-being of the group. In familial situations, ambivalence arose when the enactment of roles ceased to operate smoothly (solidarity) because of some structural alteration, but did not reach full antagonism between family members (conflict). Although historical sources document how such situations were handled at the familial level in ways that seemingly kept them from becoming conflictual, the same sources indicate that the resolutions did not dispel continuing feelings of injustice and of having been treated unfairly. Such resolutions, in other words, never successfully removed ambiguity and ambivalence from potentially conflictual social situations.

In Part II, Frank Lettke and David Klein begin by reviewing the literature on measurement of ambivalence. They argue that operationalization has to take into consideration different dimensions of ambivalence, different contexts, and the different perspectives of family members as well as of social scientists. Lettke and Klein then critically review attempts to operationalize ambivalences. Using examples from a survey on the topic, they illustrate direct and indirect measures of intergenerational ambivalence. They also show how the concept of ambivalence can be applied to existing instruments in family research. They conclude with recommendations for future development of measures for research on intergenerational relations and suggestions for their application and continued improvement.

Karl Pillemer presents data from a study of 189 mothers aged 60 and over that examined ambivalence regarding the quality of parents' relationships with adult children. Both direct and indirect measures of ambivalence were used to address two research questions. First, what is the prevalence of ambivalent assessments of the parent-adult child relationship? Second, what factors are correlated with such ambivalence? Ambivalence was uncovered in a number of domains of parent-child relationships. In addition, ambivalence in parent-child relations was strongly associated with several variables, including unequal exchange of assistance, value similarity, and educational attainment. Higher ambivalence toward children was correlated with greater negative affect.

Karen Fingerman and Elizabeth Hay examine ambivalence between parents and children in the context of the larger social network and consider whether individuals experience more ambivalence in this relationship than in other relationships. In addition, this chapter considers age differences in these patterns. A total of 187 participants, ranging in age from 13 to 99, completed separate diagrams of their close and their problematic social contacts. Diagrams were examined for three types of relationships: relationships that were listed solely as positive, relationships that were listed solely as problematic, and relationships that were considered to be both positive and problematic (ambivalent). When ambivalence is assessed across the social network, it is clear that parents and offspring do evoke a sense of mixed feelings, even at a global level. This relationship is not necessarily the most ambivalent tie throughout life; rather, the nature of the ambivalence in this tie appears to be distinct and does not stem from issues arising in the context of a shared residence. The authors argue that factors that make the parent-child tie distinct from other social ties, and the changes that parents and offspring incur as they grow older, warrant additional research attention.

Kurt Lüscher and Frank Lettke conclude this section with a report on new research findings from a survey of intergenerational ambivalence conducted by researchers at the University of Konstanz, Germany. A total of 124 respondents were interviewed (approximately 60% were parents and 40% were adult children). Findings are presented concerning the assessment of intergenerational ambivalence from the perspective of the children and from the perspective of the parents. Measures were included of "ambivalence awareness," that is, the degree to which people are themselves aware of ambivalences. In addition, the study examined strategies for "ambivalence management" looking at the different ways people handle ambivalences. Results indicate that ambivalences seem to correspond systematically to the quality of intergenerational relations in families, with unsatisfactory relationships bearing a higher potential for ambivalences. However, some degree of ambivalence was also present in relationships that were relatively harmonious. The authors recommend that researchers examine the role of different family forms and different social settings as important contexts of ambivalences.

Frieder Lang opens Part III with observations on adult children's task of reorganizing and restructuring the relationship with parents who have reached old age. Filial tasks may compete with other demands of midlife, and thus may be associated with contradictory experience in the relationship with parents. Therefore, the key filial task is often one of mastering ambivalence in the relationship to one's aging parents. Lang provides an empirical illustration, using data from the Berlin Aging Study. A cluster analysis of support exchanges, personal norms, emotional closeness, and perceived strains with parents reveals four patterns of children's relational styles towards their older parents. These patterns of child-parent relationships differ with respect to the children's age, gender, marital status, and occupational status. The patterns also predict adult children's likelihood of giving care to their parents and the degree of inconsistency of children's satisfaction with parents.

The chapter by Pauline Boss and Lori Kaplan integrates social science and clinical perspectives. The authors focus on the "ambiguous loss" of living with a parent with Alzheimer's disease. Their study found that adult children experience conflicting thoughts and feelings as their parent becomes psychologically absent while remaining physically present. The objective of this chapter is to show the linkage between ambiguity and ambivalence using dementia caregiving as an illustration. The research provides a new window for intervention studies to reduce stress and maintain health of the adult-child caregiver. The basic premise is that ambiguity regarding the absence or presence of a parent will lead to ambivalent feelings and behaviors in the intergenerational family system, especially in the adult child caregivers. Helping families to understand this intergenerational dynamic when a parent is "ambiguously lost" will lessen the negative effects of what are in fact normal feelings of ambivalence in the adult children.

Dagmar Lorenz-Meyer examines ambivalence in relation to parental care in the narratives of young adults in Germany. Following the idea that intergenerational ambivalences may be productively analyzed around status passages, the chapter aims to produce a nuanced understanding of the ambivalences that many adult children encounter with respect to dealing with possible needs of their aging parents and the consequences of those needs. Data are presented from a study of how young adults in Germany plan their intergenerational commitments in the face of the potential need for personal care of their parents. Lorenz-Meyer identifies relational strategies of managing ambivalence with respect to care.

Part IV begins with Bertram Cohler's examination of the mixed feelings experienced by parents and other family members in response the declaration of an offspring's sexual identity as lesbian or gay. Cohler explores the implications of this disclosure for the management of ambivalence within the family, focusing on the manner in which parents and children negotiate their relationship following the child's disclosure. Parental concerns regarding the implications of offspring coming out as gay or lesbian are often expressed in terms of disappointment regarding the possibility of not having grandchildren and concern regarding availability to help parents as they grow older. "Backward" socialization is often reported as offspring help parents realize that the child's life-partner will be available as a source of support as parents grow older. The chapter concludes with discussion of next steps in the study of intergenerational relations among families with a gay or lesbian offspring.

Gregory Maio, Frank Fincham, Camilio Regalia and F. Giorgia Paleari focus on the influence of ambivalence on one of the central aspects of relationships: psychological attachment processes. Attachment processes involve the formation of a strong affectional bond to another person. People's capacity to form these bonds is presumed to emerge in infancy and persist throughout the lifespan. Maio and colleagues detail how ambivalence influences psychological attachment to other people. The findings suggest that young people who possess more mixed feelings and beliefs toward a parent develop less secure attachment to other people in general, especially when the children are ambivalent toward their father. In addition, this effect of ambivalence is not attributable to other attitude properties (e.g. evaluative inconsistency) that are somewhat related to ambivalence. Moreover, ambivalence toward parents predicts the perceived quality of the relationship between the children and their parents. The perceived quality of their relationship, in turn, predicts attachment to each parent, which predicts general attachment to others when the parent is the child's father. Thus, intergenerational ambivalence has a broad potential impact on attachment to others.

Harry Segal concludes this section with a developmental model for intergenerational ambivalence and an empirical method for exploring it. He begins by proposing that our perceptions, judgements, and culture shape our understanding of social events, as do our wishes, fears and feelings. However, this understanding is also sometimes strongly influenced by our early experiences, in particular by the ways in which we came to know our parents as young children. Segal holds that the experience of our adult selves with our parents necessarily and simultaneously evokes the early experience of ourselves as children, a structural and a neural cognitive expression of ambivalence. He then presents an experimental approach that complements this theoretical model. Using a quantified approach to content analysis, the current experiences of a large cohort of young adults, as well as their imagined future lives, are shown to strongly affect the ways in which they report the earliest memories of their mothers and fathers.

ACKNOWLEDGMENTS

This volume is the result of several years of sustained interaction among many of the chapter authors. This collaboration would not have been possible without funding from the Transcoop Program of the Alexander von Humboldt Foundation. We are grateful to both the University of Konstanz and the College of Human Ecology at Cornell University for providing matching funds for that grant. Karl Pillemer's involvement in this book was also partially supported by grants from the National Institute on Aging (1 P50 AG11711-01 and 1 RO1 AG18869-01).

An effort of this scope necessarily involves the assistance of many individuals. We would like to acknowledge the able editorial assistance of Paul Cash in the preparation of this volume. Series editor Felix Berardo provided support and encouragement for our efforts. We have also benefited greatly from discussions with a number of other colleagues regarding the issues reflected in this volume, including Vern Bengtson, Johannes Bilstein, Joan Jacobs Brumberg, Ingrid Connidis, Pamela Gorkin Daepp, David Lando, Ulrich Gaier, Benjamin Gottlieb, Matthias Grundmann, Patrick Haemmerle, Rainer Heuer, Michael Honig, Ina Jekeli, Matthias Junge, Paul Kingston, Oliver König, Andreas Lange, Clare

McMillan, Phyllis Moen, David Morgan, Julie McMullin, Brigitte Pajung-Bilger, Brigitte Rockstroh, Reinhold Sackman, Ruth Meyer Schweizer, Delia Spangler, J. Jill Suitor, Clemens Tesch-Römer, and Elaine Wethington.

Finally, this project could not have been completed without the assistance of research associates and assistants on both sides of the Atlantic. Thanks are due to Leslie Schultz, Myra Sabir, Helene Rosenblatt, Amelie Burkhardt, Ruth Nieffer, and Denise Rüttinger.

REFERENCES

Abel, E. K., & Nelson, M. K. (1990). *Circles of care: Work and identity in women's lives*. Albany, NY: State University of New York Press.

Aldous, J. (1990). Family development and the life course: Two perspectives on family change. *Journal of Marriage and the Family, 52*, 571–583.

Attias-Donfut, C. (1995). Le double circuit des transmissions [The twofold circle of transmissions]. In: C. Attias-Donfut (Ed.), *Les Solidarités entre Générations* [Solidarities between Generations] (pp. 41–81). Paris: Nathan.

Bell, D. W., Esses, V. M., & Maio, G. R. (1996). The utility of open-ended measures to assess intergroup ambivalence. *Canadian Journal of Behavioural Science, 28*, 12–18.

Bengtson, V. L. (2001). Beyond the nuclear family: The increasing importance of multigenerational bonds. *Journal of Marriage and the Family, 63*, 1–16.

Bengtson, V. L., Giarrusso, R., Mabry, J. B., & Silverstein, M. (2002). Solidarity, conflict, and ambivalence: Complementary or competing perspectives on intergenerational relationships? *Journal of Marriage and the Family, 64*, 568–576.

Bengtson, V. L., & Harootyan, R. A. (1994). *Intergenerational linkages: Hidden connections in American society*. New York: Springer.

Bengtson, V. L., Rosenthal, C. J., & Burton, L. M. (1995). Paradoxes of families and aging. In: R. H. Binstock & L. K. George (Eds), *Handbook of Aging and the Social Sciences* (4th ed., pp. 253–282). San Diego, CA: Academic Press.

Bleuler, E. (1911). *Dementia Praecox oder Gruppe der Schizophrenien* [Dementia praecox or the group of schizophrenia]. Leipzig, Germany: Franz Deuticke.

Blieszner, R., Usita, P. M., & Mancini, J. A. (1996). Diversity and dynamics in late-life mother-daughter relationships. *Journal of Women and Aging, 8*, 5–24.

Blumer, H. (1969) Symbolic interactionism; perspective and method. Englewood Cliffs, NJ: Prentice-Hall.

Boss, P. (2000). *Ambiguous loss: Learning to live with unresolved grief*. Cambridge, MA: Harvard University Press.

Clarke, E. J., Preston, M., Raksin, J., & Bengtson, V. L. (1999). Types of conflicts and tensions between older parents and adult children. *The Gerontologist, 39*, 261–270.

Cleese, A. F., & Bates B. (2001). *How to manage your mother: Understanding the most difficult, complicated, and fascinating relationship in your life*. New York: Regan Books.

Cohen, E., & Cohen S. (1997). *Mothers who drive their daughters crazy: Ten types of 'impossible' moms and how to deal with them*. New York: Prima Publishing.

Cohler, B. J. (1983). Autonomy and interdependence in the family of adulthood. *The Gerontologist, 23*, 33–39.

Cohler, B. J., & Grunebaum, H. (1981). *Mothers, grandmothers, and daughters. Personality and childcare in three-generation families.* New York: Wiley.

Cole, T. (1992). *The journey of life: A cultural history of aging in America.* Cambridge, England: Cambridge University Press.

Coleman, J. S. (1990). *Foundations of social theory.* Cambridge, MA: Harvard University Press.

Connidis, I. A. (2001). *Family ties and aging.* Thousand Oaks, CA: Sage.

Connidis, I. A., & McMullin, J. A. (2002). Sociological ambivalence and family ties: A critical perspective. *Journal of Marriage and the Family, 64,* 558–567.

Coser, R. L. (1966). Role distance, sociological ambivalence, and transitional status systems. *American Journal of Sociology, 72,* 173–187.

Curran, S. R. (2002). Agency, accountability, and embedded relations: "What's love got to do with it?" *Journal of Marriage and the Family, 64,* 577–584.

Daatland, S. O., & Herlofson, K. (Eds) (2001). *Ageing, intergenerational relations, care systems and quality of life – an introduction to the OASIS project.* Oslo: Norwegian Social Research.

Demos, J. (1986). *Past, present, and personal.* New York: Oxford.

DeVault, M. L. (1991). *Feeding the family.* Chicago: University of Chicago Press.

Ehmer, J. (2000). Alter und Generationenbeziehungen im Spannungsfeld von öffentlichem und privatem Leben [Aging and intergenerational relations between private and public life] In: J. Ehmer & P. Gutschner (Eds), *Das Alter im Spiel der Generationen* [Aging and the Interplay of generations] (pp. 15–50). Wien: Böhlau.

Eidelberg, L. (1968). *Encyclopedia of psychoanalysis.* New York: Free Press.

Erikson, E. H. (1994). *The life cycle completed.* New York: Norton.

Ferree, M. M. (1990). Beyond separate spheres: Feminism and family research. *Journal of Marriage and the Family, 52,* 866–884.

Filipp, S.-H., & Mayer, A.-K. (1999). *Bilder des Alters. Altersstereotype und die Beziehungen zwischen den Generationen* [Images of aging. Stereotypes and intergenerational relationships]. Stuttgart: Kohlhammer.

Finch, J., & Mason, J. (1993). *Negotiating family responsibilities.* London: Tavistock, Routledge.

Fingerman, K. L. (1998). Tight lips? Aging mothers' and adult daughters' responses to interpersonal tensions in their relationships. *Personal Relationships, 5,* 121–138.

Fingerman, K. L. (2001a). *Aging mothers and their adult daughters: A study in mixed emotions.* New York: Springer.

Fingerman, K. L. (2001b). A distant closeness: Intimacy between parents and their children in later life. *Generations, 25,* 26–33.

Foner, A. (1986). *Aging and old age: New perspectives.* Englewood Cliffs, NJ: Prentice-Hall.

Foner, N. (1984). *Ages in conflict.* New York: Columbia University Press.

Freud, S. (1913). *Totem and taboo.* A. A. Brill (Trans.). New York: New Republic.

George, L. K. (1986). Caregiver burden: Conflict between norms of reciprocity and solidarity. In: K. Pillemer & R. Wolf (Eds), *Elder Abuse: Conflict in the Family* (pp. 67–92). Dover, MA: Auburn House.

Graff, H. J. (1995). *Conflicting paths: Growing up in America.* Cambridge, MA: Harvard University Press.

Henwood, K. L., & Coughlin, G. (1993). The construction of "closeness" in mother-daughter relationships across the lifespan. In: N. Coupland & J. F. Nussbaum (Eds), *Discourse and Lifespan Identity: Language and Language Behaviors* (Vol. 4, pp. 191–214). Newbury Park, CA: Sage.

Jonas, K., Diehl, M., & Bromer, P. (1997). Effects of attitudinal ambivalence on information processing and attitude-intention consistency. *Journal of Experimental Social Psychology, 33,* 190–210.

Kohli, M., & Künemund, H. (Eds) (2000). *Die zweite Lebenshälfte: Gesellschaftliche Lage und Partizipation im Spiegel des Alters-Survey* [The second half of life: Societal position and participation. Results from the first German Survey of Aging]. Opladen, Germany: Leske + Budrich.

Levine, D. N. (1985). *The flight from ambiguity: Essays in social and cultural theory.* Chicago: University of Chicago Press.

Litwak, E. (1965). Extended kin relations in a democratic industrial society. In: E. Shanas & G. Streib (Eds), *Social Structure and the Family* (pp. 290–323). Englewood Cliffs, NJ: Prentice-Hall.

Lüscher, K. (1997). Solidarische Beziehungen: Das "neue" Problem der Generationen [Solidaritarian relationships: The "new" problem of generations]. In: K. Gabriel, A. Herlth & K. P. Strohmeier (Eds), *Modernität und Solidarität* [Modernity and Solidarity] (pp. 59–77). Freiburg, Germany: Herder.

Lüscher, K. (1998). Postmodern societies. Postmodern families? In: E. Matthijs (Ed.), *The Family. Contemporary Perspectives and Challenges* (pp. 181–194). Leuven: University Press.

Lüscher, K. (2000). Family rhetoric in family politics. In: H. Cavanna (Ed.), *The New Citizenship of the Family* (pp. 3–13). Burlington, VT: Ashgate.

Lüscher, K., & Pajung-Bilger, B. (1998). *Forcierte Ambivalenzen: Ehescheidung als Herausforderung an die Generationenbeziehungen unter Erwachsenen* [Forced ambivalences: Divorce as a challenge to intergenerational relationships between adults]. Konstanz, Germany: Universitäts-Verlag.

Lüscher, K., & Pillemer, K. (1998). Intergenerational ambivalence: A new approach to the study of parent-child relations in later life. *Journal of Marriage and the Family, 60*, 413–445.

Lye, D. N. (1996). Adult child-parent relationships. *Annual Review of Sociology, 22*, 79–102.

Marshall, V. W., Matthews, S. H., & Rosenthal, C. J. (1993). Elusiveness of family life: A challenge for the sociology of aging. In: G. L. Maddox & M. P. Lawton (Eds), *Annual Review of Gerontology and Geriatrics: Focus on Kinship, Aging, and Social Change* (pp. 39–72). New York: Springer.

von Matt, P. (1995). *Verkommene Söhne, mißratene Töchter. Familiendesaster in der Literatur* [Degenerated sons, misguided daughters. Family disasters in literature]. München: Hanser.

Merton, R. K., & Barber, E. (1963). Sociological ambivalence. In: E. Tiryakian (Ed.), *Sociological Theory: Values and Sociocultural Change* (pp. 91–120). New York: Free Press.

Mintz, S., & Kellogg, S. (1988). *Domestic revolutions: A social history of family life.* New York: Free Press.

Moen, P. (Ed.) (2003). *It's about time: Couples and careers.* Ithaca, NY: Cornell University Press.

Myerhoff, B. (1980). *Number our days.* New York: Simon and Schuster.

Otscheret, E. (1988). *Ambivalenz* [Ambivalence]. Heidelberg: Roland Asanger.

Parker, R. (1995). *Mother love/Mother hate: The power of maternal ambivalence.* New York: Basic Books.

Pillemer, K., & Moen, P. (2000). Children after childhood: Relations between older parents and adult children. In: A. Lange & W. Lauterbach (Eds), *Kinder in Familie und Gesellschaft zu Beginn des 21sten Jahrhunderts* [Children in Family and Society at the Beginning of the 21st Century]. Berlin: Enke Verlag.

Pillemer, K., & Suitor, J. J. (1991). Will I *ever* escape my child's problems? Effects of adult children's problems on elderly parents. *Journal of Marriage and the Family, 53*, 585–594.

Pillemer, K., & Suitor, J. J. (1992). Violence and violent feelings: What causes them among family caregivers? *Journal of Gerontology, 47*, S165–S172.

Pillemer, K., & Suitor, J. J. (1998). Baby boom families: Relations with aging parents. *Generations, 23*, 65–70.

Pillemer, K., & Wolf, R. S. (1998). Elder abuse. In: J. M. Last & R. B. Wallace (Eds), *Public Health and Preventive Medicine.* Norwalk, CN: Appleton and Lange.

Priester, J. R., & Petty, R. E. (1996). The gradual threshold model of ambivalence: Relating the positive and negative bases of attitudes to subjective ambivalence. *Journal of Personality and Social Psychology, 71,* 431–449.

Roberts, R. E. L., Richards, L. N., & Bengtson, V. L. (1991). Intergenerational solidarity in families: Untangling the ties that bind. In: S. K. Pfeifer & M. B. Sussman (Eds), *Families: Intergenerational and Generational Connections* (pp. 11–46). Binghamton, NY: Haworth Press.

Rosenmayr, L. (1992). Sexualität, Partnerschaft und Familie älterer Menschen [Sexuality, partnerships and family of older peresons]. In: P. B. Baltes & J. Mittelstraß (Eds), *Zukunft des Alterns und gesellschaftliche Entwicklung* [The Future of Aging and Societal Development] (pp. 461–491). Berlin: De Gruyter.

Rosenmayr, L. (1998). Generationen. Zur Empirie und Theorie eines psycho-sozialen Konfliktfeldes [Generations. Reality and theory of a field of psycho-social conflicts]. In: M. Teising (Ed.), *Altern. Äussere Realität, innere Wirklichkeiten* [Aging. External and Internal Realities] (pp. 17–44). Opladen: Westdeutscher Verlag.

Rossi, A., & Rossi, P. (1990). *Of human bonding: Parent-child relationships across the life course.* Hawthorne, NY: Aldine de Gruyter.

Rubin, L. B. (2000). *Tangled lives: Daughters, mothers, and the crucible of aging.* Boston: Beacon Press.

Rycroft, C. (1973). *A critical dictionary of psychoanalysis.* Totowa, NJ: Littlefield Adams.

Secunda, V. (1991). *When you and your mother can't be friends: Resolving the most complicated relationship of your life.* New York: Delta.

Shanas, E., Townsend, P., Weddeburn, D., Friis, H., Milhoj, P., & Stehouwer, J. (1968). *Old people in three industrial societies.* New York: Atherton Press.

Shmotkin, D. (1999). Affective bonds of adult children with living vs. deceased parents. *Psychology and Aging, 14,* 473–482.

Silverstein, M., & Bengtson, V. (1997). Intergenerational solidarity and the structure of adult child B parent relationships in American families. *American Journal of Sociology, 103,* 429–460.

Sincoff, J. B. (1990). The psychological characteristics of ambivalent people. *Clinical Psychology Review, 10,* 43–68.

Sprey, J. (1991). Studying adult children and their parents. In: S. K. Pfeifer & M. B. Sussman (Eds), *Families: Intergenerational and Generational Connections* (pp. 221–235). Binghamton, NY: Haworth Press.

Stearns, P. N. (1986). Old age family conflict: The perspective of the past. In: K. Pillemer & R. S. Wolf (Eds), *Elder Abuse: Conflict in the Family* (pp. 1–24). Dover, MA: Auburn House.

Strauss, B. S. (1993). *Fathers and sons in Athens.* Princeton, NJ: Princeton University Press.

Suitor, J. J., & Pillemer, K. (1988). Explaining intergenerational conflict when adult children and elderly parents live together. *Journal of Marriage and the Family, 50,* 1037–1047.

Suitor, J. J., & Pillemer, K. (1996). Changes in support and interpersonal stress in the networks of married caregiving daughters: Findings from a 2-year panel study. *Journal of Gerontology, 51,* S297–306.

Sussman, M. B. (1959). The isolated nuclear family: Fact or fiction. *Social Problems, 6,* 333–347.

Thorne, B. (1992). Feminism and the family: Two decades of thought. In: B. Thorne & M. Yalom (Eds), *Rethinking the Family* (pp. 3–30). Boston: Northeastern University Press.

Weigert, A. J. (1991). *Mixed emotions: Certain steps toward understanding ambivalence.* Albany, NY: State University of New York Press.

Wolf, R. S., & Pillemer, K. (1997). The older battered woman: Wives and mothers compared. *Journal of Mental Health and Aging, 3,* 325–336.

PART I:
CONCEPTUAL AND HISTORICAL PERSPECTIVES

and how the concept can be defined. I will make a case for a definition that keeps in mind the specific purpose of analyzing what may be called "*intergenerational* ambivalence." At the same time, this definition can be situated within the broader field of using the concept of ambivalence and remains connected to other usages of the word.

The task, then, is to try what may be called an "operationalization" in the broad sense of the word. A first step requires exploring what we mean by social relations or relationships. In a second step, I will outline a schematic model of intergenerational ambivalence, developed in our research group at Konstanz. It is based on an analytical distinction of two basic dimensions of social relationships, which we term the personal-subjective and institutional-structural. Insofar as each of them can refer to two basic ambivalent polarizations, it becomes possible to distinguish four ideal-typical ways of dealing and coping with intergenerational ambivalences.

The model is meant to represent one possibility of a theoretically funded operationalization of intergenerational ambivalence. (Research based on this model is presented in Chap. 7 of this volume.) In the final section of the present chapter I briefly review the current status of research on intergenerational ambivalence and propose steps to advance the approach. I conclude by returning to my original thesis, namely that the concept of ambivalence enriches our understanding of intergenerational relations, relates it to basic issues of the social sciences, connects it with other disciplines, and has fundamental relevance for the analysis of contemporary social life.

DEFINING INTERGENERATIONAL AMBIVALENCE

Everyday Understanding of Ambivalence

What do parents mean, in everyday language, when they confess to an ambivalent relationship with their daughter or son? They feel themselves somehow tugged back and forth, torn between closeness and distance, intimacy and estrangement. Parents and children want to be independent of one another, knowing all the while that they are still mutually dependent. When both parties experience feelings of estrangement or even of hostility, they may nevertheless still feel bound together by ties of love. Under such circumstances they may be burdened by a sense of indecisiveness, uncertainty, and drifting apart.

Ambivalence offers itself as a plausible label in the context of sophisticated everyday language. The *Collins English Dictionary*, for instance, sums up ambivalence or ambivalency as "the co-existence of two opposed and conflicting emotions..." and its thesaurus refers to "contradiction...equivocation, fracturation . . . opposition, uncertainty, vacillation." *The Oxford English Dictionary* points to "the co-existence in one person or one work of contradictory emotions and attitudes towards the same object or situation (or thing)." The root syllables are "ambi," meaning dual or twofold, and "valence," which refers to value or valuation. We might conclude that it refers to a center and to opposite sides. If we equate the center with the self, this aspect of meaning is compatible, formally speaking, with the idea of personal identity as a reference of ambivalence.

To move beyond the unavoidable vagueness of everyday language and its proximity to essentialist and normative usage, turning to the brief but important history of the concept is worthwhile. Such a reconstruction suggests possible dimensions to be accounted for in research. It is also fruitful because it throws light on why ambivalence can and should be understood as a source for new experiences, and should therefore not "a priori" be seen as a negative experience.

Important Facets of the Concept's History

The Origins

As far as we know, the Swiss psychiatrist Eugen Bleuler invented and first used the concept of ambivalence for the psychiatric diagnosis of "negativism" in 1910, and subsequently as one of four core symptoms of schizophrenia (Bleuler, 1911). This specific meaning is still part of the medical nomenclature (WHO, 1992). Bleuler distinguished three types of ambivalence – in regard to affection or emotions, to cognitions, and to volition (expression of will) – and pointed out that the three are closely intermingled. His scientific usage is more differentiated than is our everyday usage, which speaks mainly of emotions or feelings, as the dictionary definitions above show.

A brief recollection of the first public debate on ambivalence, at an annual meeting of the Society of Swiss Psychiatrists (see the minutes by Riklin, 1910/1911), may illuminate another important point. Among those present at that assembly in Berne was C. G. Jung. He applauded the term, but he wanted to have it understood primarily in an abstract formalistic manner, expressing that "each tendency is counterbalanced by an opposite" (see on this Graber, 1924, p. 8). Thus, Jung equated ambivalence with dialectical opposition aiming at a balance. This interpretation entails a simplification in a way which – following Kris (2000, p. 15) – can be seen as significant for Jung's way of theorizing. Following Bleuler, ambivalence should not be seen as a disequilibrium, nor should it be equated with dialectics.

Bleuler's most comprehensive treatment of the concept is an essay simply entitled, *Die Ambivalenz* (1914, "Ambivalence"). He starts with several illustrations from clinical practice that hint at the idea of divided consciousness, and mentions the case of a mother who has killed her child, grieving and laughing simultaneously over the child's death. Yet Bleuler also argues that ambivalent affect, cognitions, and volitions can be part of ordinary, "normal" conduct. Furthermore, he points to the experience of ambivalence as a source of creative stimulus for writers, and as a topic of their writings. Goethe in his *Sorrows of Young Werther* provides an example. Relating ambivalence to creativity freed the concept from its association with a pathological condition of the mind, laying the grounds to use and to comprehend ambivalence as a neutral analytical term.

Bleuler made it clear that the inability *to cope* with ambivalence, rather than ambivalence itself, is what leads to psychic disorders. His son, Manfred Bleuler, later added that ambivalence is, in fact, a mental state inherent in the human condition. Significantly, this idea appears in a chapter entitled *Gesundes im Schizophrenen – Schizophrenes im Gesunden* (Bleuler, 1972, pp. 607–613: "The Healthy in the Schizophrenic – the Schizophrenic in the Healthy"). Here we find the statement: "Wie aber dem Schizophrenen gesundes inneres Leben nicht verloren geht, so ist dem Gesunden schizophrenes Leben nicht fremd" (p. 610). ("Just as the schizophrenic person does not lose his healthy inner life, schizophrenic life is not foreign to the healthy person.") Stotz-Ingenlath (2000, p. 156) points out: "For him (Bleuler) the schizophrenic symptomatology seemed to be only an exaggeration and disturbance of healthy psychic processes."

In the context of this chapter, it also is noteworthy that Eugen Bleuler already had connected ambivalence to mythological accounts of what he called the "father-complex." He refers to the accounts of Uranus and Saturn who destroy their children's lives, yet the children survive and become the representatives of the future, castrating and dethroning their fathers.

Psychoanalysis and Psychotherapy
Freud took up the concept from Bleuler very quickly. This is not surprising because the theme of simultaneous opposition surfaces, for instance, in an essay on "The Antithetical Meaning of Primal Words" (1910, Standard Edition, Vol. 11, pp. 155–161). Freud makes positive, complimentary remarks about the invention of the concept. Like Bleuler, Freud was aware of the ubiquity of ambivalent experiences and of the necessity to adapt their general meaning to specific cases.

Freud thought in terms of ambivalence. He first used the term in connection with a theory of "transference" (Freud, 1912/1975). This use is relevant insofar as the context is a specific social relationship (i.e. between therapist and patient) that may have some similarity, in its asymmetric structure, with intergenerational relationships. Later, he also included it in his theory of the Oedipus complex, to analyze an exemplary intergenerational phenomenon. A concise presentation appears in his short essay, "On the Psychology of the Secondary School Pupil" (Freud, 1914/1953). Furthermore, he integrated the concept into his work on mass psychology and ego analysis (Freud, 1921/1953), and his cultural-critical study "Civilization and its Discontents" (Freud, 1929/1953). He also connected it with his fundamental theory of "drives" and of "totem and taboo," and ultimately with the juxtaposition of "eros" (love) and "thanatos" (death).

Attempts to lay out in more detail Freud's concern with ambivalence have been made by Knellessen (1978) and Otscheret (1988). Without providing much detail, one can say, with Knellessen, that Freud's usage of ambivalence demonstrates his increasing preoccupation with developing a meta-psychology. He aimed to uncover the fundamental forces – or "drives" – which serve as the agents of personal and societal development. His use of the term has to be seen in parallel with its reception and development by many authors in the psychoanalytic tradition, who also applied it in psychotherapy. This tendency can be summarized in the way Knellessen sees it, that "after an initially strongly biologically conditioned orientation, it is increasingly being embedded in social relationships, in objective structures" (p. 129). This development also runs parallel to the reception of the term in sociology.

It is beyond the scope of this chapter to present the full history of the term in psychoanalysis, psychotherapy, and family therapy (for the latter, see especially Otscheret, 1988). Among recent contributions, Parker's treatise on "Mother Love, Mother Hate" merits special attention. Within a feminist frame of reference, she expands the idea, already touched upon by Bleuler as mentioned above, that dealing with ambivalence may be a source of social creativity.

Parker (1995, p. 6) refers to Melanie Klein, who "considered that ambivalence had a positive part to play in mental life as a safeguard against hate." Parker adds: "I want to go further and claim a specifically creative role for manageable maternal ambivalence. I suggest that it is in the very anguish of maternal ambivalence itself that a fruitfulness for mothers and children resides." The major mechanism can be described as follows: Given the fundamental dichotomy and the awareness of love and hate, mothers are able even in desperate situations to reactivate the forces of love.

More generally, mothers search continuously, even under difficult situations, for arrangements that serve the well-being of their children. This fundamental ability to cope with ambivalence creatively can be seen as a genuine cultural and social contribution of mothers to civilization. Contributions like Parker's make clear why – and also how – a focus on ambivalence can be compatible with feminist thinking. This field is sensitized to possible ambivalences in gender relations and to constructive, as well destructive, strategies dealing with them.

Sociology

Looking at the concept's history in sociology, we note again a rather recent appearance of the term itself: despite an awareness of the topic which dates back much further. Indeed, as Levine (1985), Luthe and Wiedenmann (1997), Junge (2000), and a number of other writers point out, classical theoreticians such as Emile Durkheim and Max Weber identified – in their critical appraisal of modernization – enduring paradoxes which are more than mere contradictions or conflicts.

The most outstanding theoretician of sociological ambivalence, however, is Georg Simmel. Although he does not use this term explicitly, an early awareness of ambivalence is apparent in many of his writings. In a general way, he can be regarded as the discoverer of what may be called the realm of "in-betweeness" in human sociality, the fields of the indeterminate (Luthe & Wiedenmann, 1997, p. 19) and of ambiguity (Levine, 1995). Simmel saw closeness and distance as basic conditions of human sociality and consequently of social relations.

More recently, Bauman (1991) shows sensitivity for possible roots of ambivalence in language as such. A quote from the opening chapter of his book on postmodernity may serve as an illustration:

> Ambivalence, the possibility of assigning an object or an event to more than one category, is a language-specific disorder: a failure of the naming (segregating) function that language is meant to perform. The main symptom of disorder is the acute discomfort we feel when we are unable to read the situation properly and to choose between alternative actions.
>
> It is because of the anxiety that accompanies it and the indecision which follows that we experience ambivalence as a disorder – and either blame language for lack of precision or ourselves for linguistic misuse. And yet ambivalence is not the product of pathology of language or speech. It is, rather, a normal aspect of linguistic practice. It arises from one of the main functions of language: that of naming and classifying. Its volume grows depending on the effectivity with which that function is performed. Ambivalence is therefore the *alter ego* of language, and its permanent companion – indeed, its normal condition (p. 1).

A dominant issue among sociologists interested in ambivalence concerns whether certain features of social structures generate ambivalent experiences. Yet, the issue is complicated.

In the literature, two notions – structures "being" ambivalent vs. structures generating ambivalence – are confused. This often goes together with a holistic, even essentialistic language that speaks of society as being a thing or an actor. Such reifications carry the danger of oversimplifying social complexities and the interplay between personality and social structure. Also, moralistic arguments such as a society or the "state" being "good" or "bad" are furthered. This line of thinking is situated on the level of general meanings and is difficult to connect to research.

The recent popular use of the term ambivalence in "postmodern" social writings demonstrates these dangers. Nevertheless, Bauman (himself a prominent representative of sociological postmodernism) adds noteworthy elements to the exploration of ambivalence. He often refers to "social types" or "modal personalities," for example, when he illustrates contemporary ambivalence. In this way, he connects the concept to the observation that many people experience themselves as fragmented, that is, they have what can be called a precarious, fragile personal identity. One is reminded of the origins of the concept in Bleuler's work with patients suffering from schizophrenia.

Along this line, reference should be made to Weigert, who published several texts on ambivalence that speak to the topic of ambivalence and identity formation and – like Bauman's works – point to connections with modernization processes (Weigert, 1988; Weigert & Franks, 1989). He primarily located ambivalence in the sphere of emotions (Weigert, 1991). This work suggests a relation to the sociology of emotions and the study of emotion management (see, for example, Hochschild, 1983).

Credit for the most influential sociological reception of the concept of ambivalence is due to Robert Merton and colleagues in the 1960s. In their seminal article, Merton and Barber (1963) first refer to Bleuler and Freud and to the cultural awareness of ambivalence in history. Then, they propose to study "which social structures generate the circumstances in which ambivalence is imbedded in particular statuses and status-sets together with their associated social roles" (Merton & Barber, 1963, p. 95). Significantly, they see the "core" of ambivalence as being in "conflicting normative expectations." Furthermore: "Since these norms cannot be simultaneously expressed in behavior, they become expressed in an oscillation of behaviors: of detachment and compassion, of discipline and permissiveness, of personal and impersonal treatment."

Speaking from our present state of understanding, however, one may argue that Merton and Barber did not distinguish ambivalence clearly enough from conflict. They did not consider the bridge to the notion of the self, a shortcoming that may be due to functionalistic role-theory. Writers in the tradition of symbolic interactionism were more outspoken on this issue. For example, Goffman's treatise on *Stigma* (1963), although without an explicit definition, analyzes the phenomenon of ambivalence and its management by people who suffer from physical or psychic anomalies and illustrates different strategies of dealing with ambivalence. Goffman also reminds us of the relevance of ambivalence for the presentation of the self in everyday situations. Furthermore, Merton and Barber wrote their essay before the "linguistic turn" showed its consequences in the social sciences. Therefore, they did not treat language simultaneously as a social phenomenon and as a means to socially construct reality – in the sense suggested by Berger and Luckmann (1966).

Along these line, Donati (1998) provides a careful critical assessment of Merton's notion of ambivalence.

The strength of Merton and Barber's approach, however, can be seen in their application of ambivalence to the characterization of specific roles for most professions, e.g. the physician, the scientist, the organizational leader, as documented by the later writings of Merton (1976, Chaps 2–5). In this way, the link to societal preconditions of ambivalence is established – certainly a genuine sociological view. Traces of this idea can also be found in works by scholars such as Rose Laub Coser (1964, 1966), Lewis Coser (1965), Jan Hajda (1968), and others who wrote on ambivalence in the 1960s.

A more recent example of the reception of Merton and Barber is Weingardt's attempt to work out the implications of "professional ambivalence" for psychotherapists. He indicates – with reference to Merton and Barber – four conditions to be challenged, namely: the open-ended continuity of the relationship, the authority of the therapists, his or her self-interests, and the difference of performance appraisal. In his account, Weingardt pleads for a two-sided apprehension: "When ambivalence is normalized . . . it can become a productive force of therapy rather than an impediment to it" (Weingardt, 2000, p. 305).

Applying the concept of ambivalence to the study of professional roles implies using it as a quality of social *relationships*. This application coincides with our concern with relations between generations. As mentioned earlier, professional relationships and intergenerational relationships have at least one feature in common, namely, a specific structure of power or authority: The patient depends upon the physician as the child depends upon the mother or father. Yet seen from the other side, the power of the physician, as well as the power of the parents, is not unrestricted and is not a "free-space" for the pursuit of self-interests. To the contrary, authority here (as elsewhere) implies a responsibility for a dependent person. It includes empathy and concern for the well-being of the client or the child. Moreover, it is a responsibility for the development of the person. It is also a personalized responsibility insofar as the patient or the child may sooner or later judge the consequences of the physician's or the parents' "care." These features represent concomitantly structural and personal preconditions of ambivalence in relationships.

Thinking about such issues draws attention toward the "logic of relationships," by which I mean the formulation of specific rules that emerge in a culture or community to establish and to ensure sociality on all levels and in all domains of societal life. Smelser (1998) has taken up the concern with ambivalence in the social sciences and addresses just this point when he juxtaposes "the ambivalent and the rational" to show the relevance of ambivalence in the social sciences as a complementary alternative to the concern with "rational choice." Smelser himself, however, remains somehow undecided. On one hand, he does not see in ambivalence "a theoretical competitor . . . opposed to the postulate of rational choice" (p. 5). On the other hand, he states:

> . . . if we move toward the broader implications of the place of the rational and the ambivalent in the social sciences, it becomes clear that we are dealing with a fundamental existential dilemma in the human condition. It is communicated in various dichotomies – freedom vs. constraint, independence vs. dependence, autonomy vs. dependence, maturity vs. infancy, and more – but ever the dichotomy, the dilemma appears to be insoluble (p. 13).

Be that as it may, Smelser's essay can be understood as supportive of two of our major concerns. First, ambivalence may be comprehended as a major condition of human sociality; second, it may be prevalent in certain kinds of social relations and situations, especially those where dependency is an issue. The latter is certainly the case for intergenerational relations.

Ambivalence in Fiction and Art

Because ambivalence refers to experiences which are deeply rooted in human life, it is also observable in the work of writers and artists. Here, the links between ambivalence, identity and creativity call for attention. Seeing through the eyes of artists and writers reminds us that the awareness of ambivalence requires specific processes of interpretation. Commentators on the lives of writers, artists, and composers also provide a connection between ambivalence-producing experiences in the life of artists and interpretations of their works, and can show that elements in the works signify ambivalences in the creator's life. Moreover, and as already referred to in passing by Bleuler, artistic works can be understood as ways of *dealing with* ambivalence.

Reinharz (1986), for example, gives an informative overview on "loving and hating one's elders" as "twin themes in legend and literature." She refers, among other examples, to the tragedy of Uranus and his sons and to the Oedipal myth. Hamlet as well, she tells us, can be read as a "portrait of intergenerational relations" (p. 38). Peter von Matt presents a colorful overview of the theme (von Matt, 1995) under the provocative title "Verkommene Söhne, missratene Töchter" (Degenerate Sons, Misguided Daughters). He draws a line from the biblical story of Absalom to the admonitory children's book *Der Struwelpeter* (Shock-headed Peter) and recalls the complex relationships described in Theodor Fontane's *Effie Briest* and in Kafka's tale "The Metamorphosis." We also can add Philip Roth's novel *American Pastoral* as an example of ambivalence in recent American literature. In so far as fictional works are or can be seen as constructions of worlds of their own, one also may see the ambivalences as deliberately constructed.

Transposed into the realm of social inquiry, this observation alerts us to be sensitive to the possibility of actually *creating* ambivalences for ourselves, and possibly for others. The notion that ambivalences can be created by writers and artists implies, as a further assumption, that they are experienced by readers or viewers. In the same way, spectators are supposed to see ambivalences in the work of painters, as in a still life by Hopper (Levin, 1981). It likewise is assumed that listeners will "hear" ambivalences in a symphony by Mahler or a string quintet by Shostakovitch. Instead of "reading," "seeing," or "hearing" ambivalences, however, it is more customary to speak of "feeling" them. In turn, this may provoke the experience of ambivalence by those exposed to the works of art and music. Thus, we may also consider that "ambivalence can breed ambivalence."

This is an insight which is also relevant for psychotherapy. Brief examples may serve as illustrations. Dagmar Hoffmann-Axthelm is a musicologist and a psychoanalyst. Her sophisticated study (1994) of Robert Schumann looks into circumstances and relationships in Schumann's life, which plausibly can be interpreted as ambivalent. Schumann was torn, for example, between a highly sensitive father and a strong mother who was absent for part of his childhood. Later, his mother opposed his intention to become a musician and forced him to study law. Furthermore, Schumann's relationship with his wife Clara was characterized by a mix of ambitious expectations for harmony and genuine rivalry between them. One can identify a certain repetition of ambivalent experiences in Schumann's life, which can be related to certain elements of his music. Hoffmann-Axthelm, as a musicologist, is able to trace creative responses to these ambivalences in compositions such as the piece for piano, entitled "Papillon." Later in his life, Schumann lost the ability to cope with his complex ambivalences and transform them creatively into music. Clara (at least in the way Hoffmann-Axthelm sees it) had to separate from Schumann, for fear of being herself pulled in to his struggles with ambivalence.

Hoffmann-Axthelm's account of Robert Schumann shows how an ultimate inability to manage or transform ambivalence can lead to the destruction of the self. The opposite can be illustrated with reference to an analysis by Gerhard Schneider (2001) of the work of the Russian painter Kasimir Malevitch. His most significant work, often called an icon of 20th century art, is entitled "Black square in front of a white background." As the title says, the work simply juxtaposes a black square to a white environment that is also a square. Thus, the painting uses two colors, black and white, which are properly speaking "non-colors." The extreme reduction in "color" goes together with an extreme reduction of form, namely to the square. One may really speak of an ultimate juxtaposition. Yet the square is not fully perfect. It shows some minor aberrations. The juxtaposition is just not fully perfect. It may be called a pending, vacillating, waving juxtaposition. For this reason, we can interpret the work as a pictorial representation of ambivalence and its dynamics.

In a second step of the analysis, Schneider relates the realization of this extreme – and in its time absolutely innovative – work to the artistic biography of Malevitch, who eagerly desired to create something new, yet the field was already taken by movements such as cubism. Malevitch's solution was extreme yet ambivalent abstraction. The act of coming to this position became a turning point in the life of Malevitch. Schneider quotes a personal note of the painter that confirms this view. Further proof of the existential relevance of that decisive, creative moment may be seen in the fact that Malevitch made three additional versions of the work. He identified himself with the black quadrangle throughout his life, although his work subsequently moved in a different direction. And conversely, he was "identified" by the artistic community and the public with the "black quadrangle": A reproduction of the picture is even painted on his gravestone. Malevitch, in the interpretation of his life by Schneider (and other art critics such as Simmen, 1998) of which this brief account is only an extremely condensed version, can be seen as having made a successful close and creative connection between the experience of ambivalence and personal development. His example confirms the links between ambivalence and self.

In sum: The role of the concept of ambivalence reveals three aspects, which are relevant for its usage in the social sciences and the study of intergenerational relations. First, ambivalence can be created, and ambivalence can be a source of creative activity. Second, the awareness and the experience of ambivalence require processes, interpretation. Third, these two aspects go together with a usage of the concept that underlines its openness and ambiguity. I will argue that this usage comes close to the notion of ambivalence as an "interpretative concept," to be distinguished from the usage as a "research construct."

Proposing a Definition

The previous section brings to light only a few facets of the rich history and diverse use of the concept of ambivalence. More comprehensive overviews call attention to many other areas into which the concept has been introduced. *The Oxford English Dictionary* (1989, pp. 387–388) mentions, for example – in addition to the social sciences references already noted above – the following first usages of the term:

1939 L. TRILLING, *M. ARNOLD* iv. 123. Rousseau's *Confessions* had laid the ground for the understanding of emotional ambivalence.

1948, M. Joos *Acoustic Phonetics* 23. The principle of ambivalence, which states that any thing which is capable of emitting acoustic power linearly will also absorb acoustic power according (to) the same rules that govern its behavior as an emitter.

1953, *Times Lit. Suppl.* 9 Oct. 645/2. What social anthropologists call "plural belonging," what literary critics call ambivalence of attitude, and what the proverb calls having your cake and eating it, is a common human phenomenon.

1956 A. L. ROWSE *Early Churchill* p. vii. There is much to be said for a certain judicious ambivalence.

1959 *Times Rev. Industry* Mar. 4/3. There is an ambivalence in the claims on promotional moneys, for the furtherance of distribution on the one hand and for the extension of advertising on the other.

Sources such as this attest to the continuing ambiguity of the concept. A multitude of meanings and a certain vagueness of meaning can be observed not only in everyday language, but also in texts where the concept is invoked as a general characterization of contemporary society. Junge (2000) goes so far as to see theories of contemporary societies converging in an analysis of ambivalences. He refers in particular to Bellah's theory of "moral economy," Münch's theory of action, Beck's theory of "reflexive modernity," and Bauman's characterization of postmodernity (p. 87).

There is much to recommend trying to formulate an explicit definition. While a "working definition" must not be taken as all-encompassing or final, it can help to clarify what is common in all appearances of what we mean by the term, and how it differs in different contexts. Furthermore, an adequate definition may serve as a useful reference point for research; insofar as an explicit definition can identify the fundamental characteristics of the creature to be studied, it also can facilitate the processes of application for research – often called "operationalization." This process goes hand in hand with a certain limitation or, in literary terms, "contextualization" of the concept.

An explicit definition may also serve to set some limits on how other terms are used in the field. The term "conflict," for instance, is much more general than what I would take as the meaning of "ambivalence." "Conflict" can range from indecisiveness, to tensions, to antagonistic interests, and to the clash of physical forces. Many conflicts may be resolved – be it by mutual agreement, by contract, by compromise, by subordination, or even by destruction. These mechanisms do not work in the case of ambivalence, however, because with ambivalence the basic tension remains; it is "pending conflict." Another way this distinction can be expressed is by characterizing ambivalence as a juxtaposition of two forces that cannot fully balanced against each other. Ambivalence expresses an incomplete, imperfect "accountability" (see also Curran, 2002).

The following proposition, then, while appropriately groomed for the application of the concept in the analysis of intergenerational relations, is also an attempt toward a general understanding of ambivalence. It is thought to provide a better sense of what precisely can be meant by ambivalence, and where possible divergences in our understanding of the term can be identified. I start with the definition to be followed by a set of explanations:

For the purposes of sociological research (on intergenerational relations), it is useful to speak of ambivalence when polarized simultaneous emotions, thoughts, volitions, actions, social relations, and/or structures that are considered relevant for the constitution of individual or collective identities are (or can be) interpreted as temporarily or even permanently irreconcilable.

In the sense that it is intended to help give direction to scholarly (scientific) analysis, and contains therefore a heuristic component, this definition can be called pragmatic. It focuses on elements that may be directly or indirectly related to empirical observations. The usefulness of the definition – its validity or truth, so to speak – is measured by the extent to which it helps to organize empirical observations, to integrate results of research, and to connect insights from different disciplines. Given this intention, it should be understood as tentative and in need of confirmation through results and their acceptance in the scientific community.

This working definition contains some elements – such as polarization or opposition – which seem obvious and generally understood. Going a step further, though, I propose to see in ambivalence not merely a formal opposition, but something that is embedded in the very processes of thinking, feeling, doing, relating, and organizing. From this perspective, ambivalences are dynamics that must be *dealt with*.

We may label this view a pragmatic, action-oriented perspective. Ambivalence is presumed to activate, or at least to appeal to the human potential for action in social structure. In other words, dealing with ambivalence requires what Giddens and other contemporary sociologists speak of as "agency" (see, for example, Malcomb Waters, 1994). In turn, agency implies the awareness of identity (be it individual or collective). It is therefore appropriate to include an explicit reference to identity in our working definition. Support for this view comes also from authors from the field of applied psychotherapy (Weingardt, 2000). The client may enter the situation reluctantly, hoping for a change, yet at the same time, he or she should accept his or her self-image. The therapist, in turn, strives to activate the creative resources of the client, being aware of the client's dependency and need for help (Linehan, 1993; Miller & Rollnick, 2002). Under these circumstances, dealing with ambivalence has the character of a dialogue which may be conducted intra- or interpersonally. Consequently, negotiation is an important mode of dealing with ambivalence. In this connection, reference should be made to Jekeli's concern with what she calls "Ambivalenztoleranz" (tolerance of ambivalence). She uses the idea of tolerating and enduring ambivalence as the point of departure for strategies to cope – more or less successfully – with ambivalence (Jekeli, 2002).

Thus, systematically speaking, the following points may be seen as core of the proposed definition:

Identity: The origin of the concept of ambivalence, as we have seen, is its use as an element in the diagnosis of schizophrenia, a disorder that severely affects person-ality. More recently, difficulties in dealing with ambivalence have been proposed to be part of the symptomatology of the borderline personality disorder (Kernberg, 1979; Linehan, 1993). The incapacity to cope with ambivalence in a proper way – that is, a way that is accepted in a given socio-cultural context – may lead to psychic disorders and severe problems in interactions, hence to difficulties in the constitution of personal identity.

The basic issue concerns the ability to handle simultaneously competing perspectives toward one and the same object, which at the personal level also can be toward the self. Sociologically, ambivalence can be ascribed to relationships. The emphasis in both cases is always on two polarized yet interdependent components. We can hypothesize that people cope with ambivalence in more or less competent, productive ways. Deliberately constructing ambivalences can also be a strategy in social interaction – another reason to view ambivalence as both an opportunity and a burden. Furthermore, the experience of ambivalence can be related to psychological well-being (Pillemer, this volume). All these considerations include a (sometimes implicit) reference to the self or identity.

Time, irreconcilability, and conflict: Adding the temporal dimension, we can speak of polarized forces that cannot be fully reconciled within a limited or even an unlimited time span. Ambivalence can be experienced in situations in which a child cares for an elderly parent, and it also can be seen in regard to the entire biographical history of the relationships between parents and their children (see Segal, this volume). The specific temporal qualities of ambivalence can also be expressed by the term "oscillation," as used in theoretical writings about family therapy (Simon, 1998). Awareness of temporary or enduring irreconcilability is an important feature; it fundamentally distinguishes ambivalence from conflict, insofar as conflict can, at least in principle, be resolved. If we regard ambivalence as conceptually prior to both harmony and conflict, then we can treat both as common ways of dealing with ambivalence. Such a view is based on the general proposition (or hypothesis) that ambivalence is both a possibility and a challenge of the *"condition humaine."*

Attribution and interpretation: Not to be comprehended as innate, ambivalence may be understood as the product or consequence of an attribution or interpretation made by actors themselves, other persons, therapists, or social scientists. This insistence on ambivalence as a product of interpretation is inspired by uses of the term in art and literature. However, it should be underscored that interpretation is a central, not disposable, element of the definition. It clarifies the epistemological quality of ambivalence as a "construct." From a social-psychological point of view, ambivalence (and a model of dealing with ambivalence as suggested below) may even be comprehended as "mental representation."

The insistence on interpretation also emphasizes the pragmatic aspects of the idea of "irreconcilability," as the processes of interpretation locate a given experience of ambivalence in a social, interpersonal context and its temporal dimension; these may be seen as more or less limited, but also may be seen as "open" or unlimited. In other words: the experience of ambivalence may persist for a certain time span, and then may lapse because the context loses its relevance. The notion of interpretation also allows us to account for cases where ambivalence is denied or repressed by the actors, yet third persons may uncover it.

Indeed, people differ in the extent to which they are aware of ambivalence. Thus, we must distinguish between manifest, explicit, overt ambivalence on one hand, and latent, implicit, covert ambivalence on the other. These two types must be studied by means of different research methods.

Overt ambivalence can be asked about directly, even in everyday language – for instance, asking a parent if he or she has feelings of being torn. Researchers encounter certain limits, however, imposed by linguistic skills, comprehension, and personal mechanisms influenced by what is considered socially desirable and acceptable. Consequently, it also is desirable and necessary to develop methods of indirect assessment for covert ambivalences. These methods are presented in several of the later chapters in this volume.

There is more at stake than just words in the attempt to produce accurate definitions. The fundamental issue here is about how closely we can bring our thinking into alignment with the reality of social life as it is lived today. In this regard, and by way of a first approximation, we may distinguish two ways that the concept of ambivalence is applied in the social sciences, including psychology and psychotherapy.

First, the term can serve as *interpretative (or explanatory)* concept. This is, in fact, its primary use in macro-sociological texts – as, for instance, in Bauman's characterization of "postmodernity" as pervaded with ambivalence. References to social reality are confined to generalizations, based mostly on highly aggregated, generalized data. Sometimes, outstanding examples are called to the fore, to be seen as enlightening illustrations. Descriptions are sometimes presented in the form of "ideal-types" or "model personalities" such as Bauman's proposed "tourist" or "player" (Bauman, 1997).

In contrast, a second approach to, or use of, the concept of ambivalence begins with viewing it as a *research construct* which is to be operationalized. The goal is to apply the concept in research – such as surveys, experiments, observations, and the analysis of documents. For this purpose, an explicit definition is necessary – one that can serve as the reference point for formulating specific hypothesis and constructing research instruments.

The definition offered here is intended to serve both of these uses, facilitating the discourse between different approaches and disciplines. It attempts to circumscribe the core meaning of the concept, and it refers to elements that are relevant for more elaborated usages.

Any definition provokes the question of differentiation from related terms. Ultimately, this issue is a matter of convention, but it may facilitate mutual understanding and transdisciplinary work to recall the epistemology and the history of a term, as well as how it is used in individual disciplines, even in different approaches or schools within a given discipline. It is beyond the scope of this chapter to offer this kind of analysis for terms associated with or similar to ambivalence such as: dilemma, paradox, or the social-psychological concept of cognitive dissonance. However, at least a brief note is appropriate in regard to the concept of "ambiguity."

Interestingly, the term ambiguity is much older than ambivalence, and its history reaches back into the 17th century. In present language, the two terms are often used synonymously. Encyclopedic sources such as *The Oxford English Dictionary* or *Websters Dictionary* highlight in ambiguity the idea of uncertainty, and that it implies having more than two meanings. In contrast, ambivalence focuses on bipolar tensions, at least in most usages of the term. In scholarly language, the concept of "tolerance of ambiguity" (Ambiguitätstoleranz), as suggested apparently by Frenkel-Brunswik in connection with the famous study of the "Authoritarian Personality" (Adorno et al., 1950, p. 461; Frenkel-Brunswik, 1949/1950), enjoys certain popularity. It refers to one's ability to endure uncertainty and contradiction in the relationships with another person. This meaning comes close to the idea of dealing with ambivalence, as discussed in more detail by Jekeli (2002). A specific clinical meaning which includes the dimension of coping is Boss' theory of "Ambiguous Loss" (see Chap. 9, this volume; also Lüscher & Pillemer, 1998, p. 416).

OPERATIONALIZING INTERGENERATIONAL AMBIVALENCE

Generally speaking, operationalization means establishing rules that specify how a concept should be used to guide systematic observation and interpretations. This involves deciding which observable facts the concept should be associated with and in what manner. In a narrower sense, the aim is to develop measurement procedures. The definition of the concept serves as a starting point, especially in regard to the explicitly addressed elements or dimensions, in which different degrees or levels of concreteness can be discerned.

Predispositions for Ambivalence in Intergenerational Relations

The working definition and the history of the term do not suggest that ambivalence is an innate, a priori, or "given" attribute or quality of any social phenomenon, not even of intergenerational relations. However, using the concept heuristically implies the assumptions that empirical indicators of ambivalence (as noted above) are likely to be found in intergenerational relations, and that dealing with ambivalence is a task or challenge often posed by them. In this section, I would like to support the case for making these assumptions by means of three arguments that address the question: Why is it useful, or even advisable, to analyze intergenerational relations under the premise that they may require dealing with ambivalence?

The first argument is general and even epistemological. It refers back to the basic meaning of the term "generation." Nash (1978, p. 1) convincingly argues:

> Our most secure standard for defining a generation rests on the Greek root of the word *genos*, whose basic meaning is reflected in the word *genesthais*, to come into existence . . . . That moment when a child is born simultaneously produces a new generation separating parent and offspring – *gonos ergo genos* – and the very concept evokes the paradox of an ever-shifting threshold in time.

Thus, "generation" stands both for continuity and for beginning. It is used in the context of family roles (parents vs. children), but it also distinguishes the older from the younger within the same population. How this differentiation is socially and culturally achieved and accentuated is a major theme of societal development. It displays a complex temporal structure composed of interplay, or interactions, between the past and the future. Both are represented in the present, as is expressed in Pinder's (1928/1961) famous dictum of the "Ungleichzeitigkeit des Gleichzeitigen" ("non-contemporaneity of the contemporary"). Generation refers not only to "procreation," but also to descent from an ancestor. New life is procreated, and at the same time the emerging individual is integrated in an existing social unity.

No matter how strongly parents and children are bonded to one another throughout their lives and experiences, the latter can never become completely identical with the former. Not only are intergenerational relations formally indissoluble, they also are characterized by this fundamental difference from other relationships. Pragmatically speaking, experiences and identities even may be in opposition to each other in intergenerational relations. The ongoing oscillation between sameness and difference which necessarily ensues, constitutes a basic epistemological and anthropological *precondition* for ambivalence.

The second argument is phenomenological and more concrete. It refers to how relationships between parents and (adult) children are experienced in everyday life. It also concerns the understanding that people may have about the characteristics and specific qualities of these relationships. Although the topic is discussed in the scientific literature on personal relationships, intergenerational relationships are seldom in the focus. This thread of my argument relates to Smelser's proposition (discussed above) regarding how "dependence" in personal relationships is likely to breed ambivalence. Closeness and intimacy may reinforce or strengthen the susceptibility for ambivalence.

Indeed, dependence is an obvious component of intergenerational relations. We see it from birth (or even during pregnancy) through childhood and youth until adulthood, and in many cases even late in the life span. It manifests very early in the needs for nurture, care, protection, and education. Beyond these immediate obligations, and in the course of fulfilling them, parents develop and acquire specific information and particular knowledge about an individual child as a person – that is, about his or her personality and self. This understanding of the child's personality is relevant for decisions that concern his or her well-being and development. It also reinforces the parents' power to control and to discipline the child, not only when he or she is small but also in later phases of life.

While many decisions are matters of daily routine, others may become of crucial importance in later life. Consider, for instance, the impact of their choice of kindergarten, or of a certain type of school, or of approving or denying the child's participation in certain cultural activities or sports. Parents should decide and act on behalf of and in the (best) interest of a child or youth who, later on, may demand that they explain or justify why they decided or acted as they did. Thus, parental authority has limitations. The awareness that they have to act on the child's behalf without knowing for certain how things will work out, and how the child may see those results later, can constitute a breeding ground for ambivalence.

In this context of dependency, power, and accountability, the closeness and physical intimacy that good parent-child relations require also can occasion ambivalence. If the line between physical intimacy and sexual intimacy is not clearly drawn and observed, for example, this area can be particularly susceptible to it. Most cultures have found themselves required to enforce taboos in this realm, most prominently with respect to incest.

Further along in the intergenerational life course, the direction of dependency between children, parents, and older or younger generations may become more complicated – support and care are specific instances explored in this book. Yet the authority of the elder, established early in life, may persist as another source of ambivalence even as situations arise that produce a possible or real reversal of dependency. Cohler and Grunebaum's studies of relationships between mothers and daughters in·Italian immigrant families (1981, pp. 120ff., 197ff.) provide many convincing illustrations of this process.

A third reason for looking at intergenerational ambivalence can be deduced from a close examination of the structural and cultural conditions of contemporary western (postmodern) societies. On the macro-sociological level, population dynamics establish a framework in which ambivalence easily emerges. The rise in life expectancy, attributable to improved living conditions for increasingly large segments of the population, was accompanied by a decrease in infant mortality. As a child's chance of survival became more likely, the possibility of seeing each child as an individual person was enhanced. The decrease in the birth rate was a logical consequence. Childhood and youth soon were seen as specific phases of the life-course calling for their own institutions – for instance, public schooling. The same observation can be made with respect to the other end of the life course via the recognition of aging as a stage of life calling for its own institutions. The rise of gerontology as a science is one indicator, as is, for instance, the popular distinction between the "young old" and the "old old." The distinction is loosely drawn in keeping with the need for intensive care. Finally, even the life period of the "middle years" began to receive attention.

This marking out of different periods or segments of the life course has led to a heightened consciousness of the importance of relationships between age groups, or in other words, between generations. This has been true especially in the realm of the family, but also in the society at large. The development of social welfare became another factor in this marking out of life-stages and of intergenerational relationships.

On the micro-social level, this differentiation of the life course into stages or segments correlates with a rising preoccupation with personal growth and the expression of personal identity. Seen through the lens of these processes, the traditional dynamics of intergenerational relationships are no longer taken for granted. They become issues requiring conscious action, and in this way they gain in importance.

Ambivalence consequently is more likely to be widespread in the general population today than it has been in the past, and is more consciously perceived and experienced. It is more important now than ever before to explicitly structure, negotiate, and organize intergenerational relationships, because the life span shared by successive generations is in general longer than in former times, and larger segments of the population are experiencing ambivalence. The rise in ambivalence is one by-product of the increasing diversity of contemporary lifestyles (Coontz, 2000).

Last, but not least, the traditional assignment to women of the responsibility to care for family members is not regarded unreflectively regarded as socially justifiable. This challenge to traditional assumptions about who "should" do what with respect to family care, in connection with changes in gender roles, is a important factor in producing a greater consciousness of intergenerational ambivalence (Connidis & McMullin, 2002a).

Any sociological work on the topic has to be aware of Karl Mannheim's seminal essay on the problem of generations (Mannheim, 1928/1993, p. 200), which serves as the point of departure for a genuinely sociological perspective in the field. Mannheim was primarily concerned about social progress and its paradoxes. He turned his attention to the dynamics inherent in the succession of generations, especially to the differences in their perspectives of what is in keeping with "the times." Out of this he elaborated a precise terminology about the notion of generation, differentiating between "generation status," "generation as actuality," and "generation unit."

Noteworthy in our context, however, is Mannheim's proposition to connect the simple fact of belonging to a generation with the awareness of "identity" (although he did not use this term). He emphasized the importance of the formative experiences of youth though, interestingly, he did not really take into account the role of the family. As a consequence, Mannheim's notion of generation is exclusively societal and does not include genealogical succession. We may speculate that this shortcoming derives from his preoccupation with the confrontation between conservative and progressive political and cultural movements (Kettler, Meja & Stehr, 1987; Mannheim, 1927). Or perhaps it is due, or partly due, to the fact that in his historical period, the family was primarily seen as an institution, based on another institution, marriage, of which parenthood was seen as self-evident consequence. This understanding of the family has changed over time. Together with the growing awareness of the consequences of longevity, and the daily awareness of an expanding common life span between the old and the young, the attention has turned to the task of organizing intergenerational relationships, particularly among kin and family members. We may locate here the "new" problem of generations.

What is Meant by "Relationships"?

Preceding discussions and considerations of ambivalence take as self-evident what is meant by "social relationships." This practice corresponds with a long tradition in the social sciences, where even classical authors only rarely gave serious thought to a systematic elaboration of the concept itself. In sociology, Max Weber, Georg Simmel, and Leopold von Wiese are among the exceptions. Since the 1970s, however, efforts have been made to establish a transdisciplinary science of personal or interpersonal relationships. These developments can be seen in reviews by Blumstein and Kollock (1988) and Berscheid (1994), among others. Donati (1990) and Emirbayer and Mische (1998) have attempted to establish the foundations for a genuine sociological approach based on the concept of relationship.

An attempt to clarify also the basic dimensions of the concept of interrelationship can profit from the seminal work of Hinde (1976), who made the following major points:

> A relationship involves a series of interactions in time. By an interaction we usually mean a sequence in which individual A shows behaviour X to individual B or A shows X to B and B responds with Y .... Interactions involving a sequence of behavioural events can be classified according to the extent to which each response by each participant was determined by the preceding behaviour of the other participant .... In studying relationships, it is a proper assumption that each interaction affects the future course of the relationship, even if only by confirming the status quo. In other words, any stability that a relationship has is dynamic in nature. Since all relationships are prone to change ... stability in a relationship is a relative matter (pp. 3–4).

Hinde also lays out the importance of control and power in the context of relationship, although he does not elaborate this point.

We commonly speak about how we get along with somebody else, or how we are related to someone. Usually we describe generalized emotional judgements, for instance by saying how close we feel to her or him as a person. Or we may speak of having "mixed feelings," often meaning that we see ourselves torn between feeling close to that person and feeling distant from them. This common way of describing relationships is often taken up in social research, and it can also be used to assess ambivalence. Questions posed in just this sort of language appear in the research instruments developed and applied in the Konstanz and Ithaca studies and by Fingerman (see Chapters by Lüscher and Lettke, Pillemer, and Fingerman and Hay in this volume). The great advantage of this approach lies in the familiarity of the language and the ease of understanding what is being asked.

But familiarity has its limits. The statements are very general and therefore evoke unequivocal responses. The information that can be gained in this way is limited to overt forms of ambivalence. From an analytical perspective, it therefore seems desirable, at least conceptually, to explore possibilities that can offer a more differentiated comprehension of what we will call "relational ambivalence."

Since relationships are self-referential and thus recursive, they not only are experienced as encounters between two (or more) subjects but also are to be seen as bound to a "system" that provides a framework for the interactions and promotes their continuity. It is therefore reasonable to distinguish two dimensions of social relationships: The first refers to the individuals involved as subjects, with their personal attributes; the second concerns the structural context. Since the latter emerges from the establishment of rules and norms, it seems appropriate to call it the "institutional" component, especially in the case of the family. Such usage is in accordance with the premises of a pragmatic-interactionist or social-constructivist notion of social institutions, as developed by Berger and Luckmann (1966, pp. 47–128).

On one hand, institutional conditions are reinforced and reproduced by the ways people live out their relationships. On the other, these conditions are influenced by general societal conditions, such as stratification into social classes and distinctions among socio-cultural units based, for instance, on ethnographic classifications. Many contemporary approaches also view gender as a structural category.

In their attempt to further extend the theory of intergenerational ambivalence, Connidis and McMullin (2002a) make a strong case for what they call "structural ambivalence." With this term they are referring to social conditions that give rise to ambivalence. They conceptualize ambivalence "as socially structured contradictions made manifest in interaction," and they see ambivalence as "created by the contradictions and paradoxes that are embedded in sets of structured social relations (e.g. class, age, race, ethnicity, gender) through which opportunities, rights, and privileges are differentially distributed" (p. 565). This notion of ambivalence comes close to the idea of conflict as developed in "critical theory," in a general sense of that term. Further discussions about the specifics of structural ambivalence in their understanding seem necessary.

These authors also held that "managing ambivalence in daily life shapes the very social structures that produce ambivalence in the first place, through either reproduction of the existing order or its transformation. Thus, a critical, sociological conception of ambivalence bridges social structure and individual lives by emphasizing the tensions between them, as individuals attempt to meet their own, their family's, and society's contradictory demands and expectations" (p. 565). This view is compatible with the intentions followed up here by putting an emphasis on relationships so as to build a bridge between the personal and the structural conditions of ambivalence. Connidis and McMullin also think that, because of cultural and linguistic differences, calling this dimension "institutional" may lead to misunderstanding (2002b, p. 600). Adding the term "structural" to the proposed working label for this dimension may help to remind us that all institutions imply social structures.

In addition, a closer look into relationships allows us to distinguish between micro- and macro-social spheres of social conduct, as well as to combine both in our view. Relationships can be conceived as taking place in face-to-face encounters between two or more persons. Relationships emerge from direct interaction and as such are, so to say, "primary" relationships. But the concept of relationship also can be used to describe the mutual influence and connectedness of different social units such as two families, or the community and the church. Relationships of this kind may be called "mediated" or "secondary."

Primary relationships can be influenced by secondary relationships. The field of intergenerational relations provides many examples of this. For instance, the way a daughter cares for her elderly mother may also reflect how older generations in a society are interrelated with the younger generations – which in turn depends, as one "mediating instance," upon the availability of social welfare institutions for care and support. Similarly, the mutual understanding of husband and wife (including, for example, their ability to eventually accept divorce) depends upon the contemporary societal and cultural view of gender relations.

The distinction between primary and secondary relationships can also be understood in terms of social time, not only social space or place. From this perspective, "primary" refers to the immediate present, "secondary" to the past and possibly also the future. Consider, for example, a concrete situation in which a mother is torn between accepting and refusing her adult daughter's help with housekeeping. Looking back on the history of how they have gotten along through the years, the mother may recall situations in which accepting her daughter's help created embarrassing feelings of dependence. In this case, the subjective-personal dimension includes a reference to the history of the relationship between the two parties.

Looking into the temporal preconditions of ambivalence draws our attention to the need to be aware of the life course as a whole. One can hypothesize, as for instance is suggested by Pillemer and Suitor (2002), that a turning point or a crisis situation may be especially sensitive to the experience of ambivalence. This approach also can take into account the institutional-structural dimension, as the passage from youth to adult is at least partially determined by sociocultural dictates and customs. If in a given society – as in, for instance, present-day Italy (see Donati & Sgritta, 2002) – the requirement to become independent is countermanded by adverse economic conditions such as widespread unemployment, ambivalence is likely and widespread. Ambivalence may be felt intensely, for example, on a beautiful morning when a father, going to work, is torn between demanding that his unemployed son "get up and do something reasonable" while also empathizing with the son's deplorable situation.

Another circumstance that breeds intergenerational ambivalence arises when a child begins the process of leaving the parental home. Grown children usually feel entitled to lead their own private lives, but at the same time they often want to continue receiving certain types of assistance from their parents – for example, financial help or benefits such as having laundry done for them or borrowing the family car. In such situations, parents may ask themselves whether they should help their children (with or without strings attached). They may sometimes even feel that they are being exploited. If they consequently make their help available on conditions of having certain demands or requests met, they may reduce their children's sense of independence. In such situations, it appears difficult to set limits. On a structural level, data show that since 1990, many adult children are getting older when they finally move out; this can be interpreted as a possible structural indicator of increasing intergenerational ambivalence (Lauterbach & Lüscher, 1999).

To summarize: Both primary and secondary relationships – in terms of behaviors, opportunities, and ways of understanding – are deeply embedded in societal structures and in individual and family mentalities. In this connection, Curran (2002) refers to the "embeddedness," of ambivalence. One is reminded of some approaches in the socio-ecological traditions, for instance, in the models sketched out by Bronfenbrenner (1979, 1995; see also Moen, Elder & Lüscher, 1995).

Intergenerational relations are embedded in a family system which is characterized, sociologically speaking, by a society's prevailing structural, procedural, and normative conditions. These structural-institutional "givens" shape familial relationships. They create a "family world" into which the individual is born.

family world

The Konstanz Model of Intergenerational Ambivalence

Many who study intergenerational relationships, including those between parents and young children, consider the tension between autonomy and dependence to be a central issue (see, for example, Cohler, 1983). Many would also agree that any aspect of the relationship that touches upon this area is a breeding ground for ambivalence. The analytical considerations of the concept of relationship that we have explored above, however, may provide a distinction and a differentiation that can prove useful in this context. Before exploring how the two dimensions of relationship provide a primary guiding idea for the Konstanz schema, we should consider several background issues.

The idea of describing the field of social interactions and relations in terms of two dimensions – an individualistic-subjective component and a structural-societal component – is well known in the social sciences. One example from the classical literature is G. H. Mead's notion of the self as emerging from the interplay between "I and Me," where "I" refers to spontaneous subjectivity and "me" refers to generalized other (Mead, 1938). Recollection of this theory is important, given the relevance for the self (i.e. one's conscious personal identity) of the experience of ambivalence. Many interpersonal models of personality explicitly refer to Mead. For example, Leary (who developed a circumplex model that describes personality between the poles of love vs. hate and dominance vs. submission), speaks of Mead as a "creative watershed to which later theories of interpersonal relations can trace their sources" (Leary, 1957, p. 101).

A more recent interpersonal circumplex model building upon this tradition is that of Benjamin (1974, 1982; Benjamin, Foster, Roberto & Estroff, 1986; Benjamin & Wonderlich, 1994), who tries to conceptualize even psychic disorders in forms of interpersonal behavior that can be analyzed using the dimensions of love/hate and dominance/autonomy. Benjamin explicitly conceptualizes ambivalence as behavior that alternates between these poles and refers to the self. The use of a two-dimensional model also can be found in the literature on family therapy. Olson's so-called circumplex model is one popular example (Olson, 1986; Olson, Sprenkle & Russell, 1979).

A note of caution is appropriate, however. It is important to remember that schematic models serve heuristic purposes. A degree of simplification (to allow for clear graphic presentation) and a certain open-endedness (due to the ambiguity or equivocal nature of generalized terminology) may bring forward contradictions and stimulate further thoughts that are fruitful for the development of a theory. These qualities are unique to schematic models and may account for their popularity, which can be traced to a long history of this kind of presentation (Bogen & Thürlemann, 1998).

Following these leads, conceptual and empirical researchers at the University of Konstanz encouraged the development of schematic models for the analysis of intergenerational ambivalence. I present the basic outlines of this research in the remaining portions of this chapter, and two other chapters in this book will provide more detail. Our intention is to offer one possible example of how one might advance the conceptualization and the operationalization of intergenerational am-bivalence. Chapter 4 (Lettke & Klein) reviews some of the methodological issues involved in this process, and Chap. 7 (Lüscher & Lettke) reports on results from studies based on the Kostanz model (see also: Lüscher & Pajung-Bilger, 1998).

The model is based on the premises discussed in the previous section of this paper. We should also recall that the concept of ambivalence has, epistemo-logically and theoretically, the status of a construct. This means, briefly stated, that it cannot be observed directly. It must be deduced from indicators that refer to attitudes, cognitions, and behaviors that we can connect with labels that designate juxtaposed poles characteristic of ambivalence. Such labels are needed for both the subjective-personal and the structural-institutional dimension of relationships (Fig. 1).

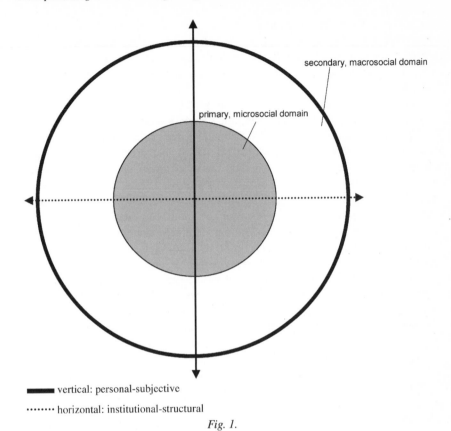

vertical: personal-subjective

horizontal: institutional-structural

Fig. 1.

The *personal* or *subjective* dimension can be characterized as follows. Parents, children, and the members of other involved generations share a certain degree of similarity. While some of this similarity can be attributed to biological inheritance, no inheritance is total, insofar as individual parents and individual children are never genetically identical. Their similarity is, however, reinforced by the intimacy of interactive learning processes, which creates the possibility for closeness and subjective identification. At the same time, and especially in the process of maturation, parent-child similarity also can be a cause of and reason for divergence. Ultimately, children develop different personal identities than their parents.

For the schematic presentation, two fairly abstract labels are needed. To account not only for the socio-spatial but also for the socio-temporal aspects, we propose the terms "convergence" and "divergence." Those two polarities can serve as umbrellas for a variety of attributes. Convergence includes such attributes as loving, warm, solicitous, reliable, and close. Divergence is illustrated by cool, easy-going, indifferent, and superficial (see also Chap. 7, Lüscher & Lettke).

For the *institution-structural* dimension, we can conceive of a polar opposition between a desire to preserve the traditional social form or structure of relationships and a desire for dramatic change. Neither is fully realizable. For instance, although children may choose a way of organizing his or her private life that is vastly different from what is customary in their family of origin, some ties to childhood experiences may remain, even if only that they provide a negative background. As technical designations, taking into account again the socio-temporal as well as the socio-spatial aspects, the terms "reproduction" and "innovation" appear useful to express the idea of a dynamic polarization. Here, reproduction includes attributes such as inflexible, restrictive, and "stuck in a rut." Innovation is expressed by terms such as open to new experiences, changeable, and so on.

The differentiation between the subjective-personal and the institutional-structural dimension (as schematic and therefore still very broad and general as it may be) suggests the analytical distinction between personal and structural ambivalences. However, in reality, the subjective-personal and institutional-structural components are interwoven. The mix of the two dimensions is especially obvious in practice, in the ways people deal with ambivalence in daily life.

As mentioned above, one possible benefit of schematic models, which has to be weighed against their shortcomings, is to encourage further ideas. Along this line, the proposed model not only distinguishes analytically two basic types of ambivalence (personal vs. institutional), but also suggests basic strategies people can call upon to deal with ambivalences. This can be observed in regard to both the primary and the secondary realms of relationship and their related activities.

In order to include the role of power and authority, we refer to ideas of Baumrind (1978, 1996), as outlined in her typology of parental styles. This author distinguishes among three parental styles: authority, authoritarian, and laissez-faire. In the case of authority, emphasis is placed on the idea that traditional structures imply a generalized orientation to the well-being of the subjects involved under the name and the general notion of the common good: Under such circumstances, ambivalences are restrained or evaded. The authoritarian perspective gives high priority to personal growth and personality development. Ambivalence can be accepted and should be discussed. Intergenerational relations in the laissez-faire mode focus on the formal equality of the involved individuals. Under such circumstances, we can assume a tendency to deny ambivalence. The fourth type suggested by our schematic model is not found in Baumrind's original typology. Yet it points to conditions that can be observed empirically and characterized as ones in which people become entangled and entrapped. Ambivalences are strongly experienced and become obvious – if not to the parents and children themselves, then at least to outside observers.

On the macro level of society, we can distinguish cultural patterns that structure intergeneration relationships. As general designations, we offer the terms solidarity, emancipation, atomization, and captivation. These labels (but not the dimensions they refer to) may be modified if they seem too general or are understood as linked to any particular culture. On the micro level, when parents and adult children interact and solve problems together in social situations, they use "situational patterns of meaning" which can be generalized to "maxims" of practical action (for these notions see Lüscher & Lettke, this volume). These must be discovered and identified through research. Based on our qualitative research to date, we offer the following initial propositions in a graphic presentation as shown in Fig. 2.

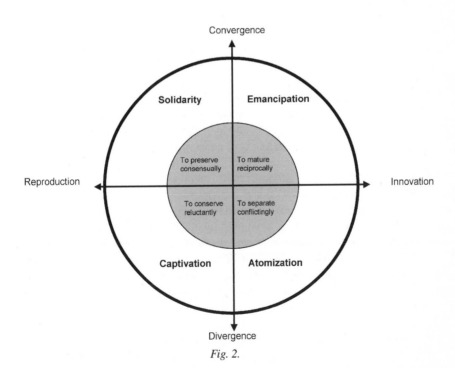

Fig. 2.

(1) *Solidarity* refers to reliable support, or the willingness of the generations to provide each other with services of a not necessarily reimbursable sort. This involves the exercise of authority, but not in the sense of a one-sided exertion of influence and power. Rather, it is understood as representative action including empathy. The maxim of action can be characterized as to "preserve consensually." The members of a family feel committed to their traditions and get along with one another quite well. Thus, "solidarity" is one possible mode of dealing with intergenerational ambivalences, which in this case may be more covert than overt. (It should be noted that this term implies a specific notion of solidarity, and that the term "loyalty" also may be appropriate for this dynamic.)

(2) Where family members strive for *emancipation*, actions predominate that support mutual emotional attachment (convergence) and openness toward institutional change (innovation). Relationships between parents and children are organized in such a way that the individual development and personal unfolding of all family members is furthered without losing sight of their mutual interdependence. This general setting contains a certain amount of direct, common purpose pursued by efforts to "mature reciprocally." Tensions can be discussed openly and temporary practical solutions can be negotiated continually.

(3) *Atomization* takes into account that family cohesiveness is no longer assured by institutional ties and the subjective experiences of relational histories. The concept expresses fragmentation of the family unit into its smallest components, specifically individual family members, who "separate conflictingly." Apart from the unalterable fact that family members are parents and children, they otherwise have very little in common. Actions follow a line of conflicting separation, although an awareness of generational bonds remains.

(4) *Captivation* designates cases where the family as an institution is invoked to support the claims of one family member against another. A fragile relationship of subordination and superiority thereby arises, in which moral demands and moral pressure are used to exert power. Usually one generation, predominantly the parental, attempts – by invoking the institutional order – to assert claims on the other or to bind them by means of moral terms without, however, basing its demands on a sense of personal solidarity. The guiding maxim here is to "conserve reluctantly" and family members may try to "instrumentalize" each other, not respecting each other as subjects, but using each other as "means to an end" or objects.

I would like to underscore the tentative heuristic character of the model. It is an attempt to synthesize and to visualize the basic assumptions about intergenerational ambivalence, and to suggest a first set of labels for the poles that characterize the dimension of simultaneously experienced juxtapositions. It also suggests ways to see how the micro- and the macro systems are embedded in a social ecology of action. As a general schematic representation, the model encourages further differentiations and adaptations to specific topics of research.

SUMMARY AND DISCUSSION: STEPS TO UNCOVER INTERGENERATIONAL AMBIVALENCE – PAST, PRESENT, AND FUTURE

This chapter's major topics are conceptualization and research strategies. The first part explored the meanings of ambivalence. Adopting the "pragmatic" ideas of Peirce's semiotic triangle (Rohr, 1993), we first pay attention to the term, its epistemology and its history, then to the phenomena that are of interest, and third to the perspectives, theories, and disciplines that connect term and phenomena by way of interpretation. This process of semiotic "triangulation" establishes and uncovers contextualized meanings of ambivalence.

This kind of analysis provides a basis for definitional considerations. Staying faithful to the "pragmatic" orientation (in the sense of pragmatism as a school of thought), definitions are understood – or we could say are "defined" – as tools to guide systematic inquiries. This kind of definition contains heuristic, hypothetical elements. Such contextual definitions are also means to promote discourse between disciplines and between approaches within disciplines.

With both functions in mind, we can formulate a comprehensive definition that explicitly labels the major elements relevant for analyzing ambivalence in the context of social sciences – particularly for the study of parent-adult child relationships. Such a proposal is ambitious because it may invoke dimensions or aspects that cannot be taken into account in specific research endeavors since any project, in practice, has to limit its scope. The attempt to produce a comprehensive definition may nevertheless be appropriate for theoretical reasons. In the context of this volume, it facilitates the comparison between the different approaches and the different research findings.

The chapter also addresses questions about the "operationalization" of ambivalence for the study of intergenerational relations. Here, one particular line of argumentation is presented. It departs from the general analysis of the notion of social relationship. The analysis, in combination with the key elements of the definition of ambivalence – namely the experience of simultaneous polarization interpreted as at least temporarily irreconcilable – leads to the design of a schematic model. It proposed heuristically, in the micro- and the macro-levels of conduct, four basic strategies of dealing with intergenerational ambivalence.

Critics may accuse this model of being static and too abstract. Such criticism, however, misunderstands the underlying intentions and the function of schematic models – at least of the kind presented in this chapter. The model is not static because it is not a guide to how to categorize personality traits or behaviors. It refers to strategies, to "considered actions" or "guidelines for conduct" that are called into play by having to deal with ambivalence. The abstract structure of the model is a consequence of its source in theoretical deduction (as contrasted with models based on induction in the form of empirical generalization). Most theories are based on comparatively simple assumptions, and representational models serve to recall these assumptions. At the same time, the simplicity can be read as an invitation for further differentiation.

One line of differentiation is contained in the proposed research strategy of "uncovering." Its point of departure may be found in the fact that "feeling (or being) ambivalent" is now part of everyday language. Furthermore, we have many virtually synonymous idiomatic phrases such as "being torn between x and y" that also express the state of being involved in enduring, irresolvable conflicts that must be dealt with. These common popular expressions make it feasible to ask direct questions about the awareness or experience of ambivalence. Several survey instruments do, in fact, make good use of this opportunity. (See, for example, research reports in chapters of this volume by Pillemer, Lüscher & Lettke.)

But this procedure, although easy to do, has its price. The common ways that people understand ambivalence are rather simplistic. They often evoke broad, unspecified references to "feelings." It is difficult in such situations to distinguish between dimensions or types of ambivalence, not to mention the specific problems in scaling and measurement to which such imprecision gives rise. It is also difficult to locate situations in specific social contexts.

It is therefore necessary to develop indirect measures of ambivalence, measures that require larger and more complicated sets of questions. Such instruments can more easily be used in personal interviews or in experimental studies. Under such circumstances, it also may become possible to operationalize the link between the experience of ambivalence and the awareness of personal identity or the impact of ambivalence on a person's sense of self. As briefly mentioned above, making this link to the notion of self – of personal identity and personal development – is, from a theoretical point of view, a highly desirable aspect of a fuller comprehension of ambivalence.

One important line of differentiation involves trying to clarify the interplay of social roles. To date, most empirical studies rely on reports concerning the experience of and the coping with ambivalence from the point of view of one respondent. However, it is highly desirable to assess the views of both people in a dyad and, if possible, of all members of a family. Indeed, a still to be explored domain concerns the element of "perspectivity" in viewing and experiencing ambivalence by the involved persons and groups. To what extent do different persons and generations, in concrete situations, agree or disagree in their awareness of ambivalence?

Moreover, it would be highly desirable to shed light upon the processes of negotiation involved in these relationships. This is a strong desideratum also in the argument of Connidis and McMullin (2002a). Some preliminary efforts have been made in the Konstanz study (see this volume, Chap. 7). Yet, the practical difficulties of gaining access to all members of a family, or even to bringing them together in a common meeting, are well known. On this point, a mixture of qualitative and quantitative methods may lead to some progress. Also, new typologies concerning the strategies of dealing with ambivalence would have to be developed, based, for instance, on theories of communication, of rhetoric, and of small-group research. The insights from family therapy may also be a source of further hypothesis.

Another task of differentiation that lies before us concerns the interplay of more than two generations. Indeed, in the realm of family and kin, any generation is a link in a chain. Processes of transfer and of inheritance guarantee – in different degrees – the passing on of goods of material and of symbolic value, as well as of experiences, skills, and family memories. Bronfenbrenner (1995) makes a strong suggestion to expand the study of intergenerational relations beyond the parent-child dyad. This would be also a fruitful approach to differentiating the theory of intergenerational ambivalence. Questions that come to mind include: Does the experience of ambivalence between two generations have an impact on the relationships among other generations? Are the applied and learned strategies of dealing with ambivalence passed on from one generation to the next as the concept of "delegation" as introduced into family therapy by Stierlin (1984) suggests? To what extent and in what way are ambivalences present in grandparent-grandchild relationships?

Another field of differentiation concerns the study of ambivalence in regard to specific activities. One important example is in the area of caregiving, as can be deduced from the large body of literature on care provided by adult children (mostly women) to their parents or parents-in-law. (See Lang in this volume and references there to recent publications.) Less attention has been given to the possible ambivalences embedded in the care of small children. Parenthood (and of late particularly motherhood) is an important field for research in which a focus on ambivalence may stimulate new insights. Parker's aforementioned essay on "Mother love, mother hate" is an excellent example of this; such work is also important for the theory of ambivalence itself, insofar as it shows that dealing with ambivalence can stimulate social creativity. In the domain of early socialization, more attention also should be paid to the implications of the presently so popular attachment theories and the overt as well as covert attention they give to ambivalence.

Care for the elderly as well as for small children is, to date, provided mostly by women. This draws attention to the correlations between gender and generations. Several studies uncover ambivalence between mothers and daughters. (See the already mentioned pioneering study by Cohler & Grunebaum, 1981, and in this volume Lorenz-Meyer and recent literature mentioned there, as well as the case study by Spangler, 2002.) Rare are studies on father-son dyads (still relevant: Nydegger & Mitteness, 1991).

Several contributions to this volume (Chaps by Fingerman & Hay; Lorenz-Meyer & Lang; Pillemer, Lüscher & Lettke) explore gender-based experiences of ambivalence, yet a profound analysis of this experience remains to be done. Specific studies on the experiences of gays and lesbians from the ambivalence perspective are already available, not least among them concerning their relationships to their parents (see in this volume Cohler and recent literature mentioned there; Connidis, 2001; Jekeli, 2000). The structural aspects of such ambivalence are particularly relevant in light of recent developments attempting to register and legalize homosexual partnerships (Lüscher & Grabmann, 2002).

The results of studies which already use the concept of ambivalence explicitly (in a more or less elaborated way), or those which report experiences and behaviors that lend themselves to being seen as indicators of ambivalence, demonstrate that ambivalence exists in intergenerational relations in different dyads, in different circumstances, and at different points of the life course. Our broad hypothesis is confirmed (as it should be, given its heuristic status) in a broad variety of ways. There are also findings that show that ambivalences seem not to exist.

From a theoretical point of view, we may even consider the idea that dealing with ambivalence is a "meta-task" in the context of intergenerational relations – a task that pervades all the concrete tasks around which intergenerational relations are organized. Ambivalence can be understood as a "dimension" which can precede or underlie any concrete action. This again is compatible with understanding intergenerational relations as an anthropologically assigned task that must be fulfilled, and one which is carried out in different ways. The modes of dealing with ambivalence can be seen as learned and internalized, and models about different strategies can eventually be comprehended as culturally transmitted "mental representations." Paradoxically speaking, this universal and abstract quality of ambivalence may be a major reason why doing research with this concept promotes the approximation to social realities – at least if we consider everyday experience, in analogy to everyday language – as their ultimate reference.

Still, a broad expanse of theoretical work lies before us. More efforts (and discussions) are needed to clarify in principle and in detail the similarities and the differences between the theories of intergenerational ambivalence and intergenerational solidarity, as referred to in the introduction of this book. Of special interest would be a closer look at the interplay between the dimensions of solidarity and patterns of dealing with ambivalence (Bengtson, Giarusso, Mabry & Silverstein, 2002). Further investigations are also necessary to clarify the structural embeddedness of ambivalence. This is also important in order to explore the fruitfulness of the concept for broader issues of social policy, such as ageing (Tesch-Römer et al., 2000), or the conceptualization of social policies for children (Lüscher, 2002). The idea of ambivalence as a bridging concept between the micro- and the macrosocial spheres (which is in agreement, for instance, with the intentions of Connidis & McMullin, 2002a), needs more elaboration, especially in regard to research. It may be a fruitful domain for cross-cultural research. Finally, the question may be asked about the extent to which we can use ambivalence as a construct that is applicable to social relations in general, or at least to specific types of social relationships. In turn, such a widening of perspective may promote our understanding of specific details of intergenerational relations.

Indeed, throughout this chapter, as in the following chapters of this book, there are many references to the relevance of the concept of ambivalence to basic issues of contemporary social science and the analysis of contemporary societies. Given the attention also paid to the concept of ambivalence in other disciplines, our studies may – in addition to helping us strengthen the professional and interdisciplinary quality of intergenerational studies – contribute to broaden intellectual horizons and promote further discourses between disciplines and between theory, research, social policy, and social practice.

ACKNOWLEDGMENTS

I would like to thank the following persons for their helpful comments on earlier drafts on this chapter: Pauline Boss, Amelie Burkhardt, Ingrid Connidis, Karen Fingerman, Helena Hurme, Ines Jekeli, Frieder Lang, Frank Lettke, Dagmar Lorenz-Meyer, and Karl Pillemer. I am especially grateful to Paul Cash for his engaged, highly professional, and empathic editorial support. Thanks also to Ruth Nieffer and Denise Rüttinger for their patient work as student assistants.

REFERENCES

Adorno, T. W., Frenkel-Brunswik, E., Levinson, D. J., & Sanford, N. F. (1950). *The authoritarian personality.* New York: Harper and Brothers.

Bauman, Z. (1991). *Modernity and ambivalence.* Ithaca, NY: Cornell University Press.

Bauman, Z. (1997). *Flaneure, Spieler und Touristen: Essays zu postmodernen Lebensformen* [Flaneurs, gamblers and tourists: Essays about postmodern life-forms]. Hamburg, Germany; Hamburg Edition.

Baumrind, D. (1978). Reciprocal rights and responsibilities in parent-child relations. *Journal of Social Issues, 34,* 179–196.

Baumrind, D. (1996). Parenting: The discipline controversy revisited. *Family Relations, 45,* 405–414.

Bengtson, V. L., Giarusso, R., Mabry, B., & Silverstein, M. (2002). Solidarity, conflict, and ambivalence: Complementary or competing perspectives on intergenerational relationships? *Journal of Marriage and the Family, 64,* 568–576.

Benjamin, L. S. (1974). Structural analysis of social behavior. *Psychological Review, 81,* 392–425.

Benjamin, L. S. (1982). Use of Structural Analysis of Social Behavior (SASB) to guide intervention in psychotherapy. In: J. C. Anchin & D. J. Kiesler (Eds), *Handbook of Interpersonal Psychotherapy* (pp. 190–214). New York: Pergamon Press.

Benjamin, L. S., Foster, S. W., Roberto, L. G., & Estroff, S. E. (1986). Breaking the family code: Analysis of videotapes of family interactions by Structural Analysis of Social Behaviors (SASB). In: L. S. Greenberg & W. M. Pinsof (Eds), *The Psychotherapeutic Process: A Research Handbook* (pp. 391–439). New York: Guilford Press.

Benjamin, L. S., & Wonderlich, S. A. (1994). Social perceptions and borderline personality: The relation to mood disorders. *Journal of Abnormal Psychology, 103,* 610–624.

Berger, P., & Luckmann, T. (1966). *The social construction of reality: A treatise in the sociology of knowledge.* New York: Doubleday.

Berscheid, E. (1994). Interpersonal relationships. *Annual Review of Psychology, 45,* 79–129.

Bleuler, E. (1911). *Dementia Praecox oder Gruppe der Schizophrenien* [Dementia Praecox or the group of schizophrenia]. Leipzig, Germany: Franz Deuticke.

Bleuler, E. (1914). Die Ambivalenz [Ambivalence]. In: Universität Zürich (Ed.), *Festgabe zur Einweihung der Neubauten* (pp. 95–106). Zurich, Switzerland: Schulthess & Co.

Bleuler, M. (1972). *Die schizophrenen Geistesstörungen im Lichte langjähriger Kranken- und Familiengeschichten* [Schizophrenia in long term medical and family studies]. Stuttgart, Germany: Georg Thieme.

Blumstein, P., & Kollock, P. (1988). Personal relationships. *Annual Review of Sociology, 14,* 467–490.

Bogen, S., & Thürlemann, F. (1998). Jenseits der Opposition von Text und Bild: Überlegungen zur Theorie des Schematischen [Beyond the opposition of text and picture: Thoughts about a theory of schemata]. Unpublished manuscript.

Bronfenbrenner, U. (1979). *The ecology of human development.* Cambridge, MA: Harvard University Press.

Bronfenbrenner, U. (1995). Developmental ecology through space and time: A future perspective. In: P. Moen, G. H. Elder & K. Lüscher (Eds), *Examining Lives in Context: Perspectives on the Ecology of Human Development* (pp. 619–647). Washington, DC: American Psychological Association.

Cohler, B. J. (1983). Autonomy and interdependence in the family of adulthood: A psychological perspective. *The Gerontologist, 23,* 33–39.

Cohler, B. J., & Grunebaum, H. U. (1981). *Mothers, grandmothers and daughters: Personality and childcare in three-generation families*. New York: Wiley.

Collins English Dictionary and Thesaurus (1993). Glasgow, Scotland: HarperCollins.

Connidis, I. A. (2001, November). The intergenerational ties of gay and lesbian adults and step kin: A conceptual discussion. Paper presented at the 54th meeting of the Gerontological Society of America. Chicago, IL: Gerontological Society of America.

Connidis, I. A., & McMullin, J. A. (2002a). Sociological ambivalence and family ties: A critical perspective. *Journal of Marriage and the Family, 64*, 558–567.

Connidis, I. A., & McMullin, J. A. (2002b). Ambivalence, family ties, and doing sociology. *Journal of Marriage and the Family, 64*, 594–601.

Coontz, S. (2000). Historical perspectives on family diversity. In: D. H. Demo, K. R. Allen & M. A. Fine (Eds), *Handbook of Family Diversity* (pp. 15–31). New York: Oxford University Press.

Coser, R. L. (1964). Authority and structural ambivalence in the middle-class family. In: R. L. Coser (Ed.), *The Family: Its Structure and Functions* (pp. 370–383). New York: St. Martin's.

Coser, L. A. (1965). *The functions of social conflict*. London: Routledge.

Coser, R. L. (1966). Role distance, sociological ambivalence and transitional status systems. *American Journal of Sociology, 72*, 173–187.

Curran, S. R. (2002). Agency, accountability, and embedded relations: "What's love got to do with it?" *Journal of Marriage and the Family, 64*, 577–584.

Donati, P. (1990). Die Familie als soziale Beziehung zwischen Öffentlichem und Privatem: Jenseits der Paradoxa [The family as social relationship between the public and the private: Beyond the paradoxes]. *Annali di Sociologia (Sociological Yearbook), 6*, 94–133.

Donati, P. (1998). Sociological ambivalence in the thought of Robert K. Merton. In: C. Mongardini & S. Tabboni (Eds), *Robert K. Merton and Contemporary Sociology* (pp. 101–121). London: Transaction.

Donati, P., & Sgritta, G. B. (2002). *Il gioco delle generazioni: Famiglie e scambi sociali nelle reti primarie* [The game of generations: Family and social exchange in primary social networks]. Milan, Italy: Francoangeli.

Emirbayer, M., & Mische, A. (1998). What is agency? *American Journal of Sociology, 103*, 962–1023.

Frenkel-Brunswik, E. (1949/1950). Intolerance of ambiguity as an emotional and perceptional personality variable. *Journal of Personality, 18*, 108–143.

Freud, S. (1910/1953–1974). The antithetical meaning of primal words. In: J. Strachey & A. Freud (Eds), *The Standard Edition of the Complete Psychological Works of Sigmund Freud* (Vol. 11, pp. 155–161). London: Hogarth Press.

Freud, S. (1912/1953–1974). The dynamics of transference. In: J. Strachey & A. Freud (Eds), *The Standard Edition of the Complete Psychological Works of Sigmund Freud* (Vol. 12, pp. 99–108). London: Hogarth Press.

Freud, S. (1914/1953–1974). Some reflections on schoolboy psychology. In: J. Strachey & A. Freud (Eds), *The Standard Edition of the Complete Psychological Works of Sigmund Freud* (Vol. 13, pp. 241–244). London: Hogarth Press.

Freud, S. (1921/1953–1974). Group psychology and the analysis of the ego. In: J. Strachey & A. Freud (Eds), *The Standard Edition of the Complete Psychological Works of Sigmund Freud* (Vol. 18, pp. 69–143). London: Hogarth Press.

Freud, S. (1929/1953–1974). Civilization and its discontents. In: J. Strachey & A. Freud (Eds), *The Standard Edition of the Complete Psychological Works of Sigmund Freud* (Vol. 21, pp. 64–145). London: Hogarth Press.

Goffman, I. (1963). *Stigma: Notes on the management of spoiled identities*. Englewood Cliffs, NJ: Prentice-Hall.

Graber, G. H. (1924). *Die Ambivalenz des Kindes* [The ambivalence of the child]. Leipzig, Germany: Psychoanalytischer Verlag.

Hajda, J. (1968). Ambivalence and social relations. *Sociological Focus, 2,* 21–28.

Hinde, R. A. (1976). On describing relationships. *Journal of Child Psychology and Psychiatry, 17,* 1–19.

Hochschild, A. R. (1983). *The managed heart*. Berkeley, CA: University of California Press.

Hoffmann-Axthelm, D. (1994). *Robert Schumann: "Gücklichsein und tiefe Einsamkeit"* [Robert Schumann: "Happiness and deep loneliness"]. Stuttgart, Germany: Reclam.

Jekeli, I. (2000). Unter Männern: Schwule Liebe als Spiel mit Ambivalenzen. [Among men: Gay love as play with ambivalences.] In: K. Hahn & G. Burkart (Eds), *Grenzen und Grenzüberschreitungen der Liebe: Studien zur Soziologie Intimer Beziehungen II* [Frontiers and Trespassing of Frontiers in Love: Studies in the Sociology of Intimate Relations II] (pp. 135–163). Opladen, Germany: Leske + Budrich.

Jekeli, I. (2002). *Ambivalenz und Ambivalenztoleranz* [Ambivalence and tolerance of ambivalence]. Osnabrück, Germany: Der andere Verlag.

Junge, M. (2000). *Ambivalente Gesellschaftlichkeit: Die Modernisierung der Vergesellschaftung und die Ordnungen der Ambivalenzbewältigung* [Ambivalent sociality: Modernization and coping with ambivalence]. Opladen, Germany: Leske + Budrich.

Kernberg, O. (1979). *Borderline-Störungen und pathologischer Narzimus* [Borderline-disorders and pathological narcissism]. Frankfurt a. M., Germany: Suhrkamp.

Kettler, D., Meja, V., & Stehr, N. (1987). Karl Mannheim et "le conservatovism" [Karl Mannheim and "the conservatism"]. *Cahiers Internationaux de Sociologie, 83,* 256.

Knellessen, O. (1978). *Ambivalenz und Doppelbindung: Eine Untersuchung des psychoanalytischen Ambivalenzbegriffes* [Ambivalence and double-bind: An analysis of the psychoanalytic concept of ambivalence]. Salzburg, Austria: Universität Salzburg.

Kris, E. (2000). *Psychoanalytic explorations in art*. Madison, CT: International University Press.

Lauterbach, W., & Lüscher, K. (1999). Wer sind die Spätauszieher? [Who is moving out late from home?]. *Zeitschrift für Bevölkerungswissenschaft, 24,* 425–448.

Leary, T. (1957). *Interpersonal diagnosis of personality*. New York: Roland Press.

Levin, G. (1981). *Edward Hopper 1882–1967: Gemälde und Zeichnungen.* [Edward Hopper 1882–1967: Paintings and drawings]. Munich, Germany: Schirmer-Mosel.

Levine, D. N. (1985). *The flight from ambiguity: Essays in social and cultural theory*. Chicago: University of Chicago Press.

Levine, D. N. (1995). *Visions of the sociological tradition*. Chicago: University of Chicago Press.

Linehan, M. (1993). *Cognitive-behavioural treatment of borderline personality disorder*. New York: Guilford.

Lüscher, K. (2002). Kinderpolitik: Mit Ambivalenzen verantwortungsbewusst umgehen [Social policy for children: Dealing responsibly with ambivalences]. In: H. Oswald & H. Uhlendorff (Eds), *Wege zum Selbst: Soziale Herausforderungen für Kinder und Jugendliche* [Pathways to the Self: Social Challenges for Children and Youth] (pp. 321–343). Stuttgart, Germany: Lucius & Lucius.

Lüscher, K., & Grabmann, B. (2002). Lebenspartnerschaften mit und ohne Kinder: Ambivalenzen der Institutionalisierung privater Lebensformen [Homosexual partnerships with and without children: Ambivalences in the institutionalization of private life-forms]. *Zeitschrift für Soziologie der Erziehung und Sozialisation, 22,* 47–63.

Lüscher, K., & Pajung-Bilger, B. (1998). *Forcierte Ambivalenzen: Ehescheidung als Heraus-forderung an die Generationenbeziehungen unter Erwachsenen* [Forced ambivalences:

Divorce as a challenge to intergenerational relationships between adults]. Konstanz, Germany: Universitäts-Verlag.

Lüscher, K., & Pillemer, K. (1998). Intergenerational ambivalence: A new approach to the study of parent-child relations in later life. *Journal of Marriage and the Family, 60,* 413–425.

Luthe, H. O., & Wiedenmann, R. E. (Eds) (1997). *Ambivalenz: Studien zum kulturtheoretischen und empirischen Gehalt einer Kategorie der Erschließung des Unbestimmten* [Ambivalence: Studies about the theoretical and empirical relevance of contingency]. Opladen, Germany: Leske + Budrich.

Mannheim, K. (1927). Das konservative Denken I [Conservative thinking I]. *Archiv für Sozialwissenschaft und Sozialpolitik, 57,* 68–142.

Mannheim, K. (1993). The problem of generations. In: K. H. Wolff (Ed.), *From Karl Mannheim* (pp. 351–395). New Brunswick: Transaction.

Matt, P. V. (1995). *Verkommene Söhne, mißratene Töchter: Familiendesaster in der Literatur* [Degenerated sons, misguided daughters: Family disasters in literature]. Munich, Germany: Hanser.

Mead, G. H. (1938). *The philosophy of the act.* Chicago: University of Chicago Press.

Merton, R. K. (1976). *Sociological ambivalence and other essays.* New York: Free Press.

Merton, R. K., & Barber, E. (1963). Sociological ambivalence. In: E. A. Tiryakian (Ed.), *Sociological Theory, Values and Sociocultural Change: Essays in Honor of Pitirim A. Sorokin* (pp. 91–120). London: Free Press of Glencoe.

Miller, W. R., & Rollnick, S. (2002). *Motivational interviewing: Preparing people for change.* New York: Guilford Press.

Moen, P., Elder, G. H., & Lüscher, K. (Eds) (1995). *Examining lives in context: Perspectives on the ecology of human development.* Washington, DC: American Psychological Association.

Nash, L. L. (1978). Concepts of existence: Greek origins of generational thought. *Daedalus, 107,* 1–21.

Nydegger, C. N., & Mitteness, L. S. (1991). Fathers and their adult sons and daughters. In: S. K. Pfeifer & M. B. Sussman (Eds), *Families: Intergenerational and Generational Connections* (pp. 249–265). London: Haworth Press.

Olson, D. H. (1986). Circumplex Model VII: Validation studies and faces III. *Family Process, 25,* 337–351.

Olson, D. H., Sprenkle, D. H., & Russell, C. S. (1979). Circumplex Model of marital and family systems I: Cohesion and adaptability dimensions, family types and clinical applications. *Family Process, 18,* 3–28.

Otscheret, E. (1988). *Ambivalenz* [Ambivalence]. Heidelberg, Germany: Roland Asanger.

Oxford English Dictionary (Vol. 1) (1989). Oxford, England: Clarendon Press.

Parker, R. (1995). *Mother love, mother hate: The power of maternal ambivalence.* New York: Basic Books.

Pillemer, K., & Suitor, J. J. (2002). Explaining mothers' ambivalence toward their adult children. *Journal of Marriage and the Family, 64,* 602–613.

Pinder, W. (1928/1961). *Das Problem der Generation in der Kunstgeschichte Europas* [The problem of generation in European history of art]. Munich, Germany: Bruckmann.

Reinharz, S. (1986). Loving and hating one's elders: Twin themes in legend and literature. In: K. Pillemer & R. S. Wolf (Eds), *Elder Abuse: Conflict in the Family* (pp. 25–48). Dover, MA: Auburn House.

Riklin, F. (1910/1911). Mitteilungen: Vortrag von Prof. Bleuler über Ambivalenz [Minutes of Prof. Bleuler's presentation on ambivalence]. *Psychiatrisch-Neurologische Wochenschrift, 43,* 405–407.

Rohr, S. (1993). *Über die Schönheit des Findens: Die Binnenstruktur menschlichen Verstehens nach Charles S. Peirce. Abduktionslogik und Kreativität* [On the beauty of finding: The internal

structure of human comprehension following Peirce's logic of abduction and creativity].
Stuttgart, Germany: M & P.

Schneider, G. (2001). Das Schwarze Quadrat auf weißem Grund von Kasimir Malewitsch [The black
square on white ground by Kasimir Malewitsch]. *Psyche, 12*, 1261–1286.

Simmen, J. (1998). *Kasimir Malewitsch: Das Schwarze Quadrat* [Kasimir Malewitsch: The black
square]. Frankfurt a. M., Germany: Fischer.

Simon, F. B. (1998). Beyond bipolar thinking: Patterns of conflict as a focus for diagnosis and
intervention. *Family Process, 37*, 215–232.

Smelser, N. J. (1998). The rational and the ambivalent in the social sciences. *American Sociological
Review, 63*, 1–16.

Spangler, D. (2002). *Ambivalenzen in intergenerationalen Beziehungen: Hochaltrige Mütter und
deren Töchter. Diplomarbeit* [Ambivalences in intergenerational relationships: Old mothers
and their daughters. Diploma thesis]. Berlin: Technische Universität Berlin.

Stierlin, H. (1984). Delegation [Delegation]. In: F. B. Simon & H. Stierlin (Eds), *Die Sprache der
Familientherapie: Ein Vokabular* [Language in Family Therapy: A Vocabulary]. Stuttgart:
Klett-Cotta.

Stotz-Ingenlath, G. (2000). Epistemological aspects of Eugen Bleuler's conception of schizophrenia
in 1911. *Medicine, Health Care and Philosophy, 3*, 153–159.

Tesch-Römer, C., Motel-Klingenbiel, A., & von Kondratowitz, H.-J. (2000). Sicherung der Solidarität
der Generationen [Ensuring solidarity between generations]. In: S. Pohlmann (Ed.), *Das Altern
der Gesellschaft als globale Herausforderung – Deutsche Impulse* [Societal Aging as Global
Challenge – German Impulses] (pp. 264–300). Stuttgart, Germany: Kohlhammer.

Walker, A. (2002). [From the editor]. *Journal of Marriage and the Family, 64*, 557.

Waters, M. (1994). *Modern sociological theory.* London: Sage.

Weigert, A. J. (1988). To be or not: Self and authenticity, identity and ambivalence. In: D. K. Lapsley
& F. C. Power (Eds), *Self, Ego, and Identity: Integrative Approaches* (pp. 263–281). New York:
Springer Verlag.

Weigert, A. J. (1991). *Mixed emotions: Certain steps toward understanding ambivalence.* New York:
State University of New York Press.

Weigert, A. J., & Franks, D. D. (1989). Ambivalence: A touchstone of the modern temper. In: D. D.
Franks & D. E. McCarthey (Eds), *The Sociology of Emotions: Original Essays and Research
Papers* (pp. 205–227). Greenwich: JAI Press.

Weingardt, K. R. (2000). Viewing ambivalence from a sociological perspective: Implications for
psychotherapists. *Psychotherapy, 37*, 298–306.

World Health Organisation (1992). International statistical classification of diseases and related health
problems. 10th Revision [ICD-10]. Geneva: WHO.

3. INTERGENERATIONAL AMBIVALENCES IN THE PAST – A SOCIAL-HISTORICAL ASSESSMENT

Andrejs Plakans

INTRODUCTION

Detecting and describing intergenerational ambivalence in historical populations is a challenge because historians are dependent, for the most part, upon the evidence that has survived, rather than on evidence elicited by researchers from participants. In this respect, the distant past is more problematic than the recent past, of course; and studies of recent (but past) generations have been able successfully to integrate documentary, statistical, and interview material (Hareven, 1982; Macfarlane, 1977). Still, such studies cover only a short stretch of past time. The purpose of this essay is to review research on family history dealing with the past three or four centuries in order to see how the subject of intergenerational ambivalence has been dealt with, if at all, and how it might need to be incorporated into historical thinking when certain kinds of situations come under scrutiny.

It should be made clear at the outset that the term "ambivalence" or any of its various synonyms is very unlikely to appear verbatim in historical documents. The term is analytical, and should be thought of, along with many similar concepts, as belonging to the historian's bag of interpretive tools (Kertzer, 1991; Smith, 1993; Wellman & Wetherell, 1996; Wetherell, 1998). What we will be looking for in the past are family situations located conceptually between solidarity and conflict. To understand these situations, and even to detect their presence, we need to

Intergenerational Ambivalences: New Perspectives on Parent-Child Relations in Later Life
Contemporary Perspectives in Family Research, Volume 4, 63–82
Copyright © 2004 by Elsevier Ltd.
All rights of reproduction in any form reserved
ISSN: 1530-3535/doi:10.1016/S1530-3535(03)04003-2

employ another set of tools, namely, the theory of family roles (Fortes, 1969; Nadel, 1957).

Historical evidence about the family seldom documents states of being that persist in time, much less the internal states of the participants of various family situations (Stearns & Stearns, 1998). In most instances, historical sources provide us with full or partial structural configurations of persons, which we take to be a "family," "household," and the like (Laslett & Wall, 1972). Depending upon its *raison d'être*, a source will contain some information about some of the relationships of the persons in the configuration. However, it will never comment on all, thus leaving the historian with the need to use guided inferences about what else could have been going on. Here is where role theory becomes useful. We infer that a particular familial configuration involved familial roles, and that these in turn involved processes of role enactment (Plakans, 1984). We impute to these roles certain rights and obligations from our knowledge of the historical society being studied. We assume that the historical record about such roles and their enactment is incomplete – as it can easily be shown to be – but we do not assume that the absence of a written record means that roles were not present or were not being enacted.

Admittedly, this procedure raises the question of whether "historical evidence" that combines within itself large doses of documentation and inference is "historical" in the true sense of the word. The question is particularly germane if we wish to use this "database" to explore the subject of intergenerational ambivalence. Absent direct evidence about how most historical actors – with the exception of those literate few who kept diaries (Macfarlane, 1970) – understood and experienced particular situations, we are treading on dangerous ground indeed. It may be that situations appearing ambivalent in retrospect (from our vantage point in the present) may not have been perceived as ambivalent by the historical actors. Conversely, situations that in retrospect look straightforward may have entailed ambivalence because we have not thoroughly understood what, historically, a role or a set of roles required (Hirschfield, 1986). To gauge whether an ambivalent situation was present, we have to be able to gauge also what values permeated a particular situation. Historically, did parental roles entail a feeling of equal responsibility toward all offspring, and did offspring expect equal treatment from parents? What was perceived as fair and what was perceived as unfair?

These questions are not mere quibbles. At the same time, we cannot allow them to become obstacles to finding new ways to look at the familial past. In what follows, we shall be looking for familial situations in which role enactment ceased to operate smoothly (that is, departed from an inferred state of "solidarity") because of some structural alteration, but did not reach a state of antagonism between family members (that is, an inferred state of "conflict"). As we shall see later, historical sources commonly used for the study of family (and intergenerational) relationships tend to skew the documentary record toward what we might term the extremes: positional configurations (derived from nominal household lists) say nothing about role enactment and thus invite interpretations highlighting solidarity, while judicial records (such as court documents) are generated by conflict situations when family relations have broken down and outside authorities have been appealed to. In contrast, our search of ambivalent situations leads us into the terrain of in-between states – dare one say "normality?" – as parental and offspring roles were adjusted to each other in the process of adaptation to changing circumstances. Ambivalence arose as parents continued to insist on receiving respect for and deference to their wishes from offspring, while among offspring individuation and differentiated expectations engendered feelings of frustration, resentment, and unfairness. At certain moments of structural change, such feelings could threaten confrontation, but at the very least could produce ambivalence in the parties concerned. The assignment for historians looking for ambivalence in this uncertain social terrain would seem to be to look at the sources in a way that assigns extreme situations to their proper place and explicates everyday life, providing some clues along the way about how in historical populations these ambivalences were resolved (if in fact they were).

CORESIDENCE PATTERNS: THE GENERAL FRAMEWORK

A logical starting point for assessing intergenerational ambivalence historically is a survey of coresidential patterns. Through rules of coresidence, generations were kept in contact with each other beyond the years during which offspring were entirely dependent on parents. It is mostly in these later phases of the family's developmental cycle that we would look for the friction between familial roles. This calls for discussion of the historical distribution of family and family household types.

Research on this subject has been a central theme of family history from the start of its "modern" phase since the mid-1960s (Laslett, 1977; Laslett & Wall, 1972; Verdon, 1998; Wall, Robin & Laslett, 1983). At that juncture, the English statistician-demographer John Hajnal introduced the notion of a Europe divided into two main marriage patterns: a "western" Europe in which marriage for both men and women was initiated relatively late (late 20s) and relatively large proportions of both sexes did not marry at all; and an "east" where marriage was relatively early and nearly universal for everyone (Hajnal, 1965; Plakans & Wetherell, 1997). An imaginary line between these two Europes ran north and south from the Gulf of Finland to the Adriatic Sea. Further refinements of this idea also explored the number of generations in coresidential groups, and found that in the east the proportion of more than two generational groups (i.e. parents and children) was always much higher than in the west (Hajnal, 1983). A subsequent modification of the bipolar typology proposed a four-part Europe: a west, a central, an east, and a Mediterranean (Laslett, 1983). Within these areas – either two or four – patterns of marriage and familial organization were assumed to be operating over a long period of time until the twentieth century, when homogenization replaced regional divisions (Watkins, 1991).

Certain consequences for intergenerational relations logically flow from these typologies; in addition, variations of many kinds were introduced by local and regional coresidence customs (or "rules") and different rates of fertility and mortality. Generally speaking, in regions where marriages were late and large proportions of the population did not marry at all, we would expect completed family size to be smaller and, by definition, a larger proportion of the population not to experience generational friction with the younger generation. These consequences could be modified by local coresidence customs: In areas where young couples were expected to establish their own households (neolocality), we would expect intergenerational frictions to be fewer than in areas where a young couple or couples normally began their married lives in the household of the parental couple (mostly patrilocality in Europe). Another example, at the other end of the familial developmental cycle, pertains to retirement decisions: Where marriage was early and universal, a retirement decision normally would resonate within a larger family group than in the regions where marriage was later and proportion remaining single larger. Assuming roughly equal mortality levels, more children in toto in an individual's family of origin meant a larger surviving sibling group when the individual reached old age; and more children in the family of procreation meant a larger number of surviving offspring to be affected by retirement and inheritance decisions. Moreover, persistence of the early age at first marriage over several generations would also lead us to expect that persons who reached the appropriate age for retirement would be at that time interacting with generally older children and grandchildren. Such permutations and combinations could be nearly endless (Ruggles, 1990), but they are important factors in assessing the historic weight and distribution of situations where intergenerational ambivalence would become socially significant.

Judging by the research to date on the historic coresidential patterns of the European continent, there is little doubt that eastern regions would provide the most fruitful ground for intergenerational friction. There, a high incidence of relatively complex family households have been found over time and space (Czap, 1983a, b; Hoch, 1986; Kaser, 1995; Kertzer, 1989; Todorova, 1993). This is not to say, of course, that simple family households did not exist in the east. But complicated family household formations have turned up in the historic populations as far separated as Finland in the north and Serbia in the south, as well as central Russia in the east and Hungary in the west (Halpern & Halpern, 1977; Moring, 1996). The reasons for their existence may have differed from place to place, but a proportion of 30–60% of all family households in the complex category in a given historical household listing (as contrasted to western proportions of 2–10%) no longer surprises (Laslett & Wall, 1972). In the European east, a variety of socio-economic regimes supported family developmental cycles in which relatively long phases included the coresidence of newly married offspring and their parents, the coresidence of married older offspring and their parents, the coresidence of married siblings (usually, but not always, brothers) after parents died, and sometimes even the coresidence of more distant married kin.

By contrast, in a simple family household regime, where custom mandated the creation of a new household upon marriage, the retirement of a head of household, for example, might affect directly only the spouse and possibly only the successor who in all probability would be living elsewhere. In a western area where the stem family was customary (a designated heir living with the parental couple, while other offspring dispersed), the number of directly affected persons in the friction among generations might be somewhat larger, but not by much. These general patterns would suggest that in the European east the population "at risk" of experiencing or feeling the effects of intergenerational friction was always substantially larger than in the west (Ruggles, 1986). But being "at risk" of participating in or feeling the effect of such friction does not mean it always developed or was always felt. This broadly-based typological framework provides an initial map of the areas where familial structures and structural change had the greatest probability of producing situations that in turn generated intergenerational ambivalence.

STRUCTURAL SITUATIONS ENGENDERING INTERGENERATIONAL AMBIVALENCE

Offspring and Servanthood

In the family-historical research of the past 30 years, historians have identified situations in which parents deliberately extruded their children from the parental home before the latter had reached young adulthood. This step did not normally mean a severing of relationships with the children, but it did mean that from that point onward parent and child were residentially separated. The enactment of parent-offspring roles would transpire over longer distances. Two well-documented cases of such extrusion both involved placing children in the homes of other people, where the children became servants or apprentices. We hypothesize that such situations engendered mixed feelings on the part of both parents and offspring, because, on the one hand, parents were deliberately placing the children under the authority of other adults; and, on the other, the children entered situations in which they could easily be mistreated.

The first example of this practice comes from the history of landed estates in eastern Europe, where very often the peasant populations contained a substantial proportion of persons who had no access to holdings of their own. Designating them as "landless" – as is normally done in the scholarly literature – is something of a misnomer, because such persons continued to work the land and therefore their everyday lives were shaped by rural circumstances as much as the lives of those who had holdings. These "landless" people worked as farmhands. They bore different designations in different places, and they could be males and females of different ages, married and unmarried. In the Russian Baltic provinces, this was a subpopulation that was constantly on the move, because their work agreements normally lasted only a year though they could be removed earlier (Plakans & Wetherell, 1988). In the Latvian language of one part of the residents of the Baltic provinces this entire subpopulation was designated as *gajeji* – literally, those who come and go.

Most farmhands were solitaries. Or, alternately, their family developmental cycle, after the initial marriage, always tended toward simplicity. Not having a permanent place of residence meant that married farmhands could not accumulate coresident relatives, because the head of the farmstead on which they worked normally refused to house more than the wife and children of a married farmhand. This meant that the normal family structure in which farmhands lived was quite simple, by contrast with the structure of the landholding peasants, whose more-or-less fixed residency in one place over several generations meant the possibility of complex family structures.

Already forced by these circumstances to remain small, farmhand families practiced widely the extrusion of very young children from even the small family circle into "jobs" in other farmsteads. The nominal household listings from such populations show very large numbers of children in the age range of 5–10 who are working as "herders" in farmsteads other than those in which their parents were living, and similarly large numbers in the age range of 10–14 working away from their parents in the capacity of "half-farmhands" or "young maidservants." While it is true that some of the young people in this category were orphans, and therefore were truly on their own, in most cases these youth had parents living somewhere else. The motivations of the parents in this instance are difficult to unearth, because we are dealing with largely illiterate populations who left no records about their feelings. But placing even young children elsewhere meant that the parental couple reduced the number of mouths it had to feed – authority and care over the young farmhand passed to the head of the recipient farmstead – and, moreover, fewer children made the couple more attractive as employees in the next round of their moves around the estate.

The second set of practices leading to the same result was identified by research on the family in the past of the British Isles, and has since come to be known as "life-cycle servitude" (Laslett, 1977). Here the custom of "putting out" children appears to have been more formalized, involved children of an older age group, and was evidently part of parental strategy of preparing children for adult life. Parents arranged for children in the mid-teen years to work in other households – girls as young maidservants, and boys as apprentices or sub-apprentices "to learn a trade." For the most part, the practice appears to have involved households in the same community, and thus very likely sets of adults who knew each other. Remuneration could flow in both directions: Parents could pay – in money or in kind – for their children to be taken in, and the children might receive some form of payment for their "services" some part of which went back to the parents and another part, especially for girls, was used in preparation of a "bridal chest."

While the motives in these cases may have involved economic necessity, more often than not the parental reasoning involved the preparation of children for adult life under the supervision of adults other than the parents. The structural consequence, however, was the same as in the Baltic example: Children left home before they "came of age" and parent-child roles were thereafter enacted over longer distances. In both cases, also, the enactment of parent-child roles now involved another set of authority figures – the adults with whom the children had been placed.

These two examples have been adduced here to stand for a much larger class of phenomena that is currently under close study by social historians – the "leaving home" question. In current research such separation is normally conceptualized as part of the life-course approach, and is seen as an important "marker" in the life courses of all the participants – the children who left parental authority, and the parents who surrendered authority over their children to other adults. The question of timing is an important one: Our examples involve separation at the younger ages of children, but a more representative set of examples could very well involve offspring who did not leave parental authority until their own marriages. It is not likely that class analysis would produce a perfect correlation between social standing and the incidence of children "leaving home" early, but this correlation was probably relatively high.

The question is whether this particular situation warrants being placed on a list of circumstances where intergenerational ambivalence came into play. We would suggest that the probability of mixed feelings in these situations was considerable, although we lack any persuasive evidence that this was the case. To assume that mixed feelings were involved at all, we would have to know far more than we do about parental and offspring expectations toward each other, and such evidence is scarce. Indeed, among social historians there is still a controversy over the question of the emotional content of parent-child relationships in the distant past: Did parents in past centuries value or love children less because of the high infant and child mortality rates? Did children view parents as little else than harsh adults dispensing strict discipline, including corporal punishment? (Ariès, 1962; Pollock, 1983). In the Baltic case, the oral tradition among Latvians contains innumerable folk songs portraying the longings of children directed toward absent parents, but such songs are understood to have been created by adults and not children. In the British case, the ubiquity of the practice may have led children from a very early age to internalize the knowledge, learned from the experience of older siblings, that in their mid-teen years they would have to leave the parental home, at least for a while.

Nonetheless, these particular structural situations have the characteristics that move them into the realm of hypothesis-testing with respect to intergenerational ambivalence. Both parental love and parental authority – the latter more than the former – must have been involved in the departure of an offspring to another residence and to the control of another set of adults. This must, in turn, have brought about changes in how the parental role was conceptualized with respect to the departing child. And this adjustment of the role must have entailed ambivalent feelings on the part of the parent: the knowledge that the parent would not be able to offer physical and emotional sustenance to the offspring on a daily basis, the fear that the offspring would have been put "into harm's way." Conversely, the offspring must have experienced some degree and confusion and fear in the new setting which no longer contained familiar adults and which may have indeed have contained rivals – the recipient adults' own children – for adult affection. The fact that such deliberate extrusion of young children from the parental home was practiced widely (in the locations that we know about) meant that the role adjustments and the mixed feeling accompanying them had become part of "normal" life.

Stepparents, Stepchildren, and Adoption

In premodern societies adult mortality rates remained high until the demographic transition, when both fertility and mortality rates began their downward slide. The most frequent way of repairing the family network, when one of its linchpin members died, was remarriage (Stone, 1977). Judging by the sources, we have to deal with three aspects of this phenomenon: remarriage of widowers, remarriage of widows, and how parental and offspring roles intermeshed in the presence of step-relationships (Dûpaquier, 1981).

Wives and mothers in their productive years periodically faced a high risk of death in childbirth, but death through others reasons was fairly frequent as well. When the death of a wife and mother occurred, the family unit faced a period of hardship; the family temporarily lost the person who was in some fashion in charge of rearing the young, who had the responsibility of taking care of the household, and who not infrequently took care of the farm animals as well, if the family was a rural one. The husband lost not only a key member of the family's economic "team," but also the person through whose body the family reproduced itself. In most instances, therefore, remarriage by the young widower was not only an economic but also a social necessity. Unfortunately, we do not know much about this phenomenon except that it was frequent. We do know that the second wife was in all likelihood substantially younger than the first wife.

In the case of first marriages, in the "western" pattern the age difference between spouses was substantially less than the age difference between spouses in the European east (Plakans & Wetherell, 1992). But in both regions remarriage offered new opportunities for the new partners. In the case of males, a substantially younger wife would ensure for the husband an extension of the period of economic partnership than would have obtained from the deceased spouse, as well as a chance to extend the period of fathering offspring. From the new wife's point of view, an older husband ensured entry into an established household and a spouse with an established reputation.

If the decision did not involve primarily romantic love, the advantages outweighed disadvantages. Among the disadvantages, however, were the strained relationships between the new wife and the husband's first set of offspring. There are probably good reasons why the image of the "evil stepmother" is a negative one in most European oral traditions, even though the new wife may have had nothing to do with forming this image and the image itself is usually overdrawn. Still, raising and disciplining children who were reluctant to accept the stepmother's authority would have been difficult, yet she would have been expected to enact those responsibilities in addition to being the "real" mother of the children she herself bore for her new husband. For the remarried husband, the normal role of husband would have become more complicated, because he had to mediate disputes between his new wife and the first set of siblings, as well as those between the two sets of stepsiblings who had different mothers.

The remarriage of young widows entailed a different set of calculations. It would seem that the frequency of widow remarriage was not quite as high as widower remarriage, but this probably depended upon the age at which widowhood came.

If the husband (and father) died when the woman was relatively young, and most of her sons were underage as well, then remarriage was probably inescapable. When, however, there was a son or sons who had reached their majority, the need for remarriage lessened. In these cases, it was entirely possible for the son(s) and the mother to form a kind of economic team to continue the family unit as an economic enterprise. Moreover, an older woman with grown children would not have attracted as many candidates for her second husband, because his calculations would have been different. There is evidence from several parts of historic Europe that some younger widows in fact chose not to remarry, having found the absence of a husband to create new freedoms that they enjoyed. In view of the male-dominated and demanding world in which married women of all social classes normally lived, the choice among women not to remarry had logic behind it, especially if children had reached young adulthood or were about to become young adults. The economic vulnerability of the mother was not as great in such circumstances, because she could count on support of her offspring who were in the process of forming their own families.

Historical sources also reveal that a family could obtain children through the mechanisms of adoption and fostering. Given the high rate of adult mortality, the appearance of orphans was not infrequent in most communities, and it was thereafter up to the adult governors of the community to reintegrate these underage persons into a family net. Speaking purely about survival from the orphans' point of view, the acquisition of a new set of parents was undoubtedly better than growing up parentless. From the receiving parents' point of view, adoption and fostering was a way of repairing the holes than had appeared in their own offspring group because of the premature death of a child.

It is not always clear, however, whether parents who adopted or agreed to foster children did so willingly or as the result of pressures from the authorities. In the serf estates of the eastern Baltic littoral, for example, sources suggest that virtually all parentless children were quickly reintegrated into existing family networks. There were few orphanages in the rural areas of this region and, in addition, estate owners could easily mandate that existing farmsteads take parentless children and raise them until adulthood.

Thus, stepmothers, stepfathers, stepchildren, and stepsiblings, as well as adopted and foster children and adoptive and fostering parents were common in most traditional European communities. These "repairs" of the family structure added a layer of roles to the "normal" roles parents and children had to enact, and created a domain rich with ambivalent intergenerational relationships. The enactment of such roles in everyday family life was modified by the distribution of power and authority within the family. For obvious reasons, stepoffspring could not give free vent to whatever negative feelings they may have had toward a stepparent, whereas a stepparent had much more latitude for subordinating the stepoffspring to his or her will. As mentioned earlier, there was also ample room for the "natural" parent to indulge in favoritism toward his or her "own" children in the enlarged (now stepsibling) group. In the subsistence conditions in which most families (at least rural families) lived, such favoritism could in fact have had significant consequences in the diets, work assignments, and living arrangements within the offspring group.

Step-relationships, as well as those created by adoption and fostering, seem to invite descriptive language that highlights conflict; but there does not exist at this writing a persuasive body of evidence that families involving step-relationships (and other quasi-familial relationships) in the long run fared more badly than families in which such relationships were not present. The ambivalent feelings these relationships engendered were in the course of time "naturalized," as offspring and parents both grew used to each other. It would not have been to anyone's advantage to heighten the significance of such cleavages, especially in those very large segments of the population in which family survival required the full energies of the whole set of persons, however combined it was. The exception to this generalization lay in the domain of property, if indeed the parental generation had any property to transfer to the offspring. Then the question of birth could easily flare up again, after having been "settled" within the everyday life of the family for many years, as we shall see later in this essay.

It should be noted finally that, for most families in the European past until relatively recent times, the ambivalence engendered by step-relationships had to be resolved by the affected parties themselves. Intervention by the state at any level, or even by custom, was rare, in part because the former was as yet weak and the latter did not address itself to the minutiae of internal family matters. When dealing with these relationships historically, therefore, we have as our sole evidence documents (such as household listings and parish registers) reporting that step-relationships were present in the family but hardly any documentary evidence that would have been generated by the intervention of authorities when the relationships became problematic. The authorities did not intervene, and the ambivalent feelings attached to these relations remained within the realm of private problems.

Retirement and Headships

Another area of family life generating considerable ambivalent feelings was the transfer of authority to a new generation. In current social-historical research, this domain has been explored most thoroughly under two related headings: what happened when the current head of the family group (usually a male) became too old or infirm to carry out the duties expected of him, and what happened as the headship of the group was transferred to another person in the next generation. Research suggests that authority transfers of this type were not smooth or predictable matters, even if local custom dictated what had to be done. The person leaving a position of authority was not altogether certain what would happen to him (and his spouse) even if the successor came from the ranks of his own offspring. Also, among the siblings-successors there were expectations that could not be met easily even if customary practice already prescribed who among them would be taking over.

In the existing literature, we can distinguish two general types of situations. The first, found most frequently in western European societies, features a document called a retirement contract (Gaunt, 1983; Plakans, 1989). When these contracts began to be used remains to be ascertained; the earliest examples come from the twelfth century and the latest from the nineteenth. In these documents, we can see that sitting household heads sought to guarantee for themselves (and usually their spouses) a place to live and sustenance in kind by making the succession contingent upon the successor's agreement to these demands. It is hardly surprising that in the transfer contracts the self-interest of the departing head should appear dominant. But these agreements also contained provisions seeking to prevent the successor from damaging the survival of the holding, or from mistreating his siblings from his new position of power. In areas where consciousness of lineage was pronounced, the documents also speak of the obligations of a successor toward the "family line" inclusively understood.

In creating these documents, the motives of the outgoing senior person were obviously mixed. They expected that after exiting from a position of authority they and their spouses would need support, and they were afraid that if the family property were parceled by the successor, such support would be increasingly harder to come by. And they were clearly afraid of physical neglect as they became more infirm: Witness in these documents the great attention to the departing seniors' later living arrangements and provisions for material support in the form of grain, agricultural products, and even sums of money. In reading such documents, one has to continually remind oneself that the parties expected to be bound by such "contracts" were in fact parents and offspring. They frequently read as if the outgoing senior had no expectation whatever that the successor-son would honorably discharge the obligations the role of "son" normally entailed. The documents are good examples of the ambivalence, engendered within the senior generation, about surrendering authority in the family group, even to their own offspring.

Outside the western and central regions of Europe, the senior generation was able to exercise far less control over its future when the prospect of giving up authority loomed large. Consider first the southern Balkan area and its property-owning familial corporations, the well-researched *zadruga* (Halpern & Halpern, 1977;

Kaser, 1995). The *zadruga* – a patrilineal descent group – could have upwards of 30–40 coresident members. The head of a *zadruga* – the *staresina* – was less powerful than we would expect and, correspondingly, he was not entirely the master of his own fate when it came time for him to surrender his authority. In advanced age the *staresina* could be removed from office when it became clear that he was no longer able to act efficiently on behalf of the group, but when this happened he did not have to fear the sudden disappearance of material support. In fact, a departing *staresina* sometimes could retain the honorary position of head even when in reality a son, or sons, had taken over the job of running the *zadruga*'s affairs (Halpern, 1958).

In the case of the *zadruga*, therefore, ambivalence was more likely to concern the way in which a senior male was displaced, rather than the material circumstances of the displacement. The communal discussions in which a sitting leader's growing weaknesses were identified, likely alternatives discussed, a successor identified and chosen, and the results of the deliberation reported to the leaders very lively involved mixed feelings – especially if the sitting leader had been effective. Of course, we are here in the realm of conjecture, because such conversations were not recorded, much less opened for inspection by scholars.

When it comes to the attitudes of the generation entering positions of authority, the documentary record is no clearer – in part because who within the offspring group should take over authority was governed by a mixture of custom and local circumstance. In western and central Europe, especially in the regions where stem-family practices held sway, a successor would have been identified much earlier than on the serf estates of eastern Europe, where the connection between headship and property rights was tenuous in the extreme, as was the right of peasant to a headship (Wetherell & Plakans, 1998; Wetherell, Plakans & Wellman, 1994). Here the peasant-serf had only use rights to the land the family worked, with ultimate ownership and the right to name successors belonging to the estate owner. But even here, heads came to their offices in a less-than-random manner. Most were the sons of previous heads; fewer were other relatives, and some were completely new to the farmstead they came to control.

What is of greatest interest to us are the attitudes within the sibling group with respect to who among them should step into the position of authority being vacated. The question was made complex by some general conditions prevailing everywhere. First, high mortality rates often prevented custom from being implemented straightforwardly, so that in areas where custom dictated succession by the "oldest son" (primogeniture), the candidate actually alive at the moment of transition may have been the "oldest surviving son." Second, in most rural areas, daughters were precluded from such successions; but throughout rural Europe there are many examples of the "in-marrying son-in-law," whose wife, the daughter of the former senior male, was in effect replacing her own mother as the dominant female in the farmstead. Third, the male offspring pushed forward by custom to be the incoming senior was not always the best candidate for the job for reasons of mental or physical incapacity or unacceptable habits. Fourth, because of the frequency of remarriage and the subsequent wide age range within the sibling group, the incoming head gained quasi-parental authority over younger brothers, even in those cases where the common father did not die but merely stepped down from his position and remained within the family group. Finally, among the sons who were the most likely candidates to succeed their fathers, there was often the phenomenon of impatience. It must be remembered that departure from authority by the senior male was not mandated by law, but was rather the result of decisions – sometimes by the landowner (if in the east) but more often than not by general consensus of the family group. While it is true that in most researched areas, heads of family groups appeared to have withdrawn from authority by the time they reached their mid-60s, there is considerable anecdotal evidence about heads "hanging on" – much to the frustration and resentment of their potential successors, who were now in their 40s and more than likely with families of their own.

All of these unremarkable features of premodern society suggest the presence of structural situations in which ambivalent emotions were engendered. The faith that the offspring generation would continue to enact the roles of "children" lovingly and respectfully when the parental generation became older was tempered by the fear that they would in fact act otherwise, and this generated retirement contracts. The hope in the senior generation that they could pass on to their successors the authority they had or had accumulated could easily, in the European east, be destroyed by unpredictable decisions on the part of the landowner. In spite of the strength of custom, the conditions of everyday life – particularly, high mortality rates – mean some degree of rivalry within the sibling group for the position of successor, even if after the succession took place the "losers" accepted their new subordinate position.

Inheritance

For some time it has been customary for researchers of the historical family to sub-sume the study of inheritance rules, customs, and practices to the larger category of "intergenerational transfers," of which "authority" – as discussed above – was one "good" and "property" another. Moreover, at the urging of the anthropologist Jack Goody, studies have also conceptualized inheritance to be more than simply the passage of goods between two adjacent generations, and to involve "the devolution of property" within family lines in real time (Goody, 1975). The subject has become exceedingly complex, involving as it does such factors as systems of inheritance customs (e.g. partible, impartible), succession practices (e.g. primogeniture, ulti-mogeniture), preferred family structures (e.g. simple, stem, extended, multiple), behavior codes pertaining to the treatment of the elderly, and conflicts between state-mandated and on-the-ground outcomes (Goody, Thirsk & Thompson, 1976).

We are, of course, interested in the states of mind that accompanied transfers of any kind, and it is precisely property transfers that we would expect to have generated the most ambivalent attitudes. If we conceive of property transfers in the broadest possible manner, then the friction between the proper enactment of parental roles and expectations within the offspring generation could arise much before the death of the parental generation. In the most inclusive conceptualization, all one-directional property flows from parents to offspring created the probability of ambivalent feelings on both sides. The "dowries" given to out-marrying daugh-ters always required considerations of type and size, and the concern that not all daughters could receive dowries of equal size. The shift of resources to sons to help in the starting of enterprises or farms, even if counted against their ultimate inheri-tance, not only raised the question of size but also the fear, in both generations, that the patrimony would be depleted before all offspring would get their "far share."

We do not have a functional explanation of why in traditional Europe there were two principal forms of inheritance – impartible and partible – since both systems could coexist within the same region and among populations which differed little from one another occupationally, economically, or culturally. Even if partible inheritance is conceptualized as an effort to introduce greater fairness in the devo-lution of property, this was not always the result in the long run. Partible inheritance practices, implemented over three or four generations, produced parcelization and threatened the economic survival and social standing of all members of the family line. In such a case, ambivalence would be created by the friction between, first, the desire to remain loyal to the principle of rough heir equality embodied in the practice; second, loyalty to the "lineage" understood as a configuration stretching backwards and forwards in time; and, third, alarm over the problems the demonstrable shrinkage of patrimonial shares was creating for the life chances of individual families in the lineage (Sabean, 1998; Segalen, 1985). An effort to cope with such ambivalent feelings can be seen in the instances where the history of landed property shows fragmentation over several generations in different family lines but also subsequent recombination of previously parceled land later on.

Without doubt, the process most charged with the ambivalent feelings was the final distribution of the patrimony in preparation of the death of the parents. We understand now that this was not simply a moment in time, involving only short-term emotions. Among those who had property, the participants in such dis-tribution were preparing themselves for it for a long time. All except the youngest knew and understood the general inheritance customs prevailing in their region, and thus the feelings about the ultimate dispensation could color intergenerational relationships for a considerable period. Even though inheritance customs privileged some of the offspring – such as the oldest son – and all offspring understood that in time their own actions would be regulated by the same rules, evidence suggests that resigned acceptance of custom was not always the case. There was resentment among the non-heirs that affected sibling relationships even while the siblings continued to live under the authority of the parents. Premortem shifts of resources to non-inheriting offspring can be read as efforts by the parents to assuage the feelings of unfairness that privileging inheritance customs generated.

The instrument of ultimate distribution among the propertied was the written testament, which frequently was prepared long before the death of its author. There is no doubt that this instrument could be used as a form of control by the senior over the junior generations because misbehavior in the latter could bring about changes in the provisions of the testament. In some respects, the written testament as an instrument of control could be used to compensate for the diminution of personal authority as the father grew older, and as male offspring entered middle age. The threat by the aging father to "change the will" and the hypocritical demonstration of filial piety this engendered in the offspring generation has been a favored theme in fictional literature, but it had many counterparts in real life as well.

After parental death, the ambivalent feelings present among unequally treated heirs toward the parents were shifted toward each other, especially if the age distribution among the male offspring was considerable. There are examples of older brothers seeking to compensate younger brothers through the creation of in loco parentis situations, which, of course, could not be guaranteed to bring success. Whatever solidarity siblings had felt earlier, the unequal life chances perpetuated by unequal distributions of the patrimony necessarily weakened it. Even though state-mandated equal inheritance – as with the Napoleonic Law in France – sought to bring greater justice within the sibling groups, the nineteenth century in France among the propertied classes was filled with legal disputes among siblings, which signifies that ambivalent feelings had been replaced by family conflict.

Yet there were regions in traditional Europe in which common people had no fixed rights to property (eastern European regions under serfdom) and were themselves a kind of property, and in which there was little occupational differentiation (Blum, 1978; Szirmai, 1961). These were also areas in which inheritance customs could at any moment be overridden by self-interested decisions of powerful people in the locality. It is quite possible, given the subsistence level of most peasants' households in these regions, that premortem distributions contributed to the prevention of any accumulation of wealth to be distributed at death. If this were so, inheritance questions here did not arise at the end of life and would not have materially affected generational relations at that time – offspring's expectations, meager though they were, having been fulfilled earlier. It is very likely that in these regions, where expectations of inheritance could not be manipulated to maintain control over the offspring generation, author-itarian aspects of the senior male's position had to be enhanced for the family unit to remain coherent when the parents were reaching old age and the male offspring had entered adulthood.

MANAGING AMBIVALENCE

Ambivalent situations in intergenerational relations have been understood here as those in which the enactment of parental and offspring roles became strained through familial changes unfolding in real time. On one hand, parents, for whatever reason, felt that the obligation to love, nurture, protect, and guide their offspring could not be exercised fully; on the other, the obligation that offspring love, respect, and obey parents was weakened or eroded. The result was tension in intergenerational relations, characterized by feelings of mistreatment, injustice, betrayal. Such tensions had to be "managed," however, to keep open conflict between the generations or between individuals from arising.

It has been argued here that these situations were commonplace historically, but also that because they were "managed," they have left little trace in the historical record. This is so because historical documentation of the family was more readily generated by conflict, and because sources that simply document the presence of a "family" (such as nominal-level household lists) do not comment on its inner workings. Much of what we have to say about ambivalent situations historically, therefore, has had to be inferential. In the final analysis, we do not have much direct information about the inner workings of families in the past, let alone about the states of mind of the individuals comprising them and participating in the tense moments of the family developmental cycle. Correspondingly, there is also little direct evidence of how intergenerational ambivalence was managed or resolved.

It is very likely that the most effective means of "managing" intergenerational ambivalence was the passage of time. If a situation did not worsen and slide into open conflict, the passage of time would decrease the intensity of emotions and allow for the gradual acceptance (perhaps as "inevitable") or forgiveness of the perceived unfairness or norm violation. In due time, offspring could become con-vinced, or could convince themselves, that parental action earlier thought to be un-fair was really done for the offspring's "own good" or "for the good of the family." As well, parents in due time and by thinking back to their own youth could become used to the idea that an offspring's challenge of their wishes was simply a normal aspect of generational replacement within the family. In both cases, ambivalent feelings would dissipate, even if they might never have disappeared entirely.

In some instances, direct action could be taken to "manage" ambivalence. This is how we would interpret, for instance, the premortem distribution of family property to non-inheriting offspring – dowries to daughters, a "stake" payment to younger sons. Though these could not equal the "share" of the patrimony eventually obtained by the principal heir, they would to some extent assuage the feelings of unequal treatment felt by non-heirs. Similarly, the general acceptance by offspring early in the family developmental cycle of the idea that elderly parents would eventually be living with the offspring can be interpreted as an effort by offspring to "manage" the ambivalence that would be created if parents throughout their adult lives had to fear eventual extrusion from the family circle.

Because the concept of "intergenerational ambivalence" is relatively new to historical interpretation, historians of the family generally have not sought to interpret their data with its help. There is persuasive evidence, however, that it can be useful for fully understanding the ebbs and flows of intergenerational emotions in the past as well as in the present.

REFERENCES

Ariès, P. (1962). *Centuries of childhood: A social history of family life*. R. Baldick (Trans.). New York: Alfred Knopf. (Original work published 1960.)

Blum, J. (1978). *The end of old order in rural Europe*. Princeton, NJ: Princeton University Press.

Czap, P. (1983a). A large family: The peasant's greatest wealth: Serf households in Mishino, Russia 1814–1858. In: R. Wall, J. Robin & P. Laslett (Eds), *Family Forms in Historic Europe* (pp. 105–151). Cambridge, England: Cambridge University Press.

Czap, P. (1983b). The perennial multiple family household: Mishino, Russia. *Journal of Family History*, 7, 5–26.

Dûpaquier, J. (Ed.) (1981). *Marriage and remarriage in populations of the past*. London: Academic Press.

Fortes, M. (1969). *Kinship and the social order: The legacy of Lewis Henry Morgan*. London: Routledge and Kegan Paul.

Gaunt, D. (1983). The property and kin relationships of retired farmers in northern and central Europe. In: R. Wall, J. Robin & P. Laslett (Eds), *Family Forms in Historic Europe* (pp. 249–279). Cambridge, England: Cambridge University Press.

Goody, J. (1975). *Production and reproduction: A comparative study of the domestic domain*. Cambridge, England: Cambridge University Press.

Goody, J., Thirsk, J., & Thompson, E. P. (Eds) (1976). *Family and inheritance: Rural society in Western Europe 1200–1800*. Cambridge, England: Cambridge University Press.

Hajnal, J. (1965). European marriage patterns in historical perspective. In: D. Glass & D. E. C. Eversley (Eds), *Population in History* (pp. 101–143). Chicago: Aldine.

Hajnal, J. (1983). Two kinds of pre-industrial household formation system. In: R. Wall, J. Robin & P. Laslett (Eds), *Family Forms in Historic Europe* (pp. 65–104). Cambridge, England: Cambridge University Press.

Halpern, J. M. (1958). *A Serbian village*. New York: Columbia University Press.

Halpern, J. M., & Halpern, B. K. (1977). *Selected papers on a Serbian village*. Amherst: University of Massachusetts, Department of Anthropology.

Hareven, T. K. (1982). *Family time and industrial time: The relationship between the family and work in a New England industrial community*. New York: Cambridge University Press.

Hirschfield, L. A. (1986). Kinship and cognition: Genealogy and the meaning of kinship terms. *Current Anthropology, 27*, 217–242.

Hoch, S. L. (1986). *Serfdom and social control in Russia: Petrovskoe, a village in Tambov*. Chicago: University of Chicago Press.

Kaser, K. (1995). *Familie und Verwandschaft auf dem Balkan: Analyse einer Untergehenden Kultur* [Family and kinship in the Balkans: Analysis of a disappearing culture]. Vienna: Bohlau Verlag.

Kertzer, D. I. (1989). The joint family household revisited: Demographic constraints and household complexity in the European past. *Journal of Family History, 14*, 1–15.

Kertzer, D. I. (1991). Household history and sociological theory. *Annual Review of Sociology, 17*, 155–179.

Laslett, P. (1977). *Family life and illicit love in earlier generations: Essays in historical sociology*. Cambridge, England: Cambridge University Press.

Laslett, P. (1983). Family and household as work group and kin group: Areas of traditional Europe compared. In: R. Wall, J. Robin & P. Laslett (Eds), *Family Forms in Historic Europe* (pp. 513–563). Cambridge, England: Cambridge University Press.

Laslett, P., & Wall, R. (Eds) (1972). *Household and family in past time*. Cambridge, England: Cambridge University Press.

Macfarlane, A. (1970). *The family life of Ralph Josselin, a seventeenth century clergyman: An essay in historical anthropology*. Cambridge, England: Cambridge University Press.

Macfarlane, A. (1977). *Reconstructing historical communities*. Cambridge, England: Cambridge University Press.

Moring, B. (1996). Marriage and social change in south-western Finland, 1700–1870. *Continuity and Change, 11*, 91–113.

Nadel, S. F. (1957). *The theory of social structure*. London: Cohen and West.

Plakans, A. (1984). *Kinship in the past: An anthropology of European family life 1500–1900*. Oxford, England: Basil Blackwell.

Plakans, A. (1989). Stepping down in former times: A comparative assessment of "Retirement" in Traditional Europe. In: D. Kertzer, J. Mayer & K. W. Schaie (Eds), *Age Structuring in Comparative Perspective* (pp. 175–195). Hillsdale, NJ: Lawrence Erlbaum Associates.

Plakans, A., & Wetherell, C. (1988). The kinship domain in an East European peasant community: Pinkenhof, 1833–1850. *American Historical Review, 93*, 359–386.

Plakans, A., & Wetherell, C. (1992). Family and economy in an early nineteenth-century Baltic serf estate. *Continuity and Change, 7*, 199–223.

Plakans, A., & Wetherell, C. (1997). Auf der Suche nach einer Verortung: Die Geschichte der Familie in Osteuropa, 1800–2000 [In search of place: The history of the family in Eastern Europe, 1800–2000]. In: J. Ehmer, T. Hareven & R. Wall (Eds), *Historische Familienforschung: Bilanz und Perspektiven* [Historical family research: Accomplishments and future direction] (1997 Festschrift for Michael Mitterauer, pp. 301–325). Frankfurt, Germany: Campus.

Pollock, L. (1983). *Forgotten children: Parent-child relationships from 1500–1900.* New York: Cambridge University Press.

Ruggles, S. (1986). Availability of kin and the demography of historical family structure. *Historical Methods, 19,* 93–102.

Ruggles, S. (1990). Family demography and family history: Problems and prospects. *Historical Methods, 23,* 22–33.

Sabean, D. (1998). *Kinship in Neckarhausen 1700–1870.* Cambridge, England: Cambridge University Press.

Segalen, M. (1985). *Fifteen generations of Bretons: Kinship and society in Lower Brittany 1720–1980.* Cambridge, England: Cambridge University Press.

Smith, D. S. (1993). The curious history of theorizing about the history of the western nuclear family. *Social Science History, 17,* 325–353.

Stearns, C. Z., & Stearns, P. N. (1998). *Emotion and social change: Toward a new psychohistory.* New York: Holmes & Meier.

Stone, L. (1977). *The family, sex, and marriage in England, 1500–1800.* New York: Harper and Row.

Szirmai, Z. (Ed.) (1961). *The law of inheritance in Eastern Europe and in the People's Republic of China.* Leyden, Netherlands: A. W. Sythoff.

Todorova, M. N. (1993). *Balkan family structure and the European pattern: Demographic developments in Ottoman Bulgaria.* Washington, DC: American University Press.

Verdon, M. (1998). *Rethinking households: An atomistic perspective on European living arrangements.* London: Routledge.

Wall, R., Robin, J., & Laslett, P. (Eds) (1983). *Family forms in historic Europe.* Cambridge, England: Cambridge University Press.

Watkins, S. (1991). *From provinces into nations: Demographic integration in Western Europe.* Princeton, NJ: Princeton University Press.

Wellman, B., & Wetherell, C. (1996). Social network analysis of historical communities: Some questions from the present for the past. *History of the Family: An International Quarterly, 1,* 97–121.

Wetherell, C. (1998). Historical social network analysis. *International Review of Social History, 43*(Suppl.), 125–144.

Wetherell, C., & Plakans, A. (1998). Intergenerational transfers of headships over the life course in an Eastern European peasant community, 1782–1850. *The History of the Family: An International Quarterly, 3,* 333–349.

Wetherell, C., Plakans, A., & Wellman, B. (1994). Social networks, kinship, and community in Eastern Europe. *Journal of Interdisciplinary History, 24,* 639–663.

PART II:
ASSESSING INTERGENERATIONAL AMBIVALENCE

4. METHODOLOGICAL ISSUES IN ASSESSING AMBIVALENCES IN INTERGENERATIONAL RELATIONS

Frank Lettke and David M. Klein

INTRODUCTION

Although ambivalence is a common experience in family relations, the conceptualization of these relations has been focused on solidarity, closeness, and attraction on one hand, and on stress, distance, disruption, and abuse on the other. Ambivalence has not often been considered systematically for the analysis of intergenerational relations. Measurement instruments are not widely available for this purpose, because they tend to focus on one dimension at a time (Berscheid, 1983, pp. 115–116).

From its beginnings in psychotherapy, followed by applications in social psychology and cognitive psychology, ambivalence has played a significant role. Its role has been significant not only in the study of pathologies, but also insofar as ambivalence relates to conflict, judgment, and decision making. Psychological research on ambivalence, however, most often has been restricted to individuals. When persons other than the individual under examination are considered, it is in the sense of seeing that individual's attitude toward these persons, and the other persons are regarded as objects. Even sociological studies of ambivalence have not concentrated on social interaction and relationships, but rather on normative structures in various social roles.

Intergenerational Ambivalences: New Perspectives on Parent-Child Relations in Later Life
Contemporary Perspectives in Family Research, Volume 4, 85–113
Copyright © 2004 by Elsevier Ltd.
All rights of reproduction in any form reserved
ISSN: 1530-3535/doi:10.1016/S1530-3535(03)04004-4

Our aim in this chapter is to discuss methodological issues concerning the measurement of ambivalence in social relations, especially in intergenerational relations. We will first provide a brief overview of standard variables in the field of intergenerational relations. Next, we will identify types of ambivalence measures in common use. Then we will discuss strengths and weaknesses of particular instruments. This discussion will lead to suggestions for new measures, and to recommendations for future research on intergenerational ambivalence.

THE TRADITIONAL STUDY OF
INTERGENERATIONAL RELATIONS

Research on intergenerational relations has been dominated so far by a few ideas, recently articulated in terms of carefully developed variables. The main ideas include the frequency of sociable interaction, emotional closeness, the amount of help given and received, the extent of agreement on beliefs and values, overt conflict between members of different generations, as well as normative obligations and opportunities to engage in interactions of various kinds. These ideas have sometimes been packaged together as a set of loosely connected dimensions of intergenerational solidarity (e.g. Bengtson & Roberts, 1991; Rossi & Rossi, 1990). This panoply of traditional measures is relevant to intergenerational ambivalence.

First, we note that there can be no ambivalence with respect to some of the standard variables. Sociable interaction and helping vary in frequency. If I combine episodes of frequent and infrequent association with my adult children, it would make sense for me to pick an intermediate score when presented with a frequency scale. But inconsistent behavior is not ambivalent behavior. A family member may do things that are both helpful and harmful to others, but this only means that he or she is acting with contradictory effects, even if the same action helps one relative and harms another. Likewise, opportunities may be great, small, or intermediate. High and low opportunities do not combine to create ambivalence. In planning for holiday visits with parents and parents-in-law, for example, couples may be faced with equal opportunities and choice dilemmas. The decision may be complicated, but it is not because the couple is ambivalent on any particular dimension of solidarity. Finally, conflict, in the sense of overt arguing, may be played out in a variety of ways and can occur more or less frequently. The combination of high and low conflict does not indicate ambivalence. Our general point is that for certain dimensions of solidarity taken separately, there is nothing peculiar about an intermediate score to suggest that it might be signaling ambivalence.

In addition, it would be incorrect to say that inconsistencies in experience across the standard variables represent ambivalence (Marshall, 2001). For example, we can spend a lot of time with our parents (or children) and not feel especially attached to them emotionally. We may have opportunities to help but no need or desire to help. We can disagree a lot with our fathers about beliefs and values, and still not argue with them. Generally speaking, the rather common inconsistencies between the facets of our intergenerational ties merely reveal the complexity of family relations. Such circumstances may at times provide a context in which ambivalence arises, but they are not inherently ambivalent. For example, I may feel that I *should* love each of my adult children equally; but one son is turning out to be particularly disappointing, so my emotional attachment to him is declining. This does not necessarily mean that I have become ambivalent toward the disappointing son. It merely suggests that our affective solidarity is lower than our normative solidarity.

As a final precaution, we note that behavioral differences among family members are not indicators of ambivalence. If there are two or more members of a generation, there is no reason to expect that all members will relate to all other members in exactly the same way. I may call my mother on the phone more than I call my father, or my mother may look after my sister's children more than my children; but such differences again merely reflect the variegated fabric of family life, not ambivalence.

So, in what ways can ambivalence be expressed in terms of the traditional tool kit of intergenerational concepts and measures? We think that the answer lies within the core ideas of emotionality, agreement, and social norms. Emotions are ambivalent when both positive and negative feelings toward an object (or a person, or a relationship between persons) are combined more or less simultaneously. The extent of agreement with another family member is ambivalent when we both agree and disagree, and tension is aroused within us because we do not know where we stand with one another. Normative commitments become ambivalent when there are multiple competing expectations for behavior that cannot all be entirely fulfilled.

Standard measures of emotional, consensual, and normative solidarity overlook the possibility of intergenerational ambivalence. For example, Bengtson and colleagues ask about the amount of affection, trust, respect, and understanding between generations, with answers ranging from low to high (Mangen, Bengtson & Landry, 1988). There is no possibility for a respondent to report mixed feelings (e.g. high understanding about some things and low understanding about others). For consensual solidarity, Bengtson and colleagues ask how much respondents agree or disagree with various beliefs about marriage, religion, politics, and racial justice, then calculate similarity of beliefs between parents and adult children. Such scoring hides instances where similarity is both high and low, depending on the specific belief. Finally, Bengtson and colleagues capture normative solidarity by asking respondents how much they agree or disagree with various statements about what family members *should* do in their relationships. Again, the scoring ignores situations in which there is a mix of contradictory expectations.

We are not suggesting that emotional, consensual, and normative solidarity are problematic constructs. They may indeed be very useful. Instead, we are arguing only that by presupposing these expressions of solidarity to be unidimensional, we miss the opportunity to fully understand the meaning of intermediate scale scores, which sometimes might reflect ambivalent attitudes.

EXISTING MEASURES OF AMBIVALENCE

Before we go into the details of ambivalence measurement, we will address two topics briefly: levels of analysis and methods of data collection. There are no correct or incorrect perspectives on these issues, but the choices that researchers make about them influence how they study ambivalence.

First, we can differentiate studies on different levels of social aggregation. The fact that they refer to ambivalence either in the individual, in social relationships, or in societies says something about the conceptualization of ambivalence.

Ambivalence is often studied in individuals, especially in psychology and psychiatry. There the interest lies in a person's personality traits, emotions, thoughts, cognitions, wishes, and desires. The insight that individuals cannot be separated from other individuals or from groups is what leads to the consideration of ambivalence in social psychology. But, here as well, the focused object is the individual. This branch of ambivalence studies, initiated by Bleuler and Freud in the early 20th century (see Lüscher, Chap. 2 in this volume), remains common in cognitive and social psychology.

Ambivalence in social relationships has been studied under the primacy of social roles and expectations, and from a normative perspective (Merton, 1976). This sociological view, in the mainstream of sociological thinking in the 1960s and 1970s, was committed to understanding the influences of social structure – usually leaving the dynamics and diversity of social relationships unexplored.

Contemporary sociological (and philosophical) scholarship also mentions ambivalence from a postmodern position with no fixed or stable status quo. Observing recent social change from a critical perspective, social relations are considered to be infused with ambivalence (Bauman, 1991). This position may be traced back to the formal sociology of Simmel, who helped pioneer the sociology of ambivalence (Frisby, 1992, p. 155; Junge, 2000).

Depending on one's perspective, ambivalence can be conceptualized as residing within persons, within relationships between persons, or within social institutions and entire societies. For our present purpose, we will restrict ourselves to ambivalence within persons, and in a family context. Therefore, we may speak of one family member being ambivalent toward another family member or toward a relationship with another family member. The ambivalence may be pervasive or focused on certain aspects of the other member or the relationship. The ambivalence of one member may or may not be reciprocated, so that we can speak cautiously about the total ambivalence in a family dyad or in an entire family. Some family-relevant ambivalence will involve two or more members of the same generation, but our focus here is on relationships between parents and adult children. Therefore we must remain sensitive to the number of such dyads in a family, as well as to variations in their age and gender compositions.

Next, we want to delineate how most empirical data on ambivalence has been collected. Even though each investigation has its special focus and procedure, studies may be subdivided according to their research design – that is, according to direct or indirect assessment of ambivalence, and using either a quantitative or qualitative paradigm (see Table 1).

In our view, all knowledge of ambivalence is socially constructed and reflexive. Ambivalence must not be regarded as a real object, but rather as an ascription made by various observers. Individuals may or may not label their own relationships or other experiences as "ambivalent." The same is true for alter egos or third persons such as scientists or therapists. The common feature among such ascriptions is that two contradictory aspects are linked together over a span of time. Lanier (1941b) showed that respondents require more time to make ambivalent judgments than to make pleasant, unpleasant, or indifferent judgments. Saying, for example, that "I feel torn in my relationship with my mother" implies that I recall positive *and* negative aspects from the past, and weigh or balance these aspects in order to give a summarizing statement. The past may entail years, hours, or just seconds.

Table 1.   Examples of Different Research Designs for Studies of Ambivalence.

	Direct	Indirect
Qualitative	In-depth interviews on dilemmas, conflicting feelings Therapeutic sessions	Secondary analysis of interviews with a different purpose. Content analysis
Quantitative	Standardized questions on conflicting feelings, mixed emotions	Comparison of contradictory items or scales. Calculation of ambivalence indices

Whereas qualitative procedures are usually designed for the detailed analysis of single cases or for exploratory investigation of social phenomena, quantitative designs concentrate on large scale analysis or the statistical estimation of correlations and predictions. Basically, direct and indirect assessments of ambivalence are applicable in both kinds of research. Unique to quantitative designs, however, is that they require much more previous knowledge and are subject to high standards of reliability and validity. Applying a highly standardized questionnaire restricts results to the assigned answer categories.

It is also clear that the direct measurement of ambivalence refers exclusively to respondents' assessments of opposing aspects. Indirect measurement, in contrast, requires that the researcher rather than the respondent link contradictory reports, who may then interpret some participants as being ambivalent.

Below, we will present and discuss the direct and indirect measurement of ambivalence in qualitative and in quantitative research, and we will go into more detail regarding quantitative instruments.

Direct Ambivalence Assessment

Qualitative sociological studies often implicitly point to ambivalences. For example, Hattery (2001, p. 58) comments on how mothers are "tugged" in two directions by their commitments to children and to paid employment. In this case, the argument is not that a mother is ambivalent toward her children, only that mothers struggle to deal with how best to maximize their children's welfare without sacrificing their other interests.

Studies such as Hattery's highlight the fundamental difference between participants talking incidentally about ambivalence and an entire interview arranged to explore the topic. The latter emphasis is rare in family research. In most cases, the observation of ambivalence is either the result of the researcher's interpretation or the focus of secondary analysis, rather than the explicit topic of the interviews. We would classify such assessments of ambivalence as being "indirect."

In contrast to sociology, the treatment of ambivalent experiences has a long tradition and a prominent position in psychotherapy. Issues may involve parent-child relations, marriage and divorce, substance abuse, domestic violence, sexual orientation, etc. Along with the treatment of the individual, partners and families often are integrated into therapeutic sessions. Some therapeutic schools, e.g. systemic therapy (Simon, Stierlin & Wynne, 1985), even consider individuals and their problems as parts and symptoms of a systemic social unit. Other approaches, for example, "paradoxical intervention," directly confront patients with potential problems in order to reduce existing pressure and to stimulate reflective processes or changes of behavior.

While ambivalence is frequently a topic in psychotherapy, it may be less obviously applicable to basic social research. In therapy, for example, an urgent exploration of the origins of ambivalence is undertaken to assist the recovery of patients. Delving too much into details of ambivalence, however, may irritate the ordinary interviewee or survey respondent in social research. In addition, the concept's origin in and relevance for therapy support an understanding of the term as referring to something pathological. Applying the concept of ambivalence to situations of everyday life, then, requires systematic exploration of different dimensions, circumstances, causes, and effects of ambivalence, which are not necessarily linked to pathological or other negative circumstances.

To date, only a few attempts have been made to assess ambivalence directly in quantitative research. The reason for this may be that ambivalence usually has been seen as a personality trait inaccessible to conscious self-report rather than as a situationally defined attitude (Sincoff, 1990, pp. 57–58).

One example of direct measurement stems from the study of Thompson, Zanna and Griffin (1995, p. 373). Their items include the following:

I'm confused about (...) because I have strong thoughts about it and I can't make up my mind one way or another.

I find myself feeling 'torn' between two sides of the issue of (...).

My mind and heart seem to be in disagreement over the issue of (...).

Brömer (1998) used a direct question about torn feelings with regard to respondents' judgments of unfamiliar consumer products. A 7-point rating scale, ranging from "not at all" to "very strong" was applied to statements such as:

In my judgment, I feel ... torn.

Another illustration is the study of Schäfer (1998, p. 386), who asked people about their attitudes toward selected foreign groups (minorities, strangers, etc.). Respondents were asked to make a choice between "clearly positive," "clearly negative," "neither positive nor negative" (indifferent), and "positive and negative" (ambivalent). Response choices were: "strong," "medium," and "lower."

One of the earliest explicit efforts to develop a direct measure of ambivalence in family studies was made by Braiker and Kelley (1979). They applied the idea to romantic relationships. The five items in the Braiker and Kelley ambivalence scale (p. 153) were:

How confused were you about your feelings toward X?
How much did you think or worry about losing some of your independence by getting involved with X?
How ambivalent or unsure were you about continuing in the relationship with X?
To what extent did you feel X demanded or required too much of your time and attention?
To what extent did you feel "trapped" or pressured to continue in the relationship?

It should be obvious that some of these items would not apply to intergenerational relationships. As adults, we may not want to be dependent on our parents or on our children, and we might feel pressured by them in various ways; but we do not usually consider the possibility of completely severing our relationships with them. Still, Braiker and Kelley offered two useful lessons. One is that ambivalence is conceptually and empirically distinct from the positive idea of love and the negative idea of interpersonal conflict. The other is the finding, similar to Orden and Bradburn (1968), that positive and negative dimensions of intimate relations may themselves be uncorrelated. This is important, because it means that positive and negative features coexist in some relationships, which opens the door to indirect measures that separately consider the two sides, but without expecting ambivalence to be present in every dyad.

Strengths and Weaknesses of Direct Measures

It is relatively easy, even if uncommon, to develop survey or interview items that directly measure ambivalent attitudes toward other persons. But we need to consider their value critically.

When respondents are asked directly about ambivalence, the most important requirements are a clear definition of ambivalence and an accurate operationalization. Although one never knows which exact associations participants have, a precise conceptualization of ambivalence is necessary for the development of valid instruments. The scientific definition has to be translated into everyday language, but this does not imply that the colloquial meaning of ambivalence is the starting point. From our perspective, not all of the illustrative protocol items mentioned earlier meet these requirements. It is important, however, to distinguish ambivalence from social conflict, confusion or uncertainty, and discordance between one's mind and heart.

Social conflict refers to interpersonal or intergroup disputes. Neither party is ambivalent so long as they are both firmly aligned with opposite sides of the dispute. Participants or bystanders who are attracted to both sides may become ambivalent, but in this case we would say that the conflict causes the ambivalence, not that the conflict is ambivalent per se.

Confusion also is not identical with ambivalence. As Camp (2002) shows, people may be confused about a fact because, for example, they do not know which one of two alternative statements is the correct one. But this does not necessarily mean that they feel torn between the two alternatives. It is possible either that they do not know about one alternative at all or that they expect to gain clarity soon. Similar comments can be made about "cognitive dissonance" (Festinger, 1957) or "ambiguity." A stimulus is ambiguous if it has no clear meaning. Ambiguity may sometimes lead to ambivalence (Boss, 1999), but the two ideas refer to different phenomena.

Finally, a disagreement between mind and heart relates two different aspects that do not belong to the same dimension, which does not accord with what Bleuler (1910/1911) saw as an important precondition for ambivalence. Ambivalence can mean disagreement either between opposing cognitions (mind) or between opposing emotions (heart), but not a conflict between one's mind and heart. Therefore, only instruments asking for torn feelings (or thoughts) between two sides of an issue will capture ambivalence directly. Note that Schäfer (1998) tried to assess relationships between social groups (or between individuals) as ambivalent without referring to real personal relationships, which would be necessary, in our view, for studying ambivalence from a sociological perspective.

Indirect Ambivalence Measures

As noted above, there are few qualitative studies that rely on the indirect calculation of ambivalence scores. In most cases, the assessment of ambivalence is the researcher's interpretation based on the secondary analysis of data collected for another purpose. One exception is Raulin's (1984) "intense ambivalence scale."

Raulin developed a structured interview in which none "of the interview questions asked about ambivalent feelings directly." It only provided "several situations in which ambivalent feelings might be displayed" – for example, the subject's home, relationships with roommates, friends, parents, and the opposite sex (p. 66). After the interview, subjects were rated on a 5-point scale for the level of ambivalence, with 1 indicating "less ambivalent than most people," 2 indicating "normal ambivalence," and 5 standing for "pathological ambivalence."

Another example is the open-ended measure developed by Maio, Fincham and Lycett (2000). Respondents are first asked to write down words that describe their feelings toward a person. In a second step, interviewees are expected to evaluate these words according to their good or bad connotations.

> Now, we would like you to think about the time you spend with your mum. How do you feel when you are with your mum? For example, do you feel safe, sad, angry, or excited? Try to think of some of your own words that show how you feel about your mum. Please tell the truth: There is no right or wrong answer. Put each word in a box. Use as many boxes as you need.
>
> My words that show how I feel about my mum are: [10 boxes are displayed].
>
> Now that you have written your words, we would like you to say if the feelings they show are good, bad, or in between. You can do this by using the marks below.

$\sqrt{}$ = little bit good, $\sqrt{}\sqrt{}$ = quite good, $\sqrt{}\sqrt{}\sqrt{}$ = very good, 0 = in between, X = little bit bad,
XX = quite bad, XXX = very bad

The amount of calculated ambivalence is essentially the sum of the checkmarks and X-marks. (We mention a more precise expression of the formula later.)

Indirect quantitative measures of ambivalence can be traced to Lanier (1941a, b), who explored the relation between memory value and different types of affective judgment for words on a free-association list. Respondents were asked to judge words such as "table," "dark," "spider," "red," and "smooth" with one of four categories: "pleasant," "indifferent," "unpleasant," and "mixed." The category "mixed" was to be used when a word seemed to arouse both pleasant and unpleasant affective reactions.

Although Lanier was not interested in ambivalence per se, his work gives important clues to the topic. One is the finding that "body" is most frequently judged as "mixed." It appears neither in the list of pleasant words nor in that of unpleasant words. This is a striking example of the importance of ambivalence to personal identity, because the body is one of the essential aspects of a person. This interpretation is supported by two other results. First, Lanier found galvanic skin responses for "mixed" judgments to be markedly higher than corresponding measures for the other three categories. Mixed words obviously cause a physical reaction, and this means that they are bothersome. Second, "mixed" words remain in memory for a longer time. This finding supports the idea that, so long as ambivalent thoughts or feelings are unresolved, they preoccupy a person's attention.

Another type of attitudinal measurement, the semantic differential scale, also has some potential for the study of ambivalence. Bipolar alternatives (e.g. favorable-unfavorable, good-bad, positive-negative) are rated on a 5- or 7-point scale (Osgood, 1952). Respondents are asked, for example, to decide which answer on a "positive-negative" scale represents their perception of, or emotion toward, an object. The middle responses reflect some degree of ambivalence, but they can also be interpreted as uncertainty or as neutrality (Klopfer & Madden, 1980). Bell, Esses and Maio (1996, p. 13) argue that bipolar scales are inappropriate for measuring ambivalence, because "they do not separate out the positive and negative dimensions of attitudes. Thus, attitudes towards two groups may be the same on a bipolar attitude measure, but differ in terms of degree of ambivalence." Another concern with bipolar scales is whether the opposing issues are really contradictory or simply orthogonal. Accordingly, "feeling close" may not be the opposite of "feeling distant" (Cacioppo & Berntson, 1994). Instead, the opposite of "close" may be "not close." For Green, Goldman and Salovey (1993), however, the independence of positive and negative affect is a statistical artifact, and they see the two as ends of a bipolar scale.

Watson, Clark and Tellegen (1988) developed a short but reliable instrument to measure self-rated moods, which they called the "Positive and Negative Affect Schedule" (PANAS). It contains 10 positive adjectives (e.g. alert, excited) and 10 negative adjectives (e.g. upset, ashamed). It also accommodates alternative time frames from feeling this way "right now" to "in general." The most important finding from studies by Watson and colleagues is that the correlation between the positive and negative scales is invariably low. This means that some people have mostly positive moods, some mostly negative moods, others a mood that is both positive and negative (ambivalent), and the remainder a mood that is neither positive nor negative.

The PANAS and adaptations of it have sometimes been used in family studies (e.g. Bedford, 1998; Fingerman, 1998), although scores on the positive and negative scales are often inversely related in these studies. Self-ratings about moods, however, are not the same as feelings about relationship partners or about relationships with partners; so we expect more efforts in the future to utilize PANAS in studies of intergenerational relations.

When family researchers challenge the assumption that positive and negative are end points on a single bipolar continuum, they may or may not find evidence for ambivalence. For example, Caldwell, Antonucci and Jackson (1998) found a strong inverse correlation between intergenerational support and conflict in a sample of teenaged mothers and their own mothers. In contrast, Johnson, White, Edwards and Booth (1986) found that the positive and negative aspects of marital quality clustered in statistically independent scales.

Still another line of family research in which indirect measures of ambivalence have received attention is the attachment literature (see Maio, Fincham, Regalia & Paleari, Chap. 12 in this volume). We wish to emphasize only that the usual conceptualization of ambivalent attachments is of questionable value. For example, Hazan and Shaver (1987) and Bartholomew and Horowitz (1991) identify an "anxious/ambivalent" style of attachment, captured by the description below:

> I find that others are reluctant to get as close as I would like. I often worry that my partner doesn't really love me or won't want to stay with me. I want to merge completely with another person, and this desire sometimes scares people away (Hazan & Shaver, 1987, p. 515).

For the present purpose, we can ignore that the focus of the excerpt above is on romantic relationships rather than on parent-child relationships, and that the description assumes a general personality trait rather than dyad-specific attitudes. If respondents endorse the description, they are combining information about themselves and about their partner. To find out if a respondent is ambivalent toward a partner, we would need a series of items about the respondent's own attraction to the partner such that it would be possible to discover some who are simultaneously attracted to and repulsed by the partner.

Perhaps the first to conceptualize ambivalence as a property of an attitude was Scott (1966, 1968), who borrowed ideas from conflict theory (e.g. Brown & Farber, 1951; Lewin & Cartwright, 1951). Scott differentiated three basic conflicts: that between two positive forces, that between two negative forces, and that between a positive force and a negative force. These insights led Kaplan (1972) to separate the positive and negative attitude components of bipolar scales and to measure them separately on two 4-point scales. In this way, the single quality of one scale (e.g. positive judgment) can be compared directly to that of another scale (e.g. negative judgment). We usually speak of ambivalence when scores on both scales are high. Difficulties in responding to a unidimensional measure, then, may reflect uncertainty rather than ambivalence.

An elaborate attempt to measure ambivalence indirectly appears in the instruments developed by Thompson, Zanna and Griffin (1995) and Thompson and Zanna (1995). The assessment of negative and positive components of attitudes toward the same object was conducted in two steps:

> Think about your attitude toward or evaluation of euthanasia, that is, allowing patients with terminal illnesses to end their own lives. Considering only the favorable qualities of euthanasia and ignoring the unfavorable characteristics, *how favorable is your evaluation* of euthanasia? Not at all favorable, slightly favorable, quite favorable, extremely favorable.
>
> Think about your attitude toward or evaluation of euthanasia, that is, allowing patients with terminal illnesses to end their own lives. Considering only the unfavorable qualities of euthanasia and ignoring the favorable characteristics, *how unfavorable is your evaluation* of euthanasia? Not at all unfavorable, slightly unfavorable, quite unfavorable, extremely unfavorable.

Analogous questions referred to the feelings or emotions and to the thoughts and beliefs toward euthanasia, with the opposing issues being satisfaction vs. dissatisfaction and beneficial vs. harmful qualities (Thompson, Zanna & Griffin, 1995, pp. 371–373).

Other authors have developed or applied similar instruments for the measurement of attitudinal ambivalence. Katz and Hass (1988) as well as Hass, Katz, Rizzo, Bailey and Eisenstadt (1991) did research on racial attitudes, with separated Pro-Black and Anti-Black scales. Sincoff (1990) asked adolescents to respond to a "Mixed Feelings Questionnaire," a 50-item measure that emphasizes a trait approach to ambivalence. Brömer (1998) has applied separate scales in order to measure attitudes towards unfamiliar consumer products.

There have been various attempts to develop an adequate formula for the calculation of an indirect ambivalence score. Breckler (1994) and Thompson, Zanna, and Griffin (1995) give a broad overview of these efforts. In the brief summary here, "A" refers to the amount of ambivalence, "S" to the stronger of the two valences, and "W" to the weaker of the two. We avoid using "positive" and "negative" because the opposing attitudes often may be equal in this respect. The ideas of strong and weak are not ideal either, because they suggest intensity when the proper interpretation sometimes may be frequency or duration, as we discuss later. For the purpose of calculation, when $W = S$, their positions in the formulas are arbitrary and interchangeable. The following are among the formulas most often considered, and we show the originators that Thompson and colleagues credit.

$$\text{Kaplan}: \quad A = 2W$$

$$\text{Katz and Hass}: \quad A = W \cdot S$$

$$\text{Jamieson}: \quad A = \frac{W^2}{S}$$

$$\text{Brown and Farber; Scott}: \quad A = \frac{W^3}{S^2}$$

$$\text{Griffin}: \quad A = \frac{S + W}{2} - (S - W)$$

The latter three formulas are all similar, and are usually strongly correlated when applied to real data. All five formulas tend to produce non-linear distributions. An advantage of the Griffin formula is that it allows one to assess separately the sizes of the attitude components and their similarity in magnitude. In general, it is important to consider not only the non-linearity that may pertain to ambivalence itself, but also non-linear relationships that ambivalence may have with other variables. For example, you may have to build up a large amount of ambivalence about helping your mother before something else happens in your relationship with your mother.

Maio, Fincham and Lycett (2000, p. 1456) have developed a formula for open-ended measures that is similar to Griffin's, such that $A = (S + W) - 2(S + W) + K$, where K is a constant to keep all scores equal to or greater than zero. The difference between the two formulas is that Griffin subtracts W from S in the second term, while Maio et al. add them. This means that Griffin places more emphasis than Maio et al. on the similarity of the strong and weak components as a positive influence on the amount of calculated ambivalence. There is no reason, by the way, to restrict the Maio et al. formula to open-ended questions.

Strengths and Weaknesses of Indirect Measures

Although the separate measurement of attitudinal components represents progress in research on ambivalence, there are still some concerns with those measures. The crucial issue is whether or not the components are opposing.

First, the instruction by Thompson, Zanna and Griffin (1995, p. 372) to concentrate on one side and to neglect the other is problematic. This inhibits an independent measurement of both aspects because the instruction is paradoxical: alerting someone to an aspect which has to be ignored. Although Kaplan as well as Thompson, Zanna and Griffin (1995) argue that this procedure is not problematic for respondents, Bell, Esses and Maio (1996, p. 17) warn that respondents have to think simultaneously of the contents of an item and of its evaluation. They suggest asking first for the contents ("stereotypes, symbolic beliefs, and emotions") in an open-ended question, and then requesting the evaluation of these aspects.

Second, linking these supposedly contradictory components implies, above all, a theoretical conceptualization of opposite issues. The tendency to assume the same origin for evaluative processes, and therefore to see, for example, positive and negative aspects as reciprocal, either is related to stereotypic antonyms of every-day knowledge or points to effects of measurement-implicit theories (Cacioppo & Berntson, 1994; see also Simon, 1998). In our view, this opposing relationship should be demonstrated empirically by means of statistical analysis after data collection, and it should not be anticipated in the corresponding questions themselves.

Interestingly, separating a bipolar scale into its two components usually results in a rather low correlation between them where a correlation of -1.0 would be expected (Kaplan, 1972; Katz & Hass, 1988; Thompson, Zanna & Griffin, 1995). Also, Watson, Clark and Tellegen (1988) have pointed out that positive and negative affect have to be regarded as orthogonal dimensions. Factor analysis is an appropriate means of finding out about the degree of opposition between items. When items load highly on the same factor, but with different signs, we could assume an antonymous relation between them. We offer a precaution here, however. If opposite words load on the same factor with strongly opposite signs, this means that respondents rarely select both words, so they are rarely ambivalent.

Diener and Emmons (1985) explained the degree of negative correlation between positive and negative affect in terms of the time period being considered. The closer in time the assessed aspects are, the more negative is their correlation. Consequently, Fincham and Linfield (1997, p. 491) argue that ambivalence assessment has to include temporal references in order to control for respondents' associations, which influence the degree of opposition in their statements.

Third, a researcher's expectation of contradictory items may cause him or her to ignore that some respondents disagree about judging positive and negative issues as opposites. Classifying the supposed contradictory issues as ambivalent neglects not only the possibility that neither choice is considered relevant, but also the possibility that the two may just exist side by side or that even more than two possibilities are relevant. This is why Breckler (1994, p. 364) differentiates between "bivalence" and ambivalence, the first simply indicating the coexistence of positive and negative aspects. In the same way, one could also speak of "trivalence" or "polyvalence." Ambivalence per se is the result of relating two aspects and therefore is a description of the relation between them, referring to their irreconcilable character. This differentiated view helps us understand the variety of respondents' judgments and the relations among them.

Fourth, these questions of validity lead to Thompson, Zanna and Griffin's (1995) suggestion to use the direct assessment of ambivalence as a validity criterion for the indirect measure. Thus, the correlation between direct and indirect measures should be as high as possible. For example, Thompson et al. (1995) found a significant Pearson's r between direct and indirect measures of 0.40, and Brömer (1998) reported a significant correlation of $r = 0.60$. This is an important point for improving the measurement of ambivalence, but only when we assume that both measures tap identical issues. Ambivalence assessments may have different origins: direct reports by respondents and indirect assessment by researchers. Also, the validation idea disregards the additional heuristic potential of connecting direct and indirect measures.

Whenever the indirect ambivalence score exceeds the direct score, an alternative interpretation is "latency" of ambivalence. While some degree of latency may be common, it is also possible for directly measured ambivalence to be more prevalent than indirectly measured ambivalence. This situation may be difficult to interpret, especially when we want to avoid the pathologization of experiences. It may simply mean that respondents are sensitized to ambivalences, or that the particular indirect measures being used miss the key contradictions.

Fifth, and finally, we want to take a closer look at the calculation of the ambivalence index score. Because existing formulas tend to produce non-linear (and non-normal) distributions of ambivalence, the question arises as to how intensity of ambivalence can be measured and how the distances between scores can be interpreted. Given positive (strong) and negative (weak) evaluations between 1 and 4, the Griffin formula produces the results in Table 2. Notice that the scores below

Table 2.   Ambivalence Index Scores Using the Griffin Formula.

Weak/Negative Component	Strong/Positive Component			
	1	2	3	4
1	1.0	0.5	0	−0.5
2	0.5	2.0	1.5	1.0
3	0	1.5	3.0	2.5
4	−0.5	1.0	2.5	4.0

the main diagonal apply only to positive-negative scales and not to strong-weak scales; this is because the weaker component cannot have a higher score than the stronger component, whereas a negative score can be higher than a positive score.

We agree with two important points. The degree of ambivalence increases with the level of identical ratings on both components (from 1/1 to 4/4). The degree of ambivalence also increases with the similarity of ratings on strong and weak components (e.g. from 4/1 to 4/4).

Some questions, however, remain unanswered. Can we, for example, be sure that ambivalence decreases linearly from 4/1 to 1/1? Doubt about this has led Priester and Petty (1996) to consider threshold effects in ambivalence, compatible with the idea of latency and with individual differences in sensitivity. For some persons, ambivalence may remain unnoticed when at a low level. Beyond a certain threshold it becomes obvious, and some individuals may even experience exponentially increasing ambivalence. Raulin (1984) found, for example, that depressed persons show especially elevated levels of ambivalence. In this respect, it is also questionable if the cases 1/1 and 2/4 should be interpreted in the same way, as the identical ambivalence index scores of 1.0 suggests. Another concern is whether the index of 2.5 in case of combination 4/3 really has to be judged less ambivalent than the combination 3/3 (index score of 3.0). When we assume that the intensity of both components increases with rising scores, the ambivalence index should do likewise so that the 3/4 case would fit between the 3/3 and the 4/4 cases. In our view, the Griffin formula places too much emphasis on the similarity of opposing attitudes. Other formulas (e.g. Kaplan's) do not have this deficiency.

Non-linearity in ambivalence is partly a function of the content being measured and partly of the response choices allowed. To illustrate the latter idea, consider Likert-type scales concerning the magnitude of "agreement" or of "applicability" of a statement with choices at the high end being "totally," "somewhat," and "partly." The ratings may differ depending on the connotations of "agreement" or "applicability." Also the number of intervals between the high and the low end may have an effect on the frequency of choices. Anchoring Likert-type scale choices with words to guide respondents also can be problematic, because the choice of "totally" may be unattractive to respondents when the other two choices are similar and more "reasonable" in connotation. In order to avoid equal-appearing intervals and to lower the constraint upon respondents to decide among relatively distant alternatives, we recommend using 7-point rather than 5-point scales, and labelling only the extremes and not each interval.

It seems likely that one formula will work better than another with a particular data set. Formulas yet to be developed may work even better, and across more data sets. Until more is known about the comparative utility of magnitude estimates for ambivalence, the safest course is to employ several formulas and discover what difference it makes to use one or another.

In general, social scientists have a blind spot when confronted with findings that seem contradictory. We tend to move in either of two directions to obliterate the contradiction rather than to treat it as a reality of human experience. One common tactic is to average opposing answers, thereby concealing the contradiction as just another intermediate score on a bipolar scale. Another common tactic is to question the reliability of the scale, and to eliminate items that retard the coefficient of internal consistency. In other words, the very psychometric principles that serve us well most of the time can be misused to steer us away from appreciating the phenomenon of ambivalence.

SUGGESTIONS FOR NEW MEASURES OF AMBIVALENCE IN INTERGENERATIONAL RELATIONS

We have seen that the concept of ambivalence plays an extensive role in understanding an individual's attitudes towards "objects," and that it has recently been applied in the context of social groups as well. When social relationships are considered, they are usually considered with respect to the normative structure of social roles or through seeing relationships as attitudinal "objects," and not with regard to interaction between two or more individuals. Inspired by Lüscher and Pillemer (1998), Lüscher and Lettke (2000) and others have begun to explore empirically the ambivalent nature of intergenerational relations (see Lüscher & Lettke, Chap. 7 in this volume). Affiliated studies have been conducted by Meyer Schweizer and Lehmann (2001), and by Pulkkinen and Hurme (2001). Intergenerational ambivalence also plays a role in the international "OASIS Study" by Lowenstein and Katz (2001).

We want to point out the innovative aspects of these instruments and make suggestions for measures that overcome some of the problems discussed above. We first concentrate on different dimensions of ambivalence, that is, frequency, duration, intensity, evaluation, and awareness. Then we present possibilities for the assessment of ambivalence in social relationships. The dimensions of ambivalence are not the same as the dimensions of attitudes (see Maio, Fincham, Regalia & Paleari, Chap. 12 in this volume).

Dimensions of Ambivalence

Frequency of Ambivalence

The appearance of ambivalence only once in a social relationship may not be very informative. An important specification is how often respondents have felt torn during a certain period of time. Ambivalent thoughts, feelings, or actions may occur periodically during a day, or they may arise repeatedly in everyday routines. Some relationships are likely to have more frequent ambivalence than others. From a life-course perspective, there may be times of crisis or critical role transitions during which respondents are especially likely to experience ambivalence.

Lüscher, Pajung-Bilger, Lettke, Böhmer, Rasner and Pillemer (2000) assess ambivalence frequency in the following two ways:

> Sometimes, family members can feel torn in two directions in their relationships with one another. Thinking about your relationship with [person], how often do you feel torn in two directions?" Categories: very often, often, now and then, seldom, never

> And how often have you already thought about such things [ambivalence, torn feelings, etc.] in the past?" Categories: very often, often, now and then, seldom, never

These measures can be made more precise by asking how often the experience happened last week, last year, or even throughout the entire relationship. When a time frame is specified, an additional question might be worth asking to determine if this period is either representative of the entire relationship or exceptional.

Duration of Ambivalence

A measure of frequency provides limited information about the prevalence of ambivalent experiences. When they occur very frequently, each experience cannot last for long. Nevertheless, ambivalences may be brief or instantaneous, but they might also last for longer periods (e.g. between parents and children throughout the latter's adolescence). Enduring ambivalent experiences have a strong impact on a relationship because of their steady and predictable character, but they also may provide more of an opportunity for coping strategies to be enacted.

We are unaware of an existing measure for the duration of ambivalence. The limitations of retrospective data are well-known, and they may increase as the time backward increases. Individuals may also differ in their sense of time. One useful question to pose to respondents might be:

> When you think of the times you felt torn, how long did these feelings generally last?" Categories: minutes, hours, days, weeks, months, years.

Intensity of Ambivalence

Frequent and longer-lasting ambivalences may become intense. In this case, ambivalence could become a "constant" quality of the relationship that requires some coping strategy (e.g. during adolescence or the chronic illness of a family member). We can also imagine periods in which ambivalence is very intense, followed by periods of only moderate or low intensity. Moderate ambivalence may be characteristic of an entire relationship, without ever becoming salient.

Lüscher et al. (2000) inquired about intensity in a follow-up question to the frequency question:

> "In this kind of situation, how stressful is it for you to feel torn in two directions regarding [person]?" Categories: very stressful, stressful, only a little stressful, not stressful at all.

Stress is only one aspect of intensity, and it may imply a negative evaluation. Therefore, questions about the "strength" of ambivalent experiences in relationships should be considered, as in the following wording:

> "When you think of the times in your relationship to [person] you felt torn, how strong were these feelings normally?" Categories: strong, moderate, weak.

An indirect way to explore the intensity of ambivalence is to ask if torn feelings in a relationship have led individuals to contact therapists or other health professionals. If so, we might conclude that ambivalence was experienced very intensely, and that individuals saw no possibility of escaping the feeling on their own.

Another indirect measure of ambivalence intensity in intergenerational relations has been presented by Lüscher et al. (2000). Respondents were asked to rate a list of attributes that describe dyadic relationships. The attributes were intended to represent contradictory ends on two different dimensions (see also Lüscher & Lettke, Chap. 7 in this volume). Ambivalence is inferred when respondents opt for opposing poles.

> "Relationships between people can be described in different ways. I am going to read you a list of descriptive terms. Please think about your current relationship with [person], and tell me to what extent the descriptions apply: solicitous, inflexible, intimate, easy-going, restrictive, full of variety, predictable, loving, reliable, unpredictable, cool, changeable, warm, superficial, stuck in a rut, indifferent, open to new experiences, close." Categories: highly apply, somewhat apply, partly apply, tend not to apply, do not apply at all.

To show first that the adjectives fit well with others in their particular set, a principal-components factor analysis was undertaken (Lettke, 2002). As a result, the following scales were constructed. *Convergence* consists of "loving," "warm," "solicitous," "intimate," and "close." *Divergence* is represented by "cool," "easy-going," "indifferent," and "superficial." The adjectives "inflexible," "restrictive," and "stuck in a rut" form the *reproduction* scale. *Innovation* consists of "open to new experiences" and "full of variety." Reliability coefficients (Cronbach's alpha) for convergence (0.87) and divergence (0.84) were reasonably high. The lower reliability of reproduction (0.64) and innovation (0.68), as well as their few items, suggest the need to develop more items for these scales.

Evaluation of Ambivalence

Ambivalence may have different meanings for different individuals. It could, for example, be judged positively or negatively, as illustrated by Lüscher et al. (2000):

> Would you say in summary that you see these 'ambivalences' as very positive, more positive than negative, equally positive and negative, more negative than positive, or very negative?

Positive and negative evaluation is a fundamental but rather unspecific distinction. A differentiation in terms such as "threat," "harm," "worry," "opportunity," or "stimulation" could be useful to find out more about the phenomenon. In addition, ambivalences may have different connotations in different relationships. Whereas in some of them it may be experienced as a heavy burden, in others it may be welcomed as part of an open-minded atmosphere. For someone with frequent and neutral or even positive experiences of ambivalence, the phenomenon may be far less problematic than for someone with moderately frequent but very negative evaluations of ambivalence. Thus, an assessment of how respondents evaluate their reports can deepen the researcher's understanding of their significance.

The fact that ambivalence is often negatively connoted is related to the concept's origin in psychiatry, especially with respect to schizophrenia (Bleuler, 1910/1911). Even though Bleuler argued that ambivalence occurs in everyday interaction, an emphasis on clinical applications suggests the importance of distinguishing between "normal" and "pathological" ambivalence. From a sociological point of view, the professional labelling of such disturbances and the import of these labels in everyday life is of special interest. Psychiatrists use standardized criteria for the diagnosis of mental disorders which are compiled in manuals (see American Psychiatric Association, 1994; World Health Organization, 1991). Laymen sometimes state that a behavior is not "normal" or that a relationship is "disrupted." Also, in family therapy we find models of "system functioning" or "homeostasis" that imply a division between functional and dysfunctional relationships (e.g. Beavers & Voeller, 1983; Olson, Sprenkle & Russell, 1979; cf. also Simon, 1998). In this view, ambivalence is an undesirable aspect of relationships.

Negative connotations, together with a normative bias in descriptions of family relations, are why reports of ambivalences may be systematically affected by social desirability response sets. If participants in a study are not encouraged to accept the possibility that ambivalence is normal, they may try to avoid the appearance of being ambivalent. Because the normative bias is due to deeply rooted cultural ideals of solidarity with respect to intergenerational relations, we would expect them to affect not only direct but also indirect measures. To control for social desirability, standard methods may be employed, such as distant spacing of opposite items, asking multiple questions, using anchor words for poles that are equal in known desirability, and allowing answers that are overly idealistic.

Using opposing concepts that are equal in social desirability is not possible when they are positive and negative emotions, due to a cultural bias against negativity in social, and especially family, relations. Concepts such as dependence and independence, however, are likely to be more closely matched in social desirability. When in doubt, we recommend an empirical assessment of social desirability before including a pair of concepts in an indirect ambivalence scale.

Awareness of Ambivalence

We define awareness of ambivalence in terms of whether or not individuals perceive contradictory aspects of a relationship. Assessing awareness is only possible, in our view, by combining direct and indirect measures. The exclusive application of direct measures may lead to artifacts, because when asked directly, even people who are unaware of what we mean as ambivalence may be prompted to appreciate something like torn feelings. The exclusive application of indirect measures raises questions of validity, because one does not know for sure if the measured ambivalence corresponds with an individual's experiences. When direct and indirect measures are linked, two requirements have to be fulfilled: Both questions must cover identical issues, and the direct questions must appear *after* the indirect questions.

As we have seen, Lüscher et al. (2000) asked directly for the frequency of ambivalence, and they infer validity if contradictory attributes for the description of a relationship are reported simultaneously (indirect measurement). But, it is doubtful that both measures tap identical issues because we find, in one case, a multi-item instrument covering several issues of a relationship, and, in the other case, a rather general report about the same relationship. In our view, one should systematically pick up the most contradictory descriptions and ask respondents to comment directly on these contradictions in another part of the interview.

MEASURING AMBIVALENCE IN SOCIAL RELATIONSHIPS

Psychological research on attitudinal ambivalence focuses on individuals. This perspective ignores the patterns of social interaction that characterize social relationships. Sociologists are more likely to ask people about their relationships. Systematically, we may differentiate the following types of information:

(1) individual reports of inner conditions ("I feel..." or "I am a..."), or about other individuals ("She is like...").

(2) individual reports about the qualities of relationships ("Normally, we talk about everything").
(3) mutual perspectives on relationships ("In our relationship my father behaves..." *and* "...my son behaves...") can be combined with self reports (son saying, "In our relationship I behave..." *and* father saying, "In our relationship I behave...").
(4) direct observations of interaction (a researcher noting that "The family members avoid talking about...").

Of these possibilities, attention to mutual perspectives offers much promise for ambivalence research. For example, Lüscher et al. (2000) asked both members of intergenerational dyads about feeling torn. Comparing the reports tells us something about the dyadic relationship. According to Elias (1978), survey questions should point to the relevant social unit. He notes that personal pronouns are especially useful for specifying the social unit. When one is interested in relationships, the personal pronoun "we" is indispensable. We prefer this version rather than talking about "my father and me," because "we" stresses the relationship itself as a unit, whereas "my father and me" represents a sum of two persons. One example from Lüscher et al. (2000) illustrates how statements about relationships can be improved, because they do not stress the "we" as the stimulus for reflections about the relationship:

Although I love my mother very much, I am also sometimes indifferent toward her.

The following example is more adequate:

Mother and I often get on each other's nerves, but nevertheless we feel very close and like each other very much.

Consequently, when one is interested in family relations, phrases such as "in our family" or "we as a family" are necessary. When "family" is the unit of analysis, the researcher is additionally forced to decide who is and is not in the family, both conceptually and for the purpose of selecting a sampling frame. Even when all of the desired participants cannot be included for practical reasons, it is usually essential to have multiple participants from the same family to permit analyses both across and within families.

When the information from different perspectives is consistent, the relationship can be described simply enough. But what if reports differ from each other? Researchers may take the individual reports and infer a description on a more abstract level. A valid abstract description has to represent the individual reports, but the abstract description is not sufficient to describe all details of a particular relationship.

Having these difficulties in mind, the classification of a relationship as "ambivalent" is an even bigger challenge. Can we conceptualize it simply by assessing contradictory reports? We do not think that one can speak of ambivalence when Person A says that the relationship is "good" and Person B says it is "not good." This situation may be conceptualized as a difference of standpoints or even as a conflict, but it does not characterize an ambivalent relationship (Marshall, 2001).

Our suggestion for defining ambivalent relationships refers to the relevance of identity as an indispensable aspect of ambivalence. The identity of a relationship can be found in ideals, in habits, or in tradition, as well as in extraordinary common experiences. Consequently, ambivalence may occur when relevant actual interaction or attitudes of the concerned parties are opposed to the common ideals of the relationship. An example would be that a father and his son both agree on the importance of harmony in their family while their daily interaction is full of anger and quarrelling. The same would apply to relationships with two parties getting along well but stating that they are suffering or that they plan to leave each other. Imagine family members all agreeing on honesty and openness while some or all of them have ulterior motives or secret strategies, and pursue only their individual goals. However, as we mentioned in our earlier discussion of solidarity, we are not arguing that discrepancies between norms and practices are ambivalent per se. Rather, we are suggesting that when the identities of family members are involved, a pattern of deviant behavior may cause ambivalence.

Here as elsewhere, ambivalence can be observed directly or indirectly. A direct assessment of ambivalence would consist of the coinciding reports of two (or more) parties that they feel torn in their relationship. An indirect assessment of ambivalence requires both information about the common "identity" of two (or more) parties and additional statements about the relationship that are contrary to the ideal. In contrast to this, we would not classify relationships as ambivalent either when the reports of two parties differ from each other or when the reports and the ideals are not contradictory. To our knowledge, there exist no attempts to measure ambivalent relationships in this way. It would be useful to study this phenomenon carefully in the future.

PROSPECTS AND CHALLENGES FOR FUTURE RESEARCH

As a result of our discussion of measuring ambivalence, we may summarize what have turned out to be the key problems. Before applying any measure, researchers have to be clear about their definition of ambivalence, namely about how ambivalence contrasts with conflict, confusion, uncertainty, irrelevance, and bi- or polyvalence. When ambivalence is conceptualized, one has to define further dimensions of the phenomenon, which may be influenced by the research question. Then a decision has to be made as to how ambivalence shall be assessed, through direct reports of respondents and/or through indirect assessments of researchers, and how both methods are best connected.

Single items and statements have to be operationalized unidimensionally so that opposing aspects can be compared. The calculation method and formula depend on the prior conceptualization of ambivalence. Important for the selection or creation of a formula is to have theoretically derived criteria for the interpretation of different ambivalence scores and of the distances between them. In order to work with empirically falsifiable measures, it is also necessary to consider the absence of ambivalence in two different situations, when one side of an opposition totally dominates the other, and when no support exists for either side.

Ambivalence may be associated with social desirability response sets or with personality traits such as tolerance for ambiguity (or for ambivalence). Consequently, such possibilities should be studied and controlled when necessary. Currently, checking the external validity of single ambivalence measures is difficult, because standard procedures are still lacking. The best way is to rely on internal checks, e.g. factor analysis and the systematic analysis of meaning structures.

When the purpose is to assess ambivalence in social relationships, in families or in larger groups and organizations, one has to choose an appropriate design. The minimum requirement is to gather the mutual perspectives of interacting respondents. The source of empirical data is in most cases the individual; but, from a sociological perspective, social relationships may have characteristics beyond those seen from the perspectives of individuals.

Another important point is the choice of a time frame or temporal contextualization for questions and answers (e.g. "last week"). We have emphasized simultaneous contradictory elements as ambivalent. But, what does "simultaneous" mean? There are reasons to assume that emotions, cognitions, and speech always happen over a period of time. One cannot speak two sentences at the same time or think two thoughts at the same time. Thus, the assessment of ambivalence is always a reflection in which two issues are related. The period between these two may be an instant, a week, or even several years. And, they may oscillate at rates that make them more or less subject to awareness.

In sum, the field of family studies is still in the early stages of exploring ambivalence. Therefore, one challenge we face is to include a range of alternative measures in a given study in order to compare them. Also, we should replicate the same measures across studies to learn more about the limits of their utility. Eventually, it may be discovered that one or more measures are reliable and valid enough to guide the field.

In this chapter, we have discussed various ways in which multiple measures can be used: quantitative and qualitative, direct and indirect, a variety of dimensions (frequency, duration, etc.), and a range of formulas for indirect measures. We think that it will be helpful, within or across studies, to combine deductive and inductive approaches. On the deductive side, we can start with general principles about ambivalence and measures used outside of family studies, as in attitudinal psychology, and then apply them to intergenerational relations. On the inductive side, we can start with ideas and measures uniquely suited to adult children and their relations with parents, and then see how well they work when applied to other family relations and other domains of human experience.

Over time, researchers will gradually or aggressively move beyond descriptive research to hypothesize and test for the correlates, causes, and consequences of intergenerational ambivalence. In the process, researchers will seek and articulate explanatory mechanisms and will address the more common responses to ambivalent conditions.

It would be useful if researchers were to focus first on situations in which ambivalence is most likely to occur. This is important because we do not expect that ambivalence is always transparent, frequent, enduring, intense, or evaluated positively. In addition to critical role transitions, another fertile topic is step-families. We can expect more ambivalence wherever social norms are less institutionalized. Thus, another promising topic should be cohabitation. Wherever opposing social norms are strong, we have fertile ground for research. Conflicting loyalties to different expectations (e.g. work vs. family) is a very relevant topic for concerted ambivalence research. The relevance to gerontology is obvious, and it will help tie ambivalence studies to practical implications for the well-being of aging persons and their caretakers.

Notice that identifying contexts of ambivalence encourages us to think about causes. Whether we view it as a cause or a context, family structure (e.g. composition and size) is certainly important, so variations in family structure should be taken into account in future research designs.

It is neither necessary nor appropriate to set definitive priorities for future research. However, because ambivalence is always "about something," a focus on intergenerational relations requires the "something" to be either the parents and the children involved, or the social relationships among them. The early studies presented throughout this volume point to many of the targets of attention that will occupy readers and authors in the years ahead. Of course, further technical advice is appropriate. For example, we have suggested in this chapter that, whenever possible, researchers should use concrete time frames in their instruments and specify appropriate units of analysis.

The attitudes of researchers toward ambivalence will affect the future course of study dramatically. We advise against blindly assuming that when something and its opposite both empirically display some magnitude, the best way to create a summary score is to subtract one magnitude from the other. Furthermore, when two sets of multiple items with opposing conceptual valences form scales that turn out to be statistically independent, we should attend to the cases for which the scale scores are mutually high, and compare them with cases that have the other possible patterns. Doing so will remind us that ambivalence is not pervasive, but shows up in some specific human relationships more than in others and in some situations more than in others. More generally, researchers will have to refrain from thinking of ambivalence as only a personal or social "problem" to be solved. Without that negative bias, we can design research tools that will encourage participants to reveal their own neutral or even positive attitudes toward ambivalence.

As we move forward, the reciprocity between theory and research, between human experiences and the methods of investigating them, will be played on the stage of intergenerational ambivalence, just as it has for other scholarly endeavors in the past. You are invited to join us in this journey.

REFERENCES

American Psychiatric Association (1994). *Diagnostic and statistical manual of mental disorders* (4th ed.). Washington, DC: Author.

Bartholomew, K., & Horowitz, L. M. (1991). Attachment styles among young adults: A test of a four category model. *Journal of Personality and Social Psychology, 61*, 226–244.

Bauman, Z. (1991). *Modernity and ambivalence*. Ithaca, NY: Cornell University Press.

Beavers, R. W., & Voeller, M. N. (1983). Family models: Comparing and contrasting the Olson circumplex model with the Beavers systems model. *Family Process, 22*, 85–98.

Bedford, V. H. (1998). Sibling relationship troubles and well-being in middle and old age. *Family Relations, 47*, 369–376.

Bell, D. W., Esses, V. M., & Maio, G. R. C. (1996). The utility of open-ended measures to assess intergroup ambivalence. *Canadian Journal of Behavioural Science, 28*, 12–18.

Bengtson, V. L., & Roberts, R. E. L. (1991). Intergenerational solidarity in aging families: An example of formal theory construction. *Journal of Marriage and the Family, 53*, 856–870.

Berscheid, E. (1983). Emotion. In: H. H. Kelly, E. Berscheid, A. Christensen, J. H. Harvey, T. L. Huston & G. Levinger et al. (Eds), *Close Relationships* (pp. 110–168). New York: W. H. Freeman.

Bleuler, E. (1910/1911). Zur Theorie des schizophrenen Negativismus [Towards a theory of schizophrenic negativism]. *Psychiatrisch-Neurologische Wochenschrift, 18*, 171–176; *19*, 184–187; *20*, 189–191; *21*, 195–198.

Boss, P. (1999). *Ambiguous loss: Learning to live with unresolved grief*. Cambridge, MA: Harvard University Press.

Braiker, H. B., & Kelley, H. H. (1979). Conflict in the development of close relationships. In: R. L. Burgess & T. L. Huston (Eds), *Social Exchange in Developing Relationships* (pp. 135–168). New York: Academic Press.

Breckler, S. J. (1994). A comparison of numerical indexes for measuring attitude ambivalence. *Educational and Psychological Measurement, 54,* 350–365.

Brömer, P. (1998). Einstellungen gegenüber unvertrauten Produkten: Selbstwirksamkeit bestimmt die Intensität der Verarbeitung relevanter Produktattribute [Attitudes towards unfamiliar products: Self-efficacy determines the intensity of processing of relevant attributes]. *Zeitschrift für Sozialpsychologie, 29,* 124–133.

Brown, J. S., & Farber, I. E. (1951). Emotions conceptualized as intervening variables with suggestions toward a theory of frustration. *Psychological Bulletin, 48,* 465–480.

Cacioppo, J. T., & Berntson, G. S. (1994). Relationship between attitudes and evaluative space: A critical review with emphasis on the separability of positive and negative substrates. *Psychological Bulletin, 115,* 401–423.

Caldwell, C. H., Antonucci, T. C., & Jackson, J. S. (1998). Supportive/conflictual family relations and depressive symptomatology: Teenage mother and grandmother perspectives. *Family Relations, 47,* 395–402.

Camp, J. L. (2002). *Confusion: A study in the theory of knowledge.* Cambridge, MA: Harvard University Press.

Diener, E., & Emmons, R. A. (1985). The independence of positive and negative affect. *Journal of Personality and Social Psychology, 47,* 1105–1117.

Elias, N. (1978). *What is sociology?* New York: Columbia University Press.

Festinger, L. (1957). *A theory of cognitive dissonance.* Stanford, CA: Stanford University Press.

Fincham, F. D., & Linfield, K. J. (1997). A new look at marital quality: Can spouses feel positive and negative about their marriage? *Journal of Family Psychology, 11,* 489–502.

Fingerman, K. L. (1998). The good, the bad, and the worrisome: Emotional complexities in grandparents' experiences with individual grandchildren. *Family Relations, 47,* 403–414.

Frisby, D. (1992). *Simmel and since: Essays on Georg Simmel's social theory.* London: Routledge.

Green, D. P., Goldman, S. L., & Salovey, P. (1993). Measurement error masks bipolarity in affect ratings. *Journal of Personality and Social Psychology, 64,* 1029–1041.

Hass, R. G., Katz, I., Rizzo, N., Bailey, J., & Eisenstadt, D. (1991). Cross-racial appraisal as related to attitude ambivalence and cognitive complexity. *Personality and Social Psychology Bulletin, 17,* 83–92.

Hattery, A. (2001). *Women, work and family: Balancing and weaving.* Thousand Oaks, CA: Sage.

Hazan, C., & Shaver, P. (1987). Romantic love conceptualized as an attachment process. *Journal of Personality and Social Psychology, 52,* 511–524.

Johnson, D. R., White, L. K., Edwards, J. N., & Booth, A. (1986). Dimensions of marital quality: Toward methodological and conceptual refinement. *Journal of Family Issues, 7,* 31–49.

Junge, M. (2000). *Ambivalente Gesellschaftlichkeit: Die Modernisierung der Vergesellschaftung und die Ordnungen der Ambivalenzbewältigung* [Ambivalent sociality: The modernization of socialization and the orders of mastering ambivalence]. Opladen, Germany: Leske + Budrich.

Kaplan, K. J. (1972). On the ambivalence-indifference problem in attitude theory and measurement: A suggested modification of the semantic differential technique. *Psychological Bulletin, 77,* 361–372.

Katz, I., & Hass, R. G. (1988). Racial ambivalence and American value conflict: Correlational and priming studies of dual cognitive structures. *Journal of Personality and Social Psychology, 55,* 893–905.

112   FRANK LETTKE AND DAVID M. KLEIN

Klopfer, F. J., & Madden, T. M. (1980). The middlemost choice on attitude items: Ambivalence, neutrality, or uncertainty? *Personality and Social Psychology Bulletin, 6*, 97–101.

Lanier, L. H. (1941a). An experimental study of affective conflict. *Journal of Psychology, 11*, 199–217.

Lanier, L. H. (1941b). Incidental memory for words differing in affective value. *Journal of Psychology, 11*, 199–217.

Lettke, F. (2002). Ambivalenz und empirische Sozialforschung: Zum Verstehen quantitativer Daten [Ambivalence and empirical sociological research: A contribution to understanding quantitative data]. *Sozialer Sinn, 1*, 137–151.

Lewin, K., & Cartwright, D. (1951). *Field theory in social science: Selected theoretical papers.* New York: Harper & Row.

Lowenstein, A., & Katz, R. (2001, November). Theoretical perspectives on intergenerational solidarity, conflict and ambivalence: The Oasis Study. Paper presented at the Annual Conference of the Gerontological Society of America, Chicago.

Lüscher, K., & Lettke, F. (2000). Keyword: Intergenerational ambivalences. Part 1. Dealing with ambivalences: Toward a new perspective for the study of intergenerational relations among adults. Arbeitspapier [Working Paper] 36. Universität Konstanz, Germany: Forschungsschwerpunkt "Gesellschaft und Familie."

Lüscher, K., Pajung-Bilger, B., Lettke, F., Böhmer, S., Rasner, A., & Pillemer, K. (2000). Generationenambivalenzen operationalisieren: Instrumente [Operationalizing intergenerational ambivalences: Instruments] Arbeitspapier [Working Paper] 34.4. Universität Konstanz, Germany: Forschungsschwerpunkt "Gesellschaft und Familie."

Lüscher, K., & Pillemer, K. (1998). Intergenerational ambivalence: A new approach to the study of parent-child relations in later life. *Journal of Marriage and the Family, 60*, 413–425.

Maio, G. R., Fincham, F. D., & Lycett, E. J. (2000). Attitudinal ambivalence toward parents and attachment style. *Personality and Social Psychology Bulletin, 26*, 1451–1464.

Mangen, D. J., Bengtson, V. L., & Landry, P. H., Jr. (Eds) (1988). *Measurement of intergenerational relations.* Thousand Oaks, CA: Sage.

Marshall, V. (2001, November). Discussant comments on "New approaches to the study of intergenerational family relations." Paper presented at the Annual Conference of the Gerontological Society of America, Chicago.

Merton, R. K. (1976). *Sociological ambivalence and other essays.* New York: Free Press.

Meyer Schweizer, R., & Lehmann, L. (2001). Familienstrukturen und Generationenbeziehungen in der Region Bern [Families and intergenerational relations in the region of Berne]. Unpublished data report, University of Berne, Switzerland.

Olson, D. H., Sprenkle, D. H., & Russell, C. S. (1979). Circumplex model of marital and family systems. *Family Process, 18*, 3–28.

Orden, S., & Bradburn, N. (1968). Dimensions of marriage happiness. *American Journal of Sociology, 41*, 715–731.

Osgood, C. E. (1952). The nature and measurement of meaning. *Psychological Bulletin, 49*, 197–237.

Priester, J. R., & Petty, R. E. (1996). The gradual treshold model of ambivalence: Relating the positive and negative bases of attitudes to subjective ambivalence. *Journal of Personality and Social Psychology, 71*, 431–449.

Pulkkinen, L., & Hurme, H. (2001). *The Jyväskylä Longitudinal Study of Personality and Social Development.* Project documentation, http://psykonet.jyu.fi/HumanDeR/laku.htm

Raulin, M. L. (1984). Development of a scale to measure intense ambivalence. *Journal of Consulting and Clinical Psychology, 52*, 63–72.

Rossi, A. S., & Rossi, P. H. (1990). *Of human bonding: Parent-child relations across the life course.* New York: Aldine de Gruyter.

Schäfer, B. (1998). Bedingungen der Ambivalenz sozialer Einstellungen [The conditions of attitudinal ambivalence in the evaluation of social groups]. In: K. C. Klauer & H. Westmeyer (Eds), *Psychologische Methoden und Soziale Prozesse* (pp. 372–400). Pabst, Germany: Lengerich.

Scott, W. A. (1966). Measures of cognitive structure. *Multivariate Behavioral Research, 1*, 391–395.

Scott, W. A. (1968). Attitude measurement. In: G. Lindzey & E. Aronson (Eds), *The Handbook of Social Psychology* (Vol. 2, pp. 204–273). Reading, MA: Addison-Wesley.

Simon, F. B. (1998). Beyond bipolar thinking: Patterns of conflict as a focus for diagnosis and intervention. *Family Process, 37*, 215–232.

Simon, F. B., Stierlin, H., & Wynne, L. C. (1985). *The language of family therapy: A systemic vocabulary and sourcebook.* New York: Family Process Press.

Sincoff, J. B. (1990). The psychological characteristics of ambivalent people. *Clinical Sociological Review, 63*, 1–16.

Thompson, M. M., & Zanna, M. P. (1995). The conflict individual: Personality-based and domain-specific antecedents of ambivalent social attitudes. *Journal of Personality, 63*, 259–288.

Thompson, M. M., Zanna, M. P., & Griffin, D. W. (1995). Let's not be indifferent about (attitudinal) ambivalence. In: R. Petty & J. Krosnick (Eds), *Attitude Strength. Antecedents and Consequences* (pp. 361–386). Mahwah, NJ: Lawrence Erlbaum.

Watson, D., Clark, L. A., & Tellegen, A. (1988). Development and validation of brief measures of positive and negative affect: The PANAS scales. *Journal of Personality and Social Psychology, 54*, 1063–1070.

World Health Organization (1991). *International classification of diseases.* Geneva, Switzerland: Author.

5. CAN'T LIVE WITH 'EM, CAN'T LIVE WITHOUT 'EM: OLDER MOTHERS' AMBIVALENCE TOWARD THEIR ADULT CHILDREN

Karl Pillemer

INTRODUCTION

There is a long history of interest in the concept of ambivalence, as the contributions to the present volume show. It is therefore somewhat remarkable that until very recently, ambivalence has not been explicitly employed in research on intergenerational relations in later life. Given the popular acceptance of contradictory feelings about parents (Cohler, 1983) and the frequent portrayal of such contradictions in cultural products (Reinharz, 1986), this may be a major gap in research. However, the question remains: Is some degree of ambivalence in fact characteristic of parent-child relationships in later life? If so, do participants in these relationships identify ambivalence when it occurs? Further, is intergenerational ambivalence related to other variables of interest? This chapter presents results from a study that addressed the issue of ambivalence in older parent-adult child relations. Measures of intergenerational ambivalence were developed and employed in a sample of 189 older women.

Intergenerational Ambivalences: New Perspectives on Parent-Child Relations in Later Life
Contemporary Perspectives in Family Research, Volume 4, 115–132
© 2004 Published by Elsevier Ltd.
ISSN: 1530-3535/doi:10.1016/S1530-3535(03)04005-6

Rationale and Primary Research Objectives

Chapter 1 of this volume highlighted several areas that point to the importance of understanding ambivalence in intergenerational relations. These included qualitative studies of parent – adult child relations, studies in family history, the clinical psychological literature on parent-child relations, and research from social psychology on ambivalent attitudes. These bodies of literature sensitize us to the possibility that the quality of parent-child relationships can be illuminated through examining ambivalence. However, to date no studies have addressed the issue of the extent of ambivalent feelings about parent child relations. Further, little is also known about factors that are associated with higher levels of ambivalence. Before a recommendation can be made for an intensive research focus on ambivalence, it is worthwhile to obtain some preliminary information regarding the extent and correlates of such feelings. Therefore, this study was guided by two major research questions:

(1) How frequent are ambivalent assessments of the parent-adult child relationship? In the study, do elderly mothers identify aspects of their relationships with adult children as ambivalent? When asked directly, to what extent do mothers acknowledge mixed or contradictory feelings? Further, to what extent does an indirect measure uncover "latent" ambivalence?

(2) What factors are related to ambivalence? First, are there characteristics of children that are more likely to lead to greater ambivalence? Second, is intergenerational ambivalence related to outcome variables for mothers, and in particular to mothers' psychological well-being?

Defining Ambivalence

Defining ambivalence can be a daunting task, and various definitions have been developed. A detailed discussion is offered by Weigert (1991), who after an extensive literature review broadly defines ambivalence as "the experience of contradictory emotions toward the same object" (p. 21). In everyday speech, the term has this connotation of holding two contradictory emotions, motivations, or values at the same time. Accordingly, as an operational definition, I have followed Raulin's (1984) formulation of ambivalence as "the existence of simultaneous or rapidly interchangeable positive and negative feelings toward the same object or activity" (p. 64). In this study, the measures were designed to examine such simultaneous positive and negative feelings *toward adult children*. Specific operationalization of the concept for the present study is discussed below.

METHODS

Sample

This study used an established panel study from which respondents were selected: The Pathways to Life Quality Study. The Pathways study focuses in particular on patterns of housing choices and residential transitions over the life course, but also collects a wide range of other data on respondents. For the research described in this article, a supplemental interview was administered to the Pathways respondents regarding parent-child relationships.

The Pathways study interviewed a community-based sample of elderly persons in Tompkins County, New York. (For a more detailed description of the Pathways study, see Moen, Erickson & Dempster-McClain, 2000.) The source of the sample for the present study was the 727 residents from the second wave of the panel study, who were interviewed in 1999–2000. Because one goal of the study was to examine differences among children, but not be overwhelmed by them, the sample for the present study was limited to Pathways respondents with either two or three living children. In addition, a decision was made to limit the sample to mothers. This decision was made because mothers are more likely than fathers to be both caregivers and "primary parents" in the younger years (cf. Hochschild, 1989; Ross & VanWilligen, 1996; Ruble et al., 1988), as well as kinkeepers throughout the life course (cf. Gerstel & Gallagher, 1993; Leach & Braithwaite, 1996; Oliveri & Reiss, 1987; Rosenthal, 1985; Rossi & Rossi, 1990). However, ambivalence among fathers is also worthy of examination, and should be an important goal of future research.

Of the 727 individuals who completed a Wave 2 interview, 248 were mothers with either two or three children. At the close of the Wave 2 interview, respondents were asked if they were willing to be contacted to participate in additional studies. Of the 248 eligible mothers, 216 agreed to be contacted. Eight of these 216 individuals (3.2%) refused the follow-up interview, and the remainder (9.1%) were either unable to be contacted or were too ill to be interviewed. Thus, the final sample for the present study were 189 mothers who completed the follow-up interview. The original Pathways interviews were conducted in person; the follow-up interview regarding ambivalence in parent-child relations was conducted by telephone (interviews lasted approximately 30 minutes).

Measures

Established measures of ambivalence in intergenerational relations do not exist. It was therefore necessary to develop various measures of ambivalence, and to experiment with adapting measures that had been developed previously. The measures employed were derived from two sources.

First, several related pilot studies were carried out to guide instrument development. These pilot studies took place in Ithaca, New York and Konstanz, Germany. (For this reason, some, but not all, of the measures discussed here are similar to those presented in Luescher & Lettke, this volume.) They included qualitative interviews with elderly parents and adult children in which issues of mixed feelings about the relationship were explored. In addition, focus group discussions were held separately with elderly persons and with adult children around the same issue. A number of items emerged from common themes in these interviews. Second, measures developed to assess ambivalence in other contexts (e.g. romantic relationships) were adapted for use in the study.

In social psychological research on ambivalent attitudes, two approaches generally have been used (see Lettke & Klein, this volume). The first approach attempts to assess subjective perceptions of ambivalence directly by asking respondents whether their attitudes toward a particular object or relationship are mixed. The second approach measures separately the positive and negative assessments of an attitude object, and then uses one of a number of mathematical formulas to create an ambivalence index from the combination of positive and negative reactions (Breckler, 1994; Priester & Petty, 1996). Both strategies were used in this study.

Direct Measures of Ambivalence
These measures asked directly about mothers' ambivalent feelings toward children, following Kelley's (1983) approach to the study of ambivalence in romantic relationships. Respondents were asked about the degree to which they felt "torn in two directions or conflicted" about each child (never, seldom, now and then, often, very often). A second item asked to what degree the respondent had "very mixed feelings" toward the child (see Sincoff, 1990). The response categories were: strongly agree, agree, disagree, strongly disagree.

In addition, three specific examples of contradictory feelings in the relationship were provided which emerged from the pilot interviews, and respondents were asked to what degree they felt this way about each child (strongly agree, agree, disagree, strongly disagree). These three items were: (a) [*child*] and I often get on each others' nerves, but nevertheless we feel very close; (b) My relationship to [*child*] is very intimate, but that also makes it restrictive; and (c) Although I love [*child*] very much, I am sometimes indifferent toward him/her. Clearly, the precise nature and wording of these items can be debated, but it was felt that they conveyed mixed and conflicting feelings to a reasonable degree.

It should be noted that a decision was made to word these items strongly, such that contradictions were highlighted. For this reason, the adjective "very" was inserted into items, and the strongly worded phrase "torn in two directions" was selected. This represents a conservative approach to measurement of ambivalence; future studies should experiment with less extreme wording. For the purpose of correlational analyses presented below, the five items were summed into a scale for each individual child, which could range from scores of 5 to 21. Reliability was acceptable for all three scales (oldest child, alpha = 0.679, mean = 9.7, sd = 2.4; second child, alpha = 0.729, mean = 9.7, sd = 2.5; third child, alpha = 0.789, mean = 9.73, sd = 2.9).

As an additional measure, at the end of the interview a summary question about parent-child ambivalence was included. The item was worded: "Please think about the topics of this interview again, especially about things like "being torn in two directions," "ambivalence" or "contradictory feelings" about your children. Prior to this interview, how often have you already thought about such things in the past regarding your relationships with any of your children?" (very often, often, now and then, seldom, never). Our goal was to capture additional ambivalent assessments that may have been missed by individual items in the interview.

Indirect Measure of Ambivalence
Direct questions are useful to assess the prevalence of intergenerational ambivalence. However, this type of approach may not detect ambivalence in some respondents, in that it requires them to be consciously aware of the ambivalence. Following the work of Thompson and colleagues, an attempt was made to measure ambivalence indirectly – that is, as a latent state that is indicated by the accessibility of positive and negative elements (Thompson & Holmes, 1996). This measurement strategy involves an attempt to "separate what have previously been considered opposite ends of a bipolar continuum, attempting to distinguish the positive from the negative aspects of experience" (Thompson & Holmes, 1996, p. 506). There is a long history within social psychology of the use of this type of measurement to assess ambivalent attitudes (cf. Kaplan, 1972; Maio, Fincham & Lycett, 2000; Priester & Petty, 1996; Thompson, Zanna & Griffin, 1995).

As one method of achieving this aim, a measure developed by Rossi and Rossi (1990) was modified. This single-item bipolar measure, used to assess affectual solidarity, asks respondents to rate parent-child relationships on a scale from 1 to 7. The low end of the scale represents relationships that are "very tense and strained," and the high end those that are "close and intimate."

The indirect measure of ambivalence was calculated by a combination of two separate items based on this measure. The first asked: "All things considered: How close do you feel to [*child*]? Please evaluate your relationship on a scale from 1 to 5, where 5 is very close and 1 is not at all close." The second item was worded: "Sometimes, no matter how close we may be to someone, the relationship can also at times be tense and strained. How about with your relationship with [*child*]? Please evaluate your relationship on a scale from 1 to 5, where 5 is very tense and strained and 1 is not at all tense and strained." Because of the small number of responses at the extreme negative end of the two scales (that is, few mothers gave the rating of 5 to "tense and strained" or the rating of 1 to "close"), the items were recoded to 4-point scales.

Several methods have been developed to compute an ambivalence score from two items formulated in this way. For analyses reported here, a formula suggested by Thompson and Holmes (1996) was employed, in which the less intense of the two scores is squared, and then divided by the more intense component (Ambivalence = (less intense attitude component)^2/more intense attitude component). This formula provides results that measure the relative similarity (or balance) of the two items, and is comparable to other ambivalence calculation methods. (For detailed discussion of the advantages of this computation method, see Thompson & Holmes, 1996; Thompson, Zanna & Griffin, 1995.) The measure reaches its maximum score when a respondent expresses the most intense scores on both variables. The minimum score is reached when a respondent expresses the most intense score on one variable, and the least intense score on the other.

To provide an example, a mother might feel close to her child, and rate the closeness item as a "3." However, she may also experience some conflict and tension, and rate that item as a "2." The score produced by the formula would thus be $2^2/3$, or 1.33. The highest possible ambivalence score emerges when both responses are "4" (resulting in a score of 4). The lowest ambivalence score occurs when one item is rated "4" and the other is rated "1" (resulting in a score of 0.25). In the first case, the respondent is extremely positive *and* extremely negative about the relationship. In the second case, the respondent is extremely positive on one pole and not at all negative on the other (or vice versa), and might thus be characterized as "certain" rather than "ambivalent."

The degree of intercorrelation between the five-item scale of relationship contradictions described above and the indirect measure of ambivalence was relatively strong (oldest child = 0.337, $p < 0.001$; second child = 0.476, $p < 0.001$; third child = 0.528, $p < 0.001$). This finding indicates a degree of consistency between the direct and indirect measure for each child, but also suggests that they to some extent tap different dimensions of the phenomenon.

Other Measures

Analyses presented in this chapter explore the degree to which the ambivalence measures are correlated with variables of interest. For these analyses, variables were selected that have been found in previous research to predict the quality of parent-adult child relations (for reviews, see Pillemer, Suitor & Keeton, 2000;

Suitor, Pillemer, Keeton & Robison, 1995). Given the lack of prior research on intergenerational ambivalence, it was not possible to justify each variable theoretically. Instead, several variables were included on which there is prior evidence that they are related to some degree to relationship quality.

Child characteristics include the child's age, gender, marital status (married/not married), parental status, educational attainment (less than high school, high school graduate, college graduate), and whether the child is employed. In addition, a single item asked whether the child had serious physical or mental problems. *Proximity* was measured as distance in miles from the parent (to a maximum of 500 miles). *Contact* was measured by an item regarding frequency the parent sees the child (ranging from every day to less than once a month). As a measure of *value similarity*, respondents were asked: "Parents and children are sometimes similar to each other in their views and opinions and sometimes different from each other. In your general outlook on life, Would you say that you and [CHILD] share very similar views, similar views, different views, or very different views?" *Help exchange* was measured by two scales. Respondents were asked if they had helped their child in the preceding year by giving advice, financial help, emotional support, and help of any other kind. The second scale asked about help received from each child in the same four areas, and one additional one: help with regular household chores. Perceived equality of help exchange was measured with the item "Do you feel that you give more than you receive in this relationship?" (strongly agree, agree, disagree, strongly disagree).

For the third analysis in this paper, two measures of parental psychological well-being were employed from the Midlife Development Inventory, which was designed for use in the Midlife in the United States Survey (MIDUS). The Positive Affect Scale measures the extent to which a person feels happy, relaxed and enthusiastic, and the Negative Affect Scale measures feelings of sadness, nervousness, hopelessness, and lethargy. Respondents are asked how frequently they experienced each item in the preceding 30 days (none of the time, a little of the time, some of the time, and most to all of the time). The scales consist of six items each, and were extensively validated (Mroczek & Kolarz, 1998); reliability was acceptable for this sample (positive affect, alpha $= 0.805$, mean $= 21.81$; negative affect, alpha $= 0.661$, mean $= 9.76$).

Sample Description

As noted earlier, all of the respondents were women. Forty-one percent of the respondents were currently married, 44% widowed, and 15% divorced or separated. Fifty-three percent had two living children, and 47% three living children. All but

5% were high school graduates, and 52% had obtained college degrees. In terms of age, 20% were between the ages of 60 and 69, 51% between 70 and 79, and 30% 80 years old and above. Eighty-six percent were not employed. Household income was generally high, with 32% receiving $60,000 or more annually, 34% in the $30,000–$59,999 range, and 34% below $30,000. Respondents were drawn from all three of the Pathways subsamples, with 8% from the continuing care retirement community, 44% from senior housing units, and 48% from the community sample.

RESULTS

Analysis I: Extent of Ambivalent Assessments of the Relationship

Direct Measures

Tables 1–4 present descriptive findings from the ambivalence items. With the exception of the summary question at the end of the interview (shown in Table 4), all items were asked separately for each child. Therefore, responses for all children are presented, given the possibility of within-family differences in parents' responses.

Table 1 presents responses on the mothers' reports of feeling "torn in two directions" about the child. Depending on the child, between 30 and 40% of parents reported that they never feel this way (however, only 18% had never felt this way with *all* children). Similar percentages of respondents reported seldomly feeling torn in two directions. Approximately 20% felt torn now and then, and between 4 and 6% felt this way often/very often. Differences among the reports for oldest, middle, and youngest children were not large, with the most notable difference occurring in the "never" and "seldom" categories. Parents were more likely never to have experienced feeling torn with their third child, and were most likely to have felt this way seldomly with their first child.

Table 1. How Often Feels Torn in Two Directions/Conflicted About Child.

	Child 1 ($n = 189$)	Child 2 ($n = 189$)	Child 3 ($n = 85$)
Never	30.9	37.0	40.0
Seldom	46.2	36.0	32.9
Now and then	18.6	20.6	21.2
Often	3.2	5.3	4.7
Very often	1.1	1.1	1.2

Note: Percent *never* torn with all three children: 18.2.

Table 2. Respondent has "Very Mixed Feelings" About Child.

	Child 1 ($n = 187$)	Child 2 ($n = 188$)	Child 3 ($n = 85$)
Strongly disagree	42.2	46.8	42.4
Disagree	50.3	45.7	43.4
Agree	6.4	6.9	11.8
Strongly agree	1.1	0.6	2.4

Between 6 and 14% of the parents agreed or strongly agreed that they have "very mixed feelings" about the child (Table 2). Interestingly, although parents were less likely to feel torn or conflicted regarding the youngest child, they were somewhat more likely to report mixed feelings toward their youngest child. Although the comparison is hindered by the different answer categories

Table 3. Specific Characteristics of Relationship.

(a) Often Get on Each Other's Nerves, but Nevertheless Feel Very Close

	Child 1 ($n = 183$)	Child 2 ($n = 184$)	Child 3 ($n = 80$)
Strongly disagree	24.6	29.3	30.0
Disagree	46.4	42.9	46.3
Agree	24.1	23.5	20.0
Strongly agree	4.9	4.3	3.7

(b) Relationship is Intimate but Also Restrictive

	Child 1 ($n = 168$)	Child 2 ($n = 164$)	Child 3 ($n = 74$)
Strongly disagree	9.5	13.4	14.8
Disagree	70.2	55.5	56.8
Agree	17.9	28.1	24.3
Strongly agree	2.4	3.0	4.1

(c) Loves Child, but Sometimes Indifferent Toward him/her

	Child 1 ($n = 187$)	Child 2 ($n = 185$)	Child 3 ($n = 84$)
Strongly disagree	32.6	35.7	39.3
Disagree	52.9	55.1	54.7
Agree	13.4	9.2	4.8
Strongly agree	1.1	0.0	1.2
Percentage agreeing with at least one of the three statements	40.6	44.4	38.4

Table 4.   Has Previously Thought About Ambivalence in Relationships
with Children.

Never	10.3
Seldom	18.9
Now and then	29.2
Often	28.1
Very often	13.5

of the two items, it is possible that these items tap two different dimensions of ambivalence.

Table 3 shows results from the three specific questions about the affective quality of the relationship. One-fifth or more of mothers agreed with the first two questions, and fewer than one-third of respondents strongly disagreed. However, mothers were substantially less likely to agree with the "loves child but also indifferent" item. The responses appear to be relatively unaffected by birth order, with two possible exceptions. Mothers were more likely to characterize relationships with later-born children as "intimate but also restrictive." Second, the respondents were somewhat more likely to report "loving the child, but also sometimes indifferent" with older children. Overall, approximately 40% of the mothers agreed with at least one of these statements for each child.

Table 4 shows results for the summary variable regarding the degree to which the respondent had previously considered ambivalence in her relationships with children. Only 10% of the sample had never considered such issues, and more than 40% had thought about such issues often or very often. These findings indicate that mothers are generally aware of some degree of ambivalent feelings regarding their adult children.

Indirect Measure
As noted earlier, the formula calculated an ambivalence score based on the separate measures of closeness and tension. Table 5 shows the values for each child. Approximately one-third of the mothers scored in the "no ambivalence" category (that is, they selected the highest value on one question, and the lowest on the other). However, there was in fact a substantial representation of respondents in the more ambivalent values. For example, the percentage of persons scoring 2 or higher is 18.3% for oldest offspring, 20.4% for next oldest, and 17.7% for youngest children. Patterns of responses were generally similar for all children, with a slight tendency in the direction of lower ambivalence toward the youngest child.

Table 5. Measure of Closeness – Tension Ambivalence.

Value	Child 1 ($N = 186$)	Child 2 ($N = 187$)	Child 3 ($N = 83$)
Low ambivalence			
0.25	31.2	34.2	38.6
0.33	12.9	14.4	15.7
0.50	4.3	3.2	2.4
1.00	14.0	12.3	14.5
1.33	19.4	15.5	10.8
2.00	3.8	2.7	3.6
2.25	7.0	7.5	6.0
3.00	5.9	8.6	7.2
4.00	1.6	1.6	1.2
High ambivalence			
Mean	1.015	1.022	0.923
Std. Dev.	0.893	0.957	0.915

Analysis II: Correlates of Ambivalence

As noted earlier, a goal of the study was to examine whether measures of intergenerational ambivalence were correlated with other variables that have been found to predict relationship quality. This analysis includes three variables: (1) The five-item scale of contradictions in the relationship discussed under "Direct Measures of Ambivalence," above; (2) the indirect measure of ambivalence based on the close/tense items; and (3) the summary measure of ambivalence.

Table 6 presents correlations between these ambivalence variables and the child-related and relationship-related variables described in the Methods section. It is clear that ambivalence is correlated with a number of variables of interest, and several patterns emerge from the analysis.

The relationship contradictions scale was most strongly correlated with variables that have been suggested to predict relationship quality, while fewer correlations were found with the indirect close/tense measure. Interestingly, the strength of the individual correlations appeared to be influenced to a degree by birth order. Although the indirect close/tense measure was not strongly correlated with any variables for the first and second child, significant correlations were found with the youngest child. The relationship contradictions scale, on the other hand, tended to correlate strongly with variables for the oldest child. Researchers should be encouraged to use multiple measures of ambivalence in future studies, given these differences.

Several variables were consistently found to be unrelated (or only very weakly related) to parental ambivalence, both across children and across different

Table 6. Relationship of Mothers' Ambivalence Variables to Child and Relationship Factors (Bivariate Correlations).

	Scale of Contradictions in Relationship with Child			Close/Tense Measure			Summary Measure of Ambivalence
	Child 1	Child 2	Child 3	Child 1	Child	Child 3	
Gender	0.0577	-0.1202	0.1177	0.0954	-0.0388	-0.0864	0.1172
Age	0.1253***	-0.0497	0.0121	0.0625	0.0212	-0.1690	-0.1272*
Married	-0.2485***	-0.1315	0.0121	-0.1179	-0.0945	-0.1330	-0.1239*
Has children	0.0648	0.0514	-0.1483	-0.0586	-0.0418	-0.1494	0.1525**
Education	-0.2275***	-0.0470*	-0.2116*	-0.0092	-0.0420	-0.3230***	0.0797
Employed	0.0510	0.1480	0.0331	-0.1014	0.1202	0.2076*	0.0561
Child problems	0.1170	0.1170	0.0110	0.1054	0.0222	0.0120	0.1119
Distance from parent	-0.0999	0.0417	-0.0409	-0.1251*	-0.0324	-0.0798	0.0006
Contact	-0.1486*	0.0662	-0.1892	-0.0073	-0.0146	-0.2295**	0.0191
Similarity in views	-0.1913**	-0.2290***	-0.4177***	-0.0928	-0.0904	-0.2385**	-0.1222*
Child help to parent	-0.0472	0.0711	0.0019	0.0480	0.0502	0.0406	0.0227
Parent help to child	0.1271	0.0759	0.1389	0.1192	0.0879	0.2013*	0.2219***
Parent gives more than receives	0.2162**	0.2935***	0.2125*	0.0446	0.1859**	0.2852**	0.0434

*$p < 0.10$.
**$p < 0.05$.
***$p < 0.005$.

measures. These were the gender of the child, child's age, whether the child is employed, whether the child has mental or physical problems, geographical distance from the parent, and the child's provision of help to the parent. It is in fact surprising that several variables generally considered to have a major impact on the parent-child relationship were not found to affect ambivalence. In particular, prior research has shown that having a female child predicts better relationship quality, whereas greater residential distance and the presence of problems in children's lives consistently decrease quality (Pillemer, Suitor & Keeton, 2000; Suitor et al., 1995). The contrast between this body of research findings and those presented in Table 6 suggests that ambivalence may not simply act as a proxy for poor relationship quality, but is instead a separate, measurable dimension in parent-child relationships.

Three variables were particularly strongly correlated with ambivalence measures: satisfaction with exchange, education, and similarity of views. Several significant correlations were found for the satisfaction with exchange variable: Parents who feel that they give more than they receive experience higher ambivalence. This finding is consistent with research suggesting that parents experience ambivalence between the desire that the child be autonomous and an obligation to help him or her (Cohler & Grunebaum, 1981).

Perceived similarity between the parent's views and the child's views was strongly negatively correlated with ambivalence. This may be consistent with the finding that child's educational attainment is also negatively correlated with ambivalence. Most of the parents in this study were relatively well educated, and the child's educational attainment may be in part a proxy for value similarity.

Analysis III: Ambivalence and Psychological Well-Being

It is also interesting to examine the relationship between ambivalence in inter-generational relations and measures of well-being. Prior research suggests that poor relationships with children can negatively affect older parents' well-being (Pillemer & Suitor, 1991; Rook & Pietromonaco, 1987; Ryff, Schmutte & Lee, 1996; Schuster, Kessler & Aseltine, 1990). It is possible that the experience of ambivalence could have a similarly negative impact on psychological well-being. There is extensive clinical evidence and empirical research suggesting that individuals experience internal psychological conflict as aversive (cf. Festinger, 1957; Maio, Fincham & Lycett, 2000), and a high level of ambivalence has been found to be associated with dysphoric states (Cacioppo, Gardner & Berntson, 1997; Raulin, 1984; Sincoff, 1990). Therefore, in a life domain as salient as the parent-child relationship, ambivalence could predict diminished psychological well-being.

To explore this possibility, we examined bivariate correlations between three ambivalence variables and the Positive and Negative Affect Scales. The ambivalence variables were again the scale of contradictions in the relationship, the indirect torn/conflicted measure, and the summary measure of ambivalence asked at the close of the interview.

The relationship contradictions scale was significantly negatively correlated with the Positive Affect Scale for all three children (oldest $= -0.1946, p = 0.013$; second $= -0.2091$, $p = 0.008$; third $= -0.2247$, $p = 0.060$). This scale was strongly positively correlated with negative affect for the youngest child (0.4037, $p < 0.001$), and also positively correlated with the oldest (0.2586, $p = 0.001$) and the second child (0.2299, $p = 0.004$). In contrast, no relationship was found between the indirect measure of ambivalence and negative affect. Correlations of the indirect measure with positive affect approached significance for the oldest child (-0.1401, $p = 0.057$) and the second child (-0.1241, $p = 0.091$). The summary item regarding the degree to which the respondent had previously thought about intergenerational ambivalence was significantly correlated with positive affect ($-0.1855, p = 0.011$), and the correlation approached significance for negative affect (0.1243, $p = 0.092$).

Although systematic multivariate analysis with larger samples is necessary to explore the relationship between ambivalence toward children and psychological well-being, this correlational analysis suggests that such relationships may indeed exist. It appears that measures of ambivalence relating to specific children may have more predictive power than global assessments of ambivalence. Further, direct measures may be more promising in predicting well-being than indirect ones.

CONCLUSIONS AND FUTURE DIRECTIONS

Several conclusions can be drawn from the analyses presented in this article.

(1) *The data offer convincing evidence that parental ambivalence regarding adult children is sufficiently widespread to be of scientific interest.*

Data were presented regarding the prevalence of parents' ambivalent assessments of parent-child relationships. In answer to the first research question posed above – whether ambivalent feelings toward adult offspring are sufficiently prevalent to merit research attention – the answer appears to be an unqualified yes.

As indicated in Table 1, only 18.2% of the mothers never felt torn with any of their children. Thus, four-fifths of the mothers in the study experienced this feeling to some degree. Similarly, approximately 40% of the mothers agreed with at least one of the contradictory statements presented in Table 2. Taken together with the fact that 90% of respondents responded affirmatively to the summary question regarding ambivalence (Table 4), and that two-thirds demonstrated at least some degree of ambivalence on the indirect measure, the phenomenon (at least at low levels of intensity) appears to be relatively widespread. In addition, it is certainly measurable using relatively simple techniques like those employed here.

(2) *The intergenerational ambivalence variables were significantly correlated with variables of interest to researchers on the aging family.*

Several statistically significant and scientifically interesting relationships were uncovered in the data analysis. Among the most striking correlational findings is the relationship between ambivalence and the exchange relationship with children. Several scholars have suggested that a dynamic tension exists in parent-adult child relations between children's continuing dependency on parents, and parents' wish to have successfully launched their offspring as independent adults (Cohler & Grunebaum, 1981; Hagestad, 1987; Pillemer & Suitor, 1991). Parents reactions to such a situation are therefore likely to involve ambivalent feelings.

Perhaps of even greater importance is the possibility that intergenerational ambivalence is negatively related to psychological well-being. Certainly in the clinical literature (Raulin, 1984), intense ambivalence is considered detrimental to mental health, and psychotherapy is suggested as a means to address ambivalence. However, in its milder, more routine forms, ambivalence in parent-child relations may be difficult to resolve for many parents. Because the parent-child relationship is in principle indissoluble, ambivalent situations may persist for years without the possibility of separation of the relationship partners (Fingerman, 1996; George, 1986; Lüscher & Pillemer, 1998). If life course transitions increase such stress, psychological distress may result. The finding that ambivalence measures are related to both positive and negative affect suggest that this is an important area for future research.

To build on these insights, researchers should be encouraged to take several steps. First, the development of reliable and valid instruments to assess intergenerational ambivalence must take high priority. For example, the measures selected for this study were free of any specific context; instead, they were measures of general feelings about the relationship. It is possible that individuals who do not identify ambivalence about the relationship in a general way may in fact do so when provided with specific dilemmas or conflicts. The qualitative pilot research conducted for this study suggests that certain events (for example, children's divorce or return to the parental household) may temporarily raise ambivalent feelings. Thus, a worthwhile field of study is the amount and nature of ambivalence generated by life-course transitions.

Second, studies of intergenerational ambivalence should be undertaken on a larger scale, with representative samples. Larger studies could incorporate at least two groups that were not considered here. First, studies should include data collection from adult children, whose responses may differ considerably from parents. Second, fathers should be included in future research. In a study of young adolescents' attitudes toward parents, Maio et al. (2000) found an effect of subjects' ambivalence toward fathers on attachment styles, but did not find this effect with ambivalence toward mothers. Thus, it may be that ambivalence has different causes and consequences for men and women.

Third, conducting studies of middle-aged parents of adult children (in addition to elderly parents) could also be enlightening. Carstensen and colleagues (Carstensen & Charles, 1998; Carstensen, Gross & Fung, 1998) have proposed the existence of socio-emotional selectivity, a process through which older adults are able to regulate their emotions more effectively than those who are younger. Through years of life experience, they may be able to achieve a better "affect balance" that minimizes negative emotion (Mroczek & Kolarz, 1998), and potentially also could minimize the ambivalence that results from parent-child relations.

A combination of these steps is likely to shed important light on the prevalence and predictors of intergenerational ambivalence. Pursuing this topic is likely to extend knowledge not only about parent-child relations in later life, but also about close relationships more generally.

REFERENCES

Breckler, S. J. (1994). A comparison of numerical indexes for measuring attitude ambivalence. *Educational and Psychological Measurement, 54*, 350–365.

Cacioppo, J. T., Gardner, W. L., & Berntson, G. G. (1997). Beyond bipolar conceptualizations and measures: The case of attitudes and evaluative space. *Personality and Social Psychology Review, 1*, 3–25.

Carstensen, L. L., & Charles, S. T. (1998). Emotion in the second half of life. *Current Directions in Psychological Science, 7*, 144–149.

Carstensen, L. L., Gross, J. J., & Fung, H. H. (1998). The social context of emotional experience. In: K. W. Schaie & M. P. Lawton (Eds), *Annual Review of Gerontology and Geriatrics: Focus on Emotion and Adult Development* (Vol. 17, pp. 325–352). New York: Springer.

Cohler, B. J. (1983). Autonomy and interdependence in the family of adulthood. *The Gerontologist, 23*, 33–39.

Cohler, B. J., & Grunebaum, H. (1981). *Mothers, grandmothers, and daughters. Personality and childcare in three-generation families.* New York: Wiley.

Festinger, L. (1957). *A theory of cognitive dissonance.* Evanston, IL: Row, Peterson.

Fingerman, K. L. (1996). Sources of tension in the aging mother and adult daughter relationship. *Psychology and Aging, 11*, 591–606.

George, L. K. (1986). Caregiver burden: Conflict between norms of reciprocity and solidarity. In: K. Pillemer & R. Wolf (Eds), *Elder Abuse: Conflict in the Family* (pp. 67–92). Dover, MA: Auburn House.

Gerstel, N., & Gallagher, S. K. (1993). Chinking and distress: Gender, recipients of care, and work-family conflict. *Journal of Marriage and the Family, 55*, 598–607.

Hagestad, G. O. (1987). Able elderly in the family context: Changes, chances and challenges. *The Gerontologist, 27*, 417–428.

Hochschild, A. (1989). *The second shift: Working parents and the revolution at home.* New York: Viking.

Kaplan, K. J. (1972). On the ambivalence-indifference problem in attitude theory and measurement: A suggested modification of the semantic differential technique. *Psychological Bulletin, 77*, 361–372.

Kelley, H. H. (1983). Love and commitment. In: H. H. Kelley, E. Berscheid, A. Christensen, J. H. Harvey, T. L. Huston, G. Levinger, E. McClintock et al. (Eds), *Close Relationships* (pp. 265–314). New York: W. H. Freeman.

Leach, M. S., & Braithwaite, D. O. (1996). Binding tie: Supportive communication of family kinkeepers. *Journal of Applied Communication Research, 24*, 200–216.

Lüscher, K., & Pillemer, K. (1998). Intergenerational ambivalence: A new approach to the study of parent-child relations in later life. *Journal of Marriage and the Family, 60*, 413–445.

Maio, G. R., Fincham, F. D., & Lycett, E. J. (2000). Attitudinal ambivalence toward parents and attachment style. *Personality and Social Psychology Bulletin, 26*, 1451–1464.

Moen, P., Erickson, M. A., & Dempster-McClain, D. (2000). Social role identities among older adults in a continuing care retirement community. *Research on Aging, 22*, 559–579.

Mroczek, D. K., & Kolarz, C. M. (1998). The effect of age on positive and negative affect: A developmental perspective on happiness. *Journal of Personality and Social Psychology, 75*(5), 1333–1349.

Oliveri, M. E., & Reiss, D. (1987). Social networks and family members: Distinctive roles of mothers and fathers. *Sex Roles, 11*(2), 719–736.

Pillemer, K., & Suitor, J. J. (1991). Will I *ever* escape my child's problems? Effects of adult children's problems on elderly parents. *Journal of Marriage and the Family, 53*, 585–594.

Pillemer, K., Suitor, J. J., & Keeton, S. (2000). Intergenerational relations. In: E. F. Borgatta & R. J. V. Montgomery (Eds), *Encyclopedia of Sociology* (2nd ed., pp. 1386–1393). New York: Macmillan.

Priester, J. R., & Petty, R. E. (1996). The gradual threshold model of ambivalence: Relating the positive and negative bases of attitudes to subjective ambivalence. *Journal of Personality and Social Psychology, 71*, 431–449.

Raulin, M. L. (1984). Development of a scale to measure intense ambivalence. *Journal of Consulting and Clinical Psychology, 52*, 63–72.

Reinharz, S. (1986). Loving and hating one's elders: Twin themes in legend and literature. In: K. Pillemer & R. S. Wolf (Eds), *Elder Abuse: Conflict in the Family* (pp. 25–48). Dover, MA: Auburn House.

Rook, K. S., & Pietromonaco, P. (1987). Close relationships: Ties that heal or ties that bind. *Advances in Personal Relationships, 1*, 1–35.

Rosenthal, C. J. (1985). Kinkeeping in the familial division of labor. *Journal of Marriage and the Family, 47*, 965–974.

Ross, C. E., & VanWilligen, W. (1996). Gender, parenthood, and anger. *Journal of Marriage and the Family, 58*, 572–584.

Rossi, A., & Rossi, P. (1990). *Of human bonding: Parent-child relationships across the life course.* Hawthorne, NY: Aldine de Gruyter.

Ruble, D. N., Fleming, A. S., Hackel, L., & Stangor, C. (1988). Changes in the marital relationship during the transition to first-time motherhood: Effects of violated expectations concerning division of household labor. *Journal of Personality and Social Psychology, 55*, 78–87.

Ryff, C. D., Schmutte, P. S., & Lee, Y. H. (1996). How children turn out: Implications for parental self-evaluation. In: C. D. Ryff & M. M. Seltzer (Eds), *The Parental Experience in Midlife* (pp. 383–423). Chicago: University of Chicago Press.

Schuster, T. L., Kessler, R. C., & Aseltine, R. H. (1990). Supportive interactions, negative interactions and depressed mood. *American Journal of Community Psychology, 18*, 423–439.

Sincoff, J. B. (1990). The psychological characteristics of ambivalent people. *Clinical Psychology Review, 10*, 43–68.

Suitor, J. J., Pillemer, K., Keeton, S., & Robison, J. (1995) Aged parents and aging children: Determinants of relationship quality. In: V. Bedford & R. Blieszner (Eds), *Handbook of Aging and the Family* (pp. 223–242). Westport, CN: Greenwood Press.

Thompson, M. M., & Holmes, J. G. (1996). Ambivalence in close relationships: Conflicted cognitions as a catalyst for change. In: R. M. Sorrentino & E. T. Higgins (Eds), *Handbook of Motivation and Cognition: The Interpersonal Context* (Vol. 3, pp. 497–530). Houston, TX: Guilford Press.

Thompson, M. M., Zanna, M., & Griffin, D. (1995). Let's not be indifferent about (attitudinal) ambivalence. In: R. E. Petty & A. Krosnick (Eds), *Attitude Strength: Antecedents and Consequences* (pp. 361–386). Hillsdale, NY: Erlbaum.

Weigert, A. J. (1991). *Mixed emotions: Certain steps toward understanding ambivalence.* Albany, NY: State University of New York Press.

6. INTERGENERATIONAL AMBIVALENCE IN THE CONTEXT OF THE LARGER SOCIAL NETWORK

Karen L. Fingerman and Elizabeth Hay

INTRODUCTION

Parents and offspring experience strong feelings for one another throughout the life span. Indeed, as other chapters in this volume suggest, this relationship is fraught with complexity. Yet, it is not clear whether ambivalence is specific to the parent-child relationship or whether it is characteristic of close relationships in general. Further, we do not know whether parents and children experience ambivalence in their tie throughout life or only at specific periods of life. In this chapter, we address two questions about ambivalence in the parent-child relationship: (1) Do individuals experience more ambivalence in their relationships with parents and offspring than they do in other social relationships? (2) Do individuals experience varying degrees of ambivalence in this relationship at different points in the life span?

We apply a definition of ambivalence that refers to a mixture of positive and negative feelings towards the same object (Weigert, 1991). Such ambivalence involves close feelings coupled with a simultaneous recognition of problems, irritation, or annoyance. This form of ambivalence is not concerned with behaviors or causes of problems. As will be discussed, we considered ambivalent social ties to be ones that were considered both positive and problematic. This approach allows for a superficial sense of how individuals generally classify their

Intergenerational Ambivalences: New Perspectives on Parent-Child Relations in Later Life
Contemporary Perspectives in Family Research, Volume 4, 133–151
Copyright © 2004 by Elsevier Ltd.
ISSN: 1530-3535/doi:10.1016/S1530-3535(03)04006-8

relationships, but it does not capture the subtle nuances and shades of feeling that may also constitute a sense of ambivalence. Thus, this chapter allows comparisons across relationships and age groups, but does not delve into the complexities of parent-child relationships that are described in other chapters.

AMBIVALENCE IN PARENT-CHILD AND OTHER SOCIAL TIES

The first question asks whether the parent-child tie involves more ambivalence than other social ties do. We considered how the parent-child tie fits into the larger social network. At a gross level, adults' social worlds consist of family members, friends, and acquaintances (Antonucci & Akiyama, 1987). At a more micro level, we might consider the social contacts that comprise each of these groups. For example, the parent-child tie lies in the family network along with spousal ties and adult siblings. Further, extended family members such as cousins, aunts, and uncles may be important social contacts. Affinal family members, such as in-laws or stepsiblings, have received little attention in the research literature, but appear to be emotionally important to adults of different ages (Fingerman & Hay, 2002). Friendship ties also vary in their psychological meaning. In early adulthood, these ties may be fraught with ambivalence as individuals struggle to accept weaknesses in their friends and select those relationships that will endure throughout adulthood (Carstensen, 1992). Finally, we have examined elsewhere (Fingerman & Griffiths, 1999; Fingerman & Hay, 2002) what we refer to as "peripheral" social ties; such relationships generally are not intimate or close, yet they may be meaningful in adults' lives. Coworkers, teachers, church members, and neighbors fit this category.

Therefore, we compared the degree of ambivalence in the parent-child tie to the degree of ambivalence in six types of social ties: intimate/romantic relationships, siblings, extended family ties (aunt, uncle, cousins, grandparent, grandchild), affinal family (in-laws, step relatives), friendships, and peripheral ties (coworkers, neighbors, church members). More specifically, we considered three possibilities: (1) ambivalence would be characteristic of close ties in general; (2) ambivalence would be more characteristic of affinal family and peripheral ties than of parent-child or other close social ties; or (3) ambivalence would be more characteristic of the parent-child tie than other social ties.

The basis for the first possibility lies in the premise that close relationships are inherently tension-laden (Rook, 1997, 1998). It is difficult to experience intimacy without allowing another party to get on your nerves from time to time (Fingerman, 2001b). Therefore, one might argue that ambivalence is no more characteristic of the parent-child tie than of any other close social tie. With regard to the second possibility, peripheral and extended family ties might be fraught with tensions because individuals have little latitude in selecting these social contacts. Indeed, affinal family ties such as in-law or step relationships may be particularly ambivalent because these relationships come pre-packaged with other, more intimate social ties. Yet, for theoretical reasons discussed below, we hypothesized that we would find the final possibility in our data: Factors that distinguish the parent-child tie from other social ties may enhance the experience of ambivalence in this tie.

As Lüscher and Pillemer (1998) suggested, ambivalence between parents and their adult children may reflect conflicts among three aspects of the relationship that cannot be easily reconciled: dependence and autonomy, norms, and solidarity. The question arises, however, as to whether these dimensions are more conflicted in parent-child ties than in other relationships. Conflicts with regard to each of these dimensions can be found in other social ties as well as in the parent-child tie. Tensions between dependency and autonomy are particularly characteristic of romantic relationships as well as the parent-child tie. Indeed, establishing intimacy involves abdicating aspects of the self and surrendering aspects of autonomy for the good of the relationship (Reis & Shaver, 1988). Of course, norms are less clear in the tie between adult child and parent than in the spousal relationship (which is legally defined). Yet, other family ties, such as ties between adult siblings and grandparents and grandchildren, are characterized by even fewer norms than the parent-child tie in adulthood. Finally, tensions over solidarity may be more characteristic of the parent-child tie than of other types of relationships. Romantic ties and friendships are predicated on the basis of an equal investment in the relationship (Moss & Schwebel, 1993). By contrast, parents are more invested in the parent-child tie than are their offspring (Bengtson & Kuypers, 1971; Fingerman, 1995, 2001a; Rossi & Rossi, 1990). This discrepancy in feelings could contribute to an overall sense of ambivalence. In sum, although the dimensions of ambivalence that Lüscher and Pillemer described are also evident in other social ties, the combination of conflicts with regard to these dimensions may render the parent-child tie more ambivalent than other ties in adulthood.

Further, while Lüscher and Pillemer described the primary basis for ambivalence in the parent-offspring tie, other taxonomies may lend insights into heightened ambivalence between parents and children when compared to other social ties. For example, Laursen and Bukowski (1997) proposed a model of relationships involving three dimensions: (1) permanence; (2) power; and (3) gender. The first two dimensions, when applied to parents and children, provide a sense of why ambivalence may be more characteristic of this tie than of other ties. The parent-child tie involves a high degree of permanence. When the child is born, the parent-child tie involves an intense emotional bond that endures over time (Bowlby, 1969). When offspring enter adulthood, the relationship could presumably be disbanded if the parties found it too stressful. With the exception of divorced fathers, however, most parents and children remain deeply involved in one another's lives throughout the life span (Rossi & Rossi, 1990; Webster & Herzog, 1995).

Marriages or friendships may disband in the face of negative feelings, but ties between parents and children persist. A daughter commented, "If my mother were my husband, I would have divorced her years ago" (Fingerman, 2001a). Further, the long history of the parent-child tie allows time for a succession of incidents to build. In addition to present irritations and annoyances, prior difficulties in the parent-child tie color its emotional hue in adulthood (Fingerman, 1997; Webster & Herzog, 1995). In sum, the permanence of this tie makes it a safe forum for negative feelings and the longevity provides fodder for such feelings to develop.

The power dimension of the parent-child tie may also contribute to the distinct ambivalence of this tie. In early childhood, the parent wields greater power in the relationship than does the child (Laursen & Bukowski, 1997). As the parties enter adulthood, the power structure shifts towards a more lateral, equitable relationship. In adulthood, parents have no direct power over their offspring's decisions or daily lives. Yet, offspring continue to crave their parents' approval and approbation until the end of life (Troll & Fingerman, 1996). This residual emotional power contributes to tensions between parents and offspring in adulthood (Fingerman, 2001a).

Finally, the parent-child tie is one in which both parties attempt to define themselves. Psychoanalytic theory suggests that the child's early sense of self is established in the context of the parent-child relationship and the parent plays a central role in the child's budding sense of identity into adulthood (Erikson, 1963; Ewen, 1993; Tyson & Tyson, 1990). Recent work also suggests that mothers and fathers derive a sense of their accomplishments as parents through their grown offspring (Ryff, Lee, Essex & Schmutte, 1994). Theorists have suggested that relationships in which individuals establish a sense of self are characterized by increased intimacy (Reis & Shaver, 1988). It seems likely that this aspect of the parent-child tie may also contribute to heightened ambivalence because parents and children not only define themselves in this tie, but also seek to differentiate themselves from one another (Fingerman, 2001b).

Thus, although ambivalence may arise in many types of close relationships, the factors that distinguish parent-child ties from other relationships may lead to a heightened level of ambivalence in this tie. Therefore, we expected to find more parent-child ties classified as ambivalent when compared to other ties in the social network.

Age Differences in Ambivalence in the Parent-Child Tie

Our second question involved age differences in the degree of ambivalence parents and their children experience at different stages of life. Although in general, the parent-child tie may be more ambivalent than other social ties, the degree of that ambivalence may vary across the life span. Lüscher and Pillemer (1998) suggested that ambivalence is heightened during periods when norms are needed but not available. In other words, ambivalence is linked to life events such as widowhood. Although such life events are not predictable at a micro, individual level, at an aggregate level, age differences in the degree of ambivalence may be evident. For example, older parents are more likely to be widowed and to incur health problems than are younger parents. Further, within a life-span framework, we might also consider individual development as a catalyst to changes in the tone of the parent-child tie. As offspring mature and parents interact with them in different ways, the likelihood of tensions arising may vary.

[handwritten margin note: non-norm, norm, events, increase ambiv.]

We examined classifications of the parent-child tie from adolescence to late old age. Using such a broad age span, it is clear that issues of non-comparability arise; adolescents are unlikely to have children, and oldest-old adults are unlikely to have living parents. Elsewhere, we have discussed the likelihood of naming different relatives as problematic social ties based on their availability (Fingerman & Birditt, 2003). Here, we compare classifications of the parent-child tie across age groups. In other words, we asked, of parents and children listed in the social networks, what proportion is listed as solely positive, as ambivalent, or as solely problematic?

Two contradictory age patterns might be expected based on extant theory and research. If we considered dimensions of ambivalence, such as conflicts involving norms, we might expect older parents and middle-aged offspring to experience greater ambivalence than younger parents and offspring. Whereas the establishment of career and family provide normative structure to early adulthood, late-life shifts tend to be less clearly proscribed societally. Further, recent findings suggest that ambivalence between parents and children in late life may stem from increasingly complex cognitive representations of this tie. Elsewhere, we reported that young adult women and their mothers viewed their relationship in globally positive terms, whereas middle-aged women and their mothers were able to incorporate negative feelings into their descriptions of their relationship (Fingerman, 2000, 2001a). These findings may reflect older women's greater ability to accept faults in the other party. Thus, in theory, we might expect to find greater ambivalence in the older age groups.

By contrast, much of the extant literature suggests a shift towards increasing positive regard in the parent-child relationship across adulthood. Longitudinal and cross-sectional data indicate that reports of negative qualities of parent-adult offspring relationships generally decrease and positive qualities increase with age (Carstensen, 1992; Suitor & Pillemer, 1987, 1988; Umberson, 1989, 1992; Weishaus, 1978). Therefore, we might expect to find that ambivalence between parents and children peaks during the adolescent years and that the relationship is increasingly viewed as solely positive across adulthood.

Discrepancies in these expected patterns may stem from methodological differences in the foci of study. Studies and theory that find increasing ambivalence with age deal with complexities and nuances within the relationship. Studies that find increasing positive regard for the tie tend to rely on global rating scales (e.g. Umberson, 1992). Given our superficial measurement involving relationship classification, we expected to find less ambivalence in older age groups here. In other words, we believe that older individuals are more likely to view their relationships with their parents or offspring as basically positive, but at the same time, to be able to recognize faults in this tie. Because we only assessed classification here, and did not consider the ability to incorporate weaknesses into this conceptualization, we expected to find a decrease in ambivalence with age.

Finally, we considered the salience of ambivalence in the parent-child tie relative to other relationships across the life span. Although characteristics of the parent-child tie suggest that there will be greater ambivalence in this relationship than in other relationships, the parent-child relationship changes over time. Whereas young adults and their parents may both be defining themselves in this tie, older parents and their middle-aged offspring may seek less definition of self in the tie. Given the paucity of studies on this topic, we did not specify hypotheses with regard to patterns of ambivalence across the larger social network, but we did examine this issue. We looked at whether ambivalence is greatest towards the parent-child tie relative to other social ties throughout life, or whether there is greater ambivalence towards different social ties at particular stages of life.

We also note that gender differences play a key role in the emotional qualities of parent-child relationships. Clearly, not all parent-child ties are the same. Rather, ties involving mothers, daughters, fathers, and sons are distinct (Troll & Fingerman, 1996). Gender differences in the experience of ambivalence are not a central focus of discussion in this chapter, but it would be irresponsible of us to consider ambivalence in this tie without acknowledging the role of gender. We examined each of our research questions separately for mothers, fathers, sons, and daughters. We estimated analyses separately for female and male participants initially. The pattern of findings did not reveal systematic gender differences; for the sake of simplicity, we focus on age differences here, and report findings with regard to the sample in general.

METHODS

Participants

This research is part of a larger study of problematic social ties in which 187 individuals ranging in age from 13 to 99 described their close and problematic social ties. The sample was distributed across five age groups: adolescents ages 13 to 16 ($n = 39$), young adults ages 20 to 29 ($n = 40$), middle aged adults ages 40 to 49 ($n = 34$), young old adults ages 60 to 69 ($n = 39$), and oldest old adults over the age of 80 ($n = 35$). Approximately equal numbers of men and women participated in the study within each age group. The study took place in a small town surrounding a large university. As in many studies conducted in the United States, participants were primarily European American and were well-educated and well-off financially relative to the general population of the United States. Although such a sample limits generalization of findings, the homogeneity of the sample allows comparisons across age groups.

Measurement

Participants completed an interview including open-ended and forced-choice questions pertaining to their social ties. Of interest in this chapter is the configuration of two social networks that participants provided. First, participants completed the Kahn and Antonucci (1980) diagram of their close social ties. In completing this measure, individuals listed their close social contacts in three concentric circles. In the innermost circle, they listed the people to whom they feel so close they could not imagine life without them. The next circle contained social contacts who are very important in participants' lives. The final circle included social contacts who are not that close, but who are still important in participants' lives. After diagramming their social contacts, participants provided information about each social contact in the network, including their relationship to the social contact, the social contact's age, and the duration of the relationship.

Participants also completed a unique adaptation of the Kahn and Antonucci measure (Fingerman & Birditt, 2003). In this adaptation, they listed the people in their lives who bother them. The innermost circle contained social contacts who bothered them most, and the two remaining circles included social contacts who bothered them to lessening degrees. Two aspects of the directions for this diagram are relevant here. First, interviewers informed participants that they could name the same social contacts they had already named or new ones. Second, interviewers provided the caveat that the people listed in these circles did not have to bother participants all of the time, just some of the time. These two caveats are important because the instructions explicitly allow participants to list social ties that are ambivalent – they were encouraged to include social contacts to whom they felt close and who irritated them from time to time. Participants then provided follow-up information about the social contacts in this second set of circles.

Independent raters then went through the social diagrams and classified participants' social contacts as belonging to one of three categories: (1) solely positive; (2) solely negative; and (3) ambivalent. The first two categories, solely positive and solely negative, involved social contacts that were named only in the close social network or in the problematic social network respectively. The ambivalent category included social contacts listed in both social networks. Raters derived these classifications based on the names of the social contacts and their relationship to the participant. For example, a participant might list "Mary" in both networks; but in one network Mary might be a spouse, and in the other network Mary might be a coworker.

For the purposes of this chapter, we considered mothers, fathers, sons, and daughters separately. We aggregated other relationships into the six types of social ties described previously: intimate/romantic relationships, siblings, extended family ties (aunt, uncle, cousins, grandparent, grandchild), affinal family (in-laws, step relatives), friendship, and peripheral ties (coworkers, neighbors, church members). Initially, we looked at stepmothers, stepfathers, stepsons, and stepdaughters separately. There were few stepparents or stepchildren in these participants' social networks, however, and patterns of findings for these-low frequency social ties did not appear meaningful. Therefore, we grouped stepparents and stepchildren with other affinal family members.

RESULTS

Descriptions of Analyses

We considered the proportion of ties across the three emotional qualities (positive only, negative only, ambivalent), rather than the absolute number of social ties within each emotional classification. For example, of the total number of friendships listed, we considered the proportion that was considered solely positive, solely negative, or ambivalent within each age group.

This approach introduces a lack of comparability across categories, and readers should be aware of limitations to understanding the data. First, available relationships vary across the life span. Only three individuals in their 20s had children, compared to nearly all individuals in their 80s. Only two individuals in their 60s had living fathers. The emotional classifications of such low-frequency events as positive are probably not meaningful. Further, some relationship categories involve within-individual comparisons and some categories involve between-individual comparisons. For example, individuals can have numerous friends, but only one father. Therefore, a given individual could classify one third of their friends as solely positive, one third as solely problematic, and one third as ambivalent. By contrast, for the father category, each *participant* appears in only one category. Finally, some relationship categories are aggregates of multiple relationships (e.g. affinal family), whereas other categories involve only one relationship type (e.g. daughters). It is possible that one relationship type (e.g. mother-in-law or coworker) might be particularly tension-laden and distort the distribution of ambivalent ties in that category.

We attempted to deal with issues of non-comparability when possible. First, we examined the distributions of relationships in the aggregate categories to ascertain that one relationship was not distorting the category. For example, the affinal ties include stepparents and in-laws. Therefore, it is possible that the ambivalent classifications involved only one relationship (stepsiblings), whereas other relationships were classified as positive only or negative only. Examination of the proportions of each individual relationship classified as positive, negative, or ambivalent revealed that the distributions of specific relationships were similar to the distributions within each category. No one relationship distorted the distributions of a given category. Next, we looked at whether some participants listed all of their relationships as ambivalent while other participants listed all of their relationships as positive or solely negative. For each participant, we estimated the proportion of ties listed in the two networks as solely positive, solely negative, or ambivalent. In all age groups, the vast majority of people classified fewer than 50% of their ties as ambivalent, with most of the remaining ties classified as solely positive and fewer classified as solely negative. Only 11 participants considered 50% or more of their relationships ambivalent and these participants were evenly spread across age groups, with the exception of the oldest-old. None of the oldest-old participants considered more than half of their social ties as ambivalent or negative; in keeping with existing research, the oldest-old disproportionately classified their social ties as solely positive.

Ambivalence in the Parent-Child Tie and the Larger Social Network

We then addressed our research questions. The proportions of each type of social tie listed as positive only, negative only, or ambivalent are found in Table 1. The first

Table 1. Proportion of Each Type of Relationship Classified as Positive, Ambivalent, or Problematic.

Relationship	Teenagers	20s	40s	60s	80s
Mothers					
Positive	0.55	0.49	0.70	0.67	–
Ambivalent	0.45	0.51	0.25	0.33	–
Problematic	–	–	0.05	–	–
Fathers					
Positive	0.54	0.34	0.50	1.00	–
Ambivalent	0.43	0.60	0.42	–	–
Problematic	0.03	0.06	0.08	–	–
Sons					
Positive	–	1.00	0.52	0.54	0.93
Ambivalent	–	–	0.48	0.46	0.07
Problematic	–	–	–	–	–
Daughters					
Positive	–	1.00	0.40	0.65	0.95
Ambivalent	–	–	0.60	0.35	0.05
Problematic	–	–	–	–	–
Romantic partners					
Positive	0.50	0.32	0.41	0.48	0.46
Ambivalent	0.50	0.64	0.55	0.52	0.54
Problematic	–	0.04	0.04	–	–
Siblings					
Positive	0.37	0.60	0.73	0.84	0.84
Ambivalent	0.63	0.37	0.21	0.11	0.16
Problematic	–	0.03	0.06	0.05	–
Extended family					
Positive	0.93	0.80	0.93	0.88	0.96
Ambivalent	0.02	0.11	0.02	0.05	0.04
Problematic	0.05	0.09	0.05	0.07	–
Affinal family					
Positive	0.53	0.75	0.69	0.72	0.93
Ambivalent	0.47	0.20	0.14	0.12	0.05
Problematic	–	0.05	0.17	0.16	0.02
Friends					
Positive	0.73	0.74	0.83	0.89	0.89
Ambivalent	0.15	0.17	0.12	0.08	0.04
Problematic	0.12	0.09	0.05	0.03	0.07
Peripheral					
Positive	0.34	0.38	0.44	0.42	0.78
Ambivalent	–	0.11	0.04	0.06	0.04
Problematic	0.66	0.51	0.52	0.52	0.18

research question asks, Do individuals feel more ambivalence towards parents and children than they do towards other social contacts? Examination of Table 1 reveals that individuals of all ages experience as much ambivalence towards romantic partners as towards their mothers, fathers, sons, and daughters. At least half of romantic partners were classified as ambivalent across age groups, even in late life. In addition, adolescents classified nearly two thirds of their siblings as ambivalent.

Participants did not appear to experience their ties to extended or affinal family members as highly ambivalent. They did, however, react negatively to some of these social contacts. Indeed, nearly as many affinal ties were considered solely problematic as ambivalent. Further, prior to late life, peripheral ties were more likely to be considered problematic than positive or ambivalent. As is discussed elsewhere, these types of ties involve less control than closer family and friendships (Fingerman, in preparation). From the perspective of understanding ambivalence, however, the parent-child tie appears to involve more ambivalence than any tie other than romantic partners until late life. In late life, parents appear to feel that their ties to their offspring are characterized solely by positive feelings.

Age Differences in Ambivalence in the Parent-Child Tie

The second research question asks, Do individuals feel more ambivalent towards their parents or children at certain stages of life? It is not possible to look at this question across the entire life span, as young people do not yet have children and older adults have lost their parents. Among individuals who had parents or children, however, age differences in ambivalence were evident.

Individuals appear to experience decreasing ambivalence towards their mothers and increasing positive regard as they grow older. More specifically, a drop in the classification of mothers as ambivalent ties is evident between the time that adults are in their 20s and in their 40s. Likewise, adults in their 40s were less likely to classify their fathers as ambivalent than were adults in their 20s. The drop-off in ambivalence was not linear with age. Rather, teenagers appeared less ambivalent towards their parents than did adults in their 20s. Although conflict with parents peaks when children are teenagers (Montemayor, 1983), teenagers may consider this conflict part of a good relationship with their parents. By contrast, adults in their 20s may view even a lesser degree of conflict as indicative of problems or complexities in their relationships with parents.

In general, fewer participants classified their ties to their mothers as ambivalent than classified their ties to their fathers as ambivalent. This finding is surprising, given the expectation that ties to mothers involve greater emotion, both positive and negative (Troll & Fingerman, 1996). The presentation of data here does not take into account dyad type, however (e.g. mother-son, mother-daughter, father-son, father-daughter) and more explicit breakdowns by gender might reveal a different pattern.

Patterns with regard to offspring showed a similar decrease in ambivalence with age. Oldest-old adults felt their ties to their offspring were globally positive, but younger adults experienced ambivalence towards their children. Only three individuals in their 20s had children, and therefore, findings with regard to this age group should be interpreted with caution. With regard to daughters, ambivalence peaked when individuals were in their 40s and decreased in a linear fashion thereafter. Individuals in their 40s and 60s classified nearly half of their sons as ambivalent ties, whereas the late-life pattern showed a considerable drop-off in classifications of ambivalence. It is important to note two issues with regard to classification of offspring. First, although individuals can only have one mother and one father, they can have more than one daughter or son. The findings with regard to children reflect the fact that individuals feel that they have positive ties with some of their children, but ambivalent ties with other children. Second, age of child and age of parent tends to coincide. Adults in their 40s are likely to have children in their teens and 20s.

To ascertain whether the age of the child was driving the parents' reports, we examined the classifications of sons and daughters based on the child's age (rather than the reporting participant's age). We grouped sons and daughters into five age groups: (1) under age 10; (2) ages 11 to 20; (3) ages 21 to 30; (4) ages 31 to 40; and (5) over age 40. We then examined the emotional classifications (positive only, negative only, ambivalent) of sons and daughters within each of these age groups. Nearly two thirds of children under age 10 were classified as solely positive, as were nearly two thirds of offspring over the age of 30. By contrast, daughters ages 11 to 20 and ages 21 to 30 were more likely to be classified as ambivalent. Two thirds of daughters ages 11 to 20 were considered with ambivalence by their parents, and just over half of daughters (52%) ages 21 to 30 were considered with ambivalence. Nearly two thirds (60%) of sons ages 11 to 20 were also classified as ambivalent, but that proportion dropped considerably when sons reached their 20s; 40% of sons in their twenties were considered with ambivalence by their parents. Therefore, the age of the child as well as the age of the parent appear to be important in parents' perceptions of the emotional qualities of their relationships with sons and daughters.

Patterns of Ambivalence within Age Groups

Finally, we considered patterns of ambivalence within each age group. In the teenage years, ambivalence appears to be greatest towards siblings. Teenagers classified nearly two thirds of their siblings as ambivalent social ties. In addition, half of teenagers classified ties to romantic partners and ties to affinal relatives (stepsiblings and stepparents) as ambivalent. Therefore, in this study, contrary to popular belief, ties towards parents were not the most ambivalent relationships in adolescence. Other close relationships were equally likely to be considered ambivalent. Relationships with friends were classified as primarily positive as were ties to extended family members (e.g. grandparents, aunts, uncles, cousins). These findings suggest that the degree of ambivalence is not associated with age, but rather with age and relationship type; teenagers considered specific relationships ambivalent.

For adults in their 20s, relationships with parents and romantic partners were equally ambivalent. Siblings were more likely to be considered solely positive by participants in this age range. Indeed, the remaining categories of social ties (with the exception of peripheral ties) were disproportionately positive.

Middle-aged adults experienced the greatest ambivalence for their fathers, sons, daughters, and romantic partners. Among participants in this age group, mothers were more likely to be considered solely positive, as were other close relationships. As was discussed previously, middle-aged adults are more likely to have teenaged or young adult children who evoke feelings of ambivalence.

Half of participants in the young-old group classified their romantic partnerships as ambivalent. They were also likely to classify sons as ambivalent, whereas daughters were viewed as disproportionately positive in this age group. The remaining categories of relationships were viewed as strongly positive, with few ties considered ambivalent.

The decrease in proportions of ambivalent ties was particularly notable among participants in the oldest-old group. Again, half of participants in this age range considered their ties to their romantic partners as ambivalent. Nearly all of their remaining relationships, including ties to their children, were considered solely positive.

DISCUSSION

Examination of the larger array of social ties revealed that parents and offspring do seem to experience greater ambivalence towards one another than they experience in many other social ties. This study makes three contributions to our understanding of intergenerational ambivalence. First, it involved assessments of the social network as a whole, rather than a specific focus on the parent-child tie. Thus, when participants listed their relationship with a parent or offspring as close or problematic, they did so spontaneously and not in response to specific task demands of the study. Second, these data allow increased attention to whether the experience of ambivalence in the parent-child relationship is more frequent than the experience of ambivalence in other types of social ties. Third, the focus on a large section of the life span (adolescence through advanced old age) allows increased attention to age differences in the parent-child relationship.

Methodology

In understanding ambivalence between parents and children, it is important to take into account the methodological approach used to assess this construct. Findings from this study reflect questions about the social network on the whole, rather than about the parent-child tie. The advantage to this approach is that we obtained information about the parent-child tie without increasing the salience of this relationship. In studies that focus specifically on parent-child relationships, participants may be more attuned to the emotional complexities of the relationship because they are thinking about the relationship so intensely. Therefore, findings pertaining to ambivalence in such studies may partially reflect the demands of the studies. These studies are like the case of the man who was told, "Do not think of a pink elephant." Even the most willing participants would have a hard time not envisioning the elephant.

On the other hand, the drawback to the approach used here involves its superficial nature. Participants did not describe the emotional qualities of their relationships. Rather, researchers inferred that ties that were listed both in a network of close social ties and in a network of problematic social ties are ex-perienced as ambivalent. Elsewhere, we have argued that open-ended approaches to understanding problematic aspects of relationships provide better data than do forced-choice approaches to understanding such complexities in relationships (Fingerman, 2001a). Indeed, different methodologies provide different types of information about the downside of parent-child ties and no single approach can be used to fully understand intergenerational ambivalence (Fingerman, 1998).

Two perplexing findings appear to stem from this methodology. First, partici-pants were more likely to report ambivalence towards their fathers than towards their mothers. Second, participants in their 20s were more likely to classify their ties to their parents as ambivalent than were participants in their teens. Both of these findings are contradictory to expected patterns in the literature. Emotional experiences with mothers are generally more complex than emotional experiences with fathers (Troll & Fingerman, 1996). Yet, findings from this study suggest that, on the whole, adults are more likely to consider their relationships with their mothers as positive, whereas they consider their relationships with their fathers to be mixed. It is likely, however, that within these generally positive relationships with their mothers, adults also experience a complex array of negative emotions (Fingerman, 2001a). Further, as mentioned previously, the findings with regard to adults in their teens and 20s may reflect a sense of the meaning of negative emotions in the relationship. When teenagers experience problems with their parents, they may consider these problems normal and part of a good relationship. When adults in their 20s experience such problems, they may view the relationship itself as problem-ridden.

In sum, the study described in this chapter provides information about whether or not individuals spontaneously think of their relationships with their parents and children in globally positive and negative terms. The study does not pursue the complexities of their emotional experiences in this relationship.

Ambivalence Between Parents and Children versus Other Social Contacts

Aside from raising questions about methodology and the construct of ambivalence, this study provides insights into the nature of ambivalence between parents and children relative to other social ties. Although many participants classified their ties to parents or offspring as ambivalent, other relationships were equally or more likely to be considered ambivalent. In particular, ties to romantic partners were considered with ambivalence throughout life and ties to siblings were considered ambivalent in adolescence. Given that nearly all romantic partners among adults over age 20 involved spouses or live-in partners, proximity may play a role in the experience of ambivalence with romantic partners and siblings. When siblings grow up and no longer live in the same household, there is a precipitous drop in the likelihood that they will be classified as ambivalent; teenagers classified their ties to siblings as ambivalent, whereas individuals in their 20s did not. It may simply be the case that individuals are more likely to experience ambivalence when they reside in the same space.

This pattern regarding proximity was not the same for parents and children, however. Adult children in their 20s, who do not reside in their parents' households, were more likely to consider their ties to their parents ambivalent than were teenagers who reside with their parents. Therefore, ambivalence between parents and children may reflect different factors than does ambivalence in other social ties. Additional research is needed to understand why participants of different ages classified each relationship as ambivalent. Possible reasons underlying unique aspects of ambivalence between parents and children relative to other social ties were delineated in an earlier section of this chapter. Future research might investigate the contribution of each of these factors to ambivalence in this tie.

Age Differences

We also considered age differences in the likelihood of experiencing ambivalence in the parent-child tie. As was discussed previously, in general, the degree of ambivalence towards parents and children decreased with age. The age of the parent and the child appear to be important, however, in understanding ambivalence.

Examination of the association between age and ambivalence revealed that parents' and offspring's ambivalence was associated with offspring's age. In general, when offspring are in their teens and 20s, parents and offspring alike appear to experience greater ambivalence towards each other than when offspring reach their 30s and 40s. There are several possible explanations for this pattern. The life tasks that parents and children face when children are in their teens and 20s may contribute to ambivalence. Beginning in their teens, children seek to establish autonomy from their parents, and tensions may erupt as they pull away (Smetana, 1995). Further, parents may view young adult offspring in their 20s as a reflection on how they did as parents (Ryff, Lee, Essex & Schmutte, 1994). Parents may experience tensions with regard to offspring who have not established themselves as their parents believe they should. When offspring are in their 30s, parents may have accepted what their offspring have achieved and who they are as adults. Further, offspring may achieve a sense of "filial maturity" (Birditt, Fingerman & Lefkowitz, 2001; Blenkner, 1963), or a greater understanding of the parent as an individual with strengths, weaknesses, and vulnerabilities. As offspring increasingly accept their parents as individuals, the overall level of ambivalence in the tie may decrease.

Although age of child plays a role in the degree of ambivalence between parents and offspring through much of life, parental age influences parents' ambivalence in the later stages. Adults over the age of 80 disproportionately reported positive ties to their offspring. These findings are in keeping with prior studies that have reported a decrease in social problems in the late stages of life (Ingersoll-Dayton & Talbott, 1992; Johnson, 1995). Although scholars have shown that older adults are generally more positive about their social ties than are younger adults (Carstensen, Isaacowitz & Charles, 1999), this pattern appears to intensify at the very end of life, at which time adults report few problematic ties. The one exception to this decrease in tensions involved marital partners; more than half of married oldest-old adults described their relationships with their spouses as ambivalent. It should be noted that all of the women in the oldest-old group were widowed, whereas all but three of the men were still married. Therefore, all reports pertaining to spouses in this age group came from men. Men and women in this group were equally positive about their offspring, however, making it unclear whether gender is a key variable with regard to the experience of ambivalence at the end of life. Rather, it may be the case that parents grow increasingly positive towards offspring as offspring step in to care for them. The sharp decline in parents' reports of ambivalent ties to offspring is another area that warrants additional research.

In summary, when ambivalence is assessed across the social network, it is clear that parents and offspring do evoke a sense of mixed feelings, even at a global level. This relationship is not necessarily the most ambivalent tie throughout life, but rather, the nature of the ambivalence in this tie appears to be distinct and does not stem from issues arising in the context of a shared residence. The factors that make the parent-child tie distinct from other social ties and the changes that parents and offspring incur as they grow older warrant additional research attention.

ACKNOWLEDGMENTS

This study was funded by Grant No. 1R03AG1448401, "Adults' Reasoning about Social Problems across Adulthood" from the National Institutes on Aging awarded to the first author. Portions of this paper were presented at the Transcoop International Workshop on Intergenerational Ambivalence, Konstanz, Germany.

REFERENCES

Antonucci, T. C., & Akiyama, H. (1987). Social networks in adult life and a preliminary examination of the convoy model. *Journal of Gerontology, 42,* 519–527.

Bengtson, V. L., & Kuypers, J. A. (1971). Generational difference and the developmental stake. *Aging and Human Development, 2,* 249–260.

Birditt, K. S., Fingerman, K. L., & Lefkowitz, E. S. (2001). Becoming a peer to your parent: Development of a scale of filial maturity (Unpublished manuscript).

Blenkner, M. (1963). Social work and family relations in later life with some thoughts on filial maturity. In: E. Shanas & G. F. Streib (Eds), *Social Structure and the Family: Generational Relations* (pp. 46–59). Englewood Cliffs, NJ: Prentice-Hall.

Bowlby, J. (1969). *Attachment and loss: Attachment* (Vol. 1). New York: Basic Books.

Carstensen, L. L. (1992). Social and emotional patterns in adulthood: Support for socioemotional selectivity theory. *Psychology and Aging, 7,* 331–338.

Carstensen, L. L., Isaacowitz, D. M., & Charles, S. T. (1999). Taking time seriously: A theory of socioemotional selectivity. *American Psychologist, 54,* 165–181.

Erikson, E. H. (1963). *Childhood and society* (2nd ed.). New York: W. W. Norton and Company.

Ewen, R. B. (1993). Alfred Adler: Individual psychology. In: *Theories of Personality* (4th ed., pp. 123–155). Hillsdale, NJ: Lawrence Erlbaum Associates.

Fingerman, K. L. (1995). Aging mothers' and their adult daughters' perceptions of conflict behaviors. *Psychology and Aging, 10,* 639–650.

Fingerman, K. L. (1997). Aging mothers' and their adult daughters' retrospective ratings of past conflict in their relationship. *Current Psychology, 16,* 131–154.

Fingerman, K. L. (1998). Tight lips: Aging mothers' and their adult daughters' responses to interpersonal tensions in their relationship. *Personal Relationships*, *5*, 121–138.

Fingerman, K. L. (2001a). *Aging mothers and their adult daughters: A study in mixed emotions.* New York: Springer.

Fingerman, K. L. (2001b). The paradox of a distant closeness: Intimacy in parent/child ties. *Generations*, *25*, 26–33.

Fingerman, K. L., & Birditt, K. S. (2003). Do age differences in close and problematic family ties reflect the pool of available relatives? *Journals of Gerontology: Psychological Sciences*, *58*, P80–P87.

Fingerman, K. L., & Griffiths, P. C. (1999). Season's greetings: Adults' social contact at the holiday season. *Psychology and Aging*, *14*, 192–205.

Fingerman, K. L., & Hay, E. L. (2002). Searching under the streetlight? Age biases in the personal and family relationships literature. *Personal Relationships*, *9*, 415–433.

Ingersoll-Dayton, B., & Talbott, M. M. (1992). Assessments of social support exchanges: Cognitions of the old-old. *International Journal of Aging and Human Development*, *35*, 125–143.

Johnson, C. (1995, November). Parent-child conflict amongst the oldest-old. Presented in the symposium "Negative Aspects of Social Relationships," K. L. Fingerman (chair), Gerontological Society of America annual meeting, Los Angeles, CA.

Kahn, R. L., & Antonucci, T. C. (1980). Convoys over the life course: Attachment, roles, and social support. In P. B. Baltes & O. C. Brim (Eds), *Life-Span, Development, and Behavior* (pp. 254–283). New York: Academic Press.

Laursen, B., & Bukowski, W. M. (1997). A developmental guide to the organisation of close relationships. *International Journal of Behavioral Development*, *21*, 747–770.

Lüscher, K., & Pillemer, K. (1998). Intergenerational ambivalence: A new approach to the study of parent-child relations in later life. *Journal of Marriage and the Family*, *60*, 413–425.

Montemayor, R. (1983). Parents and adolescents in conflict: All families some of the time and some families most of the time. *Journal of Early Adolescence*, *3*, 83–103.

Moss, B. F., & Schwebel, A. I. (1993). Defining intimacy in romantic relationships. *Family Relations*, *42*, 31–37.

Reis, H. T., & Shaver, P. (1988). Intimacy as an interpersonal process. In: S. Duck (Ed.), *Handbook of Personal Relationships* (pp. 367–389). Chichester, England: Wiley.

Rook, K. S. (1997). Positive and negative social exchanges: Weighing their effect in later life [Guest Editorial]. *Journals of Gerontology: Social Sciences*, *52*, S167–S169.

Rook, K. S. (1998). Investigating the positive and negative sides of personal relationships: Through a lens darkly? In: B. H. Spitzberg & W. R. Cupach (Eds), *The Dark Side of Close Relationships* (pp. 369–393). Mahwah, NJ: Erlbaum.

Rossi, A. S., & Rossi, P. H. (1990). *Of human bonding: Parent-child relations across the life course.* New York: Aldine de Gruyter.

Ryff, C. D., Lee, Y. H., Essex, M. J., & Schmutte, P. S. (1994). My children and me: Midlife evaluations of grown children and of self. *Psychology and Aging*, *9*, 195–205.

Smetana, J. G. (1995). Parenting styles and conceptions of parental authority during adolescence. *Child Development*, *66*, 299–316.

Suitor, J. J., & Pillemer, K. (1987). The presence of adult children: A source of stress for elderly couple's marriages. *Journal of Marriage and the Family*, *49*, 717–725.

Suitor, J. J., & Pillemer, K. (1988). Explaining intergenerational conflict when adult children and elderly parents live together. *Journal of Marriage and the Family*, *50*, 1037–1047.

Troll, L., & Fingerman, K. L. (1996). Parent-child bonds in adulthood. In: C. Malestesta-Magai & S. McFadden (Eds), *Handbook of Emotion, Adult Development and Aging* (pp. 185–205). Orlando, FL: Academic Press.

Tyson, P., & Tyson, R. L. (1990). Object relations development. In: P. Tyson & R. L. Tyson (Eds), *Psychoanalytic Theories of Development: An Integration* (pp. 97–117). New Haven, CT: Yale University Press.

Umberson, D. (1992). Relationships between adult children and their parents: Psychological consequences for both generations. *Journal of Marriage and the Family, 54*, 664–674.

Webster, P. S., & Herzog, R. A. (1995). Effects of parental divorce and memories of family problems on relationships between adult children and their parents. *Journal of Gerontology: Social Sciences, 50*, 24–34.

Weigert, A. J. (1991). *Mixed emotions: Certain steps toward understanding ambivalence.* Albany, NY: State University of New York Press.

Weishaus, S. S. (1978). Determinants of affect of middle-aged women towards their aging mothers (Unpublished doctoral dissertation). University of Southern California, Los Angeles.

7. INTERGENERATIONAL AMBIVALENCE: METHODS, MEASURES, AND RESULTS OF THE KONSTANZ STUDY

Kurt Lüscher and Frank Lettke

INTRODUCTION

This chapter reports on methods and results of an exploratory research project on intergenerational ambivalence between parents and their adult children. The study was conducted in 1998 and 1999 at the research center for "Society and Family" at the University of Konstanz. Its conceptual framework consists of the theoretical considerations and the schematic model touched upon in Chap. 2 of this book (see pp. 23–62) as one attempt to operationalize the concept of intergenerational ambivalence.

As a matter of record, we may state briefly that we realized the relevance and fruitfulness of the concept of ambivalence for the study of intergenerational relationships as three perspectives converged for us. These three are: (1) the general study of intergenerational relationships in postmodern societies (see Lüscher, 1995, brief English summary Lüscher, 2000); (2) the critical review of the status of research in Europe and the United States (Lüscher & Pillemer, 1996, 1997, 1998); and (3) our project on how parent-child relationships are reorganized after divorce in later phases of marriage, combined with a sub-study of the effects of the divorce of an adult son (Lüscher & Pajung-Bilger, 1998, brief English summary Lüscher, 2000).

Intergenerational Ambivalences: New Perspectives on Parent-Child Relations in Later Life
Contemporary Perspectives in Family Research, Volume 4, 153–179
© 2004 Published by Elsevier Ltd.
ISSN: 1530-3535/doi:10.1016/S1530-3535(03)04007-X

In the latter we explored, through a series of semi-structured interviews, how fathers and mothers on one side, and adult children on the other, coped with this event as a turning point in their lives. Our original intention was to distinguish different degrees of closeness and distance in connection with different degrees and forms of solidarity. In the course of the analysis, it became obvious that the complexity of these relationships could not be captured and explained by paying attention to solidarity alone. The obvious contradictions in the reports about the relationships suggested that we had to come up with a concept that would be more appropriate to the obvious tensions in these relationships, and to the oscillations between closeness and distance, as well as between conservation and change, that were common in them. In this context, the idea of ambivalence opened the door for a new approach.

In a secondary analysis of the interviews with the concept of ambivalence at our disposal, it became possible to offer a set of useful interpretations. These results encouraged attempts to apply the concept in a study which was especially designed around ambivalence, referring to an explicit definition, and based above all on an operationalization that would meet the requirements of quantitative research. In other words, in the first study on divorce we used ambivalence as an "interpretative concept" (see Chap. 2); in the Konstanz project, we used it as a "research construct."

As this study is one of the first to apply the concept of ambivalence in a multifaceted way in quantitative sociological research, we will comment upon its research instruments in some detail. Before looking at them, however, we will briefly review the study's basic assumptions and hypotheses.

We carefully recruited our respondents, consisting of both parents and adult children. To arrive at a sample that can be seen as approximately representative of the population in Konstanz, we had to conform strictly to strong legislation concerning the protection of personal data in Germany. For our particular study, after examining the purpose of the project and seeing its strictly academic orientation, the authorities gave us the opportunity to draw a first sample of people between the ages of 25 and 70 for a telephone survey. This survey provided the base for subsequent in-person, face-to-face interviews with a smaller number of people whom we assessed as willing and well suited to participate.

In keeping with the interpretative strategy of "uncovering ambivalence," we will present and discuss the results in a series of steps. We start with data pertaining to direct conscious experience of ambivalence and then present the results of our attempts to assess ambivalence indirectly. This approach allows us to apply the distinction between the personal and institutional dimensions of the experience of ambivalence, as deduced from the analysis of the concept of relationships (see Chap. 2). To that end, we use data that refer to specific dyads such as mother-son or daughter-father. We also will look at a third set of results having to do with patterns and strategies of dealing with ambivalence. This third set of results can be seen as suggesting another possible application for the schematic model as it is presented and explained in Chap. 2 of this volume.

Validation of the instruments is an important issue. Since many of the well-established procedures for assessing social relationships quantitatively are not appropriate for capturing the specifics of ambivalence (see Lettke & Klein, Chap. 4 of this volume), we felt it necessary to develop new ones. The validity of these instruments can be evaluated only after they have been used in future research. In the meantime, we approach this issue of validity by testing the coherence between different sets of questions.

RESEARCH DESIGN AND INSTRUMENTS

Introductory Remarks

The conceptual frame of reference suggests a certain number of consequences for the design of research instruments. They can be summarized as follows: First, the experience of ambivalence is one aspect of intergenerational relationships, but ambivalence must not be present in all relationships between parents and adult children. Ambivalence appears in different forms and with different levels of intensity. Second, people can be aware of ambivalence in intergenerational relations in daily conduct, and they can speak about them in everyday language. Hence, it is appropriate to use questions that directly address such experiences and the awareness of them. Furthermore, questions may be asked about whether the experience of ambivalence is seen as a burden or a challenge; in other words, questions can be asked regarding the judgment of ambivalence. Third, ambivalence may be hidden and unconscious. It can be concealed in how relationships are perceived and in how they are described. Thus, we need questions that allow the assessment of relationship by different, opposing and contradicting attributes and from different angles. Fourth, the elaborated definition of ambivalence (see Chap. 2) approaches ambivalence as multi-dimensional and complex. We must therefore pay attention, in the elaboration of instruments as well as in their validation, to this complexity. Fifth, ambivalence has to be coped with or dealt with. It seems plausible to distinguish different modes and strategies for doing so. The Konstanz-model is an attempt to deduce such strategies from theoretical assumptions and propositions.

Sampling

As mentioned above, the study began with a telephone survey. The main purpose of that survey was to gather data about the population between 25 and 70 years of age in the Konstanz county, in order to draw a sample of persons to be included in the main study. This initial step was necessary because no data were available on women and men in these age groups, nor was it possible to use a representative sample from other studies or to use the information from official registers. Only the names of people in this age group could be obtained, and that information could be obtained only by special permission. From a total of 162,953 persons, we drew a random sample consisting of 1,682 addresses. Of those, 528 agreed to participate in the telephone survey. The "exhaustiveness quota" after eliminating sampling neutral exceptions was 62.9%. The survey, carried out in 1998 in cooperation with ZUMA (Survey Center Mannheim, supported by the German Science Foundation) is documented in a methods report (ZUMA-Technischer Bericht Nr. 98/13 – available from the authors).

These interviews had the goal of collecting basic demographic data, information on the structure and size of the family and marital status. We also included a preliminary question about the everyday experience of ambivalence. In the responses to even these simple questions, we noticed a comparatively widespread experience and awareness of intergenerational ambivalence. Seven percent of the fathers and mothers said that they often were torn back and forth in regard to their oldest child. In turn, 18% of the children said that they felt torn back and forth. About 32% of the parents and 20% of the children said that they never felt torn back and forth. There were also preliminary findings that showed gender differences in the experience of personal ambivalence. Women reported such experiences more often than men did. Neither parents nor children judged the experience of ambivalence in a solely negative way, and there was a relatively high consciousness of thinking about the awareness of ambivalence in an everyday sense.

Of the 528 respondents of the 1998 study, we selected 90 people according to three criteria:

(1) They should be either adult children with living parents or parents of living adult children, which would increase our chances of doing follow-up interviews with members of the other generation.
(2) Assuming that the experience and the awareness of ambivalence may be related to education, we selected people with either high or low levels of education.
(3) In order to compare families with many or few experiences of ambivalence, we also included respondents who reported, in the telephone survey, either high or low intensity levels of ambivalence.

After initial interviews with these 90 people, we subsequently interviewed – as far as possible – their parents (when respondent belonged to the adult-child generation) or their adult children (when the respondent belonged to the parent generation). The resulting database of the 1999 study consisted of 52 interviews with adult children

Table 1. Age of Interviewed Family Members.

Age Class	Father	Mother	Son	Daughter	N row	(% Row)
25–29	–	–	3	4	7	(5.6)
30–34	–	–	4	7	11	(8.9)
35–39	–	–	10	6	16	(12.9)
40–44	–	–	5	5	10	(8.1)
45–49	–	3	3	1	7	(5.6)
50–54	4	4	2	1	11	(8.9)
55–59	6	8	–	–	14	(11.3)
60–64	16	8	1	–	25	(20.2)
65 and older	9	14	–	–	23	(18.5)
N column	35	37	28	24	124	(100)
(% Column)	(28.2)	(29.8)	(22.6)	(19.4)	(100)	

Source: Study 1999; $N = 124$ persons.

and 72 interviews with parents. In these 124 interviews, respondents referred to 255 dyadic relationships. (For more information, see the working paper of Lüscher, Pajung-Bilger, Lettke & Böhmer, 2000.)

The distribution of family status, age, and sex of all subjects appears in Table 1.

Research Instruments

In accordance with the interpretative strategy of "uncovering" (see Chap. 2), the core instruments of the survey were of three kinds:

(1) an instrument addressing the overt experience and awareness of ambivalence,
(2) one addressing the assessment of relationships in regard to covert ambivalence, and
(3) one addressing how ambivalence is managed and dealt with.

The topic of ambivalence itself was also addressed in some miscellaneous questions. These included a request to evaluate the interview's comprehensibility with regard to the topic of ambivalence. In addition, the questionnaire included the following topics: judgments of how younger and older people see each other, their mutual understanding of society and views of the family, and standard questions concerning personal and socio-demographic data. The following overview provides the major elements of the questionnaire (see Table 2 numbers: sequence of questions).

We developed two versions of the questionnaire, a "parents' version" and a "children's version." The contents of the questions and the sequence are identical. (For a full documentation of the instruments in German and English, see

Table 2. Overview. Major Elements of the Questionnaire of the Konstanz Study.

Level of Observation	Instruments					
	Awareness	Assessment	Management	Society	Family Image	Miscellaneous Questions
Intergenerational relationships in general				1 relationship between young and old 2 changes in this relationship 3/4 perceptions of young and old generation 5 relationship between young and old	8 morphological aspects of family 9 gender-related task distribution in the family	6 tolerance for ambiguity 49 quality of questionnaire 50 difficulties in answering 51 rating of ambivalence
Relationships in the family	15 orientation at tried and true ways vs. new ways 16 orientation at family harmony vs. allow conflicts	7 taboos in family conversation 13 how family members relate to one another	12 generalized maxims for action 14 handling of ambivalent situations		10 contrast: ideal vs. real family life 11 reasons for discrepancies	52 concern about ambivalence 53–61 demography
Specifics about parent-child relationships	18 frequency of ambivalence, feeling torn 19 judgement of ambivalence, stress	17 relationship quality (graphical illustration) 24 closeness of relationship	34–41 vignette "financial support" 42–48 vignette "choice of partner"			62 potential interview-partners in the family 63 admission for future contacts

20 typical situation of ambivalence

21 agreement with ambivalence

22 orientation at tried and true ways vs. new ways

23 orientation at family harmony vs. allow conflicts

25 contrast: ideal vs. real relationship

26 un-/pleasant aspects of relationship

27 indirectly measured ambivalence (attributes)

28 frequency of contact

29/30 desired contact

31 changes of the relationship in the past 5 years

32 reasons for this changes

33 expected future changes

Lüscher, Pajung-Bilger, Lettke, Böhmer, Rasner & Pillemer, 2000; http://www.
uni-konstanz.de/FuF/SozWiss/fg-soz/ag-fam/famsoz-i.html) A brief summary of
our methods appears in the Appendix to this chapter.

Because of the exploratory character of the study, it was not yet possible to
assess the validity and the reliability of the instruments by way of comparison
with other studies, except for some measures, which have been used in the Ithaca
study (see Pillemer, Chap. 5 of this volume). Instead, as mentioned earlier, we
attempted to look at the coherence between different sets of questions within the
interview. The results, which seem quite satisfactory at this point of development,
are reported below.

The data we present refer mainly to descriptive statements and judgments about
dyads such as father-daughter or son-mother. Our use of such statements follows
from grounding our research in a conceptualization of ambivalence that has its
focus in relationships rather than individual persons. Continuing our strategy of
"uncovering," as mentioned above, we start with data on the awareness of direct ambivalence as expressed in everyday speech. Then we include indicators of indirect
ambivalence that we assessed by indirect measures. We then present the data on the
perspective of family roles, followed by a detailed comparison of the dyadic relationships. We conclude with the results relevant to the correlation between ambivalence and the quality of relationships, and strategies of dealing with ambivalence.

As outlined in our description of the research instruments above, our approach
is exploratory in a twofold sense. First, we rely on a broad conceptualization of
ambivalence, for which the distinction between two dimensions, the personal and
the institutional, is especially relevant. We do not limit the scope of ambivalence to
feelings, and we try to bring in the theoretically deduced typology of four patterns
of dealing with ambivalence. Second, we try to develop new instruments, which
bears certain risks. In this regard, our data and their presentation differ from other
research reports in this volume.

From a critical point of view, one may reproach the study for being neither a survey based on a large sample, using a specific set of more or less established instruments, nor a clinical study focusing with in-depth instruments on a few cases. We
are willing to defend the resulting hybrid character (as it may be called) of the study,
however, in light of its sensitivity to the broadness of the concept of ambivalence.

RESULTS

Ambivalence as an Everyday Experience

Our general hypothesis implies that the experience of ambivalence is an almost
commonplace experience. Thus, we expect that parents and adult children quite

Table 3. Frequency of Ambivalence (%).

Very often	4
Often	11
Now and then	29
Seldom	35
Never	20

Source: Study 1999; $N = 255$ dyads.

often feel pulled in two directions to the extent of feeling torn, and we also expect that they are aware of these persistent tensions. The data from the preliminary telephone survey as well as the responses to different questions about the conscious experience of ambivalence confirm this assumption. Being asked to what extent they feel torn, respondents in only 20% of the dyads say that they never feel torn (Table 3).

Six contradictorily formulated statements about relationships in six different statements provide additional confirmation of the correctness of our expectation that the experience of ambivalence is common. Consider, for instance, the following statement: "[Person] and I often get on each other's nerves, but nevertheless we feel very close and like each other very much." Twenty-four percent of our respondents agreed with this statement of ambivalent emotions. Other examples are: "My relationship with my [person] is very intimate, but that also makes it restrictive," with which 11.6% agreed, and "Although I love my [person] very much, I am also sometimes indifferent toward him/her" with which 13.4% agreed. Summing the responses to all these questions, we find on the average 36% agreement with the contradictory statements (Table 4).

Although this multi-item Likert scale is only a rough indicator for the experience of ambivalence and only partly reflects the reported feeling of being torn, it nevertheless shows the presence of ambivalence in the assessments of relationships. Compared with Table 3, which entails a general judgment, the underlying reference here is to different contexts.

Table 4. Agreement with Ambivalence. Average sum of Contradictory Statements about Relationships (%).

Agree	36
Partly agree	20
Do not agree	44

Source: Study 1999; $N = 228$ dyads.

Ambivalence and Family Roles

We collected data from mothers and fathers as well as from daughters and sons, which allows us also to compare the frequency of ambivalent experiences with respect to family roles. In the existing literature of intergenerational relations, the "generational stake" hypothesis is widely cited (see, for instance, Giarrusso, Stallings & Bengtson, 1995). The hypothesis holds, generally speaking, that parents have a more positive, less critical view of their relationships with adult children than the reverse. Parents also tend to see themselves as closer to their children than their children see themselves as being toward the parents. What could we expect with respect to ambivalence in these situations? If ambivalence bears a strong negative connotation, we would expect parents to report less ambivalence than children. And what about gender? Does the well-known fact that women (especially mothers) are the "kin-keepers" suggest a lower intensity of ambivalence from females?

The findings give a more differentiated and somewhat contradictory picture, as Table 5 shows.

Two overall indicators of ambivalence – namely, the concern about ambivalence, and the frequency of consciously experienced overt ambivalence (in the sense of feeling torn) – show no significant differences between parents and children or between gender. However, the differing answers given by sons attract attention. This finding reinforces the conclusion that ambivalence should not be evaluated in solely negative terms. It is in agreement with the general conceptualization of ambivalence deduced from the history of the concept and its usage in different disciplines (see Chap. 2). However, as will be shown below, the issue is rather complicated, and further explorations are needed to get to understand it.

If ambivalence is measured in an indirect way, and if we distinguish between the subjective-personal and the institutional-structural dimensions, we are able to uncover noteworthy differences. Although the differences are not significant in regard to the *personal* dimension, the picture changes when one looks at *institutional* ambivalence. Here, the distribution shows a significant degree of differentiation. A close look suggests that this result is due mostly to a lower degree of intensity calculated from the responses of the parents, and furthermore from a higher degree of intensity in the reports of sons as compared with those of the daughters. Although a certain reticence is recommended given the comparatively small size of the sample, these results demonstrate the usefulness of the distinction between the personal and the institutional dimensions of relationships in regard to ambivalence.

Our data on the evaluation of intergenerational ambivalence provide still another interesting result of exploring ambivalence with reference to the differences

Table 5. Ambivalence Indicators and Family Roles. (Column Percent of Each Indicator).

Indicators of Ambivalence	Father	Mother	Son	Daughter	χ^2	p
(a) Concern about ambivalence						
Very often/often thought about	40	37	36	50		
Now and then thought about	32	37	50	29		
Seldom/never thought about	28	26	14	21	8.118	0.230
(b) Frequency of ambivalence						
Very often/often torn in two directions	13	12	12	**31**		
Now and then torn in two directions	31	33	25	21		
Seldom/never torn in two directions	56	55	64	48	12.307	0.055
(c) Intensity of indirectly measured personal ambivalence[a]						
−1 (low)	32	43	37	57		
0	3	1	2	2		
1	26	25	33	13		
2	25	25	12	13		
3	12	5	15	15		
4	1	1	2	0		
5 (high)	1	0	0	0	21.436	0.258
(d) Intensity of indirectly measured institutional ambivalence[a]						
−1 (low)	28	26	10	21		
0	3	7	4	13		
1	31	34	**12**	23		
2	31	26	**50**	32		
3	6	7	**25**	11		
4 (high)	2	0	0	0	36.771	0.001
(e) Rating of ambivalence						
Very/more positive than negative	**56**	36	37	29		
Equally positive and negative	37	61	51	46		
More negative than positive/very	7	4	12	**25**	23.574	0.001
(f) Judgement of ambivalence						
Very stressful/stressful	53	59	34	62		
Only a little/not stressful at all	47	41	66	39	8.227	0.042

Source: Study 1999; $N = 255$ dyads.
[a] To calculate the ambivalence values the formula developed by Griffin is employed (see Thompson et al., 1995, p. 369f.).

between family roles. First of all, parts "e" and "f" both show that ambivalence is not limited to solely negative connotations. The majority of responses to the more general question about rating (see part e) is in the middle-category of "equally positive and negative." There is, however, one notable exception of fathers who judge ambivalence predominantly as more positive (56%), and another, in the opposite direction, of daughters of whom only 29% judge ambivalence more positive than negative. These two judgments contribute mainly to the significant difference among the incumbents of the family positions.

The stronger evaluation of ambivalence as being either stressful or not also suggests a certain shift. Slightly more than half of the respondents (again with the exception of the sons) judge ambivalence as being a source of stress, although a considerable number of them do not see it in this way. This result seems even more noteworthy if one takes into account that a negative undertone does seem to characterize the common everyday understanding of ambivalence.

Dyadic Relationships

A further degree of differentiation becomes available through analysis of the eight dyadic relationships: father or mother each in relation to their daughter or son, and vice versa, as shown in Table 6.

These results confirm that overt ambivalence (in the sense of feeling torn) is frequent in the range of 32–54% of the dyads. Although the overall differences are not significant, patterns can be uncovered if both generational status and gender are taken into consideration. Adult sons and (on a slightly higher level) adult daughters report almost the same frequency of ambivalence to the father. Conversely, fathers report ambivalence in the same frequency in the relationships to daughters and sons. In contrast, the relationships between adult children and mothers, both in regard to

Table 6. Frequency of Ambivalence: "Frequently Torn" (% Related to Single Dyads).

Respondent	Person Referred to			
	Father	Mother	Son	Daughter
Father	–	–	41	48
Mother	–	–	51	39
Son	42	32	–	–
Daughter	50	54	–	–

Source: Study 1999; $N = 254$ dyads; $r = 0.693$.

frequency and reciprocity, are more differentiated. This finding is compatible with the general insight that mothers play a stronger, and apparently more outspoken role in kin-relations. More than half of the daughters report frequent feelings of being torn, considerably more than the percentage of mothers who report ambivalences with the daughters. In contrast, for son-mother dyads as compared with mother-son dyads, the pattern is quite different. All in all, opposite-sex ambivalence seems to occur more often from the perspectives of parents, whereas same-sex ambivalence seems to be more frequent from the perspectives of adult children.

For a next step of uncovering, we can differentiate these patterns by the personal and the institutional dimension of ambivalence. This requires that we take indirect measures into account and refer to the conceptual model of intergenerational ambivalence. For this purpose, we developed an indicator for inferred ambivalence based in a list of attributes that describe the relationship. We associate attributes such as "warm" or "loving" with the "convergence" pole. Attributes such as "indifferent" or "superficial" represent the "divergence" pole. "Predictable" or "inflexible" stand for "reproduction"; and "open to new experiences" or "full of variety" are examples of "innovation."

Respondents rated the applicability of each attribute on a 5-point Likert scale. Factor analysis helped in finding suitable attributes for constructing the respective scale. Each scale shows the same 5-point rating of applicability and therefore displays information about the average applicability of the four poles. When opposite poles apply at the same time, we consider this as an indicator of ambivalence. Thus, simultaneous applicability of "convergence" and "divergence" indicates "personal ambivalence." The combination of "reproduction" and "innovation" indicates "institutional ambivalence." (See appendix for a full presentation of these calculations, see Lettke, 2000a, 2002.)

Calculations show that, on average, respondents experience institutional ambivalences more frequently (47%) than personal ambivalences (31%) (table not shown). This is a first indicator for the fruitfulness of this distinction, which is confirmed by a comparison of parts a and b of Table 7. These two sections show our data on the two dimensions we are looking at, split into dyads where – with a few exceptions – the level of institutional ambivalence is higher than that of personal ambivalence.

This finding can be interpreted as an indicator that the tensions between closeness and distance are seen to be of lower frequency than those between "reproduction" and "innovation"; in other words, the tensions regarding the modes of organizing the family are higher. Moreover, it seems plausible, as the data in Table 7b show, that the younger generation feels more ambivalent than do their parents. Here, we are reminded of the thesis of "generational stake." However, the results from this study add an important additional characterization to this thesis by locating the

Table 7.   Inferred Personal and Institutional Ambivalence (% Related to Dyads).

Respondent	Person Referred to			
	Father	Mother	Son	Daughter
(a) Personal ambivalence[a]				
Father	–	–	45	36
Mother	–	–	36	23
Son	44	18	–	–
Daughter	32	22	–	–
(b) Institutional ambivalence[b]				
Father	–	–	43	37
Mother	–	–	41	30
Son	74	84	–	–
Daughter	60	44	–	–

[a] Study 1999; $N = 237$ dyads; $r = 0.201$; contingency coefficient $= 0.199$.
[b] Study 1999; $N = 237$ dyads; $r = 0.000$; contingency coefficient $= 0.325$.

difference between the young and the old in the realm of structural-institutional arrangements.

The data suggest that exploring further differentiations will be fruitful. On the personal dimension, mothers and daughters both report low levels of ambivalence in their relationships. The ratings in father-son dyads are higher. This result is compatible with the conventional "wisdom" that relationships between mother and daughters are often close, especially if the latter are mothers themselves or intend to become mothers.

In contrast, the son-mother dyad stands out, especially in regard to differences between the perspectives of sons and mothers, and the difference between the personal and the institutional dimensions. Whereas mothers report more ambivalences than sons do on the personal dimension, the opposite is the case on the institutional dimension. How can these discrepancies be explained?

We may hypothesize that, when asked directly about the feeling of being torn, respondents immediately associate this feeling with the personal aspects of their relationships, that is, with the overall sentiment of closeness vs. distance. As has been shown, personal ambivalence is least frequent in the perspective of the sons in son-mother dyads. Another explanation points to latent ambivalences. This indicator is used when respondents state that they "seldom" or "never" feel torn, even though we are able to identify ambivalences by indirect measurement. With regard to the personal dimension, we find on the average of all dyads 13.9% latent ambivalences. In the institutional dimension, the level is nearly twice as high: 24.7% (no tables given).

Table 8. Attributed Latent Ambivalence (% Related to Dyads).

Respondent	Person Referred to			
	Father	Mother	Son	Daughter
(a) Latent personal ambivalence[a]				
Father	–	–	23	11
Mother	–	–	17	10
Son	22	11	–	–
Daughter	14	0	–	–
(b) Latent institutional ambivalence[b]				
Father	–	–	18	15
Mother	–	–	18	10
Son	44	56	–	–
Daughter	30	22	–	–

[a] Study 1999; $N = 237$ dyads; $r = 0.497$; contingency coefficient $= 0.281$.
[b] Study 1999; $N = 227$ dyads; $r = 0.007$; contingency coefficient $= 0.388$.

Keeping in mind the lower degree of inferred personal ambivalence (see above), we suggest that these aspects of a relationship are more clear-cut. In other words, the chances for latent personal ambivalence to remain covert or unnoticed are rather low. A potential for personal ambivalence will give it a predominant status in relationships, so that family members feel an urgent need to deal with the situation. These aspects of the relationship are so central that they require action by the subjects.

The analysis shows almost no evidence of latent or covert personal ambivalence. In contrast to this finding, latent institutional ambivalence varies with respect to different parent-child relationships (see Table 8). Interestingly enough, latent ambivalences are here more common among children with regard to their parents than vice versa. The most striking result confirms our assumption that latent institutional ambivalence can be ascribed especially to son-mother relationships (56%) – a finding which merits more attention in future research.

Dealing with Ambivalences

The foregoing results confirm the existence of overt and covert expressions of ambivalence. The differences between parents and adult children and between genders are indicators of a multi-facetted picture of intergenerational relations which is also valid for the evaluation of ambivalence as such. Two further questions arise: What kind of correlations can be found with information on the quality of

Table 9. Ambivalence and Quality of Relationship (%).

	Quality of Relationship		
	Good	Fair	Poor
Often	29	73	72
Seldom	71	27	28

Source: Study 1999; $N = 120$ persons; $r = 0.000$; Spearman $= -0.419$.

relationships, and what kind of strategies do the respondents apply in order to deal with ambivalence?

The first of these two aspects is the subject of other studies (see, for example, Pillemer, Chap. 5 of this volume). The overall impression shows that higher frequencies of reported ambivalence go together with judgments about poorer quality of relationship. In one way, our results are in line with these findings, as shown by Table 9.

Because ambivalences may cause poor relationships, however, and because poor relationships may lead to feelings of being torn, it is difficult to determine the direction of causality in these situations. According to binary logistic regressions, the quality of a relationship is more likely to be regarded as an independent variable, and its effect is stronger for parents than for children. In addition, quality of relationship is also seen as a dependent variable. Further investigation should concentrate on the relation between these two causes. Are they linked with different kinds of relationships or families, or can we imagine combining temporal structures? One could imagine that latent ambivalences cause poor relationships and these relationships could result in manifest ambivalences that deteriorate the relationship even more. This thought points to the importance of seeing relationships in terms of their dynamic qualities. In this regard, Lettke (2000b) draws attention to the formative power of socialization for parent-child relationships throughout life. Lang (Chap. 8, this volume) concentrates on the quality of relationships in later phases of parent-child relationships and on the impact of "filial maturity." To clarify this issue, longitudinal data will be needed.

The same is true with respect to strategies people use to deal with ambivalence. The Konstanz model, as outlined in Chap. 2, shows a distinction of four basic types and uses two basic instruments to get information about this issue. The first instrument is developed around the question of how families handle ambivalent situations in general. The second instrument consists of two vignettes, namely the request for money and the choice of a partner/spouse as noted above. Answers could be given to statements that attempted to express maxims characteristic of the four strategies, namely: to preserve consensually ("solidarity"), to mature

Table 10. Strategies for Dealing with Ambivalences in Different Questions (%).

Management Questions	Strategies				N = Persons
	Solidarity	Emancipation	Atomization	Captivation	
1. How family members handle ambivalent situations	26	57	13	5	120
2. Reactions in case of requested financial support by children	54	28	10	7	116
3. Reactions to children's choice of a partner	65	25	3	8	110

Source: Study 1999.

reciprocally ("emancipation"), to separate conflictually ("atomization"), and to conserve reluctantly ("captivation").

Table 10 lays out the distribution of the answers. It shows, first, that two strategies dominate, namely solidarity and emancipation. This is plausible and understandable if we consider, first, that the interviewees were asked to respond to overt statements. We also cannot exclude the possibility that they are adapting their answers to what they perceive as a certain social desirability. Indeed, one may criticize the typology for not being neutral in regard of all four types. Nevertheless, we do acknowledge the existence of strategies that seem less favorable. Furthermore, the findings show a clear difference between the general statements and the answers to specific situations as described by the vignettes.

The strategies of solidarity and emancipation differ in the weight given to the poles of reproduction and innovation, whereas the two instruments differ in concrete situations. The findings suggest, therefore, that concreteness lowers the acceptance of or readiness for innovative conduct. Concomitantly, one may argue that both vignettes appeal to loyalty, which involves a stronger will to keep the family together, and therefore "solidarity" overbalances "emancipation." From a methodological point of view, the question is always open as to how close vignettes are to the real experiences of the respondents. Therefore, further research may include the development of alternative instruments.

Correlations Between Ambivalence Indicators

We conclude this presentation of the data with a matrix that summarizes correlations among the different measures of ambivalence used in this exploratory study.

This overview can also be interpreted as a tentative validation of the instruments (Table 11).

The major results can be summarized as follows:

- The frequency of being torn appears as a valid operationalization of ambivalence, as it has highly significant correlations with almost all other indicators: Respondents who report feeling torn judge these ambivalences as stressful, rate them negatively, and often are concerned about them. These respondents are most explicit about the ways they deal with ambivalence. (A closer look reveals that they often refer to the modes of captivation and atomization.) Furthermore, overtly reported frequent ambivalence correlates significantly with measures of indirect or covert ambivalence. Finally, these respondents accept conflict in their relationships.
- Significant correlations between judging ambivalence as stressful and the other indicators of ambivalence occur less often. This finding is consistent with the observation, mentioned above, that the existence of ambivalence as part of daily experience seems to be accepted. The frequency of experienced ambivalence is what makes it stressful and leads to a negative rating of ambivalence.
- The correlations with measures of the rating of ambivalence confirm and differentiate this finding. The comparatively high correlation with different modes of dealing with ambivalence (see above) is confirmed.
- "Dealing with ambivalence," differentiated according the four strategies, proves to be a central variable related to almost all the other indicators. This finding confirms the usefulness of attending not only to the existence of (overt and covert) ambivalence, but also to the pragmatic, action-related aspects of ambivalence, namely, how people cope with it. For the two major variables "frequency of ambivalence" and "dealing with ambivalence," distinguishing between the personal and the institutional dimensions of relationships seems to be fruitful. But the two dimensions also interact with each other. This finding suggests further efforts to develop instruments that will bear light on how these two dimensions are both independent and interdependent.

Our findings confirm that the concept of intergenerational ambivalence refers to a multi-layered phenomenon. The breadth of our approach and the instruments we used allowed us to identify some major dimensions. That this list can be expanded is shown in other research contributions to this volume. The strategy of "uncovering" seems appropriate, although the linkage of direct and indirect measurement needs further exploration. Contrary to the method (advocated in psychological literature) of using the direct measurement of ambivalence as a validity criterion for indirectly identified ambivalence and thereby classing it with the same phenomenon (see

Table 11. Intercorrelations of Different Indicators for Ambivalence (Spearman/Contingency Coefficient).

Variable 1	Variable 2								
	2	3	4	5	6	7	8	9	10
1. Frequency of ambivalence: (very often . . . never torn)	0.390***	-0.240***	0.336***	0.089	0.358***	-0.264***	-0.276***	0.015	-0.238***
2. Judgment of ambivalence: (very . . . not stressful at all)	1.000	-0.221***	0.320***	-0.072	0.233	0.078	0.084	0.010	0.060
3. Rating of ambivalence: (very positive . . . very negative)	—	1.000	-0.144**	0.004	0.348***	0.102	0.196**	-0.146**	0.068
4. Concern about ambivalence: (very often . . . never thought about)	—	—	1.000	-0.009	0.289***	-0.098	-0.070	0.042	-0.192***
5. Agreement with ambivalence: (consent with contradictory descriptions of relationships; highly agree . . . do not agree at all)	—	—	—	1.000	0.255*	0.073	-0.140**	-0.126*	-0.019
6. Dealing with ambivalence: (emancipation, atomization, captivation, solidarity)[a]	—	—	—	—	1.000	0.389**	0.450***	0.340***	0.224*
7. Intensity of indirectly measured institutional ambivalence: (-1 = low . . . 5 = high)	—	—	—	—	—	1.000	0.258***	0.015	0.126*
8. Intensity of indirectly measured personal ambivalence: (-1 = low . . . 5 = high)	—	—	—	—	—	—	1.000	-0.137**	0.035
9. Institutional ambivalence: (always rely on the past . . . always experiment with new ways)	—	—	—	—	—	—	—	1.000	0.195***
10. Personal ambivalence: (always try to preserve harmony . . . always allow conflicts to occur)	—	—	—	—	—	—	—	—	1.000

Source: Study 1999; $N = 255$ dyads.

[a] For correlations with this multiple nominally scaled variable the contingency coefficient is calculated, whose value is always between 0 and 1. All other values are ordinally scaled, so that in these cases the correlation coefficient is calculated according to Spearman.

* $p < 0.1$.

** $p < 0.05$.

*** $p < 0.01$.

Thompson, Zanna & Griffin, 1995, p. 373ff.), we emphasize the heuristic value of this distinction between direct and indirect measurement and point to new analytic possibilities. This is especially true if we attempt to explore in more detail the experience of ambivalence from the perspectives of different family members, and look more carefully at the strategies they develop together to deal with ambivalence in daily life.

SUMMARY AND CONCLUSIONS

Our exploratory quantitative study confirms that parents and their adult children experience ambivalence overtly and covertly in their relationships. These experiences vary from absence to different degrees of intensity and appear in different forms. Thus, in accordance with the other studies contained in this volume and research conducted elsewhere (Connidis, 2001; Daatland & Herlofson, 2001; Jekeli, 2002; Spangler, 2002), the empirical relevance and fruitfulness of the concept of ambivalence is confirmed. The general hypothesis that intergenerational relationships require dealing with ambivalence seems to be an appropriate general orientation for research.

Empirical work on intergenerational ambivalence is still in its beginning stage. Therefore, research by necessity is exploratory. This is true for the Konstanz project, the basic orientation of which relies heavily on conceptual work Lüscher presents in Chap. 2 of this volume. For this reason, its design and methods of analysis represent but one of several types of research strategy possible at this developmental stage of the approach. The characteristics of this strategy may be seen in the breadth of its research instruments, as presented in "Research Design and Instruments" above. Furthermore, as mentioned earlier, two different versions of the questionnaire were used: one for parents and one for adult children.

Beyond assessing ambivalence in direct and indirect ways, we tried to discover how the respondents deal with ambivalence and how they evaluate the experience of it. Given its breadth, the Konstanz project differs from research strategies that concentrate on one or two specific issues or on data representing one family role. Such strategies, in the early phase of an approach, have their advantages and their shortcomings. However, each of them may contribute in its way to the advancement of knowledge.

We see the guiding idea of "uncovering" ambivalence step by step, from the explicit to the implicit, as appropriate and useful. This approach undeniably stems from the origins of the concept of analysis in psychiatry and psychotherapy; in other words, it tends toward an interpretative mode of looking at results, even if those results are gained with quantitative instruments. Such a process allows us to build a bridge between using ambivalence as a general (interpretative) concept and using it as a research construct.

This research strategy also allows us to account for the fact that people may become aware of their ambivalence and develop a conscious attitude toward it. To that end, in the closing section of the interview, we asked people to look back and to comment on the topics we addressed. A large majority of respondents reported that our questions about ambivalence were clear, understandable, and referred to situations with which they were familiar – evidence of a widespread awareness of the topic at hand.

In this connection, it is of interest that ambivalence is judged as both positive and negative, or at least is accepted as a fact of life. This insight has to be discussed in light of the correlation, documented above, between the intensity of feeling torn and the quality of relationships. Attempts to get further clarification may include exploring the possibility of a curvilinear function between experiential awareness of ambivalence and the quality of relationships. We need to explore which conditions can activate socially creative behaviors as solutions to problematic situations, and for what kind of personalities. More generally speaking, the postulate of the interplay between creativity and ambivalence is an important and challenging issue that merits further attention on both the micro- and the macro-social levels of sociological inquiry.

Throughout our analysis, the distinction between the personal-subjective and the institutional-structural dimensions of ambivalence generated distinct findings. What does this mean? These two dimensions refer to differences in the experience, the perception, and the awareness of ambivalence. In our view, and in the light of our conceptual work, this confirms an understanding of ambivalence that includes not only emotions ("mixed feelings"), but also tension between social cognition and volitions.

One area with broad implications concerns the role of gender in the experience of ambivalence. On this point, our results, as well as those from other studies, are still far from being conclusive. The topic has several implications. One may speculate, for example, if men and women differ in their susceptibility to ambivalent feelings and thoughts. Gender research and theory is reluctant to attribute psychic traits to either of the sexes without controlling for social and cultural conditions and for the role of influence and power. But the question remains as to whether specific gender dyads are more vulnerable to ambivalence, as psychoanalytic writers have suggested historically. Our findings show results that can plausibly be interpreted to support that they are. We see, for example, more institutional ambivalence between sons and fathers and sons and mothers. The special relevance of the institutional component may be caused by specific cultural expectations both parents may have in regard to their sons because of societal customs. Yet, institutional ambivalence is also greater than subjective personal ambivalence between daughters and fathers and, to a lesser degree, between daughters and mothers. Hence, the correlation between ambivalence related to gender and ambivalence related to generational belonging may be high and may have its traces in historical developments – for instance, changes in the understanding of gender as such. The search for stronger theoretically coherent explanations about the connection and the interplay between gender (and age) is an important desideratum on the research agenda.

The Konstanz study makes an attempt to assess strategies of dealing and coping *with* ambivalence. Four different patterns, on different levels of sociality, have been deduced from the model. We applied two kinds of methods to reach the results, namely, questions about the approval and disapproval of general statements and reactions to vignettes presenting daily situations. Although the results confirm differences in the reactions, further explorations are needed; this is particularly true, for instance, with respect to the influence of social structures. Better results may also be found by focussing the attention on critical instances in the life course, and the history of the relationships (see Pillemer, Chap. 5 of this volume). To sum up:

- It is useful to differentiate between two dimensions or kinds of ambivalences: personal (referring to subjective closeness vs. distance) and institutional (referring to structural and institutional reproduction vs. innovation).
- It is also useful to distinguish between indicators for manifest (overt or direct) and latent (covert or indirect) ambivalences.
- It seems important to look closely at the interplay between gender and generation (e.g. between parents and adult children, and types of dyads).
- We need to explore further the connection between the intensity and the kind of ambivalence, the evaluation of the experience of ambivalence, and the quality of relationships. The interdependence may not be linear.
- We need further knowledge about the modes people use to deal and cope with ambivalence, including the processes of negotiations between the young and the old.

These desiderata will require multi-methodological approaches, further conceptual refinements and cooperative efforts.

ACKNOWLEDGMENTS

The research reported in this chapter has been supported by the Fritz-Thyssen-Stiftung (Köln) and the University of Konstanz. A list of all persons who have collaborated in the project is contained in the working paper [Arbeitspapier] 34.1 [Lüscher, K., Pajung-Bilger, B., Lettke, F., & Böhmer, S. (2000)] cited above. We would like to thank Paul Cash for his engaged, highly professional, and emphatic editorial support.

REFERENCES

Connidis, I. A. (2001). The intergenerational ties of gay and lesbian adults and step kin: A conceptual discussion. Paper presented at the 54th meeting of the Gerontological Society of America. Chicago, IL: Gerontological Society of America (November).

Daatland, S. O., & Herlofson, K. (Eds) (2001). *Ageing, intergenerational relations, care systems and quality of life – an introduction to the OASIS project*. Oslo: Norwegian Social Research.

Giarrusso, R., Stallings, M., & Bengtson, V. L. (1995). The "Intergenerational Stake" hypothesis revisited: Parent-child differences in perceptions of relationships 20 years later. In: V. L. Bengtson, K. W. Schaie & L. M. Burton (Eds), *Adult Intergenerational Relations: Effects of Societal Change* (pp. 227–263). New York: Springer.

Jekeli, I. (2002). *Ambivalenz und Ambivalenztoleranz* [Ambivalence and tolerance of ambivalence]. Osnabrück, Germany: Der andere Verlag.

Lettke, F. (2000a). *Generationenambivalenzen operationalisieren: Von der Messung zur Klassifizierung von Ambivalenz* [Operationalizing intergenerational ambivalences: From measurement to classification of ambivalence]. Arbeitspapier [Working Paper] 34.3. Universität Konstanz, Germany: Forschungsschwerpunkt "Gesellschaft und Familie."

Lettke, F. (2000b). Es bleibt alles anders: Zur prägenden Kraft der familialen Sozialisation auf die Generationenbeziehungen [Everything remains different: About the structuring power of familial socialization on intergenerational relations]. In: A. Lange & W. Lauterbach (Eds), *Kinder in Familie und Gesellschaft zu Beginn des 21sten Jahrhunderts* (pp. 131–154). Stuttgart, Germany: Lucius & Lucius.

Lettke, F. (2002). Ambivalenz und empirische Sozialforschung: Zum Verstehen quantitativer Sozialforschung. [Ambivalence and empirical sociological research: A contribution to understanding quantitative data]. *Sozialer Sinn, 1*, 137–151.

Lüscher, K. (1995). Postmoderne Herausforderungen der Familie [Postmodern challenges of the family]. *Familiendynamik, 20*, 233–251.

Lüscher, K. (2000). Ambivalence: A key concept for the study of intergenerational relations. In: S. Trnka (Ed.), *Family Issues Between Gender and Generations* (pp. 11–25). Luxembourg: European Communities.

Lüscher, K., & Pajung-Bilger, B. (1998). *Forcierte Ambivalenzen: Ehescheidung als Herausforderung an die Generationenbeziehungen unter Erwachsenen* [Forced ambivalences: Divorce as a challenge to intergenerational relationships between adults]. Konstanz, Germany: Universitäts-Verlag.

Lüscher, K., Pajung-Bilger, B., Lettke, F., & Böhmer, S. (2000). Generationenambivalenzen operationalisieren: Konzeptuelle, methodische und forschungspraktische Grundlagen [Operationalizing intergenerational ambivalences: Concepts, methods and basics for empirical research]. Arbeitspapier [Working Paper] 34.1. Universität Konstanz, Germany: Forschungsschwerpunkt "Gesellschaft und Familie."

Lüscher, K., Pajung-Bilger, B., Lettke, F., Böhmer, S., Rasner, A., & Pillemer, K. (2000). Generationenambivalenzen operationalisieren: Instrumente [Operationalizing intergenerational ambivalences: Instruments]. Arbeitspapier [Working Paper] 34.4. Universität Konstanz, Germany: Forschungsschwerpunkt "Gesellschaft und Familie."

Lüscher, K., & Pillemer, K. (1996). *Die Ambivalenz familialer Generationenbeziehungen: Konzeptuelle Überlegungen zu einem aktuellen Thema der familienwissenschaftlichen Forschung* [Ambivalence in intergenerational relations: Conceptual issues of an actual topic in family research]. Arbeitspapier [Working Paper] 22. Universität Konstanz, Germany: Forschungsschwerpunkt "Gesellschaft und Familie."

Lüscher, K., & Pillemer, K. (1997). Intergenerational ambivalence: A new approach to the study of parent child relations in later life. Arbeitspapier [Working Paper] 28. Universität Konstanz, Germany: Forschungsschwerpunkt "Gesellschaft und Familie."

Lüscher, K., & Pillemer, K. (1998). Intergenerational ambivalence: A new approach to the study of parent-child relations in later life. *Journal of Marriage and the Family, 60*, 413–425.

Spangler, D. (2002). *Ambivalenzen in intergenerationalen Beziehungen: Hochaltrige Mütter und deren Töchter.* Diplomarbeit [Ambivalences in intergenerational relationships: Old mothers and their daughters. Diploma thesis]. Berlin: Technische Universität Berlin.

Thompson, M. M., Zanna, M. P., & Griffin, D. W. (1995). Let's not be indifferent about (attitudinal) ambivalence. In: R. E. Petty & J. A. Krosnick (Eds), *Attitude Strength: Antecedents and Consequences* (pp. 361–386). Mahwah, NJ: Lawrence Erlbaum.

APPENDIX

This appendix summarizes the key measures in the Konstanz study. We would remind the reader that the items presented below are based on the instruments used in Germany, and thus may not appear completely idiomatically accurate. The original instruments are available from the authors in both a German and an English version.

Direct Measures of Ambivalence

These measures ask directly about overt ambivalences, i.e. ambivalences of which respondents were conscious in a variety of degrees. We asked respondents how often (*frequency*) they feel torn in a relationship (very often, often, now and then, seldom, never). Then we asked them to *judge* these situations with respect to how stressful they are (very stressful, stressful, only a little stressful, not stressful at all). Next, we asked respondents to *rate* these ambivalences in terms of whether they considered them positive or negative factors in their lives (very positive, more positive than negative, equally positive and negative, more negative than positive, very negative). As a measure of what we call their *concern* about ambivalence, we asked how often they had already thought about such things in the past (very often, often, now and then, seldom, never).

Next, we presented a series of possible contradictions in family relationships. We asked respondents to think about their relationship with a given person, and then report to what extent they agreed (highly, somewhat, partly, tend not to agree, not at all) with the statement. To uncover institutional ambivalences, we asked them to indicate the extent to which they agreed with each of the following statements:

[Person] lives her/his own life, but our relationship remains the way it has always been.

Between [person] and me everything remains the same, even when changes in relationships appear important and necessary.

[Person] can do whatever she/he wants, but she/he should not forget that family members have mutual obligations.

To assess ambivalences in the personal dimension, we asked them to indicate the extent to which they agreed (highly, somewhat, partly, tend not to agree, not at all) with each of these statements:

[Person] and I often get on each other's nerves, but nevertheless we feel very close and like each other very much.

My relationship with [person] is very intimate, but that also makes it restrictive.

Although I love [person] very much, I am also sometimes indifferent toward him/her.

Indirect Measures of Ambivalence

To assess ambivalence of which respondents may have been unaware, we developed a question that addresses a total of 14 attributes of ambivalence. The measure addresses the intensity of institutional and personal dimensions of ambivalence. In this measure, we asked respondents to think about their current relationship with a certain person and say to what extent the following descriptions apply (highly apply, somewhat apply, partly apply, tend not to apply, do not apply at all). To assess the institutional dimension, we asked about the applicability of attributes representing "reproduction" such as "inflexible," "restrictive," and "stuck in a rut," and of terms representing "innovation" such as "open to new experiences," and "changeable." To assess the personal dimension, we analogously asked about the applicability of attributes such as "loving," "warm," "solicitous," "reliable," and "close" in the sense of "convergence," and of terms such as "cool," "easy-going," "indifferent," and "superficial" in the sense of "divergence."

For the analysis of indirect ambivalence, we calculated a respective ambivalence value on the basis of 14 attributes for the institutional and personal relationship dimensions. First, on the basis of a factor analysis, for each subject we summed the ratings of the attribute of a pole, divided it through the number of attributes, and rounded off. For each pole we obtained an additive sum index (Cronbach's alpha amounts for the reproduction scale 0.636, for innovation 0.684, for convergence 0.874, and for divergence 0.837). For each relationship dimension, we calculated an ambivalence value from the respective two indices according to Griffin's formula $(P + N)/2 - (P - N)$, where P and N stand for the index values of respectively one pole. (See Thompson, Zanna & Griffin, 1995, p. 369. On methodological problems in connection with the measurement of ambivalence, see Lettke, 2002; Lettke & Klein, in this volume.)

Querying how family members respond when situations arise in which those involved aren't exactly sure how to act (because of ambivalence) provided five of the remaining ten attributes for the measure. We asked respondents to indicate which of the following statements applied to their family when such situations arise:

We almost always rely on the way we've done things in the past.

More often than not we rely on the way we've done things in the past.

We both rely on what has worked in the past and experiment with new ways.

More often than not we experiment with new ways.

We almost always experiment with new ways.

The remaining five attributes of the measure derive from asking the extent to which the respondent and the other family member will do everything possible to preserve family harmony, or whether they will allow conflicts to occur. We asked the respondents to think about themselves and a family member and say which of the following applies to how they and that family member act when situations arise that force them to choose whether to try to preserve family harmony or allow conflicts to occur:

We almost always try to preserve family harmony.

More often than not we try to preserve family harmony.

We both try to preserve family harmony and allow conflicts to occur.

More often than not we allow conflicts to occur.

We almost always allow conflicts to occur.

Dealing with Ambivalence

Our third set of measures addresses how families manage and deal with ambivalence. One measure gathers information about the general patterns of emancipation, atomization, captivation, or solidarity that may be present. We asked respondents to indicate which of the following courses of action best characterizes how members of their family respond to situations that appear contradictory to them, and to family relationships that seem to be ambivalent:

> We discuss things, above all in order to understand one another, even if in the end we cannot find clear solutions. (*emancipation*)

> Since discussions only make existing tensions worse, we prefer to avoid one another and do not talk about such things. (*atomization*)

> Our discussions usually end when someone forces the others to accept his or her viewpoint. (*captivation*)

> We look for a compromise until everyone is satisfied. (*solidarity*)

A second part of this measure employs two vignettes. The first is about parent's continuing financial support of their offspring, and the second is about the offspring's choice of partner.

The vignette concerning the issue of financial support addresses parents' uncertainty about how they should react when an adult child asks them for money, even though he/she is earning money and also lives a life that is otherwise independent of them. We ask if any of the respondent's children has asked for money, and if so, how the respondent reacted. Then we provide a choice of alternatives oriented toward the types of response suggested by the schematic model.

The vignette addressing how parents respond to their offspring's choice of (marriage) partner gathers information about a situation that can present a dilemma for parents. Parents often have mixed feelings about the partner their child has selected and vacillate between joy and reservations. Therefore, we asked: Has the choice of (marriage) partner of one of your children given you cause to think over the pros and cons of this choice?

In the children's questionnaire, we adapted the vignettes to the perspective of the children. In both cases, the answers that respondents were to choose between were worded so as to correspond to the patterns of the schematic model.

PART III:
AMBIVALENCE, CARE AND
INTERGENERATIONAL RELATIONS

8. THE FILIAL TASK IN MIDLIFE: AMBIVALENCE AND THE QUALITY OF ADULT CHILDREN'S RELATIONSHIPS WITH THEIR OLDER PARENTS

Frieder R. Lang

INTRODUCTION

Relationships between adult children and their aging parents are challenged when parents need help or care. As a consequence, adult children often experience a transition in their filial role as older parents experience functional losses and the children have to reorganize and restructure their relationship with them (Lang & Schütze, 2002). This filial task competes with other demands of midlife (such as family and career demands). As a consequence, the filial role in midlife may be associated with contradictory experiences in the relationship with one's parents, typically entailing a high potential for ambivalence.

This chapter develops the concept of ambivalence, as proposed by Lüscher and Pillemer (1998), with respect to the quality of relationships between middle-aged adults and their parents. Adult children's attitudes and behaviors towards their older parents indicate individual responses to contradictions in the filial role (e.g. the coexistence of conflict and closeness). This filial task can be described along two dimensions of children's relationship styles towards their older parents,

Intergenerational Ambivalences: New Perspectives on Parent-Child Relations in Later Life
Contemporary Perspectives in Family Research, Volume 4, 183–206
ISSN: 1530-3535/doi:10.1016/S1530-3535(03)04008-1

*2 paths -
 instrumental
 ; affective*

that is, instrumentality and affective strength. Finding ways of combining both
dimensions leads to individual solutions that may be associated with more or less
explicit ambivalent responses on the personal level. Depending on differences
in their relationship styles, for example, adult children may differ with respect
to how consistently or inconsistently they evaluate the relationship quality with
their parents.

TRANSITIONS IN THE RELATIONSHIP WITH AGING PARENTS DURING MIDLIFE

Children's relationships to their parents, in most cases, are lifelong and endure
even when children have left their parents' homes. Each phase of the child-parent
relationship is characterized by specific adaptive demands and challenges for both
the child and the parent. In early parenthood, individuals are forced to adapt their
lives to the new requirements of parental duties and responsibilities, while their
infant has to acquire the sensory-motor skills, functional capacities, and social
knowledge to grow and become an autonomous and socially integrated individual.
Throughout childhood and adolescence, children as well as parents experience role
transitions and demands associated with starting school, beginnings and endings
of friendships with peers, changing interests, first love, bodily changes in puberty,
and exit from school. The child-parent relationship faces another transition period
when aged parents eventually experience some of the hardships of old age. Adult
offspring are confronted with the question of how to respond to the possibility
that their parent might one day need daily care. This involves a transition that was
first described by Margaret Blenkner in 1965 as the filial task of midlife. Blenkner
noted that a shift in the filial role occurs in response to the aging experience of
one's parents.

Middle adulthood is characterized by many role transitions, or even turning
points, associated with marriage, divorce, parenthood, leisure, emerging health
problems, and employment shifts associated with career successes or failures (e.g.
Moen & Wethington, 1999). Some of the developmental tasks of midlife interfere
with each other, and some are even contradictory. Many midlife adults, for
example, experience a conflict between satisfactory family life and a successful
career. The filial task interferes further with such demands. Being confronted
with the task of taking responsibility for their aging parents may cause adult
children to feel torn between this and other demands that evolve from their family
and career commitments. Such contradictions of midlife have been characterized
as the sandwich position of middle-aged adults (e.g. Halpern, 1994; Rosenthal,
Martin & Matthews, 1996).

SOCIAL BEHAVIORS AND ATTITUDES OF ADULT CHILDREN TOWARDS THEIR OLDER PARENTS

How adult children respond to and behave toward their older parents' needs in everyday life is typically discussed with respect to specific characteristics of relationship quality such as emotional closeness (Lawrence, Bennett & Markides, 1992; Pruchno, Peters, Kleban & Burant, 1994), value consensus (e.g. Roberts & Bengtson, 1990), frequency of contact (Frankel & DeWit, 1989), or supportive exchanges (e.g. Ikkink, Tilburg & Knipscheer, 1999). Other researchers have pointed out potential negative or detrimental aspects of the adult child-parent relationship related to overprotection, neglect, violence, conflict, or interpersonal stress (Fingerman, 1996; Pillemer & Suitor, 1992; Suitor, Pillemer, Keeton & Robison, 1995). In general, two distinct perspectives on the parent-child relationship across the life course have emerged over the past decades. The *solidarity* perspective views positive relationships between adult children and older parents as a normative and adaptive response to the aging experience (e.g. Bengtson & Roberts, 1991; Rossi & Rossi, 1990; Silverstein & Bengtson, 1997). A second, more recent perspective is the model of *intergenerational ambivalence* (Lüscher & Pillemer, 1998) which emphasizes the pivotal function of irreconcilable contradictions as a determinant of the lifelong relationships between adult children and their parents. According to the ambivalence concept, intergenerational solidarity may be seen as just one among other prototypical responses to the filial task in midlife.

The Solidarity Model of Intergenerational Relationships

The solidarity perspective builds on a long tradition of empirical research findings suggesting that adult children not only keep contact with their parents, but continue to have close emotional relationships (e.g. Bengtson & Roberts, 1991), exchange frequent support with them (Eggebeen, 1995; Rossi & Rossi, 1990), and are among their primary caregivers when necessary. Models of solidarity imply the idea that solidarity between older and younger family generations is a desirable and adaptive strategy of coping with age-related challenges. Solidarity concepts sometimes neglect the fact, however, that some developmental tasks in midlife obstruct solidarity although they are relevant to adaptive regulation of intergenerational relationships. For example, maintaining autonomy and a sense of mastery has been identified as an important need and challenge across the entire life span (e.g. Baltes & Silverberg, 1994). On the personal level of experience, however, seeking to be autonomous while at the same time seeking solidarity may cause ambivalence.

Ambivalence in Intergenerational Relationships

The ambivalence perspective on intergenerational relationships underscores the most critical and central function of contradictions that characterize the relationships between family generations (Lüscher, 1998; Lüscher & Pillemer, 1998). A central suggestion of this perspective is that feelings of closeness and conflicts of interest both may result from individuals' social-structural and developmental opportunity structures. This implies that individuals have to seek adaptations that appear consistent with their needs, expectations, and goals.

Bengtson and Kuypers (1971), for example, proposed the concept of "developmental stake" to describe the divergence in mutual perspectives of the different generations in the family. Fingerman (1996) referred to observations of differing developmental processes between family members who belong to different generations as a "developmental schism." For example, needs and goals of middle-aged children may be quite different from needs and goals of their older parents. Middle-aged children often face developmental tasks associated with career demands or changes in their family households. Conversely, parents who are in their late life increasingly seem to seek ties that allow for emotionally meaningful experiences (e.g. Lang, 2001; Lang & Carstensen, 1994). The child's preferences for career issues and the parents' interest in maximizing emotional experience may not be easily integrated (Lang & Schütze, 2002).

The fundamental difference between the solidarity and the ambivalence perspectives lies in differing conceptions of the meaning of conflict. While the family solidarity tradition assumes that conflicts are necessarily detrimental to at least one of the partners in an intergenerational relationship, the perspective of intergenerational ambivalence suggests that experiences of strain and closeness structurally coexist within parent-child relationships. Two perspectives on ambivalence can be distinguished, one emphasizing a more institutional level, and the other a more personal level. On the institutional level, ambivalence refers to the structural contradictions in one partner's (e.g. the adult child's) life, which may not easily be resolved, if at all. On the personal level, ambivalence refers to an explicit expression of feeling torn between contradicting demands or tasks. This requires that children develop a response that entails an individual solution to the demands of the filial task. Such responses or behavioral styles of adult children towards their older parents, can be described along two dimensions of relationship styles.

Dimensions of Relationship Styles: Instrumentality and Affective Strength

A first dimension pertains to the degree of instrumentality or social control that characterizes the relationship. A second dimension relates to the affective strength.

Instrumentality in parent-child relationships refers to the extent to which children and parents respond to specific needs that could, in principle, also be fulfilled outside the parent-child dyad, and that are therefore not particular to the child-parent tie. That is, instrumentality relates to transactions associated, for example, with tangible, financial, or informational support exchanges between the child and the parents. The instrumentality of the parent-child relationship indicates the extent to which transactions or contact between children and their parents fulfill specific needs of one or both relationship partners. Whether such social transactions are perceived to be adequate, equitable, or desirable depends on subjective evaluations of the adult child and of the older parent. Such evaluations are determined and guided by different and partly competing social norms such as the norm of self-interest (Miller, 1999), the norm of reciprocity (Gouldner, 1960), the norm of filial responsibility (Blieszner & Hamon, 1992), the norm of social responsibility (Miller, Bersoff & Harwood, 1990), or the norm of social equity or justice (Montada & Lerner, 1996). Children's transactions with parents reflect the ambiguity associated with the task of complying with these differing social norms.

For example, the norm of filial responsibility refers to social expectations that children are willing to help or support their parents when needed. However, there is great latitude in how much help, support, responsibility or care is adequate to fulfill this norm. In many studies, parents were observed in the role of support-givers of their children rather than of support-receivers (e.g. Eggebeen, 1995). However, when parents become old and possibly need care, children are expected to take responsibility to help their parents, irrespective of their other obligations (e.g. Hamon & Blieszner, 1990). Simultaneously, the social norm of self-interest requires that individuals take care of themselves, which may be in conflict with norms of justice (Diekmann, Samuels, Ross & Bazerman, 1997) or the norm of social responsibility. Thus, instrumentality related to the compliance with social norms may create contradictions that require individuals to find adaptive solutions.

Affective strength refers to the extent to which adults experience intense emotions in relationships with their parents. Affective strength is unrelated to the valence of such emotional experience. That is, parent-child relationships are not uniformly positive but may also entail negative emotional experiences. Perceiving strains in the relationship to one's parents is a ubiquitous experience of children throughout their life cycles. This implies that adult children may feel very close to their parents, and yet experience at the same time much negative affect in that relationship. Mixed feelings towards one's parents represent the pivotal idea of lay conceptions of ambivalence. Note, however, that such emotional ambivalence indicates just one response to a more fundamental underlying ambiguity in the social worlds of adult children.

Adult children may respond to the contradictions of the relationship to their parents with less intense feelings and develop a sense of emotional autonomy or affective distance from their parents. Developing such distance from one's parents implies that the adult offspring leaves behind a perspective of being emotionally dependent on the parents' perspectives and starts viewing them as separate individuals who have their own biographies, personalities, and value systems. Consistent with this, Nydegger (1991) suggested that in the course of becoming independent adults, children proceed from a state of enmeshment with their parents to a state of feeling independent or resilient. In the most positive case, affective distance means that the child evaluates his or her sympathy for the parents independently of memories of earlier affective experience. However, affective distance may also refer to a state of emotional detachment from the parents and a lack of affection.

To sum up, instrumentality and affective strength are viewed as constituting distinct aspects of relationship styles towards older parents. In the following, patterns of relationship styles are explored as they emerge from three indicators of instrumentality (e.g. support exchange, personal norms) and from two indicators of affective strength (e.g. closeness, perceived strains) in adult children's relationships with their parents. It is predicted that such relationship styles differ depending on chronological age, occupational and family status of adult children, and, most importantly, with respect to indication of personal ambivalence.

One salient indicator of personal ambivalence refers to the level of inconsistency in adult children's satisfaction ratings with their parent. Inter-item variance is proposed here as an indicator of item-response inconsistency (cf. Austin et al., 1998). Typically, inconsistent answers by one individual to a set of items that aim at assessing the same underlying construct are treated as measurement error. However, such inconsistent individual responses across items may also point to systematic individual differences in this construct (Baumeister & Tice, 1988). Some individuals may express greater indecisiveness when rating similar items of the same construct in different ways. For example, individuals who feel moderate satisfaction with their parents differ from individuals who are sometimes satisfied and sometimes not satisfied with their parent. Consequently, inconsistent answers may reflect specific ways of responding to ambivalences in the relationship. For example, relationship patterns of strong instrumentality but weak affective strength (e.g. helping without liking), as well as patterns of weak instrumentality but strong affective strength (e.g. liking without helping) may be associated with greater inconsistency in subjective evaluations of the relationship. In addition, it is expected that patterns of relationship quality are also differently associated with adult children's willingness to engage in caregiving for their aging parents.

ADULT CHILDREN'S RELATIONSHIP QUALITY WITH THEIR OLDER PARENTS: AN EXPLORATORY REANALYSIS

Adult children of participants in the Berlin Aging Study (BASE) took part in a follow-up study (Lang & Schütze, 2002; Schütze & Wagner, 1995). From a total of 237 contacted adult children, 115 participants (48.5%) completed a mailed questionnaire on personal networks and on relationship quality with parents. Instrumentality in the relationship between adult children and their parents referred to supportive exchanges and the adult child's personal norm of family care. Affective strength pertained to a measure of perceived strains and a measure of emotional closeness with parents. The relationship styles of adult children towards their parents that result from levels of instrumentality and affective strength are then explored with respect to social motivations towards one's parents, contributions to caregiving of frail parents, relationship quality, and personal ambivalence. Personal ambivalence is indicated by the extent of internal inconsistency in adult children's evaluations of the relationship quality with their parents.

Participants

The mean age of adult children was 54.4 years (S.D. = 10.1; range = 28–73 years). Forty-seven participants (40.9%) had at least one living child. Most participants ($n = 82$; 71.3%) lived within the city boundaries of Berlin (i.e. in the same city as their parents), 24 (20.9%) lived outside of Berlin but in Germany and 9 children (7.8%) were currently living abroad. Most adults reported having a full-time job ($n = 51$; 44.3%) or a part-time job ($n = 16$; 13.9%), 48 participants (41.7%) did not report a professional employment. Forty-one participants (35.7%) were sons, and 74 (64.3%) were daughters. Daughters and sons were interviewed only with respect to one parent: In total, 29 daughters and 20 sons reported about the relationship to their mother; 45 daughters and 21 sons reported about the relationship to their father.

Age of their older parents was, on average, 84.7 years (S.D. $= 9.1$, $n = 83$; range $= 70$–101 years). Nine of the 83 parents were living in an institution (10.8%) and 37 parents (44.6%) lived alone.

Instruments

Support Exchange with Parent

Adult children rated, with yes or no, whether they had given to or received from their parent any of five instances of support during the past three months. These were: (1) helping with household chores; (2) helping with errands; (3) confiding about personal matters; (4) cheering up; and (5) tenderness (i.e. hugging or kissing). The sum composite of "yes" answers indicates the amount of received or given support. On average, adult children reported 1.8 (S.D. $= 1.6$) instances of support received from their parent and 3.5 (S.D. $= 1.7$) instances of given support to their parent.

Personal Norm of Family Caregiving Responsibility

Four items assessed the extent to which participants felt that the family should be held primarily responsible for taking care of older parents who need care (Schütze & Wagner, 1995). Participants indicated their agreement with each of four statements on a 7-point scale. Sample items are: "It is only natural that children give care to their parents when needed," and "Caregiving responsibilities for older people should not be burdened on the family" (inversely coded item). Internal consistency was alpha $= 0.85$. The mean composite was transformed in T scores ($M = 50$, S.D. $= 10$) with higher values indicating stronger personal norms of family caregiving.

Perceived Strains in Relationship with Parent

Six items from a subscale of a German questionnaire on quality of parent-child relationships (Angermeyer, Klusman & Walpuski, 1988) assessed the child's perceived strains and tensions with parent. Again, adult children rated items on a 7-point scale. Sample items are: "When being with my mother/father, there is much I have to swallow," and "There hardly passes a week without my being irritated about my mother/father." Internal consistency of the six items reached a Cronbach's alpha of 0.84. Normal distribution of scores was achieved after a logarithmic transformation. Higher values of T-transformed scores indicated more perceived strains with parents.

Emotional Closeness to Parent

The circle diagram questionnaire (Kahn & Antonucci, 1980) was used to assess the adult children's personal networks. The circle diagram consists of three concentric circles grouped around a small circle in which the German word "Ich" ("I") is written. Participants first included names of network members in each of the three circles. Participants then reported additional information on each network member, including sex, type of role relationship, age of partner, and frequency of contact. The circle placement of the participant's mother or father indicated the level of emotional closeness on a four-point scale ranging from 3 for "very close" to 1 for "not so close but still important" and 0 for not named in the circle diagram. About half of adult children felt very close to their parent ($n = 59$, 51.3%), 34 adults felt close (29.6%), six adults felt not so close (5.2%), and 16 did not report their mother or father in the circle diagram (13.9%). Reports on frequency of contact (including telephone contact) with the parent were transformed in a 5-point scale with 5 indicating: "daily contact" (reported by 8.7% of participants), 4 "several times in a week" (22.6%), 3 "weekly" (19.1%), 2 "at least monthly" contact (24.3%), and 1 "less than monthly" (25.2%).

Ideal vs. Real Contact Frequency with Parent

Adult children also reported what they believe is the ideal contact frequency with their parent. Ratings were transformed into a 5-point scale to match with the scale of real contact frequency. Differences between ideal and real contact frequency were obtained by subtracting ideal contact frequency from real contact frequency. Negative scores indicate that real contact frequency with parents is perceived as "less than ideal." This was true for 66.1% of participants. Positive scores indicate that the real contact frequency was "more than ideal." This pertained to 13.9% of participants.

Decisive Reasons to Have Contact with One's Parents

Adult children rated on a 7-point scale to what extent each of four reasons was decisive for them when seeking contact with their parent (Clausen, 1993): (a) "because she or he needs my help"; (b) "because I enjoy being with her or him"; (c) "because I need her or his help"; and (d) "because I feel obligated to do so." Participants used a 7-point scale with 7 indicating "very decisive" and 1 indicating "not decisive at all." Responses to each item were transformed into T scores, with higher values indicating greater importance of the respective reason to seek contact with parents.

Parents' Need of Care

Adult children reported the extent to which their parent needed help with activities of daily living (ADL) on a 5-point scale ranging from 1 for "absolutely does not need any instrumental help" to 3 for "needs some help with errands or in the house" to 5 for "needs much help and care on a daily basis." To differentiate between those adult children whose parent did not need any help (i.e. ratings 1 and 2: $n = 53$; 46.1%) and those adult children whose parent needed some help or care with daily tasks (i.e. rating 3, 4, or 5: $n = 62$; 53.9%), scores were dichotomized in subsequent analyses with 0 indicating no need of care and 1 indicating some need of help or care.

Caregiving Contribution
Adult's contribution to caregiving needs of parents were assessed with two open-ended questions: "Who gives care to the parent primarily?" and "Who assists the primary caregiver?" Among adults who had a parent in need of care, 37 reported to either partly or fully taking responsibility for parents' care needs; 25 adults did not report engaging in caregiving activities for their parents.

Satisfaction with Parents
Adult children's satisfaction with their parent and the relationship to their parent was assessed with 10 items. Most items were taken from an inventory of relationship quality between adult children and aging parents (Montada, Dalbert & Schmitt, 1988). Adult children used a 7-point scale with 1 indicating "no agreement" and 7 indicating "strong agreement" to rate items such as: (a) "I really like my mother/father"; (b) "My mother/father likes me very much"; (c) "My mother/father is full of warmth and affection for me"; (d) "My mother/father is someone to whom I feel most strongly connected"; (e) "I cannot stand my mother's/father's styles"; (f) "My mother/father is not very interested in me"; (g) "I do not feel much affection for my mother/father"; (h) "I have the sense that my mother/father rejects me"; (i) "My mother/father is not satisfied with what I do for her/him." In addition, participants used a 7-point scale (ranging from 7 for "very good" to 1 for "very bad") to respond to the question: "How would you evaluate your current relationship with your mother/father?" Internal consistency of all 10 items was alpha $= 0.90$. The mean composite of the scale was transformed into T scores with higher values indicating greater satisfaction with one's parent.

Inconsistency of Relationship Satisfaction with Parents
This factor was assessed as the inter-item variance of responses across all 10 items (Austin et al., 1998). The mean standard deviation across all 10 items was 0.974 (S.D. $= 0.631$). Low scores indicate consistency across all responses. High scores indicate inconsistency or variability across responses.

RESULTS

The statistical analyses were completed in two steps. In a first step, a cluster analysis on indicators of relationship quality with parents (i.e. emotional closeness, perceived strains, given support, received support, personal caregiving norm) was computed. Cluster solutions were then evaluated with a split-half technique of cluster analysis following a procedure suggested by Bortz (1993). In a second step of the statistical analyses, participants in the four identified patterns of relationship style were compared with respect to caregiving needs of parents, children's readiness to take responsibility for caregiving when needed, children's age, sex, marital status, and employment status.

Patterns of Relationship Styles with Older Parents – Cluster Analysis Findings

Five constructs indicating the attitudes and behaviors of adult children towards their parents were used to identify patterns of relationship style. Indicators were: (a) given support; (b) received support; (c) perceived strains with parents; (d) emotional closeness; and (e) personal family caregiving norm of children. Table 1 shows the correlations among these five constructs included into the cluster analyses on patterns of relationship style.

A hierarchical cluster analysis using the Ward algorithm and the squared Euclidian distance measure was computed. To validate the best cluster solution, a split-half technique of cluster analyses was applied (see Bortz, 1993). The centroid of each cluster solution was used to identify the clusters in the second half

Table 1. Correlations Among Indicators of Relationship Styles Towards Older Parents.

	1	2	3	4	5
1. Perceived strains with parent	–	−0.17	−0.08	0.11	−0.08
2. Emotional closeness of parent		–	**0.31**	**0.21**	**0.30**
3. Personal caregiving norm			–	**0.32**	**0.21**
4. Received support from parent				–	−0.04
5. Given support to parent					–
Means	2.7	2.2	1.8	3.5	3.2
S.D.	1.6	1.1	1.6	1.7	0.9

Note: n = 115. Coefficients printed in bold were significant ($p < 0.05$). Mean inter-item correlation is 0.11 (S.D. = 0.18).

Table 2. Replicability of Cluster of Filial Relationship Styles.

	Median Replicability (Kappa Values) of Types			
	2	3	4	5
Adult children ($n = 115$)	0.45	0.69	**0.75**	0.61

Note: Median replicability refers to kappa values of split-half cluster solutions for 10 random splits of the sample. Replicability coefficients differ significantly ($p < 0.05$, Wilcoxon signed ranks test for matched pairs).

of the sample with the k-means procedure. Cluster solutions were then compared across both randomized halves of the sample. Kappa values were determined to indicate the degree of replicability for each cluster solution. To maximize the reliability of this procedure, a total of 10 randomized split-half cluster analyses were computed.

As shown in Table 2, the four-cluster solution yielded the significantly best median replicability of 0.75 across the 10 split-half cluster solutions. Fig. 1 gives an illustration of the four observed clusters of relationship quality with older parents.

As shown in Fig. 1, adult children who belonged to the first relationship pattern reported below-average levels of closeness and supportive transactions with their parents. This pattern was named as "detached distanced" relationship style ($n = 29$; 25%). Adult children in the second pattern are characterized by giving more than average and by perceiving more than average strains with their parent, but receiving less support than other participants ("strained altruism"; $n = 25$; 22%). Participants of the third pattern were characterized by perceiving few strains, but feeling most close to their parent while reporting more supportive exchanges and personal caregiving norms than average ("close exchange"; $n = 37$; 32%). Participants who were classified into the fourth relationship pattern perceived fewer strains, received less support from parents, and expressed weaker personal caregiving norms than the average while at the same time they gave more support to parents than other adults ("resilient giving"; $n = 24$; 21%).

Patterns of Relationship Style – Gender, Age, and Satisfaction with Parents

The four relationship patterns were found to vary significantly by socio-demographic characteristics such as chronological age, sex, marital status, and employment status. The upper part of Table 3 gives an overview of the socio-demographic characteristics of adult children who belonged to the four patterns.

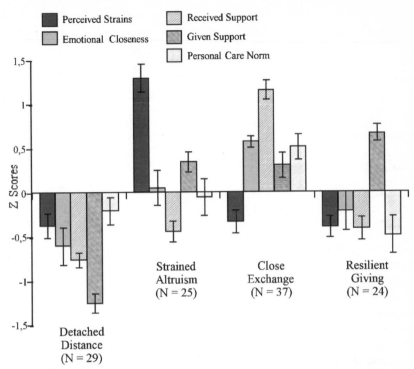

Fig. 1. Indicators Used to Identify Four Patterns of Adult Children's Relationship Styles Towards Their Older Parents in a Replicated Cluster Analysis ($n = 115$, Error Bars).

As shown in Table 3, composition by sex differed significantly between the four identified patterns ($\chi^2 = 27.3$, df = 9; $p < 0.01$). Mother-daughter dyads were most likely to be found in strained-altruistic patterns and least likely to be found in resilient giving patterns ($\chi^2 = 12.3$, df = 3; $p < 0.01$). Mother-son dyads were equally distributed across all four patterns ($\chi^2 = 0.8$, df = 3; n.s.). Father-daughter dyads were most likely to be characterized as resilient giving and least likely as strained altruism ($\chi^2 = 17.6$, df = 3; $p < 0.01$). Father-son dyads pertained most likely to detached-distant relationships and least likely to close-exchange relationships ($\chi^2 = 8.3$, df = 3; $p < 0.05$). In addition, there were also differences with respect to chronological age, marital status, and employment status. Resilient-giving offspring were older, more likely to be married, and least likely to have a full-time job than most other participants. In contrast, adult children in the close-exchange pattern were younger than average and the least likely to be married.

FRIEDER R. LANG

Table 3. Patterns of Relationship Styles Towards Older Parents: Socio-Demographic Differences, Ideal Contact Frequency, Satisfaction with Parents, and Inconsistency of Ratings.

	Detached Distance ($n = 29$)	Strained Altruism ($n = 25$)	Close Exchange ($n = 37$)	Resilient Giving ($n = 24$)	Sig.
Age of parent (years)	86	84	**81**	**89**	4.1**,c
Age of children (years)	56	53	**51**	**60**	4.6**,c
Sex dyads (percentage)					
Mother-daughter	17	**44**	32	*4*	
Mother-son	21	20	16	13	
Father-son	**35**	20	*8*	13	27.3*,b
Parents need care (%)	48	64	41	71	6.8d
Children are married (%)	75	76	*57*	**91**	8.9*,d
Have a child (%)	72	80	68	71	1.2d
Have full-time job (%)	55	56	46	*17*	10.2*,d
Real vs. ideal contact					
Ideal is less than real (%)	7	**32**	5	17	
Real is less than ideal (%)	**79**	56	70	54	13.4*,e
Satisfaction with parents					
Mean satisfaction[a] (S.D.)	50 (10)	42 (9)	**55** (8)	51 (7)	12.4**,c
Inconsistency of satisfaction with parents					
Inter-item S.D. of satisfaction (S.D.)	0.9 (0.6)	**1.4** (0.5)	*0.6* (0.6)	**1.2** (0.6)	11.3**,c
Mean inter-item correlation (S.E.)	**0.58** (0.01)	0.38 (0.02)	**0.63** (0.01)	*0.28* (0.02)	

Note: Scores printed in different style (italics, bold, normal) differ significantly ($p < 0.05$).
[a] T scores.
[b] Chi-square test with df = 9.
[c] F test with df (3;111).
[d] Chi-square test with df = 3.
[e] Chi-square test with df = 6.
*$p < 0.05$.
**$p < 0.01$.

The lower part of Table 3 displays adult children's evaluations of the relationship with their parents. On average, adult children with a *detached-distant* style reported lower satisfaction with the relationship to their parent than other adult children did. Adult children's responses to the satisfaction with parents scale represented a mean inter-item standard deviation of 0.92 (S.D. = 0.62). The mean inter-item correlation within this group ($r = 0.58$, S.E. $r = 0.01$) was stronger than in the whole sample ($r = 0.52$, S.E. $r = 0.01$). Adult children who displayed a *strained-altruistic* style, on average, expressed a preference for fewer contacts with their parents. Strained-altruists also expressed the lowest satisfaction with the relationship to their parents. Notably, mean inconsistencies of satisfaction ratings were found to be largest among adult children of this group ($M = 1.36$, S.D. $= 0.47$). In addition, inter-item correlations of the satisfaction scale, on average, were relatively low ($r = 0.38$, S.E. $r = 0.01$), indicating a strong heterogeneity within this group.

Adult children who reported a behavioral style of *close exchange* towards their parents expressed the strongest preference for more frequent contact with parents and the greatest satisfaction with their parents. Inconsistency in satisfaction ratings of this group was significantly lower as compared to the other groups ($M = 0.60$, S.D. $= 0.57$). Within this group, mean correlation among items were strongest (r(mean) $= 0.63$, S.E. $r = 0.02$), indicating great homogeneity. Finally, the *resilient-giving* adult children expressed a preference that parents live in greater geographical proximity, and that contacts occur more frequently. In the group of resilient-giving adult children, satisfaction with parents represented the average of the total sample. However, resilient-giving individuals were considerably inconsistent with respect to their satisfaction rating ($M = 1.23$, S.D. $= 0.56$). The mean inter-item correlation across the satisfaction scale was low (r(mean) $= 0.28$, S.E. $r = 0.02$), suggesting great heterogeneity of satisfaction ratings among participants in this group.

Decisive Reasons to Have Contact with Parents, Relationship Satisfaction, and Patterns of Relationship Quality

Figure 2 displays the distributions of decisive reasons for adult children to have contact with their parents separately for the four relationship patterns ($F(9; 333) = 10.1, p < 0.01, \eta^2 = 0.214$).

As shown in Fig. 2, reported reasons for having contact with parents were most consistent with other characteristics of the four relationship patterns. Adults who displayed a detached distance in relationship to their parent were not decisive with respect to the four reasons to have contact with their parent. In contrast, children of all other groups reported distinct reasons for having contact with parents. Children who displayed a close-exchange style towards parents claimed to contact parents primarily when needing help or when seeking pleasure. Strained-altruistic children had contact because their parent needed their help and because they

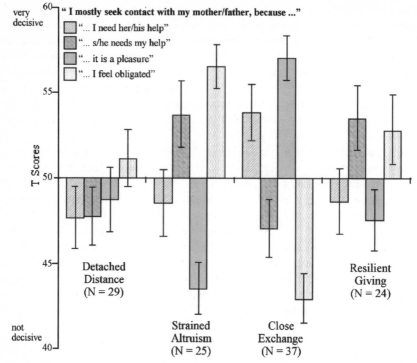

Fig. 2. Patterns of Relationship Style Towards Parents Differently Predict The Child's
Decisive Reasons for Seeking Contact with Parents (*n* = 115; Error Bars).

felt obligated. Resilient-givers reported that they seek contact with parents when
parents need help.

Giving Care to Parents and Patterns of Relationship Quality

As shown in Fig. 3, adult children's contribution to caregiving of parents who
needed care (*n* = 62) was lowest among detached-distant children and highest
among resilient givers and strained altruists ($\chi^2 = 8.9$, df = 3, $p < 0.05$).

The greater likelihood to contribute to caregiving among children in the resilient-
giving and the strained-altruistic patterns of relationship quality was found to
remain robust in a logistic regression after controlling for effects of age, sex, marital
status, and employment status. Among children in the close-exchange relationship
pattern, willingness to contribute to caregiving was not significantly different after
controlling for socio-demographic characteristics.

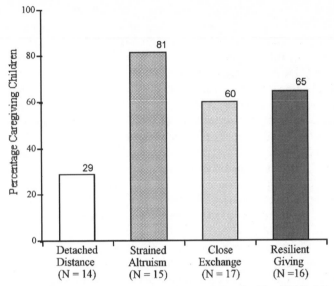

Fig. 3. Patterns of Relationship Style Towards Parents Predict The Child's Likelihood to Contribute to Caregiving of Parents, who are in Need of Care (*n* = 62, Percentages).

DISCUSSION AND OUTLOOK

Four distinct patterns of adult children's relationship styles towards their parents were identified based on indicators of support exchange, personal norms, and affective strength: close exchange, resilient giving, strained altruism, and detached distance. The four relationship styles were associated with motivations for seeking contact with parents and inconsistency of relationship satisfaction with parents. Each of the four relationship styles reflects an individual response to the challenges of the filial task in midlife. For example, among adults whose parents were in need of care, two specific relationship styles dominated, resilient giving to parents and altruistic solidarity with parents.

How Do the Four Relationship Styles Relate to
Intergenerational Ambivalence?

The four observed styles of adult children's relationship with their older parents are consistent with assumptions of the heuristic model of intergenerational ambivalence (Lüscher, 1998). According to this model, ambivalence is conceived

4 types of response:
atomization
captivation
normative (solidarity)
emancipation

as an implicit and underlying structure that may be experienced within any intergenerational relationship. For example, adult children may respond to ambivalence with detachment from their parents. Lüscher refers to this as *atomization*: "the fragmentation of the unit into its smallest parts, where coherence becomes very loose ..." (Lüscher, 1998, p. 19). This response is well reflected in the detached-distant relationship style of adult children towards their parents. Another prototypical response described in the heuristic model of ambivalence is *captivation*, which refers to feelings of being obligated to take responsibility while at the same time feeling strained by such responsibility. This response pattern is well reflected in the strained-altruistic relationship style of adult children.

A third prototypical response to intergenerational ambivalence according to the heuristic model of ambivalence is the expression of normative responsibility-taking and close supportive exchanges with the aged parent. This response pattern may be characterized as *solidarity* and is best reflected in the group of adult children who display a style of close exchange with their parents, characterized by strong emotional closeness and much supportive exchange. The relationship style of close exchange with parents comes closest to the concept of family solidarity (Bengtson & Roberts, 1991), at least with respect to the constructs of normative, functional, and affective solidarity. Adult children in this group were mostly satisfied with their relationship to their parents and displayed the strongest level of consistency across different ratings of satisfaction.

A fourth prototypical response pattern indicates *emancipation*, which refers to a pragmatic attitude of keeping an affective distance to one's parent while at the same time giving what is needed (Lüscher, 1998). This response pattern is reflected in the group of adult children who displayed a style of resilient giving towards their parents. Adult children of this group gave much support because they felt obliged to do so but also showed relative affective neutrality towards their parents. Overall, the four styles of adult children's relationships with parents represent the idea of two underlying dimensions that characterize the individual responses to contradictions of the filial role in midlife: Relationship styles represent specific ways of responding to instrumental and affective challenges in adult children's relationship with their older parents.

Manifestations of personal ambivalence as indicated by the degree of inconsistency in ratings of satisfaction with parents were differently distributed across the four relationship styles. In particular, the strained-altruistic and the resilient-giving relationship styles were found to have the greatest potential for perceptions of ambivalence (i.e. inconsistency). Both styles were associated with a basic and strong attitude towards giving support to one's parents. The strained-altruistic style differed from the resilient-giving style with respect to the affective dimension. Resilient givers, on average, appeared to maintain a more positive evaluation of their parents as compared to the group of strained altruists, who experienced more strain in the relationships to their parents. Overall, the relationship style of strained altruism comes closest to the classical notion of being "caught in the middle" (Rosenthal et al., 1996) that may characterize the kind of personal ambivalence experienced in this group. Strained altruism as well as resilient giving may serve to illustrate that ambivalence should not be equated with the occurrence of conflict in intergenerational relationships (Lüscher & Pillemer, 1998).

When interpreting the findings of this study, some caveats need to be considered. Findings are based on a post-hoc analysis of data. It is not possible to conclude in what ways the four observed relationship styles represent actual ways of coping with (institutional or personal) contradictions in the filial roles of adult children after they have occurred. Further research is warranted that more explicitly aims at assessing the instrumental and affective constraints and challenges that characterize the life situations of middle-aged children of older parents before adult children develop individual responses to such contradictions.

None of the four styles observed in this study could be characterized by a simultaneous coexistence of both emotional closeness and perceived conflict. Again, this observation ought to be interpreted with caution. The measures used in this study may not have fully captured the multifaceted and complex nature of mixed or torn feelings of adult children towards their older parents. Future studies should make use of more sophisticated methods to detect contradictions in children's attitudes and behaviors towards parents – such as, for example, the explicit use of vignettes suggesting ambivalent situations of the filial role.

Clearly, longitudinal study designs are needed for further exploration of such considerations. For example, use of event sampling techniques may be used for identifying those mechanisms, through which experiences of ambivalence in the relationship to parents are regulated and coped with across different situations. Note also that the present study focused exclusively on the adult child's perspective. However, relationship behaviors always depend on at least two partners (Aquilino, 1999). Therefore, perspectives of both the aging parent and the adult child are needed to better understand the mechanisms of intergenerational ambivalence.

Gender Differences in Relationship Styles

The four relationship styles were differently composed of sons and daughters. Most of the strained-altruistic relationship styles related to mother-daughter dyads, while most of the detached-distant styles pertained to father-son dyads. Resilient giving was predominantly observed in father-daughter dyads. These findings reflect the "gendered" structure of the relationship quality between adults and their older

202

FRIEDER R. LANG

parents (e.g. Rossi & Rossi, 1990; Silverstein, Parrott & Bengtson, 1995). For example, mother-daughter relationships are characterized by affective strength that entails both positive and negative emotional experience throughout the life course (e.g. Fingerman, 1996; Rossi & Rossi, 1990). Children's relationships with fathers were found to be generally less affectionate and more focused on specific instrumental exchange. However, this finding appears to be in contrast to other findings on father-son dyads (e.g. Nydegger & Mitteness, 1991; Welsh & Stewart, 1995).

Father-son dyads may be most complex and tense when sons are in adolescence and early adulthood (Nydegger & Mitteness, 1991). In later years, however, when sons have settled in their lives, a son's relationship with his father may have become less stressful but at the price of increased affective distance. Such distance itself may be associated with ambivalent experiences. Consistent with this point, an overwhelming majority of detached-distant adult children desired to have more frequent contact with their parent than they actually had in the present.

A Developmental Perspective on the Filial Role in Midlife: Outlook

The findings underscore the important role of gender-specific differences in parent-child relationships across the life span. Daughters and sons adapt in gender-specific ways to the aging experiences of their mother or father (e.g. Silverstein et al., 1995). The four identified relationship styles prototypically reflect responses to different sets of contradictions of the filial role in midlife. Some speculations on the developmental trajectories of such relationship styles over the life course can be suggested. For example, when mastering the challenges associated with the filial task, adult children might change the pattern of their relationship with their parents and move from a pattern of strained altruism to a pattern of resilient giving or close exchange. Clearly, longitudinal data is needed to specify in greater detail the pathways and development of the different relationship patterns throughout early, middle, and later adulthood.

The proposed ambivalence model of the filial task acknowledges the diversity and plurality of relationships between adult children and their older parents. For example, patterns of intergenerational solidarity appear to be more prominent among adult children with parents who are "young-old" rather than "old-old." Close-exchange styles may be more characteristic of child-parent relationships where resources flow from the older generation to the younger generations (e.g. Eggebeen, 1995). This is underscored by the fact that adult children in the close-exchange group received more support from parents than vice versa. Furthermore, adult children in this group, on average, reported that they prefer to seek contact with parents when in need of help. These adult children may not have developed much instrumental and emotional independence from their parents (Lang & Schütze, 2002). For example, when parents become old and eventually frail, adult children may experience greater contradictions in the relationship with their parents.

Ambivalence may be a less subtle experience when adult children actually have to cope with the challenges of caregiving responsibilities for frail parents while at the same time mastering career and other family demands. Individuals may then cope in individual ways with these contradictions of the filial role. Relationship styles with older parents such as resilient giving, strained altruism, and detached distance underscore that besides solidarity there are also other prevalent patterns of responding to the filial task in midlife.

ACKNOWLEDGMENTS

The research reported is part of the study "Adult Children with Older Parents" that was conducted by Yvonne Schütze and Michael Wagner as part of the multidisciplinary Berlin Aging Study (BASE). BASE is conducted by the Committee on Aging and Societal Development (AGE) of the Academy of Sciences and Technology in Berlin in collaboration with the Free University Berlin, Berlin, Germany, and the Max Planck Institute for Human Development and Education, Berlin, and is financially supported by the Department of Research and Technology (13 TA 011 and 13 TA 011/A) and the Department of Family and Senior Citizens. Parts of this manuscript were presented at the 2nd Humboldt Foundation Trans-Coop International Workshop on Intergenerational Ambivalence in Konstanz, Germany, February 24–27, 2000. I am grateful to Yvonne Schütze for making the data available. I am also thankful to Karen Fingerman and David Klein for comments on an earlier version of this manuscript. Correspondence concerning this article should be addressed to Frieder R. Lang, Professor of Developmental Psychology, Martin-Luther-University Halle-Wittenberg, Institute of Psychology, Brandbergweg 23A, 06099 Halle/Saale, Germany, or via e-mail to: flang@psych.uni-halle.de.

REFERENCES

Angermeyer, M. C., Klusmann, D., & Walpuski, O. (1988). The causes of functional psychoses as seen by patients and their relatives: II. The relatives' point of view. *European Archives of Psychiatry and Neurological Sciences, 238,* 55–61.

Aquilino, W. S. (1999). Two views of one relationship: Comparing parents' and young adult children's reports of the quality of intergenerational relations. *Journal of Marriage and the Family, 61,* 858–870.

Austin, E. J., Deary, I. J., Gibson, G. J., McGregor, M. J., & Dent, J. B. (1998). Individual response spread in self-report scales: Personality correlations and consequences. *Personality and Individual Differences, 24,* 421–438.

Baltes, M. M., & Silverberg, S. B. (1994). The dynamics between dependency and autonomy: Illustrations across the life-span. In: D. L. Featherman, R. M. Lerner & M. Perlmutter (Eds), *Life-Span Development and Behavior* (Vol. 12, pp. 41–90). Hillsdale, NJ: Erlbaum.

Baumeister, R. F., & Tice, D. M. (1988). Metatraits. *Journal of Personality, 56,* 571–598.

Bengtson, V. L., & Kuypers, J. A. (1971). Generational difference and the developmental stake. *Aging and Human Development, 2,* 249–260.

Bengtson, V. L., & Roberts, R. E. (1991). Intergenerational solidarity in aging families: An example of formal theory construction. *Journal of Marriage and the Family, 53,* 856–870.

Blenkner, M. (1965). Social work and family relationships in later life. In: E. Shanas & G. F. Streib (Eds), *Social Structure and the Family: Generational Relations* (pp. 46–59). Englewood Cliffs, NJ: Prentice-Hall.

Blieszner, R., & Hamon, R. R. (1992). Filial responsibility: Attitudes, motivators, and behaviors. In: J. W. Dwyer & R. R. Coward (Eds), *Gender, Families, and Elder Care* (pp. 105–119). Thousand Oaks, CA: Sage.

Bortz, J. (1993). *Statistik* (4th ed.). Berlin: Springer.

Clausen, J. (1993). Kontinuität und Wandel in familialen Generationen-beziehungen [Continuity and change in intergenerational relationships within the family]. In: K. Lüscher & F. Schulzheis (Eds), *Generationenbeziehungen in postmodernen Gesellschaften* (pp. 111–124). Konstanz, Germany: Universitätsverlag Konstanz.

Diekmann, K. A., Samuels, S. M., Ross, L., & Bazerman, M. H. (1997). Self-interest and fairness in problems of resource allocation: Allocators vs. recipients. *Journal of Personality and Social Psychology, 72,* 1061–1074.

Eggebeen, D. J. (1995). Patterns of support given by older Americans to their children. In: S. A. Bass (Ed.), *Older and Active: How Americans over 55 are Contributing to Society* (pp. 122–168). New Haven, CT: Yale University Press.

Fingerman, K. (1996). Sources of tension in the aging mother and adult daughter relationship. *Psychology and Aging, 11,* 591–606.

Frankel, B. G., & DeWit, D. J. (1989). Geographic distance and intergenerational contact: An empirical examination of the relationship. *Journal of Aging Studies, 3,* 139–162.

Gouldner, A. W. (1960). The norm of reciprocity: A preliminary statement. *American Sociological Review, 25*(2), 161–178.

Halpern, J. (1994). The sandwich generation: Conflicts between adult children and their aging parents. In: D. D. Cahn (Ed.), *Conflict in Personal Relationships* (pp. 143–160). Hillsdale, NJ: Lawrence Erlbaum.

Hamon, R. R., & Blieszner, R. (1990). Filial responsibility expectations among adult child-older parent pairs. *Journals of Gerontology, 45,* P110–P112.

Ikkink, K. K., Tilburg, T. V., & Knipscheer, K. C. P. M. (1999). Perceived instrumental support exchanges in relationships between elderly parents and their adult children: Normative and structural explanations. *Journal of Marriage and the Family, 61,* 831–844.

Kahn, R. L., & Antonucci, T. C. (1980). Convoys over the life course: Attachment roles and social support. In: P. B. Baltes & O. G. Brim (Eds), *Life-Span Development and Behavior* (pp. 254–283). New York: Academic Press.

Lang, F. R. (2001). Regulation of social relationships in later adulthood. *Journal of Gerontology: Psychological Sciences, 58B,* P321–P326.

Lang, F. R., & Carstensen, L. L. (1994). Close emotional relationships in late life: Further support for proactive aging in the social domain. *Psychology and Aging, 9,* 315–324.

Lang, F. R., & Schütze, Y. (2002). Adult children's supportive behaviors and older parents' subjective well-being – A developmental perspective on intergenerational relationships. *Journal of Social Issues, 58,* 661–680.

Lawrence, R. H., Bennett, J. M., & Markides, K. S. (1992). Perceived intergenerational solidarity and psychological distress among older Mexican Americans. *Journals of Gerontology, 47,* S55–S65.

Lüscher, K. (1998, July). A heuristic model for the study of intergenerational ambivalence. Arbeitspapier [Working Paper] 29. Universität Konstanz, Germany: Forschungsschwerpunkt "Gesellschaft und Familie."

Lüscher, K., & Pillemer, K. (1998). Intergenerational ambivalence: A new approach to the study of parent-child relations in later life. *Journal of Marriage and the Family, 60,* 413–425.

Miller, D. T. (1999). The norm of self-interest. *American Psychologist, 54,* 1053–1060.

Miller, J. G., Bersoff, D. M., & Harwood, R. L. (1990). Perceptions of social responsibilities in India and in the United States: Moral imperatives or personal decisions. *Journal of Personality and Social Psychology, 58,* 33–47.

Moen, P., & Wethington, E. (1999). Midlife development in a life course context. In: S. L. Willis & J. D. Reid (Eds), *Life in the Middle* (pp. 3–23). San Diego: Academic Press.

Montada, L., Dalbert, C., & Schmitt, M. (1988). Ist prosoziales Handeln im Kontext Familie abhaengig von situationalen, personalen oder systemischen Faktoren? [Is prosocial behavior in the family context depending on situational, personal, or systemic factors?]. In: H. Bierhoff & L. Montada (Eds), *Altruismus: Bedingungen der Hilfsbereitschaft* (pp. 179–205). Goettingen, Germany: Hogrefe.

Montada, L., & Lerner, M. J. (Eds) (1996). *Critical issues in social justice.* New York: Plenum.

Nydegger, C. N. (1991). The development of paternal and filial maturity. In: K. Pillemer & K. McCartney (Eds), *Parent-Child Relations Throughout Life* (pp. 93–112). Hillsdale, NJ: Erlbaum.

Nydegger, C. N., & Mitteness, L. S. (1991). Fathers and their adult sons and daughters. *Marriage and Family Review, 16,* 249–256.

Pillemer, K., & Suitor, J. J. (1992). Violence and violent feelings: What causes them among family caregivers? *Journals of Gerontology, 47,* S165–S172.

Pruchno, R. A., Peters, N. D., Kleban, M. H., & Burant, C. J. (1994). Attachment among adult children and their institutionalized parents. *Journals of Gerontology, 49,* S209–S218.

Roberts, R. E., & Bengtson, V. L. (1990). Is intergenerational solidarity a uni-dimensional construct? A second test of a formal model. *Journals of Gerontology, 45,* S12–S20.

Rosenthal, C. J., Martin, M. A., & Matthews, S. H. (1996). Caught in the middle? Occupancy in multiple roles and help to parents in a national probability sample of Canadian adults. *Journals of Gerontology: Social Sciences, 51B,* S274–S283.

Rossi, A., & Rossi, P. (1990). *Of human bonding: Parent child-relation-ships across the life course.* Hawthorne, NY: Aldine and Gruyter.

Schütze, Y., & Wagner, M. (1995). Familiale Solidarität in den späten Phasen des Familienverlaufs [Family solidarity in later phases of the family cycle]. In: B. Nauck & C. Onnen-Isemann (Eds), *Familie im Brennpunkt von Wissenschaft und Forschung* (pp. 307–327). Neuwied, Germany: Luchterhand.

Silverstein, M., & Bengtson, V. L. (1997). Intergenerational solidarity and the structure of adult child-parent relationships in American families. *American Journal of Sociology, 103,* 429–460.

Silverstein, M., Parrott, T. M., & Bengtson, V. L. (1995). Factors that predispose middle-aged sons and daughters to provide social support to older parents. *Journal of Marriage and the Family*, *57*, 465–475.

Suitor, J. J., Pillemer, K., Keeton, S., & Robison, J. (1995). Aged parents and aging children: Determinants of relationship quality. In: R. Blieszner & V. H. Bedford (Eds), *Handbook of Aging and the Family* (pp. 223–242). Westport, CT: Greenwood Press.

Welsh, W. M., & Stewart, A. J. (1995). Relationships between women and their parents: Implications for midlife well-being. *Psychology and Aging*, *10*, 181–190.

9. AMBIGUOUS LOSS AND AMBIVALENCE WHEN A PARENT HAS DEMENTIA

Pauline Boss and Lori Kaplan

INTRODUCTION

... the astonishing struggle that lasts forever

Francine Du Plessix Gray (2000).

... the simultaneous sound of ... both harmonies and dissonances

Kurt Lüscher (2000).

I wanted to watch my father die because I hated him. Oh, I loved him ...

Sharon Olds (1992).

The concept of absolute absence or presence is not meaningful for adult children when an elderly parent's mind is slipping away. This is a time of increased *ambiguity* in the family boundary, in which the status and roles of the demented elder are no longer clear, and often not agreed upon. Not knowing if a parent is absent or present, the potential for *ambivalence* in the adult children is high. Within this intergenerational context, the main thesis of this paper is that the ambiguous loss of a parent with dementia provides fertile ground for increased ambivalence in intergenerational relations (Boss, 1999, 2002). The heightened ambiguity and resulting ambivalence may or may not be problematic, depending on cognitive awareness and family processes.

Intergenerational Ambivalences: New Perspectives on Parent-Child Relations in Later Life
Contemporary Perspectives in Family Research, Volume 4, 207–224
Copyright © 2004 by Elsevier Ltd.
All rights of reproduction in any form reserved
ISSN: 1530-3535/doi:10.1016/S1530-3535(03)04009-3

In this paper, we first discuss these propositions by reviewing the ambiguous loss perspective. Then, we clarify distinctions between the constructs of ambiguity and ambivalence and show how they link conceptually. Along the way, we also discuss theoretical roots of the constructs in family stress theory (Boss, 2002, 2003). Finally, we propose implications for practice. Our overall objective is to further understand about how to minimize anxiety, depression, and intergenerational conflict when a parent's presence in the family remains ambiguous due to dementia. We use the inclusive term "dementia" because our focus is on the effects of psychological absence from dementia generally, rather than on the effects of one particular disease.

There are three reasons why studying the situation of ambiguous loss from dementia can broaden our understanding of ambivalence in intergenerational family relations. First, dementia is common today, as elders live longer and thus are more likely to develop cognitive and affective impairment. Second, adult children (often daughters and daughters-in-law) increasingly must care for elderly parents at home because nursing homes and assisted-living facilities are costly and can wipe out family savings. Third, studying an extreme example is useful when developing theory.

From our research and clinical observations, we have seen that family members frequently attempt to resolve the tension of living with an ambiguously lost elder by resorting to one of two extremes. They may deny the elder's illness and expect them to act as they always did. Or they may act as if the ill parent is already dead and gone, prematurely closing out the demented elder from the family system by acting as if they are already gone – no more visits, no more conversation, no more touching. Boss elsewhere gives an example of the latter: an adult son who said he could get along with his demented father as long as he considered him a piece of furniture and didn't bump into him. Sadly, this son was prematurely closing his father out of the family boundary and processes (Boss, 1999) (Fig. 1).

In this chapter, we propose a different approach. We suggest that family members can learn to increase their tolerance for ambiguity as a way to minimize their ambivalence. Specifically, this means learning to live with an elderly parent's psychological absence while appreciating that he or she is still physically present. It also means becoming more cognitively aware of one's understandable ambivalence about the elderly parent's partial presence.

THE BOSS PERSPECTIVE OF AMBIGUOUS LOSS

Boss's theoretical perspective, developed over the past 25 years, presents ambiguous loss as a special kind of loss with two basic configurations. In the

---

Ambiguity

Family members have no clarity about the absence or presence of a family member due to an externally caused situation. The ambiguity, however, is not always problematic for all families.

Qualities of the phenomenon

  Location: inside the family (structure and process)

  Source: external context

  Effect: confuses family roles and boundaries; blocks family processes of problem
       solving, communication

  Assessment: primarily familial/couple, but also may be individual

Ambivalence

An individual family member's conflicted feelings and emotions (fluctuating or simultaneous) such as love/hate, joy/sadness, anger/guilt. Ambivalence is problematic especially if not recognized by the individual experiencing it.

Qualities of the phenomenon:

  Location: inside the individual

  Source: from one's internal conflict about an external situation (in this case,
       ambiguous loss)

  Effect: Immobilizes, freezes grief; decision making and other behaviors,
       especially if ambivalence remains unconscious.

  Assessment: individual

Fig. 1. The Difference Between Ambiguity and Ambivalence.

first, a family member is physically missing and is perceived by family members as *physically absent but psychologically present* because their status as dead or alive, retrievable or irretrievable, remains unclear. Kidnapped or missing family members illustrate this type of ambiguous loss in its catastrophic form, while divorce and giving a child up for adoption are more common examples. In the second type of ambiguous loss, which is the focus of this chapter, a family member is perceived as *physically present but psychologically absent*. The person is present bodily in the family, but mind and memory are gone. This type of ambiguous or partial loss is what we see when an elderly parent is afflicted with Alzheimer's disease or another dementia (Boss, 1999; Boss, Caron, Horbal & Mortimer, 1990; Caron, Boss & Mortimer, 1999; Kaplan, 2001; Kaplan & Boss, 1999).

In this chapter, we focus only on the ambiguous loss of an older person who is psychologically absent while physically present – specifically an elderly parent who is physically with the family, but cognitively and emotionally gone. Such ambiguity provides fertile ground for increased ambivalence in intergenerational relations. Understanding the link between ambiguity and ambivalence will shed light on the tensions and immobilization that are common in such confusing family structures, and also provide a lens for envisioning therapeutic or preventive interventions.

Elsewhere Boss has written that when people suffering from an ambiguous loss seek treatment from professionals, they often are diagnosed for symptoms such as anxiety, depression, and somatic illnesses (Boss, 1999). What might be missed is *why* they have these symptoms. Questions that therapists and medical professionals might add to their assessment are: Could the external sociological context account for the symptoms? Is there a structurally ambiguous situation that could cause ambivalent feelings and behaviors in a family member? Is it "normative" for an adult child whose parent has dementia to find it difficult to make decisions, to stop being preoccupied with the ill parent, and to carry on as usual with spouse and children? Not everyone is affected to the same degree by the ambiguity surrounding a loss; but the indecisiveness, depression, anxiety, and marital tensions in adult children of demented parents might be more fruitfully explored through a lens focused less on pathology and more on the effects of stress from ambiguity. Hansen and Johnson (1979, pp. 582–603) provide one interesting early discussion on the stress of ambiguity on families (see also Boss, 1977, 1980a, b, 1987).

AMBIGUITY AND AMBIVALENCE: DEFINITIONS AND DISTINCTIONS

Ambiguity and ambivalence are conceptually distinct but interconnected constructs (Boss, 1999, 2002). Depending on research design, either can be an independent or a dependent variable. In this discussion, we place ambivalence as an outcome of an ambiguous situation, specifically ambiguous loss. The goal for intervention and therapeutic change is minimization of ambivalence to lower the incidence of individual and family problems.

Weigert (1991) distinguished ambiguity from ambivalence by noting that ambiguity is something one knows (cognition), while ambivalence is something one feels (emotion):

> Although both contradictory ideas and contradictory feelings may be experienced together, it is important to distinguish between knowing ambiguity and feeling ambivalence (p. 42).

Weigert saw ambiguity as an inability to make sense of a socio-cultural contradiction, thus interfering with cognition. This is what we call "knowing," or more precisely, "not knowing" whether an elderly parent is absent or present in one's family life.

On the other hand, Weigert sees ambivalence as an *affective* phenomenon, one often interpreted as individual failure. It results from one's internal conflict in the face of a confusing situation. Here Boss's conceptual work on ambiguous loss fits what Weigert (1991) calls "a sociological source of ambivalence" (p. 44).

Weigert (1991) writes: "Psychological ambivalence stands between socio-cultural contradictions and the decisions and actions of individuals" (p. 43). We interpret this to mean that the socio-cultural ambiguities regarding a demented parent's absence or presence create a psychological ambivalence that impedes a family member's cognitive decision-making and actions. This is the process by which an ambiguous structural situation leads to individual ambivalence and subsequent systemic immobilization. From a sociological perspective, the family boundary is no longer maintainable, roles are confused, and family tasks remain undone. From a psychological perspective, decisions are delayed, coping is blocked, grief is frozen, and ambivalence is high (Boss, 1999, 2002). The sociological source of ambivalence from dementia could, we believe, refer to the increasing incidence of dementia as a result of science and technology making it possible for elders to live longer, thus increasing the incidence of dementia and ambiguous loss for the younger generations.

What Swiss psychiatrist Eugen Bleuler called ambivalence may often be a normal reaction to a relentlessly ambiguous situation, rather than personal pathology. With an increasing life span, burgeoning numbers of adult children experience the ambiguous loss of a parent with dementia. As their elderly fathers or mothers with dementia become psychologically absent while still physically present, adult children are filled with mutually conflicting thoughts and feelings. Anticipating even more loss, they both cling and push away. They often feel guilty, because they fluctuate between wanting their parent to live – and die. They both accept and reject the caregiving role. And they are confused about family roles and status.

"Is this still my parent, or someone more like a child? Am I still the child, or am I now the parent? How can I be a good spouse and good parent to my own children, while I am trying to be 'the good child' caring for my parent?" Such questions reflect an ambivalence which can, if intense enough, immobilize and freeze family members into a behavioral and psychological helplessness. Depending on one's professional discipline, this immobilization can be operationalized as immobilization, frozen grief, low mastery, helplessness, hopelessness, blocked coping, blocked decision-making, anxiety, and/or depression.

What is most important for practitioners to recognize is that ambivalence can come from a source *outside the person*. Rather than attributing high ambivalence to individual pathology, we propose that the cause is often a situation of ambiguity beyond the individual or family's control. The tension that results from conflicting emotions can become overwhelming. By externalizing the blame, we could decrease feelings of guilt, a most problematic characteristic of ambivalence (Fig. 2).

Physical Absence	Physical Presence
Psychological presence	Psychological Absence
"Leaving without good-bye"	"Good-bye without leaving"
	Unexpected, catastrophic
• war (missing people)	dementias
• natural disasters	chronic mental illnesses
• kidnapping, hostage-taking	brain injury
• addictions	
• imprisonment	affairs
• desertion; disappearance	depression
	More common, everyday
• immigration; migration	home sickness
• divorce	preoccupation with work
• adoption	obsession with computer games; TV
• travel, relocation for work or military	
• young people leaving home	
• an elderly mate being institutionalized	

Fig. 2. Types of Ambiguous Loss.

loss structure
→ greater
ambiv.

The Link Between Ambiguity and Ambivalence

Our premise is that an ambiguously bounded structure or organization (one more difficult in which to maintain boundaries) can lead to ambivalent feelings, emotions, or behaviors on the part of the members of that organization. Thus the higher the ambiguity in family structure, the more ambivalence the individual(s) within that structure will experience. Boss (1999) writes about the sociological perspective of this linkage between ambiguity and ambivalence:

> The resolution [minimization] of ambivalence essentially hinges on helping a person to recognize his or her conflicting feelings. From the psychological view, the problem is that some feelings about a relationship [such as hoping a parent will live or die] are usually more accessible to an individual's consciousness than are others. But sociology provides another perspective. According to this view, ambivalence results from mixing elements of cognition (such as social definitions of roles and status) and emotion (which includes conditioning and learned behavior). Thus, from this perspective, ambivalence can result from the ambiguity of not knowing who is included in the structure that is supposed to be one's family. Conflicting impulses that may exist inside the psyche are often a consequence of this uncertainty (pp. 61–62).

With no clear course of action, ambivalence thrives. Offspring dread the death of a parent who has been hopelessly ill for some time; but, at the same time, they hope for death and an end to the waiting. This is understandable; but if the link is not recognized, guilt and anxiety may result.

A clinician's task is to normalize this dynamic with intentionality and awareness as part of the family's coping process. Chronic ambiguity concerning the absence or presence of a demented elder can lead to ambivalent feelings and behaviors in the younger generation; such feelings are best brought to the surface, talked about, and normalized if the family is to minimize anxiety, depression, guilt, and conflict.

We agree with Lüscher and Pillemer (1998) that ambivalence is a normal part of intergenerational family processes, but we propose that there are times when there is too much ambivalence and that it can cause trouble. While conflicted feelings are normal in human relationships, they can also be overwhelming when the status of a loved one remains ambiguous for years (Boss, 1999).

Theoretical Roots in Family Stress Theory

What we have written about ambiguous loss and ambivalence fits into the preventive realm of family stress theory, where the family's goal is to cope and remain resilient in spite of such stressors as ambiguous loss (Boss, 1987, 1992, 2002; Boss & Greenberg, 1984). To add to the tension as family members see the family boundary in differing ways, there is often conflict in the intergenerational family. In 1980, Boss wrote about "normative family stress across the life span," a topic not unrelated to what Lüscher and Pillemer (1998) address as the impossibility of an idealized form of solidarity in intergenerational relations across the life course.

Boss (1980a, b) holds that of absolute absence or absolute presence (and thus absolute solidarity) rarely occurs in families, especially during transitions when family members begin to exit (or enter) the family system. Indeed, when an elderly parent becomes demented, his or her exit begins; but it may not be completed for years, even decades. About family boundary changes over time, she wrote:

> With an obvious focus on normative function more than on normative structure, it is suggested that there may be no universals in family structural boundaries beyond the original formation of the boundary and its eventual dissolution through [death]. Between these two stages, it is variance more than universality that allows for coping and functional adaptation across the life span.... there may indeed be more than one way for families to reach the same end goal...(1980, p. 449).

Challenges to each family's capacity for boundary maintenance and solidarity in the face of change come from normal human maturation (Boss, 1980a, b), as well as from unexpected sources such as dementia. Such challenges require continuing reassessment of who is viewed as "in the family" if the family is to maintain functional interactions. The continual recalibration of the family boundary with increased tolerance for ambiguity in membership comprises the family management approach to coping. Remaining resilient in the face of long-term ambiguity is a major challenge for intergenerational families when elders suffer from dementia.

To complicate matters, there is diversity in how families perceive and reassess their ambiguous loss that results from Alzheimer's disease (Boss, Kaplan & Gordon, 1995). In a preliminary study with Ojibway Indian women who were caring for a family elder, we heard few negative descriptors about the elder's dementia. The Native women objected to the word "burden" and even to the word "stressful" when describing caring for an elder with dementia. Instead, they viewed the intergenerational situation as "the natural circle of life." Clearly, more research is necessary to document the differences in tolerance for ambiguity and levels of ambivalence in culturally diverse samples of intergenerational families.

A CURRENT DEBATE

A current debate in American psychology centers on whether coping is conscious or unconscious (see Cramer, 2000, 2001). We take interest in this debate because it relates to our conceptualization of ambivalence as being sometimes a conscious, normal response to an ambiguously lost parent, but at other times an unconscious repression, and thus problematic.

If repression (and other responses) can be *both* intentional (conscious) or unconscious, then we suggest that ambivalence also can be both conscious and unconscious. Newman (2001) and others believe that intentionality and awareness are not necessarily independent features of cognitive processes. Furthermore, experts believe that the switch from an unconscious reaction to a conscious, intentional one is a gradual process, not a categorical event (Erdelyi, 2001).

Debaters challenge Cramer's earlier idea (2000) that coping strategies (for reducing stress) are solely intentional and that defense mechanisms (for defending against stress) are solely unconscious. Yet, Cramer (2001) makes the point: "To not make the distinction between a mechanism that defends one against stress vs. strategies that help one cope with stress will causes a confusion of concepts which must be distinct before they can be empirically studied and measured" (p. 763). Erdelyi (2001) counters by saying, "Freud actually felt compelled to warn against the inference that repression is only a conscious process. For Freud, defensive repression could be conscious or unconscious" (p. 762). Cramer (2001) responds: "... the features of being unconscious and unintentional are critical for defining the defense mechanism and for differentiating this process from other methods of adaptation" (p. 763). The debate continues.

In the case of defending against ambiguous loss and the ensuing ambivalence that often results in families where an elder has dementia, we see in our research and clinical work what Erdelyi (2001) calls the *unfolding of consciousness* with no one instant when the reaction becomes intentional or cognitive. Nevertheless, we also see some "light-bulb" moments in family members who suddenly see the light and begin to do something different in their interactions with their demented elder. What matters is that change can occur either way – from a gradual unfolding of consciousness as well as from a sudden epiphany. Both processes can serve to lower ambivalence and somatic outcomes.

In the following case, it is difficult to separate the two processes:

Marie spends part of every day with her demented mother and then drives back to her own home, ten miles away. As she drives, she tells herself that she can do everything that needs to be done for her mother. She can handle it! But a few days later, she breaks out with shingles, a painful viral infection that can be exacerbated by an accumulation of stress. Marie does not link her symptoms to her ambivalence about caring for her mother. But after two more attacks of shingles and her doctor's inquiries, she suddenly sees the connection. She begins to recognize that she can't "do it all" and that her mother needs other help as well. Marie recognizes how exhausted she has become, and decides to reach out to professional care. For Marie, there was both a light-bulb experience and a gradual recognition that her body was telling her that she couldn't continue to care for her mother alone. It was simply too much work, given that she also was employed full-time. She began to enlist some professionals to care for her mother, and with their help continued to visit her mother, but with no further episodes of shingles. Today, Marie reacts to the ambiguity surrounding her mother's presence with more intentionality and awareness of not only her mother's needs, but of her own as well. Intentionally, she flows with the mood her mother is in at the time she visits, and is less concerned with her own agenda. Intentionally, she withdraws when she is overtired and returns when she is feeling more rested. Marie now does this consciously, with significant self-assessment and discussions with others along the way. We call this cognitive coping; others call it conscious coping.

There is indeed a complicated interplay between conscious and unconscious processes of stress reduction and self-protection when struggling with ambiguity and ambivalence. Discerning which construct represents intentional *coping* and which represents unconscious *defense* is no doubt necessary for research, but less necessary for clinical work. As family therapists (rather than in our role as researchers), we tend to agree with Newman (2001) who writes that "efforts to decide whether a psychological phenomenon should be categorized as a coping process [conscious] or a defense mechanism [unconscious] are more likely to hamper than facilitate efforts to understand the complicated interplay of processes involved in stress-reduction and self-protection" (p. 761).

As clinicians, we therefore have lessened our concern over whether ambiguity and ambivalence are conscious or unconscious phenomena. Instead, we intervene to bring both constructs into the family's awareness through labeling each, linking them, normalizing the stress, and then encouraging the family to start talking together to find new meaning in their structure and processes. When ambiguity and ambivalence are consciously recognized, people are more able to cope with them, manage the situation, and revise the family structure to include the ambiguity. Without such awareness and coping skills, the guilt and anxiety from the ambivalence can become overwhelming and symptomatic.

Implications for Clinical Practice

According to Canadian psychiatrist Vincenzo Di Nicola (1997), our task as family therapists is to "give structure and meaning to a family's predicament." This is challenging when a situation of ambiguity cannot be clarified and ameliorated. From the perspective of social constructionism, we merge Lazarus's cognitive appraisal model with the ambiguous loss model to help families reconstruct their view of the demented elder's presence and place in the family (Boss, 2002; Lazarus, 1977). But it is first important to distinguish between ambivalence as a normative aspect of intergenerational family life and ambivalence as a problematic aspect that needs treatment.

WHEN AMBIGUOUS LOSS AND AMBIVALENCE ARE PROBLEMATIC

From the stress perspective, there are five reasons why the ambiguity surrounding an elder's absence or presence can make offspring feel ambivalent and thus more prone to anxiety, depression, and intergenerational conflict.

(1) *Ambiguous loss is confusing*, so family members become cognitively immobilized and unable to make rational decisions. Adult children may cope by going to opposite extremes. They may, for example, try to effect premature closure, that is, closing out the demented elder, even acting as if the elder is already dead. Or they may go into denial, acting as if nothing is wrong with the parent, and still allow them to cook or drive in spite of the dementia.

(2) *The ambiguity surrounding the loss blocks the coping process.* Without knowing what the problem is, the first step in the coping process (cognition) cannot occur. Life is put on hold; family celebrations and rituals are canceled; daily routines stop.

(3) *Ambiguous loss eludes the customary markers of life or death*, so a family member's distress goes unnoticed by the larger community. People in a culture that values mastery and problem solving will often become impatient with ambiguous losses, and with those who must live with them; thus families most often are left on their own to find a way to cope.

(4) *Ambiguous loss causes even the strongest families to question their view of the world as fair and logical.* The search for meaning is difficult and requires family discussions and personal contemplation. In some cases, the meaning of the situation is that there is no rational meaning, that the situation will never make sense, and that one can learn to live with that.

(5) *Ambiguous loss of long duration is physically and emotionally exhausting for family members.*

For these reasons, there are times when the social-structural ambiguity in an intergenerational family in which an elder has dementia leads to problems. Somatic illnesses are one example. But canceled family rituals and celebrations illustrate what can occur at the systemic intergenerational level:

> For the K family, Christmas had always been a time when their large family gathered at the home of the parents. This year for the first time the adult children did not spend Christmas together, opting instead to spend it with their own families, and Mr. and Mrs. K went for the day to their eldest daughter's home. The family explained that the change resulted from their experience the Christmas before, which seemed too stressful and confusing for their father who had Alzheimer's disease. Normally he had held the central role in the fathering, deciding when gifts were to be handed out and personally selecting each present from under the tree. Last year, however, he

had been extremely irritable, had difficulty remembering why the family had gathered, and spent the time when presents were distributed sitting in another room. The family had difficulty pinpointing how the decision to spend Christmas separately was made for this year, explaining that it simply seemed to be agreed on by everyone (Boss, Caron & Horbal, 1988, p. 135).

Prior to her wedding anniversary, Mrs. L contacted each member of the family to say she did not want to celebrate the anniversary this year. She explained that her husband would not remember the date and would feel confused if a fuss were made. But when the day arrived, her husband was confused about why the anniversary was not celebrated. He said, "I'm still here, you know." Although it was not discussed further at the time, each of the adult children separately identified this date as one of the highest stress points of the past year (Boss, Caron & Horbal, 1988, p. 135).

Ambiguous loss is a problem when family dynamics freeze in place while members wait for a clarity that never comes. In such cases, adult children are caught up in a quandary of ambivalence and guilt, not knowing what they should do or how to make sense out of the situation. One moment they feel hate for a parent who demands so much care; the next they feel love and compassion. One moment they wish for recovery; the next for death. Guilt follows. The conflicting emotions, especially if not within their awareness, can immobilize. Intergenerational family life is put on hold or becomes conflictual.

As stated earlier, we agree with Lüscher and Pillemer (1998) that ambivalence in intergenerational relations is normal; we also submit that there is a level of ambivalence beyond which family members individually and collectively are put in jeopardy. But rather than viewing symptoms – or even the ambivalence – as the whole story at this time, we propose that researchers and clinicians use a more contextual view of each individual and family's unique situation. This broader lens will help us to better understand the complexities of when ambivalence in intergenerational families becomes a problem, and to target preventive interventions toward that information.

WHEN AMBIGUOUS LOSS AND AMBIVALENCE ARE NOT PROBLEMATIC

Having discussed the negative effects, it is also important to emphasize that not everyone is troubled by ambiguous loss and ambivalence, even when they must live with it on a long-term basis. It may be that factors such as personality type, learned experiences, religious and cultural beliefs, and socialization account for different responses. More research is needed to determine these effects. With a growing population of elders with dementia across diverse cultures, and thus an increased number of elderly parents who need care, it is important to identify systematically how adult children of varying cultural beliefs and personality characteristics maintain their own quality of life in spite of caring for a demented elder.

Future family-stress research involving ambiguity and ambivalence could fruitfully include measures of personality (e.g. Loevinger & Wessler's (1970) measure of ego development or Adorno et al.'s (1950) measure of authoritarianism and intolerance of ambiguity) as well as measures of social setting or culture. Donald Levine (1985) reports that researchers found "sociological implications for ambiguity tolerance" (p. 13) when they studied the subculture of a military base (where there is little tolerance for ambiguity) vs. a college setting (where students were accustomed to contradictory ideas). It appears that the adaptive qualities of "ambiguity tolerance" (thus minimizing ambivalence) may depend not only on one's personality, but also on one's context, and culture (Boss, Kaplan & Gordon, 1995).

Researchers must also study diverse situations of parental illness regarding the adult child's *lack* of ambivalence when his or her parent is slipping away. For example, Leichtentritt and Rettig (1999) found some daughters who had no ambivalence even about speeding up the death process when a parent with a terminal illness is in severe pain:

> We reached an understanding, my mother and I . . .. The day her pain will reach the level she can no longer endure, I will present her request [for medication that will end her suffering) to the physician. We give ratings to the level of pain. Today she described her physical and emotional suffering to be the level of "7" (p. 395).

It may be more common that an offspring's level of ambivalence is reduced if his or her ill parent is in severe pain. The varying contexts of parental illness, along with cultural beliefs and values, learned behavior, religious beliefs, and personality characteristics, may determine which family members can best tolerate ambiguity with minimal ambivalence.

Although such distressing situations are not what Lüscher and Pillemer wrote about when they proposed ambivalence as a normal condition of intergenerational relations, we propose that: (1) the link between ambiguity and ambivalence is crystallized in such extreme situations; and (2) even in such extreme transitions as the end of life, when ambiguity of absence and presence is likely at its peak, ambivalence is normal. That is, the ambivalence is a normal reaction to an abnormal situation.

The inability to "wrap things up" and get on with couple and family processes – decision making, coping, grieving, finding meaning – is a dilemma for many adult children today. Cohler reports that he sees this "hunger for the clarity of closure" in his clinical work with families of Alzheimer's patients: "They can't grieve yet because their parent is still alive, although barely." (personal communication, March 16, 2000). In such extreme situations of ambiguity, the ambivalence is understandable but can become problematic without some intervention.

By incorporating the constructs of ambiguity and ambivalence into the Contextual Family Stress Model (Boss, 2002), researchers and clinicians can study the normalcy (yet potential trouble) of ambivalence in intergenerational relations when family boundaries are in transition – such as when an elderly parent has dementia. Knowing that ambivalence can be exacerbated by a sociological source of ambiguity means that the confusion is not the offspring's fault. Knowing that their situation has a name – ambiguous loss – and that this is not of their doing, adult children act with less guilt and anxiety about the mixed feelings they understandably have when the parent they once knew is gone. They are less resistant and more open to adaptation.

Our emphasis in this paper on the importance of "knowing" implies a bias toward a psycho-educational model of intervention and what some call "cognitive coping" (Boss, 1993). What this means is that people can learn to cope by shifting how they perceive a distressing situation. The reconstruction of the family, when there is ambiguous loss, can only take place perceptually in their minds, because there is no official verification of status – such as a death certificate or a medical diagnosis of remission. To understand and manage the ambivalence, the main window for intervention, when an ambiguous loss persists, lies within a cognitive shift both individually and as a whole family. (For other strategies for support and intervention, see Boss, 1999, 2002.)

While we also recommend emotion-focused coping (especially centering on family ritual and symbolic interacting) we find that teaching distressed families about cognitive coping provides a beginning for empowering them when their situation is unalterably ambiguous. In clinical work, we all too often observe distress between husband and wife or between an adult child and his or her young offspring as an elder nears death. Identifying the family's situation as one of ambiguous loss (and as not their fault) and their ambivalent feelings as normal (if in their awareness) offers the intergenerational family a way to see the same situation in a new light, this time with less guilt and distress. Talking together, they begin to cope and make some meaning out of what they are experiencing.

MEASUREMENT ISSUES

To intervene appropriately and cost-effectively, health care professionals need to know which adult children are most at risk. We have operationalized family members' perceptions of psychological presence or absence as "boundary ambiguity" (Boss, 1977, 2002; Boss & Greenberg, 1984; Boss, Greenberg & Pearce-McCall, 1990. See also Touliatos, Perlmutter & Strauss, 1990). Fravel et al. also developed an observational coding system for boundary ambiguity (2000). Qualitative assessments are also being used (Boss, Dahl & Kaplan, 1996; Fravel & Boss, 1992; Garwick, Detzner & Boss, 1994; Kaplan & Boss, 1999).

Measuring ambivalence is a challenge. It is difficult to measure because individuals are not always aware that they are feeling ambivalent. Combining qualitative methods with quantitative ones in a multi-methods approach may be most useful and ethical, especially when studying families and individuals who are deeply distressed and symptomatic.

A major measurement question remains concerning how ambivalence is defined. Is ambivalence a variable of *fluctuations* between two opposite feelings/emotions ("sometimes I feel love for my parent, and at other times I feel hate"); or is ambivalence a variable of *simultaneous* conflicting feelings and emotions? This is an empirical question that begs for further study with adult children of elders with dementia. Based on clinical observations, we propose that the ambivalence of "fluctuating" conflicting feelings and roles (sociological ambivalence) may manifest fewer problems, whereas the psychological unconscious ambivalence of "simultaneous" conflicting feelings (psychological ambivalence) may be more symptomatic. Clearly, an interdisciplinary team approach would be useful to test these propositions.

CONCLUSION

Building on past research, we have argued that the greater the adult child caregiver's ambiguity regarding the demented elder's psychological presence or absence, the greater the adult child's ambivalence and increased depressive and/or somatic symptoms. While ambivalence is a normal outcome for many, it becomes troublesome, and even pathological, when depression or somatization results as family members become confused, exhausted, and immobilized.

The goal of this chapter has been to develop theory to inform interventions with intergenerational families stressed by having to live with an ambiguous loss. We discussed the conceptual linkages between ambiguity and ambivalence, and we explored when they are a problem and when not. We emphasized the need for families to become aware of ambiguous loss (naming it) and of the understandable ambivalence family members may feel as dementia creates a partial loss of the parent. Once the link between ambiguous loss and ambivalence is understood and becomes part of the adult children's cognitive awareness, the coping process can begin, and the intergenerational family has a better chance of living well in spite of a parent's dementia. In recognizing and understanding ambiguous loss and the ambivalence it may cause, these two phenomena can become more normal parts of intergenerational family life and thus more manageable.

We clearly do not propose eliminating ambiguity or ambivalence in intergenerational families, but propose instead a conceptual model for developing interventions to help intergenerational family members increase their tolerance for ambiguity to minimize their ambivalence. Helping adult children to *consciously* recognize their mixed emotions helps them to minimize and manage indecisiveness and immobilization. While the illness of dementia cannot be cured, family members can indeed reconstruct their perception of family with new meaning. They can carry on with intergenerational family life – the rituals, celebrations, and day to day interactions – even with a parent who is clearly not present.

REFERENCES

Adorno, T. W., Frenkel-Brunswick, E., Levinson, D. J., & Sanford, R. N. (1950). *The authoritarian personality*. New York: Harper.

Boss, P. (1977). Psychological father presence in families experiencing ambiguity of boundary. *Journal of Marriage and the Family, 39*(1), 141–151.

Boss, P. (1980a). Normative family stress: Family boundary changes across the life-span. *Family Relations, 29*(4), 445–450.

Boss, P. (1980b). The relationship of psychological father presence wife's personal qualities, and wife/family dysfunction in families of missing fathers. *Journal of Marriage and the Family, 42*(3), 541–549.

Boss, P. (1987). Family stress: Perception and context. In: M. Sussman & S. Steinmetz (Eds), *Handbook on Marriage and Family* (pp. 695–723). New York: Plenum.

Boss, P. (1992). The primacy of perception in family stress theory and measurement. *Journal of Family Psychology, 6*(2), 113–119.

Boss, P. (1993). Boundary ambiguity: A block to cognitive coping. In: A. Turnbull, J. Patterson, S. Behr, D. Murphy, J. Marquis & M. Blue-Banning (Eds), *Cognitive Coping, Families and Disability* (pp. 257–270). Baltimore, MD: Brooks.

Boss, P. (1999). *Ambiguous loss*. Cambridge, MA: Harvard University Press. (German translation by S. Stolzel, *Leben mit ungelostem Leid*, 2000, Munich, Germany: C. H. Beck.)

Boss, P. (2002). *Family stress management* (2nd ed.). Newbury Park, CA: Sage.

Boss, P. (Ed.) (2003). *Family stress: Classic and contemporary readings*. Newbury Park, CA: Sage.

Boss, P., Caron, W., & Horbal, J. (1988). Alzheimer's disease and ambiguous loss. In: C. Chilman, F. Cox & A. Nunnally (Eds), *Families in Trouble*. Newbury Park, CA: Sage.

Boss, P., Caron, W., Horbal, J., & Mortimer, J. (1990). Predictors of depression in caregivers of dementia patients: Boundary ambiguity and mastery. *Family Process, 29*, 245–254.

Boss, P., Dahl, C., & Kaplan, L. (1996). The meaning of family: The phenomenological perspective in family research. In: S. Moon & D. Sprenkle (Eds), *Research Methods in Family Therapy* (pp. 83–106). New York: Guilford.

Boss, P., & Greenberg, J. (1984). Family boundary ambiguity: A new variable in family stress theory. *Family Process, 23*(4), 535–546.

Boss, P., Greenberg, J., & Pearce-McCall, D. (1990). *Measurement of boundary ambiguity in families.* (University of Minnesota Experiment Station Bulletin No. 593–1990, Item No. Ad-SB-3763.) St. Paul, MN: University of Minnesota.

Boss, P., Kaplan, L., & Gordon, M. (1995). Accepting the circle of life. *Center for Urban and Regional Affairs Reporter, 25*(3), 7–11.

Caron, W., Boss, P., & Mortimer, J. (1999). Family boundary ambiguity predicts Alzheimer's outcomes. *Psychiatry, 62,* 347–356.

Cramer, P. (2000). Defense mechanisms in psychology today. *American Psychologist, 55*(6), 637–646.

Cramer, P. (2001). The unconscious status of defense mechanisms. *American Psychologist, 56*(9), 762–763.

Di Nicola, V. (1997). *A stranger in the family: Cultures, families, and therapy.* New York: W. W. Norton & Co.

Du Plessix Gray, F. (2000). The work of mourning. *The American Scholar,* 7–13.

Erdelyi, M. H. (2001). Defense processes can be conscious or unconscious. *American Psychologist, 56*(9), 761–762.

Fravel, D. L., & Boss, P. (1992). An in-depth interview with the parents of missing children. In: J. Gilgun, K. Daly & G. Handel (Eds), *Qualitative Methods in Family Research.* Newbury Park, CA: Sage.

Fravel, D. L., McRoy, R. G., & Grotevant, H. D. (2000). Birthmother perceptions of the psychologically present adopted child: Adoption openness and boundary ambiguity. *Family Relations, 49,* 425–433.

Garwick, A., Detzner, D., & Boss, P. (1994). Family perceptions of living with Alzheimer's disease. *Family Process, 33,* 327–340.

Hansen, D. A., & Johnson, V. A. (1979). Rethinking family stress theory: Definitional aspects. In: W. R. Burr, R. Hill, F. I. Nye & I. L. Reiss (Eds), *Contemporary Theories About the Family* (Vol. 1, pp. 582–603).

Kaplan, L. (2001). A couplehood typology for spouses of institutionalized persons with Alzheimer's disease: Perceptions of "We" vs. "I." *Family Relations, 50,* 87–98.

Kaplan, L., & Boss, P. (1999). Depressive symptoms among spousal caregivers of institutionalized mates with Alzheimer's: Boundary ambiguity and mastery as predictors. *Family Process, 38*(1), 85–103.

Lazarus, R. S. (1977). Cognitive and coping process in emotion. In: A. Monat & R. Lazarus (Eds), *Stress and Coping.* New York: Columbia University Press.

Leichtentritt, R., & Rettig, K. (1999). My parent's dignified death is different from mine: Moral problem solving about euthanasia. *Journal of Social and Personal Relationships, 16*(3), 385–406.

Levine, D. L. (1985). *The flight from Ambiguity: Essays on social and cultural theory.* Chicago: University of Chicago Press.

Loevinger, J., & Wessler, R. (1970). *Measuring ego development.* San Francisco: Jossey-Bass.

Lüscher, K. (2000). Ambivalence. A key concept for the study of intergenerational relations. In: S. Trnka (Ed.), *Family Issues Between Gender and Generations* (pp. 11–25). Luxembourg: European Communities.

Lüscher, K., & Pillemer, K. (1998). Intergenerational ambivalence: A new approach to the study of parent child relations in later life. *Journal of Marriage and the Family, 60,* 413–425.

Newman, L. S. (2001). Coping and defense: No clear distinction. *American Psychologist, 56*(9), 760–761.

Olds, S. (1992). *The father.* New York: Alfred A. Knopf.

Touliatos, J., Perlmutter, B. F., & Strauss, M. A. (Eds) (1990). *Handbook of family measurement techniques.* Newbury Park, CA: Sage.

Weigert, A. J. (1991). *Mixed emotions: Certain steps toward understanding ambivalence.* Albany, NY: State University of New York Press.

10. THE AMBIVALENCES OF PARENTAL CARE AMONG YOUNG GERMAN ADULTS

Dagmar Lorenz-Meyer

INTRODUCTION

A cursory look at the contemporary social scientific literature shows that the concept of ambivalence has gained prominence in analyses of contemporary societies and identities, and in analyses of interpersonal relationships and interactions. With respect to societal analyses, for example, Bauman has argued that the postmodern habitat "is a territory subjected to rival and contradictory meaning-bestowing claims and hence perpetually ambivalent" (Bauman, 1992, p. 193). "To live with ambivalence," Varga suggests (Varga, 2001), is the postmodern pronouncement. By using ambivalence as an "interpretive category" rather than as a "research construct" (Lüscher, this volume Chaps 2 and 7), however, sociologists often leave unspecified whether this way of living entails different things for different social actors.

On the level of interpersonal relationships, ambivalence has been conceived as the simultaneous presence of opposed emotions, attitudes, thoughts, or motivations that a person holds towards a person or object. It frequently is connoted negatively as creating uncertainty and indecisiveness, e.g. "negating voice and agency" (Felman, 2001, p. 123), and thereby weakening "that organized structure of understandings and emotional attachments through which we interpret and assimilate our environments" (Weigert & Franks, 1989, p. 205). The rallying

Intergenerational Ambivalences: New Perspectives on Parent-Child Relations in Later Life
Contemporary Perspectives in Family Research, Volume 4, 225–252
Copyright © 2004 by Elsevier Ltd.
All rights of reproduction in any form reserved
ISSN: 1530-3535/doi:10.1016/S1530-3535(03)04010-X

cry of many interpersonal analysts and psychologists has therefore been "against ambivalence" (McCormick, 2002).

Although ambivalence studies still lack integrated social-scientific conceptualizations, we have seen a series of increasingly rigorous formulations and measurements. The field of intergenerational relations, for example, is responding in important ways to the plea for models that go beyond an either/or dichotomy in favor of models that allow for the simultaneous presence of opposing "valences" (Lüscher & Pillemer, 1998). Earlier theorists (Freud, 1916/1989a, 1917/1989b) had highlighted the role of societal ideals and values as important constitutive forces of intergenerational ambivalence, and recent studies in this area are engaging these issues with increasing vigor.

My exploration of ambivalences in relation to parental care among young adults in Germany should be seen in the context of this discussion. Following the idea that intergenerational ambivalences can be identified on a normative-institutional dimension and a personal-biographical dimension and may be analyzed productively around status passages (Lüscher & Pillemer, 1998), this chapter aims in part to make an empirically grounded contribution to advancing and integrating the concept of ambivalence in ways that are useful for social scientific research. I also seek to produce a nuanced understanding of the ambivalences that many adult children encounter in the course of dealing with their parents' potential needs for care.

Given the increasing number of older people who require personal care, it is highly relevant to explore how ambivalences about parental care arise, to identify strategies of dealing with them, and to examine their consequences for adult children's plans of action and for governmental policy. I look at these issues in light of the multiple commitments of the younger generation and, in Germany, the simultaneous promotion and institutionalization of "individualization" (the duty of self-reliance) and "solidarity" (the duty of intergenerational support) in social policies (Lorenz-Meyer, 2001). Germany's introduction, for example, of long-term care insurance in 1995 as the "fifth pillar" of social insurance shows the state's acknowledgement of care needs that cannot be met by families alone. While instituting the care receivers' right to choose how their (physical) care needs should be met, care insurance gives explicit preference to care provided in the family over residential care.

The chapter proceeds as follows. The section "Conceptual Starting Points" highlights some important conceptual dimensions of ambivalence as personal and structural, as psychosocial and achieved, and as performative and contextual. Then, "Sample and Methods" describes the principal features of the sample we used for life-course research at the University of Bremen and outlines my research strategy and method of analysis. The next two sections analyze and contextualize multiple articulations of ambivalence with regard to its generation and its management, respectively. The chapter concludes with an outline of implications and repercussions of the analysis for socio-scientific conceptions of intergenerational ambivalence.

CONCEPTUAL STARTING POINTS

Three important but often neglected insights emerge from a review of sociological and psychological conceptions of ambivalence.

The first insight is that ambivalence not only can be diagnosed in the relationships of subjects to particular objects, persons, or ideas but can also be "built into the very structure of social relations" (Merton & Barber, 1963/1976, p. 4). Hagan (2001), for example, has recently located ambivalences in actions of the Canadian state in relation to American Vietnam-War resisters. Handel (1979, p. 858) broadly defines an ambivalent social structure as "one that simultaneously values contrary courses of action for a single actor in a given situation." Such observations show that we must analyze personal and structural ambivalences in historically specific situations – or what feminist scholars have called the "politics of location" (Rich, 1986). That is, we must carefully examine the matrix of intersecting relations of power, and potentially overlapping structural sources of ambivalence, in which individuals find themselves.

The second insight is that awareness of ambivalence can be considered as an achievement and task that results from the interaction of countervailing societal *and* psychic forces. From a psychoanalytic perspective, Becker-Schmidt (1980) has argued that the self is differentiated in different psychic registers that are ambivalently "cathected" and that these cathectic energies *blend* with affects triggered in a given situation. Following authors such as Ferenci, Becker-Schmidt suggests that a biographically acquired "tolerance of ambivalence" (Becker-Schmidt, 1993, p. 84) is a crucial resource for acknowledging, rather than denying or harmonizing, ambivalence. Achieving a tolerance of ambivalence depends on the ability to make associative links between opposing orientations in contrast to the fixity and impenetrability of schizophrenic ambivalence (Bleuler, 1910/11), on managing attendant anxiety (Parker, 1995), and on "the ratio of discriminations and encouragements" (Becker-Schmidt, 1993, p. 86) in individual biographies, that enables previous positive moments to counteract the denial of negative moments in the present. Ambivalence thereby allows for a "holistic" evaluation or representation of the person or situation that is not integrated, indifferent, or compartmentalized (Parker, 1995; Thompson & Holmes, 1996).

The third and related insight of conceiving ambivalence as "a *reaction* to competing motivations in the face of a contradictory reality" (Becker-Schmidt, 1980, p. 725, emphasis mine) is that that ambivalences are performative and contextual. By performative I mean not only that ambivalences are active processes of interpretation produced in social interaction on the individual level as well as of issuing or enforcing opposing legislation, policies, or directives on the institutional level. Rather, I wish to highlight that ambivalences *affect actions*. Ambivalences can be conceived of as situated embodied practices that keep opposing valences alive, express and enact them. Inertia or oscillating practices can be such enactments, but so can be more creative and transformative actions by individuals and institutions. Ambivalence, in this view, is not something outside of, behind, or underneath these performances that are located within and express relations of power.

With respect to the performative constitution of gender, theorists have argued that gender is a social communicative accomplishment instituted and maintained by repetitions of meaningful acts. The actuality of gender norms depends on reiterative practices of subjects "citing" or enacting these norms, a process which also offers possibilities of enacting them differently (Butler, 1993). Relating these considerations to ambivalence, the co-existence of simultaneously opposing values in a given situation can be conceived as a crucial productive resource that interrupts the seamless reproduction of norms and values. Ambivalence can be a catalyst of change that generates and maintains dynamism in societal arrangements and can facilitate social transformation.

This potentially positive effect implies that analytical attention has to identify the detailed mechanisms involved in dealing with ambivalence, without which ambivalence has little explanatory value. In a similar vein, Lüscher and colleagues (this volume, Chap. 7) have proposed four ideal-typical forms of dealing with ambivalences in the context of intergenerational relations by combining rankings of intergenerational relationships on a normative-institutional dimension and a personal-biographical dimension.

These conceptual considerations of ambivalences as personal and structural, as psychosocial and achieved, and as performative and contextual suggest directions for analysis, which I take up in Sections four and five.

SAMPLE AND METHODS

The following analysis is based on a secondary analysis of semi-structured interviews with 49 young adults who were born in Germany between 1953 and 1964. The interviews were conducted in the mid-1990s as part of three research projects that investigated changing life-course patterns in Germany of women at the age of retirement, their husbands, and their adult children. The empirical studies were conducted at the Special Research Centre "Status Passages and Risks in the Life Course" at Bremen University under the direction of Helga Krüger and Claudia Born. I developed the part of the topic guide that explored how adult children plan to deal with potential care needs of their parents and interviewed 15 young adults as part of my doctoral research. For a discussion of the research design, which combined quantitative and qualitative methods, see Lorenz-Meyer (1999).

We contacted the research participants via their mothers or fathers, who had been surveyed and sometimes interviewed in previous studies. Participants may therefore exclude children who had permanently broken off contact with their parents. On the basis of a quantitative survey of life course events and turning points of 149 adult children, we chose a theoretical qualitative sample ($n = 49$) that allowed for forming subgroups and systematically relating possible differences in interpretation patterns to the participants' gender, sibling position, and educational status, as well as to specific life-course patterns of their mothers. The sample purposely included: (a) sons ($n = 21$) and daughters ($n = 28$); (b) 10 opposite-sex sibling dyads and two same-sex sibling triads; (c) participants who were trained on the level of skilled training ($n = 23$) and participants who had a university degree ($n = 25$); (d) participants whose mothers had been predominantly employed (defined as more than 18.5 years spent in the labor market) ($n = 28$) and those who had been predominantly homemakers ($n = 21$); and (e) whose mothers had given personal support to older relatives ($n = 28$) and those who had not ($n = 21$).

At the time of our interviews, most research participants had established their own lives. More than half of them had moved away from the two regions where their parents lived (a largely Protestant urban city in northern Germany and a small town/rural Catholic district in western Germany) although their mobility was generally limited to the same region. The majority ($n = 38$) of the 49 research participants were employed, 33 were married, and 32 had children.

With respect to their age, the research participants belong to age cohorts that underwent their formative development in the mid-1970s. These years were a period of fundamental social change and destandardization of living arrangements in Germany, marked by such changes as the unprecedented expansion of part-time work; a radical decline in birth rates; and a sharp increase in cohabitation, divorce rates, and one-parent families. Consequently, the research participants are members of the cohorts who are currently held responsible for the "detraditionalization of family bonds" (Kaufmann, 1993, p. 107) and were expected to be either unwilling or unable to uphold the intergenerational "caring contract."

The method we adopted is theme-centered analysis. It begins by identifying common themes in the interviews, and then proceeds to explore systematically the similarities and differences in the research participants' interpretation patterns; these are related both to their context in the interview and to the participants' socio-demographic variables and familial characteristics. Theme-centered analysis thereby allows investigating whether interpretation patterns differ systematically between subgroups with different socio-structural characteristics, so we can examine the impact of gender, sibling status, and intra-familial traditions of care arrangements for older relatives on interpretations of ambivalence. For that purpose, I attached a summary of socio-structural and familial identifiers to the interview passages that are cited, as will be seen below.

Overall, the analysis is oriented toward examining the structure and "social logic" of ambivalences in relation to parental care rather than towards reconstructing individual or family biographies. The following presentation includes one longer case study, however, to illustrate the multifaceted nature of ambivalences of parental care.

The analysis takes, as a point of departure, respondents' spontaneous articulations of ambivalence as they thought about the possibility of their parents requiring personal care. Manifest ambivalence appears as a nodal point, often triggering a series of reflections on the history and legacies of family relationships, but also on the nature of cultural norms and social institutions and their cumulative demands and cross-pressures.

HOW MULTIPLE AMBIVALENCES ARISE AND INTERACT

The Impact of Socio-Familial Positionality on Articulations of Ambivalence

The majority of the 49 research participants, across gender and educational background, identified their parents' potential need for care as a pressing dilemmatic "choice" for the respondent – between institutionalizing the parent and personally providing in-home care. Both options were considered undesirable and were multiply constituted: The option to "shunt off" parents into a nursing home was negatively evaluated because of the belief that people deteriorate when they leave their familiar environment, the conviction that parents did not want to go into a home, and the felt obligation to reciprocate support received previously. Residential care appeared as a violation of the normative orientation of solidarity. The option to provide co-residential (in-home) care was negatively evaluated because it was expected to conflict with respondents' family and career commitments and could stir up personal conflicts. Co-residential care violated the normative orientation of individualization.

Interestingly, although respondents evidently were aware of the newly introduced care insurance scheme that offers people (partial) support in kind or in cash if their needs for help in basic and instrumental activities for daily living are assessed, care insurance was not considered as an institutional mechanism sufficient to resolve this dilemma.

As a result, anticipating their parents' need for care appeared to generate decisional ambivalence in our respondents regarding two simultaneously valued courses of action: the wish and felt responsibility to support parents personally and the structural and personal inability and unwillingness to do so (e.g. the wish to lead one's own life). The majority of participants prefaced their articulation of these irresolvable orientations with a reference to a personal strategy of consciously not dealing with or planning for parental care, and of "repressing" their thoughts and feelings about it. While this strategy of dealing with ambivalence seems indeed to point to the generation of widespread uncertainty and indecisiveness, a closer investigation of the narratives reveals that opposing options were phrased quite differently. I will examine these differences before I turn to the nine participants who did not express ambivalence.

In the excerpts from interviews provided in the rest of this chapter, the identifier after each excerpt denotes the participant's gender (w = woman, m = man), his or her identification number and sibling position (a, b, c) if several siblings were surveyed and interviewed, number and gender of siblings, educational level (university degree, skilled training), family status (married, cohabiting, single), current employment status (full-time employed, part-time employed, homemaker), number of children, and the presence or absence of a history of maternal caregiving to older relatives (maternal caring tradition).

> Int: Have you ever had thoughts about how it would be if your parents were in need of care, or could be, or what should happen then?
>
> Mrs. U: Yes. Thoughts, yes. Partly. On the one hand, you always repress it a bit, because you don't know how to solve it. Well, I also would be reluctant to put my parents in a nursing home. That would be the very last resort for me ... but if it would be a severe case, you'd have to give up. When I will work again sometime, give my job up again ... I wouldn't like to do it.
>
> *W831b, one brother, one sister, skilled training, married, homemaker, one child, maternal caring tradition*
>
> Mr. S: Yes, of course I have thought about it. And either I've repressed it or I've come to the conclusion that there is no satisfactory solution. Well, what I actually wouldn't like to do would be to move back home, because my parents needed care. Because that would mean a change of job. That would mean changing your whole life context .... That would be out of the question.

M508b, one sister, university degree, cohabiting, f/t employed, no children, maternal caring tradition

Although the option of changing or giving up one's job to provide parental care was with one exception negatively evaluated in the sample, there is an important difference between asserting that one "wouldn't like to do it" (W831b) and stating that it "would be out of the question" (M508b). Not all undesirable options are equally impossible, which points to the fact that if care needs arise, a choice will have to be made, even if ambivalence persists.

Contextualizing such passages in relation to participants' socio-structural characteristics and their family histories shows that respondents' social positionality noticeably influenced whether residential or in-home care was considered a less likely path of action. Positionality was constituted by parameters such as gender, employment status, and residential proximity, and also by familial factors such as the expected commitments of other siblings and parental expectations.

While both Mrs. U and Mr. S shared a legacy of intra-familial care provided by their mothers (which may have had a more "stimulative nature" for the female research participant), Mrs. U lived in relative proximity to her parents and did not expect any caregiving commitment from her siblings – who, in her own words, had a more "ambivalent" relationship with the parents. Geographical closeness and regular contact, together with her interrupted employment history, failed to provide "objective" hindrances – or what Finch and Mason (1992) termed a "legitimate excuse" for not providing co-residential care. Mr. S, on the other hand, lived about 400 kilometers from his parents, where he had built up a career and was in a long-term relationship. He also had a sister who lived in close proximity to the parents and relied on them for childcare. For this reason, Mr. S expected his sister to assume primary caring responsibility, which probably made it much easier for him to be firm that personal caregiving was "out of the question."

It follows that even though both men and women in our study said the choice involved a dilemma, the extent of their ambivalence – that is, its constitutive and mitigating factors – can be understood only in the context of how respondents were *relationally positioned* in their families and in societal relations of power. (Similar systematic variations in ambivalence in relation to socio-structural factors have been explored in ambivalent class identities in Britain (Savage, Bagnall & Longhurst, 2001) and in ambivalent national identities of American draft dodgers in Canada (Hagan, 2001).)

The fact that nine of our respondents did not articulate manifest ambivalence is interesting to look at in this context. This group included one woman, who anticipated full-time caregiving, and about a third of the male participants, who considered their subsidiary practical assistance to their parents as a solidaristic and consensual fulfillment of their filial responsibilities. Their lack of, or unawareness of, ambivalence lends weight to the hypothesis that the socio-familial positionality of adult sons is structurally less "saturated" with ambivalence with respect to parental care than is that of daughters. Yet, as we will see below, the interaction of gender with other parameters is what proves decisive for the degree of ambivalence.

The Interaction of Opposing Socio-Structural and Affective Forces

Opposing orientations were frequently expressed in the narratives through direct speech, which allows – quite literally – for expressing or enacting different voices without needing to integrate them into a coherent pattern of interpretation. The following extract with Mrs. A shows in more detail how socio-structural and familial parameters interacted with emotional needs and affective investments in intergenerational relations (a pattern which has been emphasized in psychoanalytically oriented conceptions of ambivalence).

Mrs. A: This is what I'm dealing with most at the moment, apart from work. Because they [parents] have always worked so much, suddenly you realize that in the last 1 or 2 years they have declined rapidly.... I'm very concerned. And I always have the feeling because I'm the only girl I'm responsible. Because they keep close contact with me, too. And I have already talked to my brother, the second youngest. I say: "What are we going to do?" I say: "I know, this makes me sick. I don't know what to do. On the one hand, I can't leave here. I have the job, don't want to give it up either. Or if I have a family, whatever is going to happen? The big house, no one is at home." I only know this: I don't want them to go into a nursing home, on any account.... I think everybody pushes it aside. Well, I also feel stressed because I think: They've done so much for us, they were always there for us. If I knew they weren't well, I don't know, I think that would cause a terrible conflict.

Int: Have your parents talked about it?

Mrs. A: Not directly. They do all the renovations in the house ... and write "Would you like *this*, or *that*?"... And I have seen it with my granny – it worked out well in our household. She was well-integrated. Sometimes it was hard for my mother, too, but somehow the woman had a nice life in old age.... I think all the family members should – whether it's a woman or man – I think all have the responsibility because they are the parents of all and were there for their children.

Int: Could you imagine, because you said they have converted the flat upstairs, moving in with them and taking care of them?

Mrs. A: There the problem with my husband has a part to play again. We have talked about it and then he said, "Well we can move in with your parents." At first I thought he wasn't serious. And I said, "Yes, but it wouldn't work." Because my mother and I are attached, but there is some friction between us. I think it would be difficult with my parents, not with me but with *him*. I do things here where my mother perhaps would say, "This isn't my daughter." And that's a problem because often you want to please

> your mother, [but] you do something, get into inner conflicts, get angry, and come to
> blows. But as to the caring, I'd like to do it, right away.
>
> *W516a, four brothers, skilled training, married, f/t employed, no children, maternal caring
> tradition*

Mrs. A's ambivalent account that she feels responsible and "would like to" but
yet cannot provide parental care highlights some of the ways in which opposing
socio-cultural and personal and affective forces reinforce but also destabilize and
reconfigure each other. Mrs. A identifies actual parental care needs as an issue
of high concern next to concerns about her work. The first part of her narrative
focuses on the socio-structural side of filial ambivalence generated by incompatible social roles, opposing socio-cultural demands, and a lack of resources to
reconcile them.

Resulting ambivalence propelled Mrs. A. into action: Her attempts to share her
concerns and filial duties with her brother can be considered as an effort to mitigate
ambivalence. His refusal to share responsibility ultimately reinforced Mrs. A's
sense of responsibility that was thus generated by a set of *mutually reinforcing
familial and cultural factors*: (a) the perceived parental expectation of filial
caregiving; (b) her endorsement of the norm of reciprocity and filial repayment;
(c) her status as the only daughter, which becomes meaningful in a cultural and
family context where women were held responsible for, and in her family had
actually assumed, the role of providing family support; (d) the positive memory
of the co-residence of her grandmother; (e) her rejection of institutional care;
and (f) the absence of any proposed alternative shared-caring arrangements from
her brothers.

While appearing to create cumulative familial-cultural pressure counteracted
by socio-structural hindrances of her full-time job and geographical distance,
achieving rather than denying ambivalence also enabled Mrs. A. to *question
the dominant socio-cultural order*: If filial responsibility is the moral duty to
repay for care received by parents, how can this repayment be solely the task of
adult daughters? In the interview, this potentially subversive question does not
become a transformative force: Feelings of filial responsibility remain stronger
than considerations of filial injustice.

The second part of the narrative offers some insights into Mrs. A's emotional investments in the relationship with her parents. These reconfigure the
socio-structural account given earlier. Mrs. A recalls a discussion with her
husband, which suggests that structural hindrances to parental care could, in
principle, be rectified. Now maintaining that the parents' non-acceptance of her
husband is what would "objectively" impede co-residence, Mrs. A substantiates
this claim by describing her emotional ambivalences in the relationship with
her mother.

Her mother's anticipated remark, "This isn't my daughter," points to the mother's (perceived) fundamental criticism and rejection of Mrs. A – possibly because Mrs. A had failed to reproduce and continue, and thereby seemingly devalued, the mother's own life choices and commitments. Dealing with her wish for maternal acceptance and her awareness of personal difference is described as a no-win situation: Mrs. A finds it equally impossible to express personal difference where intergenerational sameness is desired and to exhibit sameness where differences are present.

Irresolvable personal ambivalence in this case does indeed seem to foster self-knowledge – in that it psychologically forestalls the anticipation of mutually beneficial shared living arrangements. Psychological ambivalence thereby buttresses, yet also displaces, the socio-structural hindrances to personal care cited before. However, in the closing remark that she would "like to do it, right away," the willingness to provide filial care is finally re-affirmed and filial ambivalence is sustained.

Mrs. A's account illustrates some of the complexities of *multiple ambivalences* that can come to the fore and interact when anticipating the prospect of filial caregiving. To be sure, not all research participants who articulate ambivalence with respect to parental care refer to personal ambivalences in the relationships with their parents. But women did so more often than men in our study – whether because women tend to be more "emotionally literate" in western societies, or because the relationships with their mothers tend to be more conflicting and entangled than those of sons. (The quantitative findings of the Konstanz study similarly show that daughters reported more feelings "of being torn in two directions" in relation to their mothers than did sons. See Lüscher & Lettke, Chap. 7 in this volume.)

Two emerging findings are especially important for conceptualizing ambivalence with respect to parental care. First, in conjunction with the conceptual distinction of a normative-institutional and a personal-biographical dimension in the generation of ambivalence (Lüscher, Chap. 2 this volume), the social-familial positionality of social actors analyzed in the previous section as a constitutive factor of ambivalence with respect to care is more adequately conceptualized as *psychosocial positionality*. The concept of psychosocial positionality draws analytical attention to the *interaction* of socio-structural characteristics, familial factors, and affective investments of social actors in intergenerational relations as producing different degrees of ambivalence with respect to parental care.

Second, ambivalences in relation to parental care diagnosed by respondents both on the societal and on the personal level carry the seeds for social transformation: Contradictory normative guidelines may lose their legitimacy, and personal ambivalences in adult intergenerational relationships may prevent injurious or harmful care arrangements.

I shall now turn to the respondents' identification of structural ambivalences and their effects.

Identifications of Multiple Structural Ambivalences

Ambivalences in Socio-Historical Generational Positions

Our interviews posed the question of anticipated parental care arrangements in the broader thematic context of how adult children see their own lives in relation to the life-course model of their parents. Ambivalences were often located already *within* the generational position of their parents as well as their own, rather than merely in the relation between the respondents' lives and those of their parents. I will discuss these different forms of ambivalence in turn.

Inspired by the social references of the term "generation" in German usage, research participants linked individual lives to historical times. From this perspective, they often identified their parents as members of the postwar "reconstruction generation" (*Aufbaugeneration*), which they saw as characterized by a predominantly materialistic orientation and lifestyle. Ideal-typically and with explicit references to social changes in the 1970s, the research participants characterized their own generation as post-materialistic in distinction from the reconstruction generation; one participant termed it the "break-out generation" (*Ausbruchsgeneration*).

From their current perspective, adult children – especially adult daughters – were ambivalent about the life-course model of their mothers. They were particularly ambivalent about the strong work ethic of the women of the reconstruction generation. Whereas participants tended to evaluate positively their mothers' strength and support given in the family, daughters simultaneously viewed their mothers' actions as exploitative and self-limiting. Mothers were seen to have struggled with multiple commitments, standards of perfection, and a quest for material security that did not allow for quality time or other social activities for the mothers themselves. More often than fathers, mothers were characterized as "dominant"; but personal dominance was seen as co-existing with institutional subordination, particularly as involving a subordinate position in their marital relationship, which the respondents unanimously rejected. (In comparison, the paternal lifestyle model – characterized by frequent absences of the father and his inability to voice emotions, on the one hand, and institutional dominance and often a more "liberal" attitude on the other – was not perceived as, in itself, a cause of ambivalence.)

Ambivalences toward the maternal life-course model arose in the context of currently prevailing values, such as gender equality. They also cut across the distinction between personal and institutional dimensions: Participants contrasted solidaristic institutional behavior and personal exploitation, and personal dominance and institutional subordination. The maternal life-course – including, for some, a tradition of co-residential caregiving – offered multiple points of identification and disidentification for adult children, such as identification with strength and rejection of allowing oneself to be exploited. Given its inherently ambivalent structure, this model carried seeds for transformation; or, minimally, it did not lend itself to being reproduced by women of the younger generation in its entirety.

The research participants also identified structural ambivalences in their own generational position, for example, the opposing imperatives of being a full-time mother and a paid worker. While these opposing demands were generally located in radically changed social conditions, resulting ambivalence was sometimes seen as aggravated by the internalization of traditional values from the parental and grandparental generation.

> Ms. D: I didn't want to live like my mother, on no account. That I knew from when I was little.... Well at school in the '70s you should, wanted, had to break out. You were almost frowned upon if you didn't. And I went along with it. But it is completely torn. I think this is also a dilemma of our generation, that our parents and grandparents passed on quite traditional things, which we have somehow in us and wish for, but at the same time there is this break from outside. I think particularly as a woman you are completely at sea somehow – always this decision: occupation or motherhood."
>
> *W821a, two brothers, university, single, f/t employed, no children, no caring tradition*

The fact that other respondents interpreted their radically different lifestyle as univalent and independent from the parental model suggests that it is not the degree of similarity or difference in lifestyle and personal characteristics, in itself, that is decisive for manifest *intergenerational* ambivalence, but the way in which similarities and differences were evaluated by the research participants. Thus, the respondents considered their active counterformation of their parents' personal characteristics and lifestyle organization as univalent if they either were ambivalent about the maternal lifestyle or saw it as irrelevant for their own lifestyle. This counterformation generated ambivalence if respondents perceived their parents as strongly rejecting it (and this mattered emotionally, or in terms of personal identity, as Lüscher explores in Chap. 2 of this volume), or if it appeared to be imposed upon them through societal changes in face of which respondents lacked resources for reconciling such changes with family traditions.

In conclusion, two findings are particularly relevant for conceptualizing how intergenerational ambivalence is generated. First, research participants assess ambivalences in intergenerational relations in their specific historical context, and this often includes the assessment of structural ambivalences inherent in specific socio-historical generational positions. The interpretation of these positions and context conditions is a further crucial ingredient for the analysis of how ambivalences are generated *between* generations. Comparative analysis of their responses shows that, second, the research participants' *evaluation* of differences and similarities between their lifestyle and personal characteristics and those of their parents' is crucial for respondents' assessments of intergenerational ambivalences; and this evaluation is made in comparison to the relationship they wished for and saw as appropriate in the context of specific historical conditions.

influence of historical context

Ambivalences in Cultural-Normative Guidelines

The research participants also reflected on arrangements for parental care in the context of opposing normative guidelines. They endorsed the norm "that you repay what you received from the parents in affection and investments if there is a reason for it" (W811); but, at the same time, they also supported the legitimacy of living one's own life and the right to choose whether or not to provide personal support.

Overall, analyzing the narratives of young German adults confirmed findings from a British study that family members do not believe there are stable, unbreakable, normative rules for filial conduct (Finch & Mason, 1992). Male participants tended to emphasize individualization and the dissolution of binding social norms – "You have to decide for yourself" what you do and there are many different possibilities! (M022) Female participants, however, across educational and family status, more often insisted that side by side with individualization there exists a normative guideline of solidaristic intergenerational assistance that applies in times of personal need.

Women were more likely than men both to be aware of ambivalence on the normative level and to express personal ambivalence in relation to prevailing norms. In particular, women's awareness that choosing not to provide parental care would cause feelings of guilt led them to reflect on the existence of opposing normative values around caregiving.

Gender differences in the interpretation of normative guidelines and in reported care arrangements of their grandparents suggest that the participants were aware of, and positioned themselves within, a normative "hierarchy of carers" (George, 1986; Qureshi & Walker, 1989). In western societies, this hierarchy assigns caregiving responsibilities to spouses before adult children; and, among adult children, it assigns them to daughters before daughters-in-law and sons.

In the context of contradictory normative guidelines, the hierarchy of carers can be considered as a *cultural-normative mechanism* to "manage" or channel ambivalence on the level of society. It mitigates contrasting orientations of action for those whose responsibilities are considered secondary, by normatively freeing them from caring responsibilities; at the same time, it contributes to increasing ambivalence for those who are held primarily responsible.

As in the account of Mrs. A, some female respondents saw the normative ranking of responsibilities according to gender as being in conflict with the norm of reciprocity. While women's identification of normative ambivalence thus may lead them not to reproduce the hierarchy of carers model, this outcome seems to depend on the women's psychosocial postionality, as discussed above. If adult brothers, for example, implicitly or explicitly endorsed the normative hierarchy of caring responsibility, *and* this was identified as unfair, this actually *increased* rather than mitigated ambivalence for their sisters.

To sum up, the research participants' psychosocial positionality not only influences the assessment of normative ambivalence in relation to parental care, it also can help to produce highly critical reflections about conflicting cultural values. More specifically, ambivalences on the experiential level may be a prerequisite for identifying ambivalences in guidelines on the cultural and structural level.

Ambivalences in Institutional Structures of Care

Thinking about potential parental care arrangements inevitably involves thinking about different ways in which care can be provided. The interviews show that even though no reference is made to care insurance, the proliferation of in-home care options in Germany served as an institutional mechanism for mitigating personal ambivalence among both male and female research participants. Indeed, ambivalence on the experiential level appears to peak when anticipated parental needs can no longer be met by in-home care services.

At this point, significant gender differences again appear. Women formed the majority of those *explicitly* advocating residential care, whereas men were more likely to leave care arrangements beyond arranging in-home care unspecified. Concurrently, women with lower educational status formed the only group who prospectively committed themselves to co-residential care. For both groups of women, the expected availability and quality of care institutions was a main concern. Moreover, both groups of women were more likely than men to identify structural ambivalences between the relative benefits and inadequacies of family vs. residential care.

Advantages and disadvantages of different kinds of care were given different emphasis, depending on what was taken as the relevant dimension of comparison. Family care was seen as preferable to residential care because it was more personal and, as mentioned earlier, parents were expected to deteriorate outside of their familiar environment. Residential care appeared preferable to home care when seen in light of the lack of family carers' professionalism, the strains that in-home care may entail for adult children and their families, and how the multiple commitments of caregivers could result in social isolation of the care receiver at home.

> Mrs. C: I probably would not take my parents. I thought about this very specifically, because my sister had an experience, she had to take her mother-in-law into the house, seriously disabled, and that ruined the marriage . . . . I would see that they get into a good home. That might sound hard but they have it better there. And I would do everything to keep them in their familiar environment as long as possible with these community workers . . . because as soon as they lose the security within their own four walls, they go into a rapid decline . . . . But in a decent nursing home, they have speech therapists, they have carers who can give time and attention to the old people, right? I think you can't do it that way [at home]. Basically the person sits in front of the TV all day. It's so isolated, it's a [prison] cell, a family cell although it is not depicted like that (Krüger et al., 1987).

> *W546c, four sisters, skilled training, married, p/t employed, three children, maternal caring tradition*

Some female respondents were aware that both the institutions of the family and elder care homes could be sites of care and neglect. As with ambivalences identified in the maternal life-course model, structural ambivalence in care institutions cuts across the institutional and the personal dimensions. Family members were sometimes seen as personally better suited to provide intimate care but lacking professional skills, as well as being available for fewer hours throughout the day and night than are professional carers who are always on call.

Identifying structural ambivalences with respect to kinds of care poses dilemmas and offers new choices for transforming traditional gendered caring roles. The fact that prospective family caregivers and those opting for residential care often differed by educational status points to the hypothesis that the *ability to afford quality care* is what makes residential care a more viable option for some women. Given adequate economic resources, social institutions can indeed structurally mitigate the level of ambivalence for women – as Krüger and colleagues (1987) have shown in the case of institutional child care. This is so even if ambivalence persists between the beliefs that parents are best cared for in the family vs. in an elder care home.

In summary, it is the research participants themselves who offer far-reaching structural and historical contextualizations of ambivalences with respect to parental care. In reflecting on kinds of care, women again appeared to be the most aware of structural ambivalence. I would suggest that because younger women could be expected to continue a nurturing family role more than their brothers or partners, many had reflected on the ambivalent possibilities and perils this role had entailed for their mothers, on the tensions and ambivalences inherent in this cultural-normative expectation, and on the legitimating and delegitimating aspects of family and institutional care.

The extent to which the identification of structured ambivalences fostered (potentially) transformative practices appeared to depend significantly on material resources, amplifying the importance of material and symbolic resources arising from employment in constituting psychosocial positionality.

In the final section, I shall return to relational strategies research participants used to deal with ambivalences, the resources they require, and the consequences they entail.

STRATEGIES OF DEALING WITH AMBIVALENCES

Relationality

Earlier I noted that analytical attention has to be paid to how ambivalences are enacted and dealt with. Not thinking about or planning for parental care, evident among many male respondents, can be considered a strategy of dealing with ambivalence. Similarly, the more or less tentative parental care arrangements that some research participants developed prospectively can be considered as attempts to deal with ambivalences. In both cases, participants often spontaneously referred to concrete care arrangements in their families of origin as reference points for their own anticipations. This allows relating their strategies to the four ideal-typical strategies of dealing with intergenerational ambivalences identified in the Konstanz studies. "Emancipation," "solidarity," "captivation," and "atomization" were derived from combining the ranking of intergenerational relationships on the continuum between institutional innovation and reproduction, and between personal convergence and divergence.

In the following section, I will particularly focus on possible differentiations within and relations between those strategies of management that are posited as diametrically opposed in the Konstanz model: Captivation ("to preserve reluctantly") as the predominance of personal divergence and institutional repro-duction was diametrically opposed to emancipation ("to mature reciprocally") as the predominance of personal convergence and institutional innovation; and solidarity ("to preserve consensually") as the predominance of convergence and reproduction was diametrically opposed to atomization ("to separate conflict-ually") as the predominance of divergence and innovation. While the multiplicity of management strategies in this model helps to free ambivalence of normative connotations, it is evident that these labels themselves have strong, and perhaps unwarranted, normative connotations.

With respect to anticipating parental care arrangements that might be required, the research participants were concerned not only with institutionally reproducing or transforming (sometimes ambivalent) previous residential or family care arrangements; they also were concerned with how these arrangements were personally negotiated. The idea that siblings should share the responsibility for any agreed-upon course of action, and that communication in the family should start before care needs actually occurred, was of central importance in terms of mitigating filial ambivalence.

> Ms. N: I quickly push it aside. Because I think that will be very difficult. Three years ago, we had the experience that my grandfather required care – lived in his own house till the end, and my parents and brother were very involved. And that was basically a horrible time, which also had to do with the fact that in this family many things have gone wrong for 30 years. Which means things, important things weren't talked about, which was simply catastrophic in this situation. But I think if there is more communication from the beginning it doesn't have to get that bad. But the subject actually gives me stomach aches, because I have the feeling that I'm stuck with it because my brother, I'd simply say, has a disturbed relationship to it, or not disturbed but is very withdrawn from my parents. And so I fear a bit that I'm stuck with it. And I think in my relationship to my parents there are also a few things to work through. I saw it with my grand-dad. If you have to care for somebody who is so helpless, and then you carry with you so many unresolved conflicts that it doesn't work or I can't imagine it.
>
> Int: So you probably haven't talked about this with your brother?
>
> Ms N: Yes, sure, I have, um, attempted, or let's say, I let him know my worries or that I thought about it in this context. And, well, what I learned from the situation with my grand-dad is that you can never plan it anyway.
>
> *W707a, one brother, university degree, cohabiting, f/t employed, no children, maternal caring tradition*

Striving to transform patterns of previous solidaristic *and* "catastrophic" care arrangements (in this case to initiate communication in the family and possibly residential care) and not having the power or resources to do so, can be seen to lead to what Lüscher and colleagues have conceptualized as "captivation," the reluctant conservation of family legacies. As in the Konstanz study, captivation was found solely among adult daughters. However, independently of whether or not parents asserted moral pressure, the label "captivation" might conceal efforts toward transformation – such as the respondents' initiation of communication with siblings and parents.

Whereas in Ms. N's case open discussion remained absent despite her intent of counterformation, non-communication was also a strategy adult children used to evade making specific personal commitments. This was often facilitated by the tacit or explicit assumption that somebody else, usually a sister, would assume major caring responsibilities – and was not based on atomization or conflicting separation. As one respondent put it, "The ideal case, of course, would be that my parents move to my sister's" (M816a). If co-residential care provided by a sister were realized, it could enable personal closeness with parents and institutional innovation on the part of those who were set free from day-to-day caring responsibilities. What then appears as "emancipation," or reciprocal "maturation" in the Konstanz typology, could, in fact, be based on the reproduction of traditional gendered patterns of family interaction. Strategies of dealing with ambivalences therefore have to be analyzed in their interdependence with strategies pursued not only by parents but also by other siblings.

Another important aspect of relationality that appeared with respect to potential care arrangements is that (anticipated) institutional innovation and reproduction were not necessarily opposing ends of a continuum. Sometimes elements of previous arrangements were combined in new and dynamic ways. This is illustrated in the account of Mrs. T, who draws on both a solidaristic model of shared responsibilities in her family of origin and a model of in-home care provided in her husband's family. These models were combined and modified by considerations of intergenerational fairness.

Mrs. T and her husband felt that in adult life her parents had given assistance with child care exclusively to one of Mrs. T's sisters. With reference to the principle of intergenerational justice, primary caring responsibility was thus assigned to this sister. In her family of origin the maternal grandparents had lived part of the time with a co-resident son who took over the family business, but they also had stayed for longer periods with other adult children. Merging these experiences with that of the in-home care that had been provided for her mother-in-law, Mrs. T envisions an arrangement where she and her sisters would "proportionally" commute to their parents to provide care in conjunction with social services, with one sister taking the bulk of caring responsibility.

If this arrangement were realized, it might be interpreted as "solidarity" or as the consensual preservation of family traditions in the Konstanz typology. Yet the label "solidarity" would obscure moments of innovation and of proportional repayment in terms of received benefits. Indeed, the reference to the idea of intergenerational justice – relevant in a number of cases where the commitments of siblings and parents are concerned – can be seen as one important means of dealing with intergenerational ambivalence. While seeming to mitigate ambivalence for Mrs. T, considerations of injustice can also increase ambivalence.

In the current study, "atomization," the conflicting separation of parents and adult children, was not described as a way of dealing with parental care needs. However, five participants had broken off contact completely with their parents in the past, which in retrospect was considered vital for continuing and transforming the relationship. From the point of view of these participants, atomization did not mean that intergenerational relationships had low relevance for their own lives and was not necessarily perceived as antithetical to long-term solidarity. Rather, conflict and temporary separation often were considered as part and parcel of indissoluble family ties. As one respondent succinctly put it, "Well, family *is*. Sometimes you can argue with them or discuss or something, also fall out and say nothing to for years. But it is family. They are always still somewhere to be reached or – whereas everything else is often final, right" (W857a).

In terms of analytically distinguishing strategies of dealing with ambivalence in relation to parental care, these findings re-emphasize the need to situate and contextualize multiple and changing strategies, a possibility conceded by the Konstanz group (Lüscher, Pajung-Bilger, Lettke & Böhmer, 2000, pp. 18–19). Research participants' interpretations of their actions draw attention to relations of power, transformative and reproductive elements within and interdependence between the strategies they and their siblings pursue. Given that, for example, "captivation" can be the result of failed transformation of previous care arrangements and their negotiation, and "emancipation" can be based on the reproduction of traditional behavior that relies on the caregiving commitments of another sibling, or that "atomization" maybe a temporal strategy subsumed under long-term "solidarity," I suggest that analysts specify enabling or constraining conditions within which particular strategies are achieved and get meaning. As the presence or absence of family communication appears to be a crucial factor for distinguishing strategies of dealing with ambivalence, I will now look at it more closely.

The Role of Family Communication

Whatever the care arrangement anticipated, the narratives suggest that the *interpretation* of an anticipated care model as solidaristic mitigated personal ambivalence in the present. Actual non-communication with parents, siblings, and service providers could be highly functional because: (a) an assumed family consensus could not be threatened; and (b) as with those who did not specify possible care arrangements, the question of whether responsibilities will be fairly distributed could not be posed.

In the case of Mrs. T, interviews with two of her sisters indicated that her anticipated arrangement of proportional sharing of responsibilities with her sisters had not been discussed in the family. Significantly, the sister who is assumed will take primary responsibility is Mrs. C who had forcefully argued for a residential care arrangement, drawing on the experiences with co-residential care of her older sister.

The narrative of Mrs. M, another sister of Mrs. T and Mrs. C who lived geographically more distant, exposes an important dimension of family communication; namely, that communication is not merely a strategy deployed at will but is highly charged emotionally and itself involves ambivalence. While communication is considered necessary to deal effectively with and plan for potential care needs, it simultaneously is considered to contradict the idea of unconditional family solidarity. Patterson (1997) succinctly speaks of the "norm of non-articulation" in close kin relations. In a similar vein, Finch and Mason (1992) have argued that family members usually can not openly ask for family support or assistance, as this normatively is considered to impinge on the right of the giver to give or withhold support.

More specifically, the research shows that communication is difficult with respect to talking about personal feelings. As one respondent put it, "[In our family], nobody harasses the other with his feelings" (M011). It follows that family communication about potential needs and responsibilities is not merely a means to mitigate ambivalence but is an achievement in itself, namely, the transformation or different enactment of the norm of non-articulation that may require strategic planning.

> Mrs M: I didn't dare to ask whether they have registered somewhere. Years ago my father talked about a senior citizens' home . . .. I don't dare ask because I'm anxious that if you make suggestions they think you don't want to look after them. I'll go there at Christmas, perhaps I'll raise it then. Because my sister [Mrs. C] has asked me to talk to them because she doesn't dare to either. Because they have a house and when the children move out they even would have the space. Well she is the one who is concerned there, and is a bit anxious . . .. And of course when they raise it, it's something different from when I raise it. Because I'm so far away, I wouldn't be available for long-term care . . .. But I think this is a subject that you simply must talk about with your parents in time.
>
> *W546d, four sisters, university degree, cohabiting, f/t employed, one child, maternal caring tradition*

To sum up, one crucial step for dealing productively with ambivalences in relation to parental care is to resolve the ambivalence that exists with respect to the norm of non-communication. Reproducing the cultural norm of non-articulation seems to secure openness and choice, while in practice it may actually conceal decisions already made or tacitly assign responsibilities to other family members. Ritual non-communication is therefore functional for those not considered the first line of resort, and is likely to hold ambivalence in suspense or increase it on the part of adult daughters who feel – and, according to a normative hierarchy of carers, are held – most responsible.

At the same time, the interviews show that enacting this norm differently and achieving communication alone does not necessarily resolve the dilemma of how to achieve a consensual and mutually beneficial outcome. The testimonies of adult children and their mothers show that children tend to distrust their parents' plans to move into an elder care home and mothers do not trust their children's assurances that they will not be "sent" to a home.

But even if it does not resolve intergenerational ambivalence, communication not only is a way of sharing concerns but also of promoting individual accountability – a prerequisite to distribute caring work in a more equitable manner (which in itself tends to mitigate ambivalence). Importantly, it is necessary: (a) to access various forms of services that are given not necessarily according to need, but often to those who most effectively articulate their needs (Twigg & Atkin, 1994); and (b) to mobilize personal support, which, as the narratives of the research participants' mothers impressively show, will be needed for whatever course of action is taken.

Of the three strategies of dealing with ambivalences in relation to parental care discussed here – avoiding the issue in the hope that it will not arise, individually anticipating residential and (shared) co-residential care arrangements, and initiating open discussion about them with other family members – the latter strategy appears most likely to create opportunities for new forms of family interaction and institutional transformation.

CONCLUSIONS

Through narratives of young adults in Germany, we have explored the generation of ambivalences and strategies of dealing with them in relation to prospective parental care. The aim was both to provide a more nuanced understanding of the effects that this potential transition has on the lives of adult children, and to further an empirically grounded conceptual advancement of ambivalence as a research construct. Conceptions of ambivalences as personal and structural, as psychosocial and achieved, and as performative and contextual provided general perspectives for interpreting the narratives.

The analysis shows that many adult children in contemporary Germany perceive the (anticipated) transition of parents' requiring personal care as a structurally ambivalent situation. They see it as a situation that simultaneously values two opposing courses of action and leads to decisional ambivalence between personally supporting their parents in old age and accommodating them in a home. Participants' reflections on viable and consensual care arrangements that can be interpreted as an attempt to deal with decisional ambivalence involved a multifaceted process of taking stock of: (a) the personal relationship between parents and children, often in comparison with the relationship between parents and siblings; (b) the living situation of older parents; (c) the respondent's own living situation; (d) past family care arrangements; (e) cultural-normative guidelines; (f) care institutions; and (g) expected commitments of other siblings (and partners).

The narratives reveal that personal and/or structural ambivalences can be assessed on each of these levels. For example, participants reported that they sought both personal closeness and distance from their parents, they identified increasing frailty and the insistence of parents to remain in their own homes, and they characterized care institutions as sites of both care and neglect. Thus in the context of parental care we deal with multiple personal and structural ambivalences that underlie decisional ambivalence.

Personal ambivalences refer to the simultaneity of opposing feelings and orientations such as closeness and distance that came to the fore when participants imagined co-residential living arrangements with their parents. Crucial factors for personal ambivalence included the perception that parents strongly rejected the different lifestyle (choices) of the respondent and that they had given more support to a sibling than to the respondent. This latter example indicates that personal ambivalences are assessed not on the basis of (perceived) parental behavior, feelings, or judgments in themselves, but in comparison to what respondents saw as socially appropriate for intergenerational relationships. Naming and assessing opposing feelings and orientations therefore already has a social dimension.

Structural ambivalences refer to the simultaneity of opposing offerings, directives, or guidelines for action inherent in institutional structures, such as state agencies or social policies. In the context of parental care needs, participants identified structural ambivalences in care institutions and also more broadly in cultural-normative guidelines and socio-historical generational positions. Importantly, these institutional or quasi-institutional structures not only generate ambivalences for certain groups of actors but also make available mechanisms for managing ambivalence. For example, in-home services or residential care can mitigate decisional ambivalence when the respondents focused on the availability and professionalism of qualified carers but sustain it when they focused on the institutional lack of intimate and emotional care. Structural ambivalences were likewise assessed in comparison to what respondents desired and saw as appropriate in specific situations, thereby emphasizing the relevance of affective investments and personal identity for the interpretation of structural ambivalence.

The notion of *multiple ambivalences* refers to overlapping personal and structural ambivalences that constitute multiple sources of, rather than a single cause for, decisional ambivalence. Even though the research participants distinguished different kinds of ambivalences (in the overall context of parental care), sometimes the source of the ambivalence was identified as emerging from opposing personal and institutional dimensions. For example, research participants assessed ambivalence in the life-courses of their mothers as arising from the simultaneity of their mothers' personal strength and marital subordination. Analysts must therefore specify if and when ambivalences cut across the personal and institutional dimensions. Moreover, the analysis indicated that multiple ambivalences do not necessarily merely add up and reinforce decisional ambivalence, but that the multitude of ambivalences increases the likelihood of transformative outcomes. Strong personal ambivalence may decrease the possibility of potentially harmful co-residential care arrangements, for example, and supplant institutional ambivalences.

Last but not least, the interviews show that research participants interpreted ambivalences not just in a biographical but also in a socio-historic context. Participants' localization of intergenerational positions and relationships in concrete historical conditions can serve to de-personalize and possibly mitigate personal ambivalences. More generally, such contextualizations highlight that intergenerational ambivalence with regard to dependence and independence, for example, is likely to have different meanings in different historical times. Analysts of ambivalence therefore need to take into account specific societal contexts that frame action and opportunity structures in intergenerational relations and distinguish between intra- and intergenerational ambivalences.

Specifying and contextualizing different kinds of ambivalences must address the question of who identifies them and how they were enacted and dealt with. Ambivalences effect actions and can be conceived as embodied practices. The analysis shows that if and how ambivalences were perceived and assessed depended noticeably on what I have called the psychosocial positionality of the participants – their location in relations of power constituted by socio-structural variables such as gender, educational and employment status, affective investments, and familial position. With respect to parental care, women were significantly more likely than men to assess ambivalences on all levels – possibly because they were culturally and socially expected to assume caring responsibilities more than their brothers.

However, this does not mean that all women dealt with ambivalences in the same way. Rather the respondents' specific psychosocial positionality entailed different material and symbolic resources that not only limited but also enabled creative actions. In this context, the analysis also focused on points of connection and differentiation with the four strategies of dealing with ambivalence identified in the Konstanz studies.

Displaying inaction and not planning for parental care needs, for example, was not considered as contradicting a solidaristic orientation (and could be even interpreted as "emancipation" in the Konstanz typology if previous familial care arrangements were not reproduced and personal contact maintained). It was a strategy of dealing with ambivalence that was used mainly by men. The assumption that other siblings, usually a sister, would provide co-residential care tended to facilitate inaction and mitigate decisional ambivalence. Conversely, it was exclusively women (with intermittent employment) who committed themselves to providing co-residential care (that can be interpreted as "solidarity" or, if the initiation of alternative arrangements had failed, as "captivation"). Women were also the majority who explicitly anticipated accommodating the parent in a home while committing themselves to complementary emotional care (which can be interpreted as "emancipation" if elder care had been provided in the family). For both groups of women the perceived absence of care commitments from other siblings increased decisional ambivalence. A crucial factor for planning residential (rather than co-residential) care was the availability of material resources to afford quality care among women (and some men) with more continuous employment that thereby had a mitigating effect on decisional ambivalence.

These findings throw into relief the context-dependency and relationality of strategies of managing ambivalence among siblings: Prospectively assuming primary caring responsibility frees other family members from planning and or even discussing parental care. In the case of parental care arrangements, "emancipation" of one sibling can be based on the "captivation" of another. This fact not only calls analytical attention to linked lives and interlocking trajectories of siblings but it also highlights that developing viable parental care arrangements, in principle, requires negotiating and reconciling different viewpoints and different strategies of dealing with ambivalence among family members.

Women's reported difficulties and failures to achieve communication with other family members highlight the strength and functionality of the norm of non-communication in close kin relationships and cast doubts on the claim that intergenerational relations are increasingly based on open negotiations between equal partners (Du Bois-Remond, Büchner & Krüger, 1993) For while communication with parents, partners, and siblings was identified as a necessary (but not sufficient) condition to develop consensual models and mitigate ambivalence, it was also feared: It could provoke emotional conflict by bringing irreconcilable differences in expectations and action patterns out into the open. (I have shown elsewhere (Lorenz-Meyer, 1999) that non-communication is also upheld with respect to regular grandparental child care. Older women simultaneously want to support their daughters' (in-law) employment careers by providing child care, and they want to lead their own lives independently from child care responsibilities without raising this issue with their children.)

Drawing attention to effects of reproducing non-communication, namely that it increased ambivalence on the part of those who were considered and who felt most responsible, the analysis indicates that its transformation (or differential performance) is one crucial way of dealing with decisional ambivalence productively. Dealing with decisional ambivalences through communication may not fully resolve it – communication cannot resolve underlying ambivalences in institutional structures, which can only be addressed on the level of social policy. But it can promote accountability and collective action in the family that may serve to transform institutional structures.

The uncovering of multiple ambivalences and multiple contextual strategies of dealing with ambivalences in the context of parental care needs thus points to the need of extending multidimensional analytical frameworks, such as the one pioneered by the Konstanz group.

Such frameworks need to take into account multiple, overlapping personal and structural ambivalences, as well as their contextual and relational nature, and the resources and effects of strategies of dealing with ambivalences. Understanding these issues is critical if the task is, as I think it must be, to understand ambivalences also from the perspective of and in the frames of meaning of social actors, and to promote its transformative potential. Simply calling for an end of ambivalence, or prioritizing one strategy of dealing with ambivalence, obfuscates its potential for transforming intergenerational relations. Insofar as scientific research has repercussions on social relations, a more fruitful approach would be to call for an open communication in dealing with ambivalence.

ACKNOWLEDGMENTS

My work has been greatly helped through exchanges with members of the International Network on Intergenerational Ambivalence. I would like to thank Kurt Lüscher and Karl Pillemer, in particular, for their invitation to the Transcoop workshops. Kurt Lüscher offered many helpful comments throughout the writing of this chapter, and Uta Brauckmann provided valuable ideas for thinking about some conceptual aspects of ambivalence.

REFERENCES

Bauman, Z. (1992). *Intimations of postmodernity*. London: Routledge.

Becker-Schmidt, R. (1980). Widersprüchliche Realität und Ambivalenz: Arbeitserfahrungen von Frauen in Beruf und Familie [Contradictory reality and ambivalence: Women's work experiences in occupation and family]. *Kölner Zeitschrift für Soziologie und Sozialpsychologie, 32*, 702–725.

Becker-Schmidt, R. (1993). Ambivalenz und Nachträglichkeit: Perspektiven einer feministischen Biographieforschung [Ambivalence and deferred action: Perspectives for feminist biographical research]. In: M. Küger (Ed.), *Was Heisst hier Eigentlich Feministisch? Zur Theoretischen Diskussion in den Geistes- und Sozialwissenschaften* [What is really meant by feminist? On the theoretical discussion in the humanities and social sciences] (pp. 80–92). Bremen, Germany: Donat Verlag.

Bleuler, E. (1910/11, July 30, August 13). Zur Theorie des schizophrenen Negativismus [On the theory of schizophrenic negativism]. *Psychiatrisch-Neurologische Wochenschrift*, 171–198.

Butler, J. (1993). *Bodies that matter: On the discursive limits of 'sex.'* London: Routledge.

Du Bois-Remond, M., Büchner, P., & Krüger, H. (1993). Die moderne Familie als Verhandlungshaushalt: Zum Wandel des Generationenverhältnisses im interkulturellen Vergleich [The modern family as a household of negotiation: On the change of intergenerational relations in an intercultural comparison]. *Neue Praxis, 27*, 32–42.

Felman, J. L. (2001). *Never a dull moment: Teaching and the art of performance*. London: Routledge.

Finch, J., & Mason, J. (1992). *Negotiating family responsibilities*. London: Routledge, Tavistock.

Freud, S. (1916/1989a). 13. Vorlesung: Archaische Züge und Infantilismus des Traumes [Lecture 13: Archaic traces and infantilism of dreams]. In: A. Mitcherlich, A. Richards & J. Strachey (Eds), *Sigmund Freud Studienausgabe, Vorlesungen zur Einführung in die Psychoanalyse und Neue Folge* [Sigmund Freud study edition, Lectures on the Introduction to Psychoanalysis and New Series] (pp. 204–216). Frankfurt a. M., Germany: Fischer.

Freud, S. (1917/1989b). 33. Vorlesung: Die Weiblichkeit [Lecture 33: Femininity]. In: A. Mitcherlich, A. Richards & J. Strachey (Eds), *Sigmund Freud Studienausgabe, Vorlesungen zur Einführung in die Psychoanalyse und Neue Folge* [Sigmund Freud study edition, Lectures on the Introduction to Psychoanalysis and New Series] (pp. 544–565). Frankfurt a. M., Germany: Fischer.

George, L. K. (1986). Caregiver burden: Conflict between norms of reciprocity and solidarity. In: K. A. Pillemer & R. S. Wolf (Eds), *Elder Abuse: Conflict in the Family* (pp. 67–92). Dover, MA: Auburn House.

Hagan, J. (2001). Cause and country: The politics of ambivalence and the American Vietnam war resistance in Canada. *Social Problems, 48*, 168–184.

Handel, W. (1979). Normative expectations and the emergence of meaning as solutions to problems: Convergence of structural and interactionist views. *American Journal of Sociology, 84*, 855–881.

Kaufmann, F.-X. (1993). Generationenbeziehungen und Generationenverhältnisse im Wohlfahrtsstaat [Intergenerational relationships and relations between generations in the welfare state]. In: K. Lüscher & F. Schultheis (Eds), *Generationenbeziehungen in Postmodernen Gesellschaften: Analysen zum Verhältnis von Individuum, Familie, Staat und Gesellschaft* [Intergenerational relations in postmodern societies: Analyses of the relation between individual, family, state, and society] (pp. 95–107). Konstanz, Germany: Universitätsverlag Konstanz.

Krüger, H., Born, C., Einemann, B., Heintze, S., & Saifi, H. (1987). *Privatsache Kind – Privatsache Beruf: "Und dann hab' ich ja noch Haushalt, Mann und Wäsche!" Zur Lebenssituation von Frauen mit kleinen Kindern in unserer Gesellschaft* [Private matter child – private matter occupation: "And then I also have household, husband, and laundry!" On the lives of women with small children in our society]. Opladen, Germany: Leske & Budrich.

Lorenz-Meyer, D. (1999). *The gendered politics of generational contracts: Changing discourses and practices of intergenerational commitments in West Germany.* Unpublished doctoral dissertation, The London School of Economics and Political Science, London.

Lorenz-Meyer, D. (2001). Zur Relationalität von Individualisierung und Verflechtung: Eine historische Betrachtung deutscher sozialer (Alters-) Sicherungssysteme [On the relation between individualization and interconnection: A historical analysis of German social security systems in old age]. In: H. Krüger & C. Born (Eds), *Individualisierung und Verflechtung. Geschlecht und Generation im Deutschen Lebenslaufregime* [Individualization and Interconnection. Gender and generation in the German life course regime] (pp. 233–253). Munich, Germany: Juventa Verlag.

Lüscher, K., Pajung-Bilger, B., Lettke, F., & Böhmer, S. (2000). Generationenambivalenzen operationalisieren: Konzeptuelle, methodische und forschungspraktische Grundlagen [Operationalizing intergenerational ambivalences: Conceptual, methodical, and practical foundations]. Arbeitspapier [Working Paper] 34.1. Universität Konstanz, Germany: Forschungsschwerpunkt "Gesellschaft und Familie."

Lüscher, K., & Pillemer, K. (1998). Intergenerational ambivalence: A new approach to the study of parent-child relations in later life. *Journal of Marriage and the Family, 60,* 413–425.

McCormick, B. (2002). Against ambivalence. Retrieved March 22, 2002, from: http://www.cloud9.net ~bradmcc/ambivalence.html

Merton, R. K., & Barber, E. (1963). Sociological ambivalence. In: E. A. Tiryakian (Ed.), *Sociological Theory, Values and Sociocultural Change: Essays in Honor of Pitirim A. Sorokin* (pp. 91–120). London: Free Press of Glencoe.

Parker, R. (1995). *Mother love, mother hate: The power of maternal ambivalence.* London: Basic Books.

Patterson, N. T. (1997). Conflicting norms in modern British kinship: Cases of domestic violence and competition for care in North Wales 1920–1996. *The History of the Family, 2*(1), 1–29.

Qureshi, H., & Walker, A. (1989). *The caring relationship: Elderly people and their families.* London: Macmillan.

Rich, A. (1986). Notes towards a politics of location. In: A. Rich (Ed.), *Blood, Bread, and Poetry* (pp. 210–231). London: Virago.

Savage, M., Bagnall, G., & Longhurst, B. (2001). Ordinary, ambivalent and defensive: Class identities in the Northwest of England. *Sociology, 35,* 875–892.

Thompson, M. M., & Holmes, J. G. (1996). Ambivalence in close relationships: Conflicted cognitions as a catalyst for change. In: R. M. Sorrentino & E. T. Higgins (Eds), *Handbook of Motivation and Cognition: The Interpersonal Context* (Vol. 3, pp. 497–530). New York: Guilford Press.

Twigg, J., & Atkin, K. (1994). *Carers perceived: Policy and practice in informal care.* Buckingham: Open University Press.

Varga, I. (2001). To live with ambivalence, or aren't we all barbarians? A response to Aziz Al-Azmeh. *International Sociology, 16,* 95–114.

Weigert, A. J., & Franks, D. D. (1989). Ambivalence: A touchstone of the modern temper. In: D. D. Franks & D. E. McCarthy (Eds), *The Sociology of Emotions* (pp. 205–207). Greenwich, CT: JAI.

PART IV:
INTERGENERATIONAL AMBIVALENCE INVOLVING YOUNG ADULTS

11. THE EXPERIENCE OF AMBIVALENCE WITHIN THE FAMILY: YOUNG ADULTS "COMING OUT" GAY OR LESBIAN AND THEIR PARENTS

Bertram J. Cohler

> ...my family remained blissfully blind to this reality [of being gay]. The news could be heartbreaking to them...as much as I believed in my rights [taking another boy to the prom], I valued my relationship with my parents too much to have it abruptly severed. After all, for years I had hidden my sexuality for fear of losing my parents' love As a child it had been *the* most important thing to me (Aaron Fricke, 1981, p. 71).

> Hopefully, they [gay children] will understand, or come to understand, that as hard as it was for them to look at themselves while growing up gay and say, "I am gay," it is a thousand times more difficult for you to look at yourself and say, "My son is gay." That doesn't mean you love them any less. You must love them as the individuals you've always loved, capable of every emotion you are capable of. If loving another person of the same sex is what they lean toward, then the least you can do is be thankful they are capable of love (Walter Fricke, 1991, p. 66).

Contemporary society provides unique opportunities for enhanced intergenerational social ties within the family of adulthood. It also presents unique challenges in relations among parents and their adult offspring. Viewed from a life-course perspective (Bengtson & Allen, 1993; Elder, 1974/1999, 1996; George & Gold, 1991; Hagestad, 1981) the family consists of kin including generations of great grandparents, grandparents, parents, and offspring representing birth cohorts whose outlook and life-experiences have been shaped by quite different

Intergenerational Ambivalences: New Perspectives on Parent-Child Relations in Later Life
Contemporary Perspectives in Family Research, Volume 4, 255–284
© 2004 Published by Elsevier Ltd.
ISSN: 1530-3535/doi:10.1016/S1530-3535(03)04011-1

social and historical circumstances (Boxer & Cohler, 1989; Mannheim, 1928). Understanding of self, others, and social life is a consequence of an interplay between one's place in the generations that comprise the family and one's life-long experiences as a member of a particular generation (Elder, 1995, 1996). From the perspectives of their own unique interplay of cohort and generation, parents, grandparents, and offspring each maintain different ideas regarding how offspring should live (Thompson, 1993).

The postwar period has seen dramatic changes regarding issues of value and lifestyle across the generations within the family. The time between the mid-1960s and the mid-1970s was one of particularly rapid social change (Gitlin, 1987; Tipton, 1982), leading to what has been characterized as post-modernity (Bauman, 1991; Foucault, 1973). The present time is one of questioning traditional values and norms, in which issues of how to maintain a sense of personal integrity and coherence have become major sources of concern (Gergen, 1994; Kohut, 1985). There is new awareness of the extent to which roles and identities are fluid, constructed and performed within an ever-changing social environment (Holland, Lachicotte, Skinner & Cain, 1998; Mishler, 1999; Sarup, 1996). Contested identities inevitably lead to contradictions, as family members across generations struggle to make sense of new conceptions of traditional roles – and seek to preserve solidarity and consensus as these new conceptions challenge unexamined presuppositions about the life course of parents and offspring alike (Coser, 1966; McCall & Simmons, 1978). As Lüscher (2000) observed, this new terrain of postmodernism inevitably leads to uncertainty and to ambivalence within the family, as traditional understandings of roles are called into question.

Among the most dramatic of these social changes has been reconsideration of the fundamental concepts of gender and sexual orientation. The Civil Rights movement of the 1960s provided a model for how other minority groups could obtain social recognition and respect. In the years following patron resistance in June, 1969, to a police raid on New York's gay bar, the Stonewall Inn, for example, younger gay men and women took advantage of this signal resistance to police harassment as the foundation for "Gay Liberation" (Duberman, 1993; Kaiser, 1997; Katz, 1995). In this socio-political movement, which led to at least partial public recognition and normalization of gay and lesbian sexual identity (Sullivan, 1995), many gay and lesbian young adults found support in the emerging Gay Rights movement for their own struggle to realize enhanced personal integrity. They stopped trying to hide their gay or bisexual identity and started disclosing it to friends, parents, and other family members (Boon & Miller, 1999).

Lüscher (2000) has observed that dependent situations inevitably lead to ambivalence; young adult offspring inevitably remain dependent upon their parents, including both emotional and financial support (Blos, 1979; Stierlin, 1974). Offspring concerned about their parents' welfare worry about the impact of this disclosure of alternative sexual identity upon family morale and solidarity (Ben-Ari, 1995a); they also are concerned about the impact of this disclosure upon their parents' continued provision of support. While young adults struggle to disclose their gay identity, fearing both loss of love and overt parental disapproval, parents of gay or lesbian young adults often express feelings of consternation following this disclosure. They often feel guilt at having "produced" gay or lesbian offspring as well as concern with the implications of this disclosure for relations within the intergenerational family and between family and community (Dew, 1994; Fricke & Fricke, 1991; Herdt & Koff, 2000; LaSalle, 2000; Savin-Williams, 2001; Shyer & Shyer, 1996; Strommen, 1989; Whyte, Merling, Merling & Merling, 2000).

Understood in terms of a structural perspective, this offspring disclosure appears to threaten expectable role transitions within the family such as becoming a parent and, for parents, becoming grandparents. This is so even though, as Patterson (2000) has reported, it is increasingly common for gay couples to become parents. Adoption, donor insemination, and bringing children from a heterosexual relationship into a gay or lesbian domestic union are all routes to parenthood and for transition into the role of grandparent.

From an emotional perspective, this disclosure leads to conflicting feelings on the part of both offspring and parents, as is well documented in the observations of Aaron Fricke (1981) and his father (Fricke & Fricke, 1991). Each generation seeks to maintain feelings of love and support. Nonetheless, young adults fear parental disappointment and are concerned that this disclosure will hurt their parents; and their parents are caught between feelings of love and concern for their offspring and feelings of disappointment and disapproval.

The tension between trying to maintain family solidarity and parental concern and suffering personal distress about such disclosure is a particularly salient example of ambivalence within the family. This chapter explores the implications of offspring disclosure of same-gender sexual identity for management of ambivalence within the family. It shows the significance of the concept of ambivalence as portrayed in social analysis (Lüscher, 2000; Lüscher & Pillemer, 1998; Merton & Barber, 1963; Smelser, 1998) for understanding the impact upon the relationship between parents and young adult offspring of the offspring's disclosure of a non-normative sexual identity.

Throughout this chapter, I often use the term "gay" to refer both to gay men and to lesbians. I do this because the terms used for alternative or minority sexual identity have changed over the past decade, and many young people identifying with alternative sexuality eschew any binary classification for their sexual identity. Even the term "gay" may be superseded by other terms referring to alternative or minority sexualities. Embracing the concept reflected in the work of E. Stein (1999), and maintaining that sexual orientation cannot be understood as either heterosexual or "straight normal," many young people use terms such as "spectrum" or "trans," indicating their refusal of any bipolar classification scheme for sexual identity.

LINKING THE PERSONAL AND THE SOCIAL: AMBIVALENCE AND INTERGENERATIONAL TIES

Understood as the simultaneous experience of necessarily conflicting attitudes, wishes, feelings, or intentions, the concept of ambivalence has a complex history in psychological and social analysis. Lüscher (2000) reviewed the history of this concept, initially used in the study of abnormal states, and then generalized to the realm of the usual and expectable in social life. It should be noted at the outset that the term "ambivalence" presents two problems for social analysis: adoption of a term initially intended to portray abnormal states for the expectable course of adult life, and the extension of a concept founded on the study of personal states to social analysis. Consistent with Bleuler's (Riklin, 1910/1911) initial discussion of the term ambivalence,[1] Freud (1909, 1912, 1912–1913, 1914) attempted to resolve the first problem by showing that ambivalence – as the experience of mixed and conflicting sentiments regarding those who are particularly important in one's own life – inevitably emerges out of the child's effort to resolve the tension between social reality and his or her own desire focused on the parents of early childhood. At the same time, Freud compounded the second problem by regarding the realm of the social as the personal writ large.

Understood in terms of contemporary social analysis, the concept of ambivalence was introduced into social study by Merton and Barber (1963), who observed that:

> In its most extended sense, sociological ambivalence refers to incompatible normative expectations of attitudes, beliefs and behavior assigned to a status (i.e. social position) or to a set of statuses in a society. In its most restricted sense, sociological ambivalence refers to incompatible normative expectations incorporated in a single role of a single social status . . . . In both the most extended and the most restricted sense, the ambivalence is located in the social definition of roles and statuses, not in the feeling-state of one or another type of personality (p. 6).

In their discussion of sociological ambivalence as incompatible normative expectations of attitudes, beliefs, and behavior assigned to a status (i.e. social position) or to a set of statuses in a society, Merton and Barber (1963) and Coser (1966) extended the concept of ambivalence from the personal realm to the social realm, and focused on the circumstances created by the social structure in which ambivalence is embedded. Attempting to resolve the problem of extending to social analysis a concept formulated for the study of the psychology of the individual, Merton and Barber (1963) are concerned with the structural context within which personal ambivalence arises such as generation within the family (Parsons, 1955), and those imposed by norms related to gender, age, and social prestige which change over time together with the changing historical and social context through which particular lives are fashioned.

Educated in both social theory and research as well as psychoanalysis, Smelser (1998) has suggested that the distinction between ambivalence at the level of individual motivation and ambivalence at the level of social position may be more difficult to maintain than Merton and Barber (1963) and Coser (1966) had thought. Reviewing the concept of ambivalence as Freud had portrayed it, Smelser suggested that ambivalence at the level of individual motivation: (a) is particularly powerful; (b) challenges present adaptation; and (c) requires protection against awareness of the intense feelings which are evoked in the wake of ambivalent feelings (Holder, 1975; Kris, 1984). Study of intergenerational relations within the family of adulthood provides an ideal context for integrating ambivalence as understood in terms of both personal motivation and social structure. Smelser (1998) suggests that situations emphasizing dependence, commitment, and loyalty breed ambivalence; disclosure of alternate sexual identity further increases the intergenerational ambivalence common in our society as young people and their parents struggle together to reconcile commitments to family, school, and community.

Lüscher and Pillemer (1998) and their colleagues have extended previous formulations of ambivalence to the study of intergenerational relations within the family. Consistent with Merton and Barber's (1963) initial discussion of ambivalence in social relations, Lüscher and Pillemer focus on ambivalence within the family and observe that:

> As a general concept, we use the term "intergenerational ambivalence" to designate contradictions in relationships between parents and adult offspring that cannot be reconciled. The concept has two dimensions: (a) contradictions at the level of social structure, evidenced in institutional resources and requirements; and (b) contradictions at the subjective level, in terms of cognitions, emotions, and motivations (1998, p. 416).

Lüscher and Pillemer emphasize that the concept of ambivalence includes portrayal of both solidarity and conflict in relations among family members. They comment that within the family we are able to see norms in action and what Hagestad (1981, 1986) has portrayed as the intersect of personal, family, and social time or lived experience of family members representing contrasting generation-cohorts. However, Lüscher and Pillemer also observe that focus on family conflict reflects only one aspect of complex family processes, expressed as ambivalent sentiments such as those among parents and their young adult offspring. Most often, important issues in the interpersonal world of the family include *both* positive and negative sentiments.

Emphasis upon family solidarity and consensus is clearly an important goal for family members. But conflict is also an inevitable element of relations within the intergenerational family of adulthood in which, inevitably, one generation depends upon another – as young adults depend upon their parents for love, affection, and support. Rather than viewing ambivalence in terms of a dualistic conception of solidarity vs. conflict, Lüscher (2000) and Lüscher and Pillemer (1998) maintain that because both solidarity and conflict remain central issues for the intergenerational family, ambivalence is never fully reconciled and for that very reason is a necessary focus of family study.

Study of offspring disclosure of alternative sexual identity provides an "ideal type" of situation in which to see management of ambivalence within the family, to study the tension between solidarity and conflict. Affection, concern with maintaining solidarity within the family, and yet strong personal and family impact are inevitably aspects both of the disclosure itself and of characteristic parental responses to it (Fricke & Fricke, 1991; Whyte, Merling, Merling & Merling, 2000).

Young adults closely associate emotional autonomy with capacity for maintaining a firm sense of self as separate and vigorous, even in the physical absence of the supportive caregivers of early childhood and their approval or disapproval (Blos, 1979). Feeling both connectedness and separation was understood by these young adult offspring as the capacity for maintaining an empathic and mutually satisfying relationship with middle-aged and older parents. Consistent with this shared value on autonomy, Lye (1996) has concluded in reviewing recent literature on adult child-parent relationships "that adult offspring and parents define their obligations to each other in a manner which is supportive of individual independence and that in this way norms of obligation are reconciled with norms of independence" (p. 97). The reality is that family life presumes what Boszormenyi-Nagy and Spark (1973) have termed "invisible loyalties" which conflict with shared value on self-provision (Ewing, 1990, 1991). In a culture in which the "Marlboro Man" is the icon, alone with his horse, silhouetted against the sun setting over the distant mountains, the notion that one might need or depend upon other family members becomes a source of ambivalence (Cohler, 1983; Pruchno et al., 1984).

COMING OUT GAY: DISCLOSURE AND AMBIVALENCE

Consistent with Simmel's (1908) concept of the stranger, and Bauman's (1991) portrayal of the construction of ambivalence within society, gay men and women are particularly likely to be viewed in an ambivalent manner by family and, more generally, the larger society. With the freedom of the outsider, and perceived as indeterminate in terms of normative sexual definitions, gay men and women are regarded by mainstream society as indeterminate, and even dangerous, because unfamiliar. As a consequence, gay men and women experience uncertainty regarding their own place in society. They must struggle to attain individual identity which is "never securely and definitely possessed – as it is constantly challenged and must be ever anew negotiated" (Bauman, 1991, p. 201). Bauman (pp. 60–61) also observes that:

> The stranger's unredeemable sin is, therefore, the incompatibility between his presence and other presences, fundamental to the world order; his simultaneous assault on several crucial oppositions instrumental in the incessant effort of ordering. It is this sin which throughout modern history rebounds in the constitution of the stranger as the bearer and embodiment of incongruity . . . the stranger is, for this reason, the bane of modernity.

Gay men and women represent an incongruous category of sexuality, indeterminate from the perspective of the well-ordered socio-sexual life world of bourgeois society.

Bauman also notes that stigma, emphasizing difference, becomes the most frequent manner for dealing with the unwelcome ambiguity of the stranger. Stigma emphasizes exclusion and the effort to keep the stranger "outside." However, because at odds with the precepts of modern liberal society, it is practiced on the sly. Following Bauman's discussion, society becomes impatient with such indeterminate categories as non-normative sexual orientation, and resolves the ambivalence reflected in such diversity through inclusion and assimilation. Within the family, over time, gay men and women become accepted once again and their status as indeterminate stranger is resolved as being "one of us." This acceptance is accorded to the partners of gay offspring who are welcomed in a similar manner as the spouses of straight offspring.

Viewed in terms of intergenerational relations within the family of adulthood, such continuing young adult emotional dependence might best be understood as interdependence – as family members continue to struggle in reconciling conflicting cultural demands between dependence and concern with those emphasizing personal autonomy and independence from others. However, consistent with the observations of Stierlin (1974) regarding variation in patterns of emotional separation more and less adaptive among adolescents and young adults and their parents, Frank, Laman and Avery (1988) suggest that emotional autonomy and the experience of connectedness-separation might be separate dimensions of emotional ties within the family.

This discussion of positive and negative sentiments within the family consisting of middle-aged parents, their young adult offspring recently disclosing gay or lesbian sexual identity, and often both grandparents and even great-grandparents as well, takes place in the context of changes that are becoming generally characteristic within the family of the adult years at the present time (Johnson, 1988). George and Gold (1991) have summarized these changes as: (a) an increased number of generations within the family, accompanied by fewer members of each generation; (b) the emergence of an "age-gapped" family structure, with ever greater age differences between adjoining generations, leading possibly to a diminished sense of shared family values as a consequence of the differential impact of cohort and social change upon adjoining generations; (c) a truncated family structure, in which ever larger numbers of both men and women offspring elect either not to marry or to remain voluntarily childless (Veevers, 1979); (d) an ever greater number of reconstituted families emerging out of divorce and remarriage; (e) continuing low intensity within the family of men across generations; and (f) an ever less predictable point in the course of life that marks the transition from youth to the full role portfolio of "settled adulthood" (Cohler & Boxer, 1984).

Reciprocal Socialization and the Expression of Ambivalence

Ambivalence can be viewed in a number of different ways in terms of roles and functions of the modified extended family within contemporary Western European and American society. Lüscher and Pillemer (1998) note caregiving for the oldest by the middle generation as one such issue. Brody (1990), Cohler (1987–1988), and Cohler and Grunebaum (1981) have illustrated this ambivalence in their study of middle-aged mothers and grandmothers within a particular cohort, their adult offspring, and their grandchildren. This perspective may also be applied in the study of the relationships involved with the middle generation caring for their young adult offspring. At the same time, it should be noted that such ties are likely to be particularly complex. Parental expectations of their obligation regarding continuing forward socialization of offspring may conflict with their effort to maintain close ties which are so important for the morale of each generation.

While the social changes of the past three decades have led to particular attitudes founded on the experiences of a particular cohort (such as cynical attitudes regarding the stability and safety of lifetime employment within "Generation-X"), the values of offspring are, overall, more closely allied with those of their parents than with any other single source of influence such as community or peer group (Bengtson, 1986; Bengtson, Cutler, Mangen & Marshall, 1985; Jennings & Niemi, 1981; Schaie & Willis, 1995). Indeed, one of the major factors leading to enhanced ambivalence within the multigenerational family of adulthood is the expression of cohort-based conflict regarding values (Rossi & Rossi, 1990), while seeking to maintain generational affectional closeness.

Backward socialization efforts among young adult offspring trying to foster change in their parents' understanding of self and experience in the light of their own enhanced contact with social change may also conflict with the effort to maintain family loyalties and morale (Boszormenyi-Nagy & Spark, 1973; Cook & Cohler, 1986) and to foster enhanced family ambivalence. For example, young adults coming out gay try to win their parents over to new conceptions of the parental role that focus on the meaning of being a parent of a gay offspring. Gay offspring often give their parents books to read and provide them with pamphlets and information about groups such as PFLAG (Parents and Friends of Lesbians and Gays) which can be sources of support as parents are socialized into new conceptions of their roles as parents of gay and lesbian offspring (Beeler & DiProva, 1999; Herdt & Koff, 2000). At the same time, this intergenerational struggle regarding reciprocal socialization necessarily leads to the expression of ambivalent sentiments accompanying the effort to change the other generation. Most often, this ambivalence is resolved in terms of shared agreement not to seek to influence the other generation regarding lifestyle issues, including choice of friends and romantic partner.

In the effort to avoid such conflict, parents and offspring both guard against the emergence of conflict in their respective family roles (Merton & Barber, 1963) including avoidance of discussing such issues as lifestyle or friendships among the offspring generation. Findings reported by Aldous and Klein (1991) suggest that even where there may be some intergenerational disagreement regarding lifestyle issues, this disagreement need not affect frequency of contact or expression of affection across generations. Parents try to fulfill their offsprings' expectations yet they ultimately may become resentful, which takes its toll both on parental morale and on affection expressed through continuing parental-offspring personal relationships (Aldous & Klein, 1991; Pillemer & Suitor, 1991).

Relations Among Gay and Lesbian Young Adults and their Parents

Much of the discussion regarding ambivalence within the family of adulthood focuses on affectional ties across generations. Suitor, Pillemer, Bohanon and Robison (1995) have observed that as children become older, there is greater closeness between parents and their young adult offspring. Discussing the issue of parental experience of disappointment, Pillemer and Suitor (1991) review findings from a Canadian survey study of elderly parents which shows a direct impact upon parental morale attendant upon offspring distress. Indeed, offspring personal distress emerged as a more important predictor of parental morale than any problem in their own present life.

Considering the possible factors which would lead to enhanced parental experience of distress upon learning of offspring problems, Pillemer and Suitor (1991) review three possible factors which might explain such distress: the possibility that parents might have to provide continued care and support which might impose additional burden on parents' own available energy and resources, the possibility that offspring difficulties might prevent these offspring from providing assistance for parents themselves as parents grow older and require help from their offspring, and the possibility that offspring difficulties might lead to increased conflict between the generations which might threaten family affectional solidarity. While the first and second possible factors might be issues in the instance of gay and lesbian offspring (particularly in the instance of HIV-positive gay offspring), the factor of threat to family solidarity is what seems to be the most significant when lesbian and gay offspring disclose their sexual identity to their parents.

While such disclosure may threaten family solidarity, both systematic study and first-person accounts suggest that, over the course of time, this disclosure leads to continuing residual ambivalence within the family. Further, the impact of the offspring's disclosure is most often profound parental sense of disappointment, followed by gradual adjustment to the reality that gay and lesbian offspring will not realize the expectable transition into the normatively presumed full role portfolio of adulthood, including marriage and parenthood. It also requires adjustments in thoughts about grandparenthood for the parents, which as Cohler and Grunebaum (1981) have shown, is itself an ambivalently regarded role transition for the generation of middle-aged and older parents.

The significance of enhanced role complementarity as a means for resolving ambivalence within the multigenerational family of adulthood is highlighted when, as Umberson (1992) has noted, the role portfolio of offspring does not become more congruent with that of parents over time. Offspring who continue unmarried into that time in their lives when they have moved from young adulthood to the years of settled adulthood pose problems for their parents, who worry that they may in some way have contributed to what is regarded as a problem in terms of the norms of the larger society. Indeed, consistent with findings reported by Aldous, Klaus and Klein (1985), offspring whose role portfolio does not come in time to complement that of the parental generation, through either misfortune or choice, are regarded as a "disappointment" to parents.

Sexual identity is not a fixed or essential characteristic of personal experience and has assumed quite different meanings over time (Chauncey, 1994). Following the Stonewall Inn riots of June, 1969, and the emergence of the Gay Rights movement, young people aware of same-gender desire found support for their desire in this growing social movement. Galatzer-Levy and Cohler (2002) have discussed the emergence of the gay identity over the three decades since then. The term "gay" (or "queer") may itself be traced to efforts to turn a "spoiled" into a positive identity (Goffman, 1963). Disclosure of a gay identity, most often first to friends as a kind of trial acceptance, then to brother(s) and sister(s), then to mother and, finally, to father (Herdt & Koff, 2000; Savin-Williams, 2001) is most often experienced as fostering enhanced personal coherence and no longer dissembling. At the same time, there is often considerable pain and conflict as the young person struggles with his or her own conflicting sexual desires and, often, with community opprobrium as well. Our continuing study of gay and lesbian adults across the second half of life has shown that men and women may report first awareness of same-gender sexual desire at any point, from earliest childhood through middle and later life. At least in part, the very social change which has made same-gender desire "virtually normal" (Sullivan, 1995) has contributed to enhanced awareness of alternative sexualities.

The present discussion focuses on the impact upon family affectional solidarity and ambivalence as related to the disclosure by young adult offspring of their gay or lesbian sexual identity. While this currently is regarded as the "ideal type" of coming-out to family, it must be emphasized that important issues are also posed for middle-aged men and women only presently aware of their gay or lesbian sexual identity, perhaps disclosing this identity to much older parents or to middle-aged and older brothers and sisters. Equally important is the impact for the marital family when husbands or wives disclose their sexual identity to spouse and offspring. Each of these circumstances poses additional issues for the study of family ambivalence in response to a family member's disclosure of alternative sexual identity (Sennett, 1977).

Study is also required of parents who disclose adoption of non-normative sexuality, and the impact of this non-normative sexuality for the social life of the family of adulthood similar to that posed by parents who divorce. Review of the study to date (Cohler & Galatzer-Levy, 2000; Drucker, 1998; Laird, 1993; Tasker & Golombok, 1997) has focused on the impact of such parental non-normative sexuality for the lives of children and adolescents, primarily among mothers of young children who end heterosexual marriages and begin a lesbian relationship. Initial study of men who begin gay relationships first in middle-adulthood has been anecdotally reported by Gochros (1989); additional study of middle-aged and older parents and grandparents who seek gay and lesbian sexual lifeways (Herdt, 1997; Hostetler & Herdt, 1998) remains an uncharted area of study (Galatzer-Levy & Cohler, 2002; Herdt & Beeler, 1998).

MANAGING AMBIVALENCE WITHIN THE FAMILY:
GAY YOUNG ADULTS AND THEIR PARENTS

Offspring disclosure of an alternative sexual identity provides an important means for understanding how contemporary families manage ambivalence. Coming-out gay involves both the emotional ambivalence of maintaining close emotional ties and the structural ambivalence that accompanies renegotiating roles as gay offspring or as parent or sibling of that family member. Although, as noted, Merton and Barber's (1963) initial conception of ambivalence was posed in terms of structural constraints imposed on linked social positions within such social systems as the family, people not only enact normatively constructed social positions but also assign meanings to these roles (Berger & Luckmann, 1966; Schutz & Luckmann, 1973, 1989). Indeed, as Garfinkel (1967), Gubrium (1988), Gubrium and Holstein (1993), and Holstein and Gubrium (1994, 1995) have suggested, how these roles are enacted is what particularizes their meanings within the family.

Meanings attached to these roles are refashioned over time as a consequence of induction, performance, and exit or loss of these cardinal adult roles. These roles are managed over a lifetime within the context of expectable and eruptive life changes characterizing both a cohort and the lives of members of this cohort. Lüscher (1998) and Lüscher and Pillemer (1998) have shown the significance for social analysis of integrating these structural and intersubjective perspectives. Subsequent role negotiations and both forward and backward socialization are consequences of the structural and emotional ambivalence which follows offspring disclosure of non-normative sexuality.

Recognizing the penchant for normalizing possibly disruptive, often eruptive, and presumably adverse life-events, both the social sciences and the general public seek to make sense of such adversity through the construction of stages (DeVine, 1984; Robinson, Walters & Skeen, 1989). This concern with construction of stages, already noted regarding the formation of sexual identity as gay or lesbian, further essentializes a complex social process and fails to account for the great variation as a function of social position, cohort, and the quite different vicissitudes of life experiences. Indeed, just as there is a host of factors leading to gay or lesbian sexual identity, there is a variety of ways in which gay and lesbian young people and their parents make sense of this experience – as expressed in the coming-out stories of both offspring and parents across cohorts (Davies, 1992).

Based on the detailed study of four families in which a young adult offspring had recently disclosed his or her gay sexual identity to parents, Beeler and

DiProva (1999) identified 12 salient family themes (Hess & Handel, 1959) of struggling with ambivalence. These include family efforts to normalize offspring non-normative sexual orientation and reconcile offspring gay identity with stereotypes regarding the gay lifestyle; shared ambivalence on the part of each generation regarding disclosure of the offspring's gay identity to grandparents and other relatives; parental reconciliation of feelings of guilt, sadness, blame, and loss consequent upon learning of the offspring's sexual orientation; reconciliation of the offspring's disclosure with a with non-normative life-course on the part of each generation which, for parents of an only child or whose other children can't or won't have children, means not having grandchildren and foreclosing other options requisite upon particular lifestyles. While many of these issues focus primarily on parental response to offspring disclosure, each has implications for the management of structural and subjective expressions of ambivalence within the family (Lüscher & Pillemer, 1998; Smelser, 1998).

First-person accounts of going gay or lesbian, and the process of disclosing this sexual identity to family ("coming-out" gay or lesbian), is most often recounted in the context of life-experiences and told in the terms of the present social and historical context (Plummer, 1995). Gay young adults report a sense of being indeterminate in terms of the larger society, reflecting this quality of the stranger (Bauman, 1991; Simmel, 1908) whose sexuality is threatening because indeterminate in terms of presently understood categories of sexual identity (Fricke, 1981; Kantrowitz, 1977; Miller, 1997; Porter & Weeks, 1991; Reid, 1973). As Liang (1998) and Plummer (1995) have shown, the discourse of "coming-out" stories is socially constructed; influences ranging from emergence of the AIDS pandemic to popular accounts of possible "causes" of alternative sexualities become a part of these narratives of coming-out. For example, a common parental response to offspring disclosure in this time of AIDS is to be afraid that offspring who go gay will be at increased risk for this terrible illness. Parents who are members of a local chapter of PFLAG tell a story of offspring disclosure and its impact upon the family very much in accord with the ideology of this organization. This discussion reviews first the young adult's perspective on disclosure and then the response of parents and siblings to it.

The experience of such disclosure has been well stated by one gay young man, Christopher Dew, as reported by his mother (Dew, 1994). Discussing the manner in which his parents might tell their friends and colleagues at work that he had come out gay:

> . . . you don't get any privacy if you're gay and come out. Your life is immediately everybody's property. Everybody likes gossip. But people are more comfortable if you stay in the

closet . . . but you and Dad don't have to feel responsible for any of this. You shouldn't do
anything that makes you feel uncomfortable (p. 187).

While there has been some systematic study of the young adult's perspective on disclosure (Cohen & Savin-Williams, 1996; Savin-Williams, 1996c, 1998a), there has
been little systematic study of the impact of this disclosure upon parents and other
family members. Much of the information to date has come from a small number
of first-person accounts, nearly always written by mothers of gay sons, regarding
the impact upon the family. There is much less information available regarding the
impact of daughters disclosing lesbian identity to parents and brothers and sisters.
    Offspring are generally reluctant to inform their fathers, preferring first to tell
their close friends, then brothers and sisters and their mother, and somewhat later
to tell their father (Ben-Ari, 1995a; Boxer, Cook & Herdt, 1991; Savin-Williams,
1996c). Indeed, in this as in other aspects of the study of lesbian and gay offspring
and their family, fathers most often are portrayed as distant but disapproving of the
offspring's lifestyle and social values. In the case of each generation, this discussion
takes advantage both of available systematic accounts and of first-person accounts.

Systematic Study of Gay Adult Offspring Coming-out to their Parental Family

Study of offspring disclosure of being gay has focused primarily upon the young
person's struggle to make the disclosure. There has been little systematic study of
the parental experience of the disclosure (Savin-Williams & Dubè, 1998). Findings
from two research programs focusing on young adults coming-out to their parents
have been reported: the Ithaca study of Savin-Williams and his colleagues (Cohen
& Savin-Williams, 1996; Savin-Williams, 1989a, b, 1996a, b, c, 1998a, 2001) and
the study of young people and their parents attending a drop-in program (Herdt &
Boxer, 1996; Herdt & Koff, 2000).
    In a series of papers published over the past decade, Savin-Williams and his
colleagues have reported findings from a study of students in two colleges initially
recruited into the study through the innovating technique of a picnic for gay and
lesbian students. They discuss findings regarding the process of coming-out to
family members of gay young adults within the cohort roughly identifying itself as
"Gen-X," born in the late 1960s and early 1970s. Cohen and Savin-Williams (1996)
and Savin-Williams (1989a, 1998a) report an association between the decision to
disclose sexual orientation and the probability of parental acceptance: Gay and
lesbian young adults make what they believe to be a prudent decision that their
parents can or cannot accept offspring sexual orientation. Few young adults expect
that their parents will react with overt hostility.

Findings regarding the probability of disclosing sexual orientation to parents vary considerably across studies (Savin-Williams, 1998a). While more than 80% of activist gay or lesbian teens have disclosed their sexual identity to their parents, less than a fifth of non-activist college students surveyed had made a similar disclosure. Many of these young people, however, believe that their parents are aware of their gender-atypical interests and have tacitly recognized their non-normative sexual orientation. Disclosure becomes particularly important when a young adult seeks to bring a lover or partner home for important family gatherings. Further, the offspring's lifestyle and romantic interests become increasingly visible in the post-college years as parents visit with their young adult offspring. Efforts to hide the reality of same-gender sexual orientation become ever more awkward. Parents may become increasingly concerned with their adult children's plans with respect to marrying and having children of their own; persistent parental inquiries and concern regarding offspring lack of heterosexual romantic interests often force offspring disclosure of same-gender sexual identity.

Savin-Williams (1998a, c, 2001) reported findings from both his own study of college-age youth and comparative findings from other such studies (D'Augelli, Hershberger & Pilkington, 1998) which shows that up to three-fourths of gay and lesbian young adults disclose their same-gender sexual identity to friends before telling any family members. Some studies (Cramer & Roach, 1988; DeVine, 1984) have suggested that gay or lesbian young adults are more likely to disclose their non-normative sexual orientation to brothers and sisters before disclosing to parents. Gay offspring implicitly assume that, as members of the same generation, brothers and sisters will be most likely to understand and support a non-normative sexual identity and lifestyle. However, when brothers and sisters are told, it is most often after coming-out to friends (Savin-Williams, 1998c). What is clear is that once learning of gay or lesbian sexual identity, more than three-fourths of brothers and sisters are supportive of this decision (Savin-Williams, 1998c). First disclosure within the family is more often to mothers than to fathers (Savin-Williams, 1998a, c); young people believe that mothers are more likely than fathers to respond in a supportive manner (Savin-Williams & Dubè, 1998).

Studying gay teenagers at a drop-in center, Herdt and Boxer (1996) report that these young people most often reported their mother as the family member most likely to be aware of their non-normative sexual orientation. Girls were more likely than boys to report parental awareness of their alternative sexual orientation, whether stated or unstated, but were also more likely than boys to disclose their alternative sexual orientation. Those young people who did disclose their alternative sexual orientation also reported less conflicted relationships with parents prior to such disclosure. Further, as Savin-Williams (1998a, c) notes, young people are likely to tell their mother in person, while either writing to their father or hoping that their mother will tell their father. Daughters appear to have particular difficulty telling their fathers about their lesbian sexual identity (Savin-Williams, 1998a). Boxer, Cook and Herdt (1991) and D'Augelli, Hershberger and Pilkington (1998) have reported similar findings. Boxer, Cook and Herdt (1991) report that offspring at best experience their father as emotionally "absent" from their lives, so that the response of fathers was less salient for them than that of their mother. Cramer and Roach (1988) speculate that many fathers are relatively distant figures in the lives of their offspring; the relationship may be strained even prior to the disclosure of offspring non-normative sexual identity.

Young people from fundamentalist religious backgrounds were particularly unwilling to disclose non-normative sexual orientation to their family. Striking in this study is the report of a "silent disclosure" in which neither the young person nor the parents explicitly acknowledge the young person's sexual identity as gay or lesbian, although each generation tacitly recognizes this reality (Wilkerson, 2000). One young person reported his parents' continual inquiries regarding his "social life," while another young man reported his parents' continuing efforts to arrange dates with eligible girls – daughters of family friends. Whether implicitly or explicitly acknowledged, lesbian young people reported that their relationship with their father had deteriorated. Negative changes with parents were less common among gay boys.

Where young people felt supported by fathers, such support may have reflected a previous strong relationship. In general, young adults reported better relations with parents after disclosure than adolescents did. Further, these young people report that focus on maintaining family unity was more significant for the family than any problems posed by offspring being gay or lesbian. This finding conflicts, however, with a report by Newman and Muzzonigro (1993), also based on offspring self-report, showing that the presence of traditional family values within both mainstream and ethnic families was associated with increased family conflict regarding offspring disclosure. Tragically, in the study reported by D'Augelli, Hershberger and Pilkington (1998) and Pilkington and D'Augelli (1995), as in reports by Remafedi (1987), young people who disclose their sexual orientation in school and at work are more likely to suffer physical abuse, more likely to have suicidal wishes, and more likely to make suicidal gestures than youth who conceal their gay sexual identity from straight society.

Among young adults not disclosing their sexual orientation, fear of the father's response was the reason most often cited. Herdt and Boxer (1996) report similar findings from a study of gay youth and their family. Fathers appear to experience greater guilt than mothers upon learning of their offspring's gay or lesbian sexual identity (Ben-Ari, 1995a). Parents of daughters coming out lesbian appear to feel greater guilt and anguish than parents of boys coming out gay (Ben-Ari, 1995a;

Boxer, Cook & Herdt, 1991). Perhaps because a daughter is presumed to have children and carry on the family lineage, disappointment regarding daughters becoming lesbian is greater than that regarding sons becoming gay.

Cohen and Savin-Williams (1996) report that parental response to offspring disclosure is often idiosyncratic. Reflecting offspring ambivalence regarding the impact of disclosure on emotional closeness with their parents, Savin-Williams (1996c) observes further that young adults who choose to disclose to parents have quite different relations with their parents than those choosing not to make such disclosure. Those young people fearing the impact upon their relationship with their parents following disclosure may or may not be accurate in their appraisal of parental responses. This issue has not been well-studied; there is very little information available on the impact upon the family of the process of coming out where the *same* offspring disclosing their alternative sexual identity and their own parents have been studied as a whole family. Available findings come mainly from families involved with PFLAG (Beeler & DiProva, 1999; Herdt & Koff, 2000) where both generations are likely to have had better relations prior to disclosure. This implies both reduced conflict regarding offspring disclosure and greater effort at resolving the inevitable ambivalent feelings which parents express regarding it (Wilkerson, 2000).

Systematic Study of Parental Response to Disclosure

With the passage of time after self-identifying as gay or lesbian, pressure to come-out to parents increases (D'Augelli, Hershberger & Pilkington, 1998). It may become increasingly difficult for offspring to "hide" their alternative sexual orientation. It is also generally known that self-esteem and the sense of personal coherence increase after telling parents and other family members (Savin-Williams, 1989a, 2001).

Reviewing extant findings regarding parental response to offspring disclosure, Cohen and Savin-Williams (1996) note that some negative response is likely even among those parents who consider themselves to be liberal and accepting. While a good relationship with parents prior to this announcement is a reliable predictor of parental response to the information, nevertheless this disclosure leads to marked ambivalence among parents who worry about what it will mean for their children's future; it also brings out structural ambivalence in terms of what it will mean for the parents' own lives across their middle and later years, and for provision of care by their offspring when they grow old.

A long history of gender-atypical interests and lack of interest in heterosexual dating among boys are often regarded as evidence of non-normative sexual orientation. To date, there have been only three systematic studies of parental response to offspring disclosure regarding gay or lesbian sexual identity (Ben-Ari, 1995a, b; Boxer, Cook & Herdt, 1991; Savin-Williams, 2001). Parents interviewed in the study by Boxer, Cook and Herdt (1991) expressed concern primarily about the discrimination and presumed increased risk for AIDS attendant upon the offspring's chosen lifestyle. Their principal concern appeared to be for their offspring rather than for themselves. There was less emotional ambivalence than structural ambivalence in these parental reports: Parents reported that offspring disclosure led them into a period of increased self-reflection and reordering of priorities and expectations for themselves, as these middle-aged and older parents struggled with such implications as the possibility of having fewer grandchildren. As many of the parents in this study were active members of a local PFLAG group, they represent an unusual group; with the support of other PFLAG parents, they had been able to deal with many of the ambivalent feelings elicited by having a gay or lesbian offspring.

Once again, as in other reports, parents of daughters disclosing lesbian sexual orientation had greater difficulty reordering their own expectations and priorities than was reported among parents of sons. Reflecting issues of structural ambivalence, daughters are seen as the key to realizing grandchildren: For fathers, grandparenthood means the possibility of carrying on family traditions; while for mothers, as daughters first marry and then become parents, there is enhanced role complementarity (Cohler, 1987–1988; Low, 1978). Boxer, Cook and Herdt (1991) also report that parents had the greatest difficulty accepting non-normative sexuality in somewhat older offspring. Among offspring who are younger at the age of disclosure, there may be some hope that this is a transient experience of youth; with offspring who are older at the age of disclosure, it is more difficult to maintain such hope.

Significant in this report is the extent to which parents had implicitly acknowledged the reality of the offspring's sexual identity. Many of the offspring in the study reported by Boxer, Cook and Herdt (1991) were in their mid-twenties at the time that they and their parents explicitly acknowledged their gay or lesbian sexual identity. It was clear, however, that each generation had implicitly acknowledged this reality prior to formal explicit acknowledgment. Boxer, Cook and Herdt (1991) see such tacit acknowledgment as evidence of a "DMZ" – a term initially used in this context by Hagestad (1981) – reflecting ambivalence regarding the offspring's non-normative sexual identity, and seeking to preserve family solidarity while disapproving of the offspring's disclosure and lifestyle. Explicit acknowledgment of the offspring's gay or lesbian sexual identity is avoided, but at the cost of not realizing greater closeness between the generations.

Study of relations between young adults and their parents more generally in contemporary society suggests that this shared agreement regarding subjects not discussed contributes to reduced conflict between generations, since cohort related social change inevitably leads to different perspectives between generations regarding issues of offspring lifestyle and increases ambivalence on the part of both generations as they struggle to understand each other's perspective on family and relationships (Hagestad, 1981). Issues of parental response to offspring disclosure of non-normative sexual identity must be understood within the context more generally of relations between young adults and their parents; systematic study of intergenerational relations among otherwise comparable groups of gay and straight offspring and their parents is required in order to understand the particular impact upon intergenerational relations explicitly related to offspring disclosure of alternative sexual orientation (Savin-Williams & Dubè, 1998). In this as in so many areas of the study of family life, cross-sequential study of whole families is an urgent task (Baltes, 1968; Baltes, Cornelius & Nesselroade, 1979; Schaie, 1996).

While the Chicago area parents interviewed by Boxer and his colleagues (Boxer, Cook & Herdt, 1991) were often isolated from contact with the gay community, the families interviewed by Ben-Ari were living in the midst of the San Francisco Bay area community which had become a center of gay life through the preceding two decades. Most parents in this study reported an improved relationship with their offspring following offspring disclosure, and most often when offspring were in their twenties. Just as in the Chicago study, parents were most concerned about the impact upon offspring of possible social stigma and discrimination, followed by concern with the possibility that offspring would be at increased risk for AIDS which, by the 1990s, had become a pandemic in the Bay area. However, Ben-Ari (1995a) maintains that this concern regarding the impact of AIDS was less significant than was concern regarding social discrimination. Once again, perhaps reflecting issues of structural ambiguity focused on concern that they wouldn't realize grandparenthood, parents of lesbians expressed greater difficulty accepting their offspring's disclosure than did parents of gay sons. The greatest guilt regarding one's own presumed contribution to offspring non-normative sexual identity was expressed, however, by mothers of gay sons and fathers of lesbian daughters.

Fear of rejection appeared to be an important determinant of parental response to offspring disclosure of gay or lesbian sexual identity in Ben-Ari's study. Offspring anticipating the possibility of parental rejection found confirmation of their concerns, in the sense that their parents reported that it was difficult to accept their offspring's disclosure. Parents more isolated from the liberal attitudes and lifestyle of the Bay area were also less able to accept offspring disclosure. Mothers in this study also found it easier than fathers to accept offspring non-normative sexual identity. Significantly, within this Bay area group of parents, more than three-fourths of the parents had found a parent support group in dealing with their offspring's disclosure. Mothers are most likely to spur this effort to join support groups and to be able to use support groups in dealing with their own feelings ambivalent feelings following offspring disclosure (Henderson, 1998).

Regarding the resolution of parental ambivalence in response to offspring disclosure, Savin-Williams and Dubè (1998) report that parental response was primarily one of denial, maintaining that the offspring was in a "phase." Consistent with Ben-Ari's (1995a, b) reports, in which parents of younger offspring were more likely than parents of older ones to view this disclosure as a phase. Savin-Williams' study (1998b, c) suggested that fathers were at least as likely as mothers to respond in a positive manner.

Clearly, mothers and fathers of gay and lesbian adolescents and young adults react in quite different ways to this disclosure. Savin-Williams (1998b, c, 2001) suggests that parents initially react with feelings of guilt when hearing of their offspring's gay or sexual identity. Systematic study and published anecdotal parental narratives (Baker, 1998; Dew, 1994; Whyte, Merling, Merling & Merling, 2000) suggest, however, that parents gradually accommodate offspring non-normative sexual orientation. Apparently, over time, a process of reciprocal socialization takes place: While parents continue efforts at forward socialization into expectable adult roles, their gay or lesbian offspring induct their parents into modified understandings of these roles.

These findings suggest that continuing efforts at reciprocal socialization on the part of each generation is an important means for resolving ambivalence regarding the offspring's gay identity. For example, parents or parents-in-law are generally responsible for the forward socialization of offspring and spouse into the role of married offspring. When a gay man or woman finds a partner, the offspring more often helps his or her parents modify their understanding of the role of spouse or "in-law," now understood in terms of relations both with the partner and the partner's family (Serovich, Skeen, Walters & Robinson, 1993; Whyte, Merling, Merling & Merling, 2000). Within families in which offspring have gay or lesbian partners, such socialization is more likely to be reciprocal, but also more likely to lead to increased structural and affectional ambivalence regarding these new roles than in more traditional families.

CONCLUSION

Disclosure by young adult offspring of same-gender sexual desire to family members provides a unique opportunity for the study of ambivalence within the family. Ambivalence is understood as a paradox arising from the need to renegotiate roles within the family as offspring become adults, and from conflicting sentiments engendered by ambiguity between young adults, their parents, and other relatives within the modified extended family characteristic of contemporary urban society (Lüscher & Pillemer, 1998; Merton & Barber, 1963). Study of young adult offspring and their parents is likely to yield important information regarding the expression and management of this ambivalence. Young adults are particularly close to sources of social change, which inevitably requires renegotiation of long-standing meanings inherent in continuing reciprocal socialization across generations.

Young adulthood represents an important point for the study of ambivalence within the family (Stierlin, 1974). As young adults begin to establish a life beyond their parental family, and to assemble an adult role portfolio, particular structural strains are introduced within the larger family. These issues are compounded when a young adult comes out gay or lesbian. Reciprocal resocialization following initial offspring disclosure requires imparting information about what it is like to be involved in the gay and lesbian community, and about issues of partnership and caring for a same-gendered life partner; it also requires restructuring of expectations regarding the place of the gay or lesbian family member within the larger family group. For example, other family members may be concerned that gay or lesbian offspring will not be willing to provide care for older parents or grandparents, or that the life partner of these gay and lesbian offspring will not feel the same role pressures as a spouse by marriage in assisting with this care of parents as they grow older.

Findings reported to date show that young adults experience considerable personal struggle prior to disclosure to other family members of gay or lesbian sexual identity (Cohen & Savin-Williams, 1996; Savin-Williams, 1998a, 2001). In the first place, such disclosure generally follows a period of intense reflection regarding the meanings for oneself of being gay or lesbian. Offspring may have learned to hide their sexual orientation from family and friends or even from themselves; often, while parents read cues such as lack of interest in heterosexual dating or atypical gender interests as evidence of a non-normative sexual orientation, offspring may continue to deny this reality (Reid, 1973). Common concerns regarding reluctance to disclose a non-normative sexual orientation include concern whether parents will be able to accept it, fear of emotional or physical abuse or outright rejection following disclosure, concern with loss of status within the family, guilt regarding the presumed burden this announcement might impose on other family members, and concern regarding the implications for relations with grandparents and other extended kin following this announcement.

Reciprocal socialization, an inevitable aspect of intergenerational relations through the course of life, is a source of particular structural or role ambivalence within families in which offspring disclose gay or lesbian identity. While young

adults within each cohort or generation have to teach their parents a new role
of parenthood within the family of adulthood, gay and lesbian young adults are
confronted with the additional task of teaching their parents what it means to
be gay, and how to relate to gay friends and partners and their partners' family.
Emotional ambivalence becomes particularly evident as parents and offspring
continue to negotiate such issues as bringing home a gay or lesbian partner.
Parents are then confronted with the task of redefining relations with kin and
within the community as they inevitably find themselves disclosing their son
or daughter's gay identity to neighbors and coworkers. Accompanying this role
negotiation, parents also confront the task of rewriting their own story of their
relationship with their gay son or daughter, too often accompanied by unwarranted
feelings of guilt at "having made" a son or daughter gay.

Parental response to offspring disclosure as gay or lesbian reflects concern
both for self and for the offspring. Difficulties in accepting non-normative sexual
identity may be a problem for families with more traditional values, although
this issue of value differences is complex and reflects the interplay of social
change across cohorts or generations within the family. Concerned that they will
become alienated from their gay or lesbian offspring, parents may have difficulty
integrating the offspring's lover or partner and his or her own relatives within
the family, and may have concerns regarding the impact of this disclosure for
status within both the extended family and the larger community (Boxer, Cook &
Herdt, 1991).

Even after leaving home, reciprocal socialization continues as offspring succes-
sively acquire the roles associated with work, marriage, and parenthood (Hogan,
1981; Hogan & Astone, 1986). Parents and offspring often implicitly understand
that lifestyle issues such as choice of friends, income, and sexual identity are
not to be discussed in the interest of preserving feelings of family solidarity
(Hagestad, 1981). While implicit and covert, each generation recognizes that such
discussion may lead to increased tension and increased structural and emotional
ambivalence. Particular problems in maintaining these boundaries regarding
topics for intergenerational discourse are introduced when offspring have a
non-normative sexual orientation. Issues of disclosure of same-gender sexual
identity challenge the ordinary proscription against discussing offspring lifestyle
(Beeler & DiProva, 1999; Boxer, Cook & Herdt, 1991; D'Augelli, Hershberger
& Pilkington, 1998; Savin-Williams, 1996c). As a consequence, additional
structural and emotional ambivalence within the family arises which is much
less characteristic within those families in which offspring maintain a normative
sexual orientation.

As they begin to redefine their relationship with their gay or lesbian offspring, parents may struggle with a sense of loss and grief regarding such prior

expectations as having grandchildren from this offspring (although both social change and medical advances have led an increasing number of gay and lesbian offspring to be able to have children of their own). These efforts at renegotiating the relationship are accompanied by concerns regarding the psychological well-being of their offspring, including concern that offspring will suffer from anti-gay prejudice, concern that offspring will grow old lonely and alone, and concern that he or she will be rejected by brothers, sisters, and other family members. Parents also express concern that their gay offspring will be at increased risk for sexually transmitted disease, including HIV/AIDS.

In all these respects, offspring disclosure of a non-normative sexual identity poses a challenge for intergenerational solidarity.

NOTES

1. The concept of ambivalence is founded in Bleuler's (Riklin, 1910/1911) discussion of schizophrenia and was adopted by Freud (1912) in his discussion of the dynamics of the transference in clinical psychoanalytic intervention. Freud observed that negative and positive feelings often are directed at the same time towards the same person. He elaborated this concept of ambivalence in terms both of individual psychodynamics and of cultural institutions in his essay, *Totem and Taboo* (1912–1913). This conjunction of loving and hating feelings is but one of three kinds of ambivalence initially described by Bleuler who refers to intention, intellect, and sentiment as the three arenas of mental life in which ambivalence or contradictory feelings within the same person might be observed. This concept has been discussed in terms of the psychoanalytic literature by Holder (1975) and Kris (1984). Coser (1966, p. 176) suggests a parallel concept of ambivalence within social life reflecting contradictory (and inevitably irreconcilable) expectations among two or more role partners.

REFERENCES

Aldous, J., Klaus, E., & Klein, D. M. (1985). The understanding heart: Aging parents and their favorite children. *Child Development, 56,* 303–316.
Aldous, J., & Klein, D. (1991). Sentiment and services: Models of intergenerational relationships in mid-life. *Journal of Marriage and the Family, 53,* 595–608.
Baker, J. M. (1998). *Family secrets: Gay sons – A mother's story.* New York: Haworth Press, Harrington Park Press.
Baltes, P. H. (1968). Longitudinal and cross-sequential sequences in the study of age and generation effects. *Human Development, 11,* 145–171.
Baltes, P., Cornelius, S., & Nesselroade, J. (1979). Cohort effects in developmental psychology. In: J. R. Nesselroade & P. B. Baltes (Eds), *Longitudinal Research in the Study of Behavior and Development* (pp. 61–87). New York: Academic Press.
Bauman, Z. (1991). *Modernity and ambivalence.* Ithaca, NY: Cornell University Press.

278 BERTRAM J. COHLER

Beeler, J., & DiProva, V. (1999). Family adjustment following disclosure of homosexuality by a family member: Themes discovered in narrative accounts. *Journal of Marital and Family Therapy, 25,* 443–459.

Ben-Ari, A. T. (1995a). The discovery that an offspring is gay: Parents', gay men's and lesbians'. *Journal of Homosexuality, 30,* 89–112.

Ben-Ari, A. T. (1995b). It's the telling that makes the difference. In: R. Josselson & A. Lieblich (Eds), *The Narrative Study of Lives: Interpreting Experience* (Vol. 3, pp. 153–172). Thousand Oaks, CA: Sage.

Bengtson, V. L. (1986). Sociological perspectives on aging, families and the future. In: M. Bergener (Ed.), *Perspectives on Aging: The 1986 Sandoz Lectures in Gerontology* (pp. 237–263). New York: Academic Press.

Bengtson, V. L., & Allen, K. R. (1993). The life course perspective applied to families over time. In: P. G. Boss, W. J. Doherty, R. LaRossa, W. R. Schumm & S. K. Steinmetz (Eds), *Sourcebook of Family Theories and Methods: A Contextual Approach* (pp. 469–499). New York: Plenum Press.

Bengtson, V. L., Cutler, N. E., Mangen, D. J., & Marshall, V. W. (1985). Generations, cohorts, and relations between age groups. In: R. Binstock & E. Shanas (Eds), *Handbook of Aging and the Social Sciences* (pp. 304–338). New York: Van Nostrand Reinhold.

Berger, P., & Luckmann, T. (1966). *The social construction of reality.* Garden City, NY: Doubleday Books.

Blos, P. (1979). *The adolescent passage.* Madison, CT: International Universities Press.

Boon, S. D., & Miller, J. A. (1999). Exploring the links between interpersonal trust and the reasons underlying gay and bisexual males' disclosure of their sexual orientation to their mothers. *Journal of Homosexuality, 37,* 45–68.

Boszormenyi-Nagy, I., & Spark, G. N. (1973). *Invisible loyalties: Reciprocity in intergenerational therapy.* Hagerstown, MD: Harper and Row.

Boxer, A., & Cohler, B. (1989). The life course of gay and lesbian youth: An immodest proposal for the study of lives. In: G. Herdt (Ed.), *Gay and Lesbian Youth* (pp. 315–355). New York: Harrington Park Press.

Boxer, A., Cook, J., & Herdt, G. (1991). Double jeopardy: Identity transitions and parent-child relations among gay and lesbian youth. In: K. Pillemer & K. McCartney (Eds), *Parent-Child Relations Throughout Life* (pp. 559–592). Hillsdale, NJ: Lawrence Erlbaum.

Brody, E. (1990). *Women in the middle: Their parent care years.* New York: Springer.

Chauncey, G. (1994). *Gay New York: Gender, urban culture and the making of the gay male world, 1890–1940.* New York: Basic Books.

Cohen, K. M., & Savin-Williams, R. C. (1996). Developmental perspectives on coming out to self and others. In: R. C. Savin-Williams & K. M. Cohen (Eds), *The Lives of Lesbians, Gays, and Bisexuals* (pp. 113–151). Fort Worth, TX: Harcourt Brace.

Cohler, B. (1983). Autonomy and interdependence in the family of adulthood. *The Gerontologist, 23,* 33–39.

Cohler, B. (1987–1988). The adult daughter-mother relationship: Perspective from life-course family study and psychoanalysis. *Journal of Geriatric Psychiatry, 21,* 51–72.

Cohler, B. J., & Boxer, A. (1984). Middle adulthood: Settling into the world – Person, time, and context. In: D. Offer & M. Sabshin (Eds), *Normality and the Life-Cycle* (pp. 145–204). New York: Basic Books.

Cohler, B., & Galatzer-Levy, R. (2000). *The course of gay and lesbian lives: Social and psychoanalytic perspectives.* Chicago: University of Chicago Press.

Cohler, B., & Grunebaum, H. (1981). *Mothers, grandmothers, and daughters: Personality and childcare in three-generation families*. New York: Wiley.

Cook, J., & Cohler, B. (1986). Reciprocal socialization and the care of offspring with cancer and with schizophrenia. In: N. Datan, A. Greene & H. Reese (Eds), *Life-Span Developmental Psychology: Intergenerational Relations* (pp. 223–244). Hillsdale, NJ: Lawrence Erlbaum.

Coser, R. L. (1966). Role distance, sociological ambivalence, and transitional status systems. *American Journal of Sociology, 72*, 173–187.

Cramer, D. W., & Roach, A. J. (1988). Coming out to mom and dad: A study of gay males and their relationships with their parents. *Journal of Homosexuality, 15*, 79–91.

D'Augelli, A. R., Hershberger, S. L., & Pilkington, N. W. (1998). Lesbian, gay, and bisexual youth and their families: Disclosure of sexual orientation and its consequences. *American Journal of Orthopsychiatry, 68*, 361–371.

Davies, P. (1992). The role of disclosure in coming out among gay men. In: K. Plummer (Ed.), *Modern Homosexualities: Fragments of Gay and Lesbian Gay Experience* (pp. 75–86). New York: Routledge.

DeVine, J. (1984). A systematic inspection of affectional preference orientation and the family of origin. *Journal of Social Work and Human Sexuality, 2*, 9–17.

Dew, R. F. (1994). *The family heart: A memoir of when our son came out*. New York: Ballentine Books.

Drucker, J. (1998). *Families of value: Gay and lesbian parents and their children speak out*. New York: Plenum, Insight Books.

Duberman, M. (1993). *Stonewall*. New York: St. Martin's Press.

Elder, G. (1974/1999). *Children of the great depression: Social change in life experience* (15th anniversary ed.). Boulder, CO: Westview Press.

Elder, G. (1995). The life-course paradigm: Social change and individual development. In: P. Moen, G. H. Elder, Jr. & K. Lüscher (Eds), *Examining Lives in Context: Perspectives on the Ecology of Human Development* (pp. 101–139). Washington, DC: American Psychological Association.

Elder, G. H., Jr. (1996). Human lives in changing societies: Life course and developmental insights. In: R. Cairns, G. H. Elder, Jr. & E. Costello (Eds), *Developmental Science: Multiple Perspectives* (pp. 31–62). New York: Cambridge University Press.

Ewing, K. P. (1990). The illusion of wholeness: Culture, self, and the experience of inconsistency. *Ethos, 18*, 251–278.

Ewing, K. P. (1991). Can psychoanalytic theories explain the Pakistani woman? Intrapsychic autonomy and interpersonal engagement in the extended family. *Ethos, 19*, 131–157.

Foucault, M. (1973). *The order of things: An archeology of the human sciences*. E. Gallimard (Trans.). New York: Random House, Vintage Books.

Frank, S., Laman, M., & Avery, C. (1988). Young adults' perceptions of their relationships with their parents: Individual differences in connectedness. *Developmental Psychology, 24*, 729–737.

Freud, S. (1909/1955). Notes upon a case of obsessional neurosis. In: J. Strachey (Ed. & Trans.), *The Standard Edition of the Complete Psychological Works of Sigmund Freud* (Vol. 10, pp. 158–250). London: Hogarth Press.

Freud, S. (1912/1958). The dynamics of the transference. In: J. Strachey (Ed. & Trans.), *The Standard Edition of the Complete Psychological Works of Sigmund Freud* (Vol. 13, pp. 99–108). London: Hogarth Press.

Freud, S. (1912–1913/1953). Totem and taboo. In: J. Strachey (Ed. & Trans.), *The Standard Edition of the Complete Psychological Works of Sigmund Freud* (Vol. 13, pp. 1–161). London: Hogarth Press.

Freud, S. (1914/1953). Some reflections on schoolboy psychology. In: J. Strachey (Ed. & Trans.), *The Standard Edition of the Complete Psychological Works of Sigmund Freud* (Vol. 13, pp. 241–244). London: Hogarth Press.

Fricke, A. (1981). *Reflections of a rock lobster*. Boston, MA: Alyson.

Fricke, A., & Fricke, W. (1991). *Sudden strangers: The story of a gay son and his father*. New York: St. Martin's Press.

Galatzer-Levy, R., & Cohler, B. (2002). Making the gay identity: Coming-out, social context, and psychodynamics. In: J. W. Winer, J. W. Anderson, B. J. Cohler & R. D. Shelby (Eds), *Rethinking Psychoanalysis and the Homosexualities*. Hillsdale, NJ: Analytic Press.

Garfinkel, H. (1967). *Studies in ethnomethodology*. Englewood Cliffs, NJ: Prentice-Hall.

George, L., & Gold, D. (1991). Life course perspectives on intergenerational and generational connections. In: S. P. Pfeifer & M. B. Sussman (Eds), *Families: Intergenerational and Generational Connections* (pp. 67–88). New York: Haworth Press.

Gergen, K. (1994). *Realities and relationships: Sounding in social construction*. Cambridge, MA: Harvard University Press.

Gitlin, T. (1987). *The sixties: Years of hope, days of rage*. New York: Bantam Books.

Gochros, J. S. (1989). *When husbands come out of the closet*. New York: Haworth, Harrington Press.

Goffman, E. (1963). *Stigma: Notes on the management of spoiled identity*. New York: Simon and Schuster.

Gubrium, J. F. (1988). The family as project. *The Sociological Review, 36*, 273–296.

Gubrium, J. F., & Holstein, J. A. (1993). Phenomenology, ethnomethodology, and family discourse. In: P. G. Boss, W. J. Doherty, R. LaRossa, W. R. Schumm & S. K. Steinmetz (Eds), *Sourcebook of Family Theories and Methods: A Contextual Approach* (pp. 651–675). New York: Plenum Press.

Henderson, M. G. (1998). Disclosure of sexual orientation: Comments from a parental perspective. *American Journal of Orthopsychiatry, 68*, 372–375.

Herdt, G. (1997). *Same sex different cultures*. Boulder, CO: Westview Press.

Herdt, G., & Beeler, J. (1998). Older gay men and lesbians in families. In: C. J. Patterson & A. R. D'Augelli (Eds), *Lesbian, Gay and Bisexual Identities in Families: Psychological Perspectives* (pp. 177–196). New York: Oxford University Press.

Herdt, G., & Boxer, A. (1996). *Children of horizons* (Rev. ed.). Boston, MA: Beacon Press.

Herdt, G., & Koff, B. (2000). *Something to tell you: The road families travel when a child is gay*. New York: Columbia University Press.

Hess, R., & Handel, G. (1959). *Family worlds*. Chicago: University of Chicago Press.

Hogan, D. (1981). *Transitions and social change: The early lives of American men*. New York: Academic Press.

Hogan, D., & Astone, N. (1986). The transition to adulthood. *Annual Review of Sociology, 12*, 101–130.

Holder, A. (1975). Theoretical and clinical aspects of ambivalence. *Psychoanalytic Study of the Child, 30*, 197–220.

Holland, D., Lachicotte, W., Jr., Skinner, D., & Cain, C. (1998). *Identity and agency in cultural worlds*. Cambridge, MA: Harvard University Press.

Holstein, J. A., & Gubrium, J. F. (1994). Constructing family: Descriptive practice and domestic order. In: T. R. Sarbin & J. I. Kitsuse (Eds), *Constructing the Social* (pp. 232–250). Thousand Oaks, CA: Sage.

Holstein, J. A., & Gubrium, J. A. (1995). Deprivatization and the construction of domestic life. *Journal of Marriage and the Family, 57*, 894–908.

Hostetler, A., & Herdt, G. (1998). Culture, sexual lifeways, and developmental subjectivities: Rethinking sexual taxonomies. *Social Research, 65,* 249–290.

Hagestad, G. (1981). Problems and promises in the social psychology of intergenerational relations. In: R. W. Fogel, E. Hatfield, S. B. Kiesler & E. Shanas (Eds), *Aging: Stability and Change in the Family* (pp. 11–46). New York: Academic Press.

Hagestad, G. (1986). Dimensions of time and the family. *American Behavioral Scientist, 29,* 679–694.

Jennings, M. K., & Niemi, R. G. (1981). *Generations and politics: A study of young adults and their parents.* Princeton, NJ: Princeton University Press.

Johnson, C. L. (1988). Post-divorce reorganization of relationships between divorcing children and their parents. *Journal of Marriage and the Family, 50,* 221–231.

Kaiser, C. (1997). *The gay metropolis, 1940–1996.* Boston, MA: Houghton Mifflin.

Kantrowitz, A. (1977/1996). *Under the rainbow.* New York: St. Martin's Press.

Katz, J. N. (1995). *The invention of heterosexuality.* New York: Dutton, Plume Books.

Kohut, H. (1985). *Self-psychology and the humanities: Reflections on a new psychoanalytic approach.* In: C. Strozier (Ed.). New York: Norton.

Kris, A. O. (1984). The conflicts of ambivalence. *Psychoanalytic Study of the Child, 39,* 213–224.

Laird, J. (1993). Lesbian and gay families. In: F. Walsh (Ed.), *Normal Family Processes* (Rev. ed., pp. 282–328). New York: Guilford Press.

LaSalle, M. C. (2000). Gay male couples: the importance of coming out and being out to parents. *Journal of Homosexuality, 39,* 47–71.

Liang, A. C. (1998). The creation of coherence in coming out stories. In: A. Livin & K. Hall (Eds), *Queerly Phrased: Language, Gender, and Sexuality* (pp. 287–309). New York: Oxford University Press.

Low, N. (1978). The relationship of adult daughters to their mothers. Paper presented at the Annual Meetings of the Massachusetts Psychological Association, Boston (April).

Lüscher, K. (1998). A heuristic model for the study of intergenerational ambivalence. Invited address, 15th Biennial Meeting, International Society for Behavioral Development (ISSBD), Berne, Switzerland (July).

Lüscher, K. (2000). Ambivalence: A key concept for the study of intergenerational relations. In: S. Trnka (Ed.), *Family Issues Between Gender and Generations: Seminar Report, European Observatory on Family Matters at the Austrian Institute for Family Studies* (pp. 11–25). Luxembourg: Office for Official Publications of the European Communities.

Lüscher, K., & Pillemer, K. (1998). Intergenerational ambivalence: A new approach to the study of parent-child relations in later life. *Journal of Marriage and the Family, 60,* 413–425.

Lye, D. N. (1996). Adult child-parent relationships. *Annual Review of Sociology, 22,* 79–102.

Mannheim, K. (1928/1993). The problem of generations. In: K. H. Wolff (Ed.), *From Karl Mannheim* (2nd expanded ed., pp. 351–398). New Brunswick, NJ: Transactions Books.

McCall, G., & Simmons, J. (1978). *Identities and interactions: An examination of human associations in everyday life* (Rev. ed.). New York: Free Press.

Merton, R., & Barber, E. (1963). Sociological ambivalence. In: E. Tiryakian (Ed.), *Sociological Theory, Values, and Sociological Change: Essays in Honor of Pitirim A. Sorokin* (pp. 91–120). New York: Free Press.

Miller, T. (1997). *Shirts and skins.* Los Angeles, CA: Alyson Books.

Mishler, E. G. (1999). *Storylines: Craftartists' narratives of identity.* Cambridge, MA: Harvard University Press.

Newman, B. S., & Muzzonigro, P. G. (1993). The effects of traditional family values on the coming out process of gay male adolescents. *Adolescence, 28,* 213–226.

Parsons, T. (1955). Family structure and the socialization of the child. In: T. Parsons & R. F. Bales (Eds), *Family, Socialization and Interaction Process* (pp. 35–131). New York: Free Press.

Patterson, C. (2000). Family relationships of lesbians and gay men. In: R. M. Milardo (Ed.), *Understanding Families into the New Millennium: A Decade in Review* (pp. 271–288). Lawrence, KS: Alliance Communications Group and the National Council on Family Relations.

Pilkington, N. W., & D'Augelli, A. R. (1995). Victimization of lesbian, gay, and bisexual youths in community settings. *Journal of Community Psychology, 23,* 33–56.

Pillemer, K., & Suitor, J. (1991). "Will I ever escape my child's problems?" Effects of adult children's problems on elderly parents. *Journal of Marriage and the Family, 53,* 585–594.

Plummer, K. (1995). *Telling sexual stories: Power, change, and social worlds.* New York: Routledge.

Porter, K., & Weeks, J. (1991). *Between the acts: Lives of homosexual men, 1885–1967.* London: Routledge.

Pruchno, R., Blow, F., & Smyer, M. (1984). Life events and interdependent lives. *The Gerontologist, 27,* 31–41.

Reid, J. (1973/1996). *The best little boy in the world.* New York: Ballantine Books.

Remafedi, G. (1987). Male homosexuality: The adolescent's perspective. *Pediatrics, 79,* 326–330.

Riklin, F. (1910/1911). Mitteilungen: Vortrag von Prof. Bleuler über Ambivalenz [Minutes of Prof. Bleuler's presentation on ambivalence]. *Psychiatrisch-Neurologische Wochenschrift, 43,* 405–407.

Robinson, B. E., Walters, L. H., & Skeen, P. (1989). Response of parents to learning that their child is homosexual and concern over AIDS: A national study. In: F. W. Bozett & M. B. Sussman (Eds), *Homosexuality and Family Relations* (pp. 59–80). New York: Haworth Press.

Rossi, A. S., & Rossi, P. H. (1990). *Of human bonding: Parent-child relations across the life course.* New York: Aldine de Gruyter.

Sarup, M. (1996). *Identity, culture, and the postmodern world.* Athens, GA: University of Georgia Press.

Savin-Williams, R. C. (1989a). Coming out to parents and self-esteem among gay and lesbian youths. In: F. W. Bozett & M. B. Sussman (Eds), *Homosexuality and Family Relations* (pp. 1–36). New York: Haworth Press.

Savin-Williams, R. C. (1989b). Gay and lesbian adolescents. In: F. W. Bozett & M. B. Sussman (Eds), *Homosexuality and Family Relations* (pp. 197–216). New York: Haworth Press.

Savin-Williams, R. C. (1996a). Memories of childhood and early adolescent sexual feelings among gay and bisexual boys: A narrative approach. In: R. C. Savin-Williams & K. M. Cohen (Eds), *The Lives of Lesbians, Gays, and Bisexuals* (pp. 94–112). Fort Worth, TX: Harcourt Brace.

Savin-Williams, R. C. (1996b). Ethnic and sexual-minority youth. In: R. C. Savin-Williams & K. M. Cohen (Eds), *The Lives of Lesbians, Gays, and Bisexuals* (pp. 152–165). Fort Worth, TX: Harcourt Brace.

Savin-Williams, R. C. (1996c). Self-labeling and disclosure among gay, lesbian, and bisexual youths. In: J. Laird & R. J. Green (Eds), *Lesbians and Gays in Couples and Families: A Handbook for Therapists* (pp. 153–184). San Francisco: Jossey-Bass.

Savin-Williams, R. C. (1998a). Lesbian, gay, and bisexual youths' relationships with their parents. In: C. J. Patterson & A. R. D'Augelli (Eds), *Lesbian, Gay and Bisexual Identities in Families: Psychological Perspectives* (pp. 75–88). New York: Oxford University Press.

Savin-Williams, R. C. (1998b). Parental reactions to the child's disclosure of a gay, lesbian, bisexual identity. *Society for Psychological Study of Lesbian, Gay, and Bisexual Issues, American Psychological Association, 14*, 16–19.

Savin-Williams, R. C. (1998c). The disclosure to families of same-sex attractions by lesbian, gay, and bisexual youths. *Journal of Research on Adolescence, 81*, 49–68.

Savin-Williams, R. C. (2001). *Mom, Dad, I'm gay: How families negotiate coming out.* Washington, DC: American Psychological Association.

Savin-Williams, R. C., & Dubè, E. M. (1998). Parental reactions to their child's disclosure of a gay/lesbian identity. *Family Relations, 47*, 7–13.

Schaie, K. W. (1996). *Intellectual development in adulthood: The Seattle longitudinal study.* New York: Cambridge University Press.

Schaie, K. W., & Willis, S. L. (1995). Perceived family environments across generations. In: V. L. Bengtson, K. W. Schaie & L. M. Burton (Eds), *Adult Intergenerational Relations: Effects of Societal Change* (pp. 174–209). New York: Springer.

Schutz, A., & Luckmann, T. (1973). *The structures of the life world.* Evanston, IL: Northwestern University Press.

Schutz, A., & Luckmann, T. (1989). *The structures of the life world* (Vol. 2). Evanston, IL: Northwestern University Press.

Sennett, R. (1977). Destructive gemeinschaft. In: N. Birnbaum (Ed.), *Beyond the Crisis* (pp. 171–197). New York: Oxford University Press.

Serovich, J. M., Skeen, P., Walters, L. H., & Robinson, B. E. (1993). In-law relationships when a child is homosexual. *Journal of Homosexuality, 26*, 57–76.

Shyer, M. F., & Shyer, C. (1996). *Not like other boys: Growing up gay: A mother and son look back.* Los Angeles, CA: Alyson Books.

Simmel, G. (1908/1950). The Stanger. In: K. H. Wolff (Ed.), *The Sociology of Georg Simmel* (pp. 402–408). New York: Free Press.

Smelser, N. (1998). The rational and the ambivalent in the social science. *American Sociological Review, 63*, 1–16.

Stein, E. (1999). *The mismeasure of desire: The science, theory, and ethics of sexual orientation.* New York: Oxford University Press.

Stierlin, H. (1974). *Separating parents and adolescents: A perspective on running away, schizophrenia, and waywardness.* New York: Quadrangle Books.

Strommen, E. (1989). Hidden branches and growing pains: Homosexuality and the family tree. In: F. W. Bozett & M. B. Sussman (Eds), *Homosexuality and Family Relations* (pp. 9–34). New York: Haworth Press.

Suitor, J., Pillemer, K., Bohanon, K. S., & Robinson, J. (1995). Aged parents and aging children: Determinants of relationship quality. In: V. Bedford & R. Blieszner (Eds), *Handbook of Aging and the Family* (pp. 223–242). Westport, CT: Greenwood Press.

Sullivan, A. (1995). *Virtually normal: An argument about homosexuality.* New York: Knopf.

Tasker, F. L., & Golombok, S. (1997). *Growing up in a lesbian family: Effects on child development.* New York: Guilford Press.

Thompson, P. (1993). Family myths, models, and denials in the shaping of individual life paths. In: D. Bertaux & P. Thompson (Eds), *Between Generations: Family Models, Myths, and Memories* (pp. 13–38). New York: Oxford University Press.

Tipton, S. (1982). *Getting saved from the sixties: Moral meaning in conversion and social change.* Berkeley, CA: University of California Press.

Umberson, D. (1992). Relationships between adult children and their parents: Psychological consequences for both generations. *Journal of Marriage and the Family*, *54*, 664–674.

Veevers, J. (1979). Voluntary childlessness: A review of issues and evidence. *Marriage and Family Review*, *2*, 1–26.

Whyte, D., Merling, A., Merling, R., & Merling, S. (2000). *The wedding: A family's coming out story*. New York: Avon Books.

Wilkerson, W. S. (2000). Is there something you need to tell me? Coming out and the ambiguity of experience. In: P. M. L. Moya & M. R. Hames-Garcia (Eds), *Reclaiming Identity: Realist Theory and the Predicament of Postmodernism*. Berkeley, CA: University of California Press.

12. AMBIVALENCE AND ATTACHMENT IN FAMILY RELATIONSHIPS

Gregory R. Maio, Frank D. Fincham, Camillo Regalia and F. Giorgia Paleari

INTRODUCTION

Parents and children can drive each other mad. At one moment, a parent may be encouraging and affectionate toward the child; in the next, the parent may be sending the child to his or her bedroom. Similarly, a child who seems helpful and cooperative can suddenly turn belligerent. Parents and children may partly resolve the mixture of negative and positive feelings they experience in such situations by remembering their basic love for each other. Nevertheless, the conflicting sentiments will be stored in the memory of both parties, contributing to a long-lasting melange of conflicting beliefs, feelings, and behaviors. What are the psychological consequences of this state of affairs in relationships?

This issue is relevant to research on attitudes, which are tendencies to favor or disfavor objects or ideas in the environment (Olson & Maio, 2003). People spontaneously form attitudes toward just about everything, ranging from other people and pets to abstract ideas and issues. These evaluative tendencies subsume positive and negative beliefs, feelings, and past behaviors toward the objects (Zanna & Rempel, 1988). When this mental assortment simultaneously contains a high amount of positive and negative elements, the attitude is said to

Intergenerational Ambivalences: New Perspectives on Parent-Child Relations in Later Life
Contemporary Perspectives in Family Research, Volume 4, 285–312
ISSN: 1530-3535/doi:10.1016/S1530-3535(03)04012-3

be ambivalent (Conner & Sparks, 2002; Esses & Maio, 2002; Priester & Petty, 1996). In our view, this construct of attitudinal ambivalence helps yield special insights into the working of relationships.

This chapter focuses on the influence of ambivalence on one of the central aspects of relationships: psychological attachment processes. Attachment processes involve the formation of a strong affectional bond to another person (Bowlby, 1969). People's capacity to form these bonds is presumed to emerge in infancy and persist throughout the life span. As a result, the attachment of children to parents has received considerable attention from researchers. These particular attachment bonds are the primary focus of this chapter.

Before examining the relations between attitudinal ambivalence and attachment to parents, it is essential to consider in detail the meaning of each construct. Consequently, the first section of this chapter describes conceptualizations of attitudes and attitude ambivalence, and is followed by conceptualizations of attachment style. The remainder of the chapter then presents evidence on the relation between these constructs and highlights some important directions for future research.

ATTITUDES AND ATTITUDE AMBIVALENCE

As noted above, many researchers argue that attitudes have three conceptually distinct components (Eagly & Chaiken, 1998; Esses & Maio, 2002; Zanna & Rempel, 1988): cognition, affect, and behavior. The cognitive component subsumes positive and negative *beliefs* about attributes of the attitude object; the affective component subsumes positive and negative *feelings* about the attitude object; and the behavioral component subsumes positive and negative *behaviors* toward the attitude object. For instance, a daughter who dislikes her father may hold negative feelings toward him (e.g. resentment, shame), negative beliefs about him (e.g. he is hot-tempered and violent), and negative behaviors toward him (e.g. avoidance, yelling). Together, these cognitions, affects, and behaviors express an unfavorable attitude toward the child's father.

Often, these three components are similar in overall valence (i.e. negativity vs. positivity; Eagly & Chaiken, 1993, 1998). In the present example, it would be logical for the daughter to develop negative feelings and behaviors toward her father because of his bad temper and violence. It would seem to be psychologically difficult for her to hold positive feelings and behaviors in the face of these characteristics. Nonetheless, the potential prevalence of synergistic beliefs, feelings, and behaviors does not necessarily preclude the occasional existence of conflicting beliefs, feelings, and behaviors. In fact, children's needs for succor can be so strong that they may regard positively a caregiver who is abusive to them (Lyons-Ruth & Jacobvitz, 1999). Thus, despite the tendency for these components to be similar in valence, exceptions may occur.

Such exceptions can be labeled as instances of *inter*component ambivalence, which is conceptually and empirically distinct from *intra*component ambivalence (Esses & Maio, 2002; MacDonald & Zanna, 1998; Maio, Esses & Bell, 2000). Intracomponent ambivalence exists when there are conflicting reactions within an attitude component. In our example, the daughter might harbor some positive feelings toward her father (e.g. awe) in addition to the negative feelings. Similarly, she might possess some positive beliefs about him (e.g. he is strong) and perform some positive behaviors toward him (e.g. hugging) despite the negative beliefs and behaviors. In such a case, each of these three components (i.e. beliefs, feelings, and behaviors) would be marked by some degree of ambivalence.

Theoretically, such intracomponent ambivalence can be high even when intercomponent ambivalence is low. This situation can arise because all of the components may be equally positive or negative on average, while each component possesses high or low levels of ambivalence within itself (see Maio, Esses & Bell, 2000). In fact, although many of the effects of intracomponent ambivalence have been conceptually replicated in studies of intercomponent ambivalence (e.g. MacDonald & Zanna, 1998; Maio, Esses & Bell, 2000; Maio, Fincham & Lycett, 2000; Maio, Greenland, Bernard & Esses, 2001), they may also produce distinct effects on occasion (e.g. Hodson, Maio & Esses, 2001). For this reason, it is important to examine both types of ambivalence in research on this construct.

Nonetheless, prior research has often examined intracomponent ambivalence. This type of ambivalence has been associated with a variety of important consequences outside of the relationship context. For example, people who are ambivalent to members of a different ethnic group tend to respond in a polarized manner to members of the group; that is, behaviors performed by a different ethnic group will lead to more extreme positive or negative reactions than if the same behaviors were performed by the in-group (Bell & Esses, 1997, 2002). In addition, people with greater ambivalence toward a group react more negatively to derogatory language directed at the group (Simon & Greenberg, 1996). Also, ambivalence about an issue causes people to scrutinize persuasive messages about the issue more carefully (Jonas, Diehl & Brömer, 1997; Maio, Bell & Esses, 1996).

Overall, such evidence supports the significance of the ambivalence construct, and it is possible that this significance extends to the formation of attachment bonds in relationships. Before addressing this issue, however, it is essential to consider the psychological nature of attachment processes.

ATTACHMENT STYLES

According to Bowlby's (1969) seminal theorizing, attachment processes begin in infancy as part of a biological behavioral system. This system is designed to protect infants from predation, facilitate learning, and provide comfort from stress. To achieve these aims, the infant bonds with a primary attachment figure who is the most familiar, available, and responsive person in the infant's environment.

Several types of attachment bonds can be formed between infant and parent, however. Each type of attachment bond reflects a unique mental representation of the parent that is held by the child. Ainsworth, Blehar, Waters and Wall (1978) identified three types of attachment styles in infant-parent relations: secure, avoidant, and anxious-ambivalent. The secure style exists when the caregiver is regarded as being consistently warm and responsive; the avoidant style exists when the caregiver is seen as rejecting and withdrawn; the anxious-ambivalent style exists when the caregiver is regarded as being inconsistent and insensitive to the child's needs.

To identify the existence of these styles in an infant-parent relationship, Ainsworth et al. (1978) developed the Strange Situation. In this situation, a caregiver (usually the mother) and an infant from 12 to 18 months old interact briefly in a laboratory. The caregiver then withdraws from the room briefly and returns. The infant's response to the caregiver on her return is used as an indicator of the infant's attachment style. If the infant is easily comforted and willing to be close after separation, the child is classified as being secure. If the child shows little distress at separation and resists contact afterward, the child is classified as avoidant; if the child seeks closeness while expressing discomfort and anger, she or he is classified as anxious-avoidant.

These attachment styles in children may persist into adulthood (Bowlby, 1969). For this reason, procedures also have been developed to assess attachment styles in adults. For example, Main, Kaplan and Cassidy (1985) developed the Adult Attachment Interview (AAI) to classify parents' attachment styles, using their recollections of their own childhood. Amazingly, these attachment scores predicted the behavior of the adults' children in the Strange Situation (see van IJzendoorn, 1995), suggesting some transmission of attachment styles across generations (cf. Elicker, Englund & Sroufe, 1992; Shaver, Collins & Clark, 1996).

Such continuity indicates that the measurement of adult attachment styles provides a useful glimpse of a deep, well-rooted psychological process, which may spill over and affect relations with others in addition to relations with children. In fact, since the mid-1980s, several groups of researchers have demonstrated the value of assessing adults' attachment to romantic partners and to others in general (e.g. Hazan & Shaver, 1987, 1990). For example, Bartholomew (1990) developed a measure of general adult attachment that assesses four attachment styles: secure, dismissing (i.e. avoidant/indifferent), fearful (i.e. avoidant), and preoccupied. These four styles reflect internal working models of the self *and* the other. The secure style subsumes positive models of the self and other; the dismissing style subsumes a positive model of the self and a negative model of the other; the fearful style subsumes negative models of the self and other; the preoccupied style subsumes a negative model of the self and a positive model of the other.

There is abundant evidence that adult attachment styles predict many psychological processes and relationship features. For example, adults with more secure attachment styles tend to indicate higher amounts of relationship commitment, relationship satisfaction, relationship stability, and sexual activity (see Shaver & Hazan, 1993). In contrast, adults with secure attachment styles are less likely to exhibit anger, depression, neuroticism, and romantic jealousy (Shaver & Hazan, 1993). Thus, attachment styles possess many important psychological correlates.

AMBIVALENCE AND ATTACHMENT

Despite the importance of attachment styles to many psychological processes, we know comparatively little about variables that contribute to the formation of different attachment styles. Bowlby's (1969) attachment theory indicates that the child-parent relationship is the first place to look for important predictors, because this relationship sets the patterns of interaction that are the foundations for the child's mental representations of others. Nonetheless, an interesting issue is exactly how these patterns of interaction become translated into the mental representations of others.

Attitudes may be an important intervening variable, because children should spontaneously form attitudes toward their parents during the course of interaction with them. These attitudes should reflect the children's positive and negative (a) beliefs about the parent, (b) feelings about the parent, and (c) past behavioral experiences with the parent. Furthermore, the positive and negative elements (e.g. beliefs, feelings) of children's attitudes may be at least somewhat independent. As a result, children who possess high amounts of positivity may possess high or low levels of negativity. That is, children's attitudes are not necessarily positive or negative; they can be both positive and negative at the same time. In fact, Freud (1926/1948) speculated that this ambivalence is a vitally important aspect of children's views of their parents, and a plausible hypothesis is that such ambivalence uniquely shapes the affectional bonds between children and parents. In other words, children who are simultaneously positive and negative toward their parents (i.e. ambivalent) may develop different affectional bonds with their parents than children who are either solely positive or solely negative toward them (i.e. nonambivalent).

This possibility becomes more concrete when we consider different attachment styles. In particular, attachment theory predicts that children are "securely" attached to their parents when the children possess positive beliefs, feelings, and behavioral experiences regarding the parents (see Collins & Read, 1994). In contrast, children who are ambivalent toward their parents should have a mixture of positive and negative elements in their attitudes, which should result in less "secure" attachment. Consequently, ambivalence toward a parent should be negatively correlated with secure attachment toward the parent.

What about the relations between attitudinal ambivalence and the other attachment styles? Bartholomew's (1991) conceptualization of attachment helps with predictions about these relations, because it explicitly separates the model of self from the model of other. Theoretically, ambivalence toward a parent should make the model of other (i.e. the parent in this example) more negative and ambivalent than is typical in relationships. Consequently, ambivalence should increase the likelihood of "fearful" attachment and "dismissing" attachment because each of these styles involves negativity and ambivalence in the model of other. In contrast, ambivalence should decrease the likelihood of "preoccupied" attachment because this style involves a very positive model of other, which is less likely to occur as the ambivalence in the model of the other increases.

These predictions have been partly supported. Levy, Blatt and Shaver (1998) asked undergraduates to describe their perceptions of each parent and then scored these reports on several dimensions, including attitudinal ambivalence. They also assessed participants' secure, dismissing, fearful, and preoccupied attachment to romantic partners.

On one hand, as predicted by attachment theory, participants who were ambivalent toward their father were less securely attached to others. A similar trend was evident in the relation between ambivalence toward the mother and secure attachment, but this relation was significant only in one of two measures of attachment. People who were ambivalent toward their father were also significantly more likely to exhibit fearful attachment. On the other hand, ambivalence toward the mother did not predict fearful attachment, and there was a positive (not negative) relation between ambivalence toward the parents and preoccupied attachment, but only for one measure of attachment. In addition, ambivalence did not predict dismissing attachment. Thus, the relations between ambivalence toward the parents and each insecure attachment style were not clear-cut.

Nevertheless, because many significant, theoretically expected relations were obtained, Levy et al.'s (1998) findings provided excellent initial support for the importance of examining the relations between ambivalence and attachment style in relationships. These findings also opened some complex issues for understanding the role of ambivalence in attachment processes. These issues form the basis for the studies that are reported in this chapter.

ISSUES ADDRESSED IN PRESENT RESEARCH

Other Attitude Properties

Perhaps the most important caveat is that ambivalence is not the sole attitude property that might conceivably predict attachment style, and the effects of ambivalence might be attributable to some other attitude property. Research has found that attitudes vary in numerous ways other than their subsumed ambivalence (Esses & Maio, 2002; Wegener, Downing, Krosnick & Petty, 1995). For example, attitudes vary in valence. In the relationship context, this property is important because people tend to have positive attitudes toward their parents, partners, and children. As a relationship deteriorates, people may mix negative elements with the positive elements in their attitude (Fincham, Beach & Kemp-Fincham, 1997). As a result, the overall attitude becomes more negative in valence, while also becoming ambivalent. Thus, it is important to verify that effects of ambivalence (i.e. the combination of high positivity and negativity) are distinct from effects of a more negative net attitude per se.

Of course, attitudes vary in many ways other than valence. For example, people vary in the extent to which they feel subjectively committed to their attitude. To assess attitudinal commitment, people can be asked to rate the certainty, clarity, and intensity of their attitudes (see Wegener et al., 1995). In addition, attitudes vary in evaluative consistency (see Chaiken, Pomerantz & Giner-Sorolla, 1995). High consistency exists when the net attitude is consistent with the evaluation implied by an attitude component. For example, consistency between the net attitude and relevant cognitions can be examined. This variable often is labeled evaluative-cognitive inconsistency, and it is operationalized as the magnitude (absolute value) of the difference between the favorability implied by one's overall attitude and the favorability implied by one's beliefs about the attitude object (Chaiken, Pomerantz & Giner-Sorolla, 1995; Rosenberg, 1968).

Also, attitudes vary in the extent to which they are embedded in or linked to a lot of attitude-relevant information (e.g. beliefs and feelings about the target; Esses & Maio, 2002; Wood, Rhodes & Biek, 1995). When attitudes are highly embedded, people can easily retrieve many beliefs, feelings, or behaviors relevant to their attitudes. Thus, counts of these beliefs, feelings, and behaviors can be used to quantify embeddedness (Esses & Maio, 2002).

In theory, these attitude properties and other attitude properties (e.g. accessibility; Fazio, 2000) might explain some of the relation between ambivalence toward parents and general attachment styles. For this reason, it is useful to measure these properties in attitudes toward parents and test whether ambivalence predicts attachment styles independently of these properties. In fact, we expect that ambivalence does uniquely predict attachment. Prior studies have shown that ambivalence uniquely taps the psychological conflict within an attitude (even more than the constructs tapping evaluative consistency; Maio, Esses & Bell, 2000). Furthermore, ambivalence uniquely predicts other phenomena that are presumed to occur as a result of internal psychological conflict, including attitudinal polarizations (Bell & Esses, 1997, 2002) and the processing of persuasive messages (Maio et al., 1996). These findings are important because the attachment system is sensitive to psychological conflict (Simpson, Rholes & Phillips, 1996) and, therefore, ambivalence should uniquely predict attachment processes.

Measurement of Ambivalence

In Levy et al.'s (1998) research, ambivalence was subjectively inferred by coders of the participants' descriptions of their parents. In contrast, the attitudes literature has utilized two approaches that are more direct operationalizations of ambivalence. One general approach asks participants to describe the amount of ambivalence that they feel (e.g. Cacioppo et al., 1997; Newby-Clark, MacGregor & Zanna, 2002). A disadvantage of this approach is that it relies on people's descriptions of their internal processes (i.e. ambivalence), and these descriptions can be influenced by a variety of factors – including personal theories about the variables that should influence how people feel (Bassili, 1996; Nisbett & Wilson, 1977; Ross, 1989).

Another general approach partly avoids this pitfall by calculating ambivalence based on participants' endorsement of positive and negative responses toward a target (Bassili, 1996). For example, one technique asks participants to rate their positivity on a single unipolar scale (from "not at all positive" to "extremely positive") and their negativity on an additional scale (from "not at all negative" to "extremely negative"). An additional technique asks participants to list their beliefs, feelings, and/or behaviors regarding a target and then rate the positivity or negativity of each response (see Esses & Maio, 2002). The ratings then are used to calculate the total positivity and the total negativity across the responses. For both techniques, the positivity and negativity scores can be combined by means of formulas that calculate the extent to which there are high amounts of ambivalence (i.e. high simultaneous positivity and negativity). Interestingly, regardless of which formulas are used, correlations between subjective ambivalence ratings and calculated ambivalence scores tend to be moderate (Newby-Clark et al., 2002; Priester & Petty, 1996). Thus, in research on the relations between ambivalence and attachment, it is important to utilize both types of ambivalence measures.

Differences Between Mother and Father

Levy et al. found that the relations between ambivalence toward each parent and general attachment styles differed across parents. For instance, ambivalence to the father predicted fearful attachment, but ambivalence to the mother did not predict fearful attachment. Before interpreting this result, however, it is important to test whether ambivalence toward the father and mother are *independent* predictors of general attachment style. This issue is important because children's level of ambivalence toward their father may be similar to the level of their ambivalence to the mother, making it conceivable that any relations between ambivalence toward each parent and attachment are partly due to ambivalence toward the other parent. The Levy et al. data did not indicate whether ambivalence toward the father is related to ambivalence to the mother. Consequently, it is an open issue whether effects of ambivalence to the father on attachment to others are independent of effects of ambivalence toward the mother.

Nevertheless, there are reasons to suspect that ambivalence toward the father independently predicts attachment to others. In particular, ambivalence toward the father may be unique because fathers assume different roles in the rearing of children than do mothers (Lamb, 1982; Phares & Compas, 1992; Rohner, 1998). In fact, some perspectives suggest that fathers' roles often provide a key link between the family unit and the external world. For example, Parsons and Bales (1955) suggested that fathers are more likely to have an action-oriented approach to child rearing, and this focus includes an emphasis on helping children succeed in the external world. Similarly, Albelin (1980, as cited by Mächtlinger, 1981) argued that fathers offer young children "a stable island of practicing reality" (p. 153). If such speculations are correct, ambivalence to fathers may indeed account for variance in general attachment that cannot be explained by ambivalence to mothers.

Mediating Mechanisms

In theory, ambivalence toward parents predicts general attachment styles because ambivalence toward parents affects attachments to parents, which, in turn, influence attachment to others (see, e.g. Bartholomew & Horowitz, 1991; Hazan & Shaver, 1990). That is, according to attachment theory, the mental representations of parents become the basis for mental representations of the self and others. Therefore, ambivalence should influence attachment to others through the mental representations of the parents. Prior research has not examined directly this potential role of attachment to parents, making it an important issue for the present research.

Relations with Insecure Attachment Styles

It is also important to examine attachment to parents, because these attachment styles might help identify why Levy et al. (1998) found only weak relations between ambivalence toward parents and general insecure attachment styles This result suggests that the general insecure attachment styles tap mental representations of others that are psychologically distinct from ambivalence toward parents. Before confidently reaching this conclusion, however, it is necessary to replicate the weak relations between ambivalence toward parents and the general insecure attachment styles.

If these weak relations are obtained again, it would be useful to begin looking for factors that may dampen the strength of these relations. One possible explanation is that ambivalence toward parents is simply too far removed from insecure attachment to other people in general. Perhaps ambivalence toward parents is more closely tied to the mental representations encompassed by insecure attachment to the parents. This possibility can be examined using measures of attachment to the parents. If these measures were more strongly related to ambivalence toward parents, it would be apparent that part of the reason for the low relations is the target of the general attachment measures.

Childhood vs. Young Adulthood

Levy et al. warned that their results should be extended to younger samples. This issue is important partly because it has been suggested that children's capacity for attachment to others increases as they age (Hazan & Zeifman, 1994; Steinberg & Silverberg, 1986). From this perspective, the early teenage years provide an interesting period of transition, because teenagers have only recently begun to form more general attachments. Thus, it is interesting to test whether relations between ambivalence and general attachment styles emerge before the general attachment styles crystallize in adulthood.

Cultural Differences

There are notable differences in family practices across cultures, and some of the differences may be reflected in various demographic statistics across countries. For example, Italy has one of the lowest birth rates in Europe, whereas Britain has one of the highest (UNESCO, 1998). In addition, Italian children (especially boys) are more likely to maintain high dependency and closeness to their parents well into adulthood (Scabini, 2000). As a result of such differences, Italian attachment bonds might exhibit different relations to other variables (e.g. ambivalence) than we find in countries like Britain.

STUDY 1: BASIC RELATIONS BETWEEN AMBIVALENCE AND ATTACHMENT

To begin addressing these issues, our first study examined 66 young adolescents (12 to 14-year-olds) in Wales (Maio, Fincham & Lycett, 2000). We tested whether children's ambivalence toward their parents predicted the children's general attachment styles, while statistically controlling for the valence, commitment, embeddedness, and consistency in the children's attitudes toward their parents. During a 30-min break in their classes, the participants completed an open-ended questionnaire asking them to list their feelings and beliefs about their mother. They also filled in a thermometer-like scale designed to assess the valence of their attitudes toward her. Participants rated their commitment to these attitudes as well, using scales that asked them to rate the certainty and intensity of their feelings. Similar measures were presented to assess attitudes and attitude commitment regarding the father. A third questionnaire assessed general attachment styles, and it was placed randomly between or after these questionnaires.

After listing their feelings and beliefs regarding each parent, participants were asked to go back and rate the positivity or negativity of each feeling and belief. These ratings were then entered into a previously validated formula for measuring ambivalence from open-ended measures (see Bell, Esses & Maio, 1996). In addition, to estimate attitudinal embeddedness, we counted the number of feelings and beliefs that were listed. We also calculated the extent to which participants' responses to the question assessing attitude valence were consistent with the net valence of the beliefs and feelings (evaluative consistency). Together with the index of attitudinal commitment derived from the self-report scales, we used these measures to predict participants' general attachment styles.

We used Bartholomew and Horowitz's (1991) Relationship Questionnaire to assess secure, dismissing, fearful, and preoccupied attachment styles in participants' general relationships with others. Each style was described in a brief paragraph. For each paragraph, participants rated the extent to which the description reflected them, using a 7-point scale from 0 (not at all like me) to 6 (very much like me). For example, the description of a secure relationship with people in general was as follows:

> It is easy for me to have close friendships with other people. I am comfortable depending on other people to do things for me. I feel OK if other people depend on me. I don't worry about being alone or if people don't like me.

As expected, the results indicated that children who were ambivalent toward their father or mother were less likely to endorse the general secure attachment style than were children who were not ambivalent (see Maio, Fincham & Lycett, 2000). In addition, children who were more ambivalent toward their father were less likely to endorse the preoccupied (i.e. ambivalent) attachment style. Interestingly, none of the other correlations between ambivalence and the insecure attachment styles were statistically significant. In addition, a regression analysis revealed that participants' ambivalence toward their father predicted general secure attachment independently of ambivalence toward their mother, but ambivalence toward their mother did not predict secure attachment independently of ambivalence toward the father.

Given these results, we conducted regression analyses to test whether ambivalence toward the father predicted general secure attachment independently of the other attitude properties. In each analysis, ambivalence and one other attitude property (e.g. attitude commitment) were entered as simultaneous predictors of attachment. Results indicated that the relations between ambivalence and secure attachment remained significant when the other attitude properties (e.g. commitment, embeddedness) were statistically controlled. Thus, higher ambivalence predicted less secure attachment independently of these other properties.

Overall, then, the results of this first study extended Levy et al.'s (1998) findings in several ways. First, our direct measure of ambivalence replicated their observation of a negative relation between ambivalence toward the father and general secure attachment. In addition, as in their research, ambivalence was not consistently related to the insecure attachment styles, despite our use of an objective, direct measure of ambivalence. Interestingly, however, we also found that ambivalence toward the father predicted secure attachment independently of ambivalence toward the mother. This new finding supports prior theories that fathers tend to act more as a model of how to relate to others (e.g. Parsons & Bales, 1955) and begs further investigations of role asymmetries in child rearing. Another important finding was that ambivalence predicted secure attachment independently of the other attitude properties. Thus, the effects of ambivalence to parents are not attributable to some other property of attitudes to parents.

STUDY 2: THE ROLE OF ATTACHMENT TO PARENT

Before interpreting the effects of ambivalence further, we wished to replicate our results in a second study (Maio, Fincham & Lycett, 2000). This new study also was used to address the lack of evidence assessing the mediating mechanism through which ambivalence predicts general attachment. Specifically, this study tested our hypothesis that relations between ambivalence toward parents and general secure attachment are mediated by attachment to the parents. For example, if this hypothesis is correct, the negative relation between ambivalence toward the father and general secure attachment should be eliminated when attachment to father is statistically controlled.

Our second study tested such possibilities by including a measure of attachment to parents, in addition to the measures of general secure attachment and ambivalence toward each parent that were used in Study 1. Specifically, 44 adolescents (12 to 14-year-olds) in Wales completed a measure of attachment to parents that was similar to the measure of general attachment styles, except that the wording was changed to refer to parents, rather than people in general. For example, the paragraph describing a secure relationship with participants' father was as follows:

> It is easy for me to be close with my Dad. I am comfortable depending on him to do things for me. I don't worry about being alone or if my Dad does not accept me.

As expected, participants who were highly ambivalent toward their father were once again less securely attached to others. Surprisingly, participants who were more ambivalent toward their mother were also less likely to exhibit fearful attachment, unlike the results in our first study. The remaining relations between ambivalence toward the parents and general attachment styles were nonsignificant. Thus, across both studies, the sole consistent relation was the negative correlation between ambivalence toward the father and general secure attachment. Moreover, as in Study 1, this correlation was not eliminated when other attitude properties were statistically controlled using regression analyses.

Given this evidence, our next goal was to test whether this relation between ambivalence toward the father and secure attachment was mediated by attachment to the father. As expected, participants who were ambivalent toward their father exhibited less secure attachment to him, and those who possessed less secure attachment to the father were less securely attached to people in general. More importantly, the negative relation between ambivalence and general secure attachment was eliminated when attachment to the father was statistically controlled in a regression analysis that utilized ambivalence and attachment to the father as simultaneous predictors of general secure attachment. Thus, attachment to the father mediated the relation between ambivalence toward the father and general secure attachment.

Importantly, this result does not preclude the possibility that ambivalence toward the father directly influences general secure attachment, which, in turn, influences attachment to the father. Although this possibility is not consistent with attachment theory's assumption that the interactions with parents form the basis for mental representations of others, this possibility is empirically testable using a regression analysis that includes ambivalence and general secure attachment as predictors of attachment to the father. Consistent with our expectations, the application of this regression analysis to our data revealed that ambivalence predicted attachment to the father independently of general secure attachment. Thus, general secure attachment did not fully mediate the relation between ambivalence toward the father and attachment to him, and the more sustainable explanation for our data is that attachment to the father mediated the relation between ambivalence toward the father and general secure attachment.

STUDY 3: LATE ADOLESCENTS IN ANOTHER CULTURE

Together, Study 1 and Study 2 demonstrate a unique effect of attitudinal ambivalence on general attachment and on attachment to parents. The next challenge involved discovering the limitations of ambivalence effects. For example, do the effects of ambivalence occur in older adolescents, who tend to experience more conflict with parents and struggle with their transition to adulthood? Also, do these relations occur in different cultures with different family styles?

It was also worthwhile to examine the effects of ambivalence toward parents on the quality of the relationship between children and parents. Relationship quality is one of the most frequently examined variables in relationships, and it has been linked to ambivalence (Fincham et al., 1997) and attachment style (Collins & Read, 1990; Shaver & Hazan, 1993). In fact, attachment theory predicts that poor relationship quality between children and parents causes less secure attachment (Bowlby, 1969). Consequently, one explanation for why ambivalence toward the father may increase insecure attachment is that ambivalence induces a lower-quality relationship with him. In other words, ambivalence toward the father may cause a less positive relationship with the father, which should cause the development of less secure attachment. Thus, the effect of ambivalence on secure attachment to the father may be mediated by the quality of the relationship to him.

Nonetheless, there are other ways that relationship quality might relate to ambivalence and attachment. For example, it is conceivable that relationship quality is an antecedent of the relation between ambivalence and attachment to parents. That is, children who have a poor relationship with their parents might develop more ambivalence toward them, leading to less secure attachment to them. In addition, relationship positivity may be a consequence of the relation between ambivalence and attachment to the parent. For instance, ambivalence to a parent may lead to less secure attachment to the parent, thereby causing a poor relationship with him or her. Indeed, there is evidence that insecure attachment styles predict poor relationship quality in adult relationships (see Shaver & Hazan, 1993, for a review).

In short, there are three potential mechanisms that may link ambivalence toward parents, attachment to them, and the quality of the relationship with the parent, and it is important to test all three models empirically. We began examining these mechanisms using a sample of 218 15 to 19-year-old adolescents in the north of Italy (Regalia & Paleari, 2002). (As indicated above, Italy was a useful choice because the parenting and family styles in Italy are quite different from those in the United Kingdom.) Participants completed our measures of ambivalence and attachment toward each parent in addition to a measure of the quality of their relationship with each parent. The measure of relationship quality was based on the Positive Affect Index (PAI; Bengtson & Schrader, 1982), which assesses the amount of positive affect that the respondent has for another person and the positive affect that he or she perceives the other person has toward him or her. In this study, respondents indicated the extent to which five positive attributes (e.g. love, trust, understanding) described their relationship with each parent. Participants responded to each item using a 6-point scale from 1 (almost not at all) to 6 (very, very much). Responses to these items were summed, such that higher scores indicated higher relationship quality.

As in Study 2, the results indicated that participants who were more ambivalent toward their parents were less securely attached to them. In addition, participants who were more ambivalent toward their parents exhibited more dismissing, fearful, and preoccupied attachment to them. Also, participants who were more ambivalent toward their parents perceived the relationship with their parents more negatively. Finally, participants who perceived lower relationship quality exhibited less secure attachment, but more dismissing, fearful, and preoccupied attachment to them.

Because these results indicated that ambivalence was associated with secure attachment and relationship quality, we tested whether relationship quality mediates the relation between ambivalence and secure attachment to each parent. Interestingly, the relations between ambivalence and secure attachment to each parent were significantly reduced when we controlled for relationship quality. Thus, relationship positivity mediated the link between ambivalence and attachment to each parent. Relationship quality also mediated the relation between ambivalence and fearful attachment or dismissing attachment.

As noted above, it is also conceivable that relationship positivity is an antecedent of the relation between ambivalence and attachment to parents. It is also possible that relationship positivity is a consequence of the relation between ambivalence and attachment to the parent. We tested these models using regression analyses similar to those described above. Results indicated no consistent support for the hypothesis that relationship quality is an antecedent of ambivalence and attachment, but they did reveal consistent support for the hypothesis that relationship quality is a consequence of the link between ambivalence and attachment. That is, secure, fearful, and dismissing attachment at least partly mediated the link between ambivalence and relationship quality in all of our analyses. Overall, then, these data support the notion that ambivalence affects both attachment and relationship quality, which may have bi-directional effects on each other.

STUDY 4: ROMANTIC ATTACHMENT IN ANOTHER CULTURE

Thus far, we have focused on children's ambivalence and attachment to their parents, which are intergenerational variables because they focus on the relationship between children and parents. It is also possible to examine intragenerational manifestations of ambivalence and attachment. For example, it would be interesting to uncover the relation between ambivalence and attachment among people who are in a close relationship, but who are not offspring and progenitors. Do high levels of ambivalence predict less secure attachment even in these relationships?

To answer this question, many types of intragenerational relationships can be examined, including close friendships, sibling relationships, and romantic relationships. Attachment in romantic relationships has received the bulk of experimental attention so far (see Shaver, Collins & Clark, 1996), making it interesting to consider whether ambivalence predicts attachment styles in these relationships. This was the primary aim of our fourth study.

A secondary aim was to re-examine the mediating role of relationship quality in the relation between ambivalence and secure attachment. In Study 3, we found that adolescents' ambivalence toward their parents predicted their attachment to the parents and the quality of their relationship with the parents, with the latter two variables predicting each other. Given these results, we wished to test whether married partners' ambivalence toward one another predicts attachment to each other and the perceived relationship quality, while showing a bi-directional causal relation between attachment and relationship quality.

Participants were 160 Italian married couples who had at least one adolescent child attending the last three years of high school (Regalia & Paleari, 2000). From these couples, 146 wives and 141 husbands returned completed questionnaires. Remarkably, the average length of the marriages was 21.3 years, thereby ensuring that these couples had been together long enough to form strong attachment bonds.

The participants completed the measures of ambivalence and attachment from our prior studies, except that these measures were modified to ask about ambivalence and attachment to each participant's spouse, rather than to enquire about a parent. In addition, they completed Norton's (1983) Quality of Marriage Index. This 6-item inventory assesses marital quality through broadly worded, global items (e.g. "We have a good marriage"). Following Norton's recommendations, responses to each item are standardized and then summed, such that higher scores indicate higher relationship quality.

The results indicated that spouses' ambivalence was negatively related to both marital quality and secure attachment, while being positively related to fearful, preoccupied, and dismissing attachment to the spouse. That is, husbands and wives who exhibited more ambivalence toward a spouse were less likely to be satisfied with their marriage, less likely to be securely attached to the spouse, and more likely to have a fearful, preoccupied, or dismissing attachment style to the spouse. Additional results supported the hypothesis that marital quality mediates the relation between ambivalence and attachment to the spouse. Specifically, the relations between ambivalence and the secure, fearful, and preoccupied attachment styles were eliminated when we controlled for the effect of ambivalence on attachment. Thus, the impact of ambivalence on secure, fearful, dismissing, and preoccupied attachment styles occurred via relationship quality.

Of course, it is also conceivable that marital quality is an antecedent of the relation between ambivalence and attachment to the partner. In other words, people who have a poor relationship with a partner might develop more ambivalence toward him or her, leading to less secure attachment. In addition, it is possible that marital quality is a consequence of the relation between ambivalence and attachment to the partner. That is, ambivalence may lead to less secure attachment with a partner, which can cause a poor relationship with him or her. Similarly to the results from Study 3, however, regression analyses similar to those described above did not support the role of relationship quality as an antecedent to ambivalence and attachment. In contrast, these analyses indicated that the four attachment styles partly mediated the effects of ambivalence toward the partner on relationship quality, although these partial mediation effects were weaker among the wives. Thus, as in Study 3, we obtained evidence that ambivalence toward a family member predicts attachment to the family member and the quality of the relationship with the person, and that the latter two variables are reciprocally related.

GENERAL ISSUES

At the outset of our research, we sought to discover whether ambivalence toward parents predicts general attachment to others. This issue was important partly because abundant theory has suggested that ambivalence and attachment are important characteristics of close relationships, but no prior research had examined the empirical link between these constructs. In addition, our curiosity was piqued by the idea that a simple property of attitudes toward parents (i.e. ambivalence) may have a potent impact on general attachments to people in general. Our results not only supported this provocative idea, they also draw attention to several substantive issues. Below, we outline the issues and their current status.

Predicting Secure Attachment

As it turns out, both of the first two studies obtained evidence to support our prediction that ambivalence toward parents is related to general attachment style. In particular, children who were more ambivalent toward their father tended to be less securely attached to others. Moreover, ambivalence toward the father predicted general secure attachment independently of ambivalence toward the mother. Interestingly, ambivalence toward the mother was not consistently associated with general attachment to others (see also Levy et al., 1998). Thus, there is something unique to the child-father relationship that affects the secure attachment to others.

What is the unique feature of child-father relationships? As noted earlier, both theory and research suggest that fathers assume different roles in child rearing than do mothers (Lamb, 1982; Phares & Compas, 1992; Rohner, 1998), but we know comparatively little about the implications of these differences for child development. Several researchers have suggested that fathers may act uniquely as a model of what to expect from the outside world (Albelin, 1980, as cited by Mächtlinger, 1981; Parsons & Bales, 1955). If this hypothesis is correct, then ambivalence towards fathers may tap distinct variance in a variety of variables, in addition to uniquely predicting general attachment style. For example, ambivalence towards fathers may tap distinct variance in extroversion, because extroversion is a personality dimension that taps a willingness to interact with others in general, outside of the family unit (e.g. Eysenck, 1970). Similarly, ambivalence toward fathers might uniquely predict openness to experience, which is a personality dimension that reflects willingness to seek new intellectual and emotional stimulation (Costa & McCrae, 1992). In short, any variable that taps an orientation to the social world outside of the family should be affected by ambivalence toward fathers, if the father does indeed act as a model for understanding people outside of the family. This issue remains an important topic for future research.

Regardless of the implications of ambivalence toward the father for understanding variables other than attachment, the link between ambivalence toward fathers and general attachment is merely an encapsulation of a longer process. In particular, if fathers come to act as a model for representing others, then children's general secure attachment should reflect the attachment style they have developed with their fathers. Moreover, according to attachment theory (e.g. Bowlby, 1969), different attachment styles emerge because they are mental representations that are built on long-standing patterns of interaction. Consequently, the perceived nature of the quality of the relationship with a caregiver should determine the style of attachments to the caregiver. Thus, the effects of ambivalence on relationship quality and attachment to each caregiver may mediate effects of ambivalence on general attachment.

Studies 2–4 collected evidence that could be used to test this reasoning. In Study 2, because children who were ambivalent toward their fathers were less securely attached to him, the relation between ambivalence to the father and general secure attachment was reduced when secure attachment to the father was statistically controlled. In other words, the effect on general secure attachment depended on the effect on secure attachment to the father.

In Study 3, Italian adolescents who were ambivalent toward their parents perceived lower relationship quality in their interactions with their parents and less secure attachment to their parents. In addition, the effects of ambivalence on secure attachment to the parents and the quality of the relationship with them were reduced when either of the two criterion variables was statistically controlled (e.g. controlling for attachment in the analysis of the effect of ambivalence on relationship quality). A similar pattern was obtained in Study 4, except that Study 4 utilized Italian married couples as participants. In this study, participants who were ambivalent toward their spouse perceived lower relationship quality in their interactions with the spouse and reported less secure attachment to him or her. Moreover, the effects of ambivalence on secure attachment to the partners and the quality of the relationship with them were reduced when either of the two criterion variables was statistically controlled (e.g. controlling for relationship quality in the analysis of the effect of ambivalence on attachment).

A three-stage model best summarizes the results across studies (Fig. 1). In this model, the first two stages apply across parent-parent and child-parent relationships, and the third stage applies only to the father-child relationship and the secure attachment style. In the first stage, ambivalence toward a parent or caregiver causes lower perceived quality of the relationship with the person and less secure attachment to the caregiver or spouse. In the second stage, the

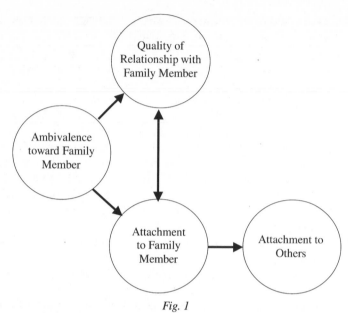

Fig. 1

Note: This figure is a representation of the chain of events through which ambivalence toward family members affects general attachment to others. The rightmost path applies only when the child-father relationship and the secure attachment style are examined.

perceived quality of the relationship influences attachment and vice-versa. In the third stage, which applies only to child-father relationships and the secure attachment style, attachment to the father predicts general attachment to others. Thus, ambivalence toward a family member predicts the quality of the relationship with the family member and the level of secure attachment to him or her, and this specific attachment predicts general attachment styles when the target of the specific attachment is the father and the secure attachment style is examined.

Of course, this model is an abstraction across the results of our four studies. Future research should test the complete model in a single study. In addition, our causal hypotheses about the sequence of the stages are currently supported only by the logic underlying path analyses of correlational data (e.g. Baron & Kenny, 1986; Cohen & Cohen, 1983), and it is important to obtain support using experimental paradigms that can manipulate the presence or absence of each factor. Also, it remains vital to determine why the third step applies only to father-child relationships. Perhaps some aspect of the father-child relation is a crucial mediator of the father's unique effect. For instance, ambivalence toward the father may predict general attachment because fathers tend to be less involved in child rearing and activities around the home. This absenteeism may make fathers seem to be more like individuals from outside the home and, therefore, more appropriate models for attachments to people outside the familial home. If this hypothesis is correct, then ambivalence toward the mother might predict general attachment styles more strongly in families where the mother is absent more than the father. Future research should consider this and other hypotheses.

The Insecure Attachment Styles

The inconsistent relations between ambivalence toward parents and the insecure attachment styles to others (e.g. fearful attachment) are interesting. This pattern was not obtained only in our studies; Levy et al. (1998) also obtained this pattern. Thus, these weak relations are replicable across studies.

In contrast, ambivalence did predict insecure attachment to the target of ambivalence across the studies that examined these relations. In Studies 2–4, people who were ambivalent toward parents and spouses were preoccupied, fearful, and dismissively attached to them. (These results for Study 2 are described in Maio, Fincham & Lycett, 2000.) Thus, when the target of the attachment style is specifically relevant to the target of the ambivalence, consistent relations emerge.

Nonetheless, only two of the three relations are in directions consistent with prior theory. According to Griffin and Bartholomew's (1994) prototype model of attachment, each attachment style is a mental representation of the self and the other, who could be a caregiver or an abstract representation of people in general. In this model, dismissive and fearful attachment styles subsume negative beliefs, feelings, and behavioral experiences regarding the other. Consequently, it makes sense that children who are ambivalent toward their parents should have developed more negativity in their model of the other, causing more dismissive and fearful attachment. Nevertheless, the prototype model suggests that preoccupied attachment subsumes a positive model of the other; thus, ambivalence should decrease the likelihood of forming this model. Yet, we obtained positive relations between ambivalence to the other and preoccupied attachment.

One possible explanation for this result is that preoccupied attachment toward parents reflects mixed perceptions of them, rather than positive perceptions of them and negative views of the self. Indeed, operationalizations of preoccupied attachment are often open to this interpretation. For example, in our research, we adapted Bartholomew and Horowitz's (1991) Relationship Questionnaire to assess the preoccupied attachment style. Specifically, children indicated the extent to which their father "doesn't want to be as close to me as I want him to be. Sometimes, I worry that he doesn't care about me as much as I care about him."

Although affirmative responses to this item may reflect positive feelings about the father and worries about the self, they also could reflect mixed feelings about the target person. In particular, a child with the preoccupied attachment style might describe his or her father as emotionally distant and uncaring, which are negative traits that would create ambivalence when mixed with other positive traits.

Alternative measures of attachment may help to resolve this issue. Because attachment styles subsume complex metacognitive processes and patterns of emotional self-regulation, many different measures of attachment have been proposed (e.g. Bartholomew, 1990; Hazan & Shaver, 1987). Most recently, Fraley, Waller and Brennan (2000) reviewed past measures and used item analyses to construct a new measure that is more reliable and valid than the past measures. It is therefore worthwhile to test whether the current results are replicated with this new measure.

It is also worthwhile to utilize alternative measures of ambivalence. Perhaps a measure that explicitly asks participants about their feelings of ambivalence would predict the attachment styles more strongly. Measures that ask participants to report their ambivalence are only moderately correlated with measures that calculate ambivalence from positive and negative responses, and it is possible that the subjective measures tap bases of ambivalence that are untapped by the calculations of ambivalence from positivity and negativity (Priester & Petty, 1996). Nevertheless, given the consistency in our principal findings (e.g. relation between ambivalence to the father and general attachment) across studies, we would be surprised if the current results were not replicated with alternative measures of ambivalence and attachment.

Intergenerational vs. Intragenerational Relations

Together, the results across studies indicate that the relations between ambivalence toward parents and attachment to parents are similar to the relations between ambivalence to partners and attachment to partners. Moreover, perceived relationship quality mediated the effects of ambivalence on secure attachment styles in both types of relationships. Thus, the role of ambivalence in intragenerational marital relationships is at least partly matched within intergenerational parent-child relationships.

Nonetheless, these data should not be taken to suggest that there is nothing that distinguishes between intragenerational and intergenerational relationships. One of the most obvious differences between these types of relationships is the differential power status in the intergenerational relationships. For example, because parents have more power than children in their relationships, the sources of children's ambivalence frequently may reflect this power differential. In our sample, for instance, children sometimes believed that their parents are "bossy." Although people in marital relationships can perceive an imbalance of power in the relationship (e.g. Blumstein & Schwartz, 1983), the negative effects of such asymmetries might be superseded by a communal focus (Mills & Clark, 1994). This focus emphasizes the warmth toward the partner and concern for common welfare, rather than a concern about fair outcomes for each individual. Consequently, the *sources* of ambivalence in intragenerational marital relationships may be concerns about warmth and mutual support, whereas the sources of ambivalence in intergenerational parent-child relationships might be concerns about fair treatment and outcomes. Clearly, more research is needed on the sources of ambivalence in both types of relationship.

The Role of Other Attitude Properties

In Study 1 and Study 2, we demonstrated that ambivalence toward the father predicts general secure attachment styles independently of several other attitude properties, including attitudinal inconsistency, embeddedness, and commitment. An interesting issue is whether ambivalence should always exert a unique effect on attachment styles, independently of other attitude properties. Although ambivalence often does exert unique effects on a variety of variables (see Esses & Maio, 2002), we suspect that it will not always do so.

In theory, independent effects of ambivalence should become less likely as people's overall attitudes become extreme. For example, in very close relationships, people may feel so positively toward the other person that their attitudes are mostly nonambivalent and positive. In these close relationships, the presence of any negativity would lead to some ambivalence, resulting in a strong negative relationship between ambivalence and attitude valence. Indeed, we observed moderate negative correlations between attitude valence and attitude ambivalence in our first two studies. Nonetheless, despite these moderate relations, ambivalence toward the father predicted general secure attachment styles independently of attitude valence.

In other samples, however, the people within a relationship might become so fond of each other that the measures of ambivalence and valence become redundant. In such an event, it is not possible to reveal unique effects of each variable, because of problems of collinearity in regression analyses. Fortunately, in our studies, the thermometer measure of attitude valence was not related so strongly to the measure of ambivalence that collinearity was a problem. Nonetheless, this issue could arise when the measures of attitude valence and ambivalence are strongly correlated. Consequently, one avenue for future research would assess the unique role of ambivalence using multiple measures of ambivalence and other attitude properties. In this manner, the unique variance attributable to each property can be confidently tapped. Such an approach may reveal that the unique effects of ambivalence are even stronger than we observed.

CONCLUSION

In this chapter, we have described how ambivalence influences psychological attachment to other people. As expected, the findings suggest that children who possess more mixed attitudes toward a parent develop less secure attachment to other people in general, especially when the children are ambivalent toward their father. In addition, this effect of ambivalence is not attributable to other attitude properties (e.g. evaluative inconsistency) that are somewhat related to ambivalence. Moreover, a specific process can explain this effect. In particular, ambivalence toward parents predicts the perceived quality of the relationship between the children and their parents. The perceived quality of their relationship, in turn, predicts attachment to each parent, which predicts general attachment to others when the parent is the child's father. Thus, intergenerational ambivalence has a broad potential impact on attachment to others.

Interestingly, our evidence suggests that a similar process also occurs in married couples, showing that ambivalence is important for both inter and intragenerational relationships. This result qualifies the example used at the beginning of our chapter. Not only can parents and children experience a mixture of negative and positive feelings that affect the quality of their affectional bonds, but spouses can similarly experience mixed feelings towards each other, with similar psychological consequences. An essential agenda for future research involves uncovering the antecedents of this ambivalence in both types of relationships, perhaps helping to alleviate problems of relationship conflict and satisfaction at their source.

REFERENCES

Ainsworth, M. S., Blehar, M. C., Waters, E., & Wall, S. (1978). *Patterns of attachment: A psychological study of the strange situation*. Mahwah, NJ: Lawrence Erlbaum.

Baron, R. M., & Kenny, D. A. (1986). The moderator-mediator variable distinction in social psychological research: Conceptual, strategic, and statistical considerations. *Journal of Personality and Social Psychology, 51*, 1173–1182.

Bartholomew, K. (1990). Avoidance of intimacy: An attachment perspective. *Journal of Social and Personal Relationships, 7*, 147–178.

Bartholomew, K., & Horowitz, L. M. (1991). Attachment styles among young adults: A test of a four-category model. *Journal of Personality and Social Psychology, 61*, 226–244.

Bassili, J. (1996). Meta-judgmental vs. operative indices of psychological attributes: The case of measures of attitude strength. *Journal of Personality and Social Psychology, 71*, 637–653.

Bell, D. W., & Esses, V. M. (1997). Ambivalence and response amplification toward Native peoples. *Journal of Applied Social Psychology, 27*, 1063–1084.

Bell, D. W., & Esses, V. M. (2002). Ambivalence and response amplification: A motivational perspective. *Personality and Social Psychology Bulletin, 28*, 1143–1152.

Bell, D. W., Esses, V. M., & Maio, G. R. (1996). The utility of open-ended measures to assess intergroup ambivalence. *Canadian Journal of Behavioural Science, 28*, 12–18.

Bengtson, V. L., & Schrader, S. S. (1982). Parent-child relations. In: D. J. Mangen & W. A. Peterson (Eds), *Research Instruments in Social Gerontology* (Vol. 2, pp. 115–185). Minneapolis: University of Minnesota Press.

Blumstein, P., & Schwartz, P. (1983). *American couples: Money, work, sex.* New York: Pocket Books.

Bowlby, J. (1969). *Attachment and loss: Attachment* (Vol. 1). New York: Basic Books.

Cacioppo, J. T., Gardner, W. L., & Berntson, G. G. (1997). Beyond bipolar conceptualizations and measures: The case of attitudes and evaluative space. *Personality and Social Psychology Review, 1*, 3–25.

Chaiken, S., Pomerantz, E. M., & Giner-Sorolla, R. (1995). Structural consistency and attitude strength. In: R. E. Petty & J. A. Krosnick (Eds), *Attitude Strength: Antecedents and Consequences* (pp. 387–412). Mahwah, NJ: Lawrence Erlbaum.

Cohen, J., & Cohen, P. (1983). *Applied multiple regression/correlation analysis for the behavioural sciences* (2nd ed.). Mahwah, NJ: Lawrence Erlbaum.

Collins, N. L., & Read, S. J. (1990). Adult attachment, working models, and relationship quality in dating couples. *Journal of Personality and Social Psychology, 58*, 644–663.

Collins, N. L., & Read, S. J. (1994). Cognitive representations of attachment: The content and function of working models. In: H. Bartholomew & D. Perlman (Eds), *Advances in Personal Relationships* (Vol. 5, pp. 53–90). London: Jessica Kingsley.

Conner, M., & Sparks, P. (2002). Ambivalence and attitudes. *European Review of Social Psychology, 12*, 37–70.

Costa, P. T., Jr., & McCrae, R. R. (1992). *Revised NEO Personality Inventory (NEO-PI-R) and NEO Five-Factor Inventory (NEO-FFI) professional manual.* Odessa, FL: Psychological Assessment Resources.

Eagly, A. H., & Chaiken, S. (1993). *The psychology of attitudes.* Fort Worth, TX: Harcourt Brace Jovanovich.

Eagly, A. H., & Chaiken, S. (1998). Attitude structure and function. In: D. T. Gilbert, S. T. Fiske & G. Lindzey (Eds), *Handbook of Social Psychology* (Vol. 1, pp. 269–322). Boston: McGraw-Hill.

Elicker, J., Englund, M., & Sroufe, L. A. (1992). Predicting peer competence and peer relationships in childhood from early parent-child relationships. In: R. D. Parke & G. W. Ladd (Eds), *Family-Peer Relationships: Modes of Linkage* (pp. 77–106). Mahwah, NJ: Lawrence Erlbaum.

Esses, V. M., & Maio, G. R. (2002). Expanding the assessment of attitude components and structure: The benefits of open-ended measures. *European Review of Social Psychology, 12*, 71–102.

Eysenck, H. J. (1970). *The structure of human personality* (3rd ed.). London: Methuen.

Fazio, R. H. (2000). Accessible attitudes as tools for object appraisal: Their costs and benefits. In: G. R. Maio & J. M. Olson (Eds), *Why we Evaluate: Functions of Attitudes* (pp. 1–36). Mahwah, NJ: Lawrence Erlbaum.

Fincham, F. D., Beach, S. R. H., & Kemp-Fincham, S. I. (1997). Marital quality: A new theoretical perspective. In: R. J. Sternberg & M. Hojjat (Eds), *Satisfaction in Close Relationships* (pp. 275–304). New York: Guilford.

Fraley, R. C., Waller, N. G., & Brennan, K. A. (2000). An item response theory analysis of self-report measures of adult attachment. *Journal of Personality and Social Psychology, 78,* 350–365.

Freud, S. (1948). *Inhibitions, symptoms and anxiety.* A. Strachey (Trans.). London: Hogarth. (Original work published 1926.)

Griffin, D. W., & Bartholomew, K. (1994). The metaphysics of measurement: The case of adult attachment. In: K. Bartholomew & D. Perlman (Eds), *Advances in Personal Relationships* (Vol. 5, pp. 17–52). London: Jessica Kingsley.

Hazan, C., & Shaver, P. R. (1987). Romantic love conceptualized as an attachment process. *Journal of Personality and Social Psychology, 52,* 511–524.

Hazan, C., & Shaver, P. R. (1990). Love and work: An attachment-theoretical perspective. *Journal of Personality and Social Psychology, 59,* 270–280.

Hazan, C., & Zeifman, D. (1994). Sex and the psychological tether. In: K. Bartholomew & D. Perlman (Eds), *Advances in Personal Relationships: Attachment Processes in Adulthood* (Vol. 5). London: Jessica Kingsley.

Hodson, G., Maio, G. R., & Esses, V. M. (2001). The role of attitudinal ambivalence in susceptibility to consensus information. *Basic and Applied Social Psychology, 23,* 197–205.

Jonas, K., Diehl, M., & Brömer, P. (1997). Effects of attitudinal ambivalence on information processing and attitude-intention consistency. *Journal of Experimental Social Psychology, 33,* 190–210.

Lamb, M. (1982). *The role of the father in child development.* New York: Wiley.

Levy, K. N., Blatt, S. J., & Shaver, P. R. (1998). Attachment styles and parental representations. *Journal of Personality and Social Psychology, 74,* 407–419.

Lyons-Ruth, K., & Jacobvitz, D. (1999). Attachment disorganization: Unresolved loss, relational violence and lapses in behavioural and attentional strategies. In: J. Cassidy & P. R. Shaver (Eds), *Handbook of Attachment* (pp. 520–554). New York: Guilford.

MacDonald, T. K., & Zanna, M. P. (1998). Cross-dimension ambivalence toward social groups: Can ambivalence affect intentions to hire feminists? *Personality and Social Psychology Bulletin, 24,* 427–441.

Mächtlinger, V. J. (1981). The father in psychoanalytic theory. In: M. E. Lamb (Ed.), *The Role of the Father in Child Development* (2nd ed., pp. 113–153). New York: Wiley.

Main, M., Kaplan, N., & Cassidy, J. (1985). Security in infancy, childhood, and adulthood: A move to the level of representation. *Monographs of the Society for Research in Child Development, 50*(1 & 2, Serial No. 209), 66–104.

Maio, G. R., Bell, D. W., & Esses, V. M. (1996). Ambivalence and persuasion: The processing of messages about immigrant groups. *Journal of Experimental Social Psychology, 32,* 513–536.

Maio, G. R., Esses, V. M., & Bell, D. W. (2000). Ambivalence and inconsistency are distinct constructs. *Canadian Journal of Behavioral Science, 32,* 71–83.

Maio, G. R., Fincham, F. D., & Lycett, E. J. (2000). Attitudinal ambivalence toward parents and attachment style. *Personality and Social Psychology Bulletin, 26,* 1451–1464.

Maio, G. R., Greenland, K., Bernard, M., & Esses, V. M. (2001). Effects of intergroup ambivalence on information processing: The role of physiological arousal. *Group Processes and Intergroup Relations, 4,* 355–372.

Mills, J., & Clark, M. S. (1994). Communal and exchange relationships: Controversies and research. In: R. Erber & R. Gilmour (Eds), *Theoretical Frameworks for Personal Relationships* (pp. 29–42). Mahwah, NJ: Lawrence Erlbaum.

Newby-Clark, I. R., MacGregor, I., & Zanna, M. P. (2002). Thinking and caring about cognitive inconsistency: When and for whom does attitudinal ambivalence feel uncomfortable? *Journal of Personality and Social Psychology, 82*, 157–166.

Nisbett, R. E., & Wilson, T. D. (1977). Telling more than we can know: Verbal reports on mental processes. *Psychological Review, 84*, 231–259.

Olson, J. M., & Maio, G. R. (2003). Attitudes in social behavior. In: T. Millon & M. Lerner (Eds), *Handbook of Psychology: Personality and Social Psychology* (Vol. 5, pp. 299–325). Hoboken, NJ: Wiley.

Parsons, T., & Bales, R. F. (1955). *Family, socialization, and interaction process.* Glencoe, IL: Free Press.

Phares, V., & Compas, B. E. (1992). The role of fathers in child and adolescent psychopathology: Make room for daddy. *Psychological Bulletin, 111*, 387–412.

Priester, J. R., & Petty, R. E. (1996). The gradual threshold model of ambivalence: Relating the positive and negative bases of attitudes to subjective ambivalence. *Journal of Personality and Social Psychology, 71*, 431–449.

Regalia, C., & Paleari, G. (2000). Attachment, ambivalence and marital well-being. Paper presented at the 3rd National Congress of Social Psychology, Parma, Italy (September).

Regalia, C., & Paleari, G. (2002). *The role of ambivalence in parent-child relationships.* Unpublished Paper.

Rohner, R. P. (1998). Father love and child development: History and current evidence. *Current Directions in Psychological Science, 7*, 157–161.

Rosenberg, M. J. (1968). Hedonism, inauthenticity, and other goads toward expansion of a consistency theory. In: R. P. Abelson, E. Aronson, W. J. McGuire, T. M. Newcomb, M. J. Rosenberg & P. H. Tannenbaum (Eds), *Theories of Cognitive Consistency: A Sourcebook* (pp. 73–111). Chicago: Rand McNally.

Ross, M. (1989). The relation of implicit theories to the construction of personal histories. *Psychological Review, 96*, 341–357.

Scabini, E. (2000). New aspects of family relations. In: C. Violato, E. Oddone-Paulucci & M. Genious (Eds), *The Changing Family and Child Development* (pp. 3–24). Aldershot, England: Ashgate Publishing Ltd.

Shaver, P. R., Collins, N., & Clark, C. L. (1996). Attachment styles and internal working models of self and relationship partners. In: G. J. O. Fletcher & J. Fitness (Eds), *Knowledge Structures in Close Relationships: A Social Psychological Approach* (pp. 25–61). Mahwah, NJ: Lawrence Erlbaum.

Shaver, P. R., & Hazan, C. (1993). Adult, romantic attachment: Theory and evidence. In: W. J. Jones & D. Perlman (Eds), *Advances in Personal Relationships* (Vol. 4, pp. 29–70). London: Jessica Kingsley.

Simon, L., & Greenberg, J. (1996). Further progress in understanding the effects of derogatory ethnic labels: The role of pre-existing attitudes toward the targeted group. *Personality and Social Psychology Bulletin, 22*, 1195–1204.

Simpson, J. A., Rholes, W. S., & Phillips, D. (1996). Conflict in close relationships: An attachment perspective. *Journal of Personality and Social Psychology, 71*, 899–914.

Steinberg, L., & Silverberg, S. B. (1986). The vicissitudes of autonomy in early adolescence. *Child Development, 57*, 841–851.

UNESCO (1998). *World culture report*. Retrieved March 27, 2002, from http://www.unesco.org/
    culture/worldreport/html_eng/index_en.shtml
van IJzendoorn, M. H. (1995). Adult attachment representations, parental responsiveness, and infant
    attachment: A meta-analysis on the predictive validity of the Adult Attachment Interview.
    Psychological Bulletin, 117, 387–403.
Wegener, D. T., Downing, J., Krosnick, J. A., & Petty, R. E. (1995). Measures and manipulations of
    strength-related properties of attitudes: Current practice and future directions. In: R. E. Petty &
    J. A. Krosnick (Eds), *Attitude Strength: Antecedents and Consequences* (pp. 455–487).
    Mahwah, NJ: Lawrence Erlbaum.
Wood, W., Rhodes, N., & Biek, M. (1995). Working knowledge and attitude strength: An information
    processing analysis. In: R. E. Petty & J. A. Krosnick (Eds), *Attitude Strength: Antecedents and
    Consequences* (pp. 283–313). Mahwah, NJ: Lawrence Erlbaum.
Zanna, M. P., & Rempel, J. K. (1988). Attitudes: A new look at an old concept. In: D. Bar-Tal & A. W.
    Kruglanski (Eds), *The Social Psychology of Knowledge* (pp. 315–334). Cambridge, England:
    Cambridge University Press.

13. THE ONCE AND FUTURE PARENTS: EXPLORING THE IMPACT OF EARLY PARENTAL MEMORIES ON THE ANTICIPATED LIFE HISTORIES OF YOUNG ADULTS

Harry G. Segal

INTRODUCTION

In this volume, researchers have brought their expertise to bear on the ambivalence enacted and expressed by adult children and their parents towards each other. As Lüscher and Pillemer note in their seminal article (1998), using *ambivalence* as an organizing concept for the study of intergenerational relationships allows researchers to explore the inherent contradiction of roles and obligations. For example, at what point does a child become an *adult* child? Is this a judgment that both parent and child make? What happens when parent and child disagree? Even raising the question misses the point: One can never unidimensionally be an "adult child." In the subtle and dynamic consciousness within which each of us dwells, we are always an adult *and* a child to ourselves and to our parents, as they were to theirs.

In this chapter I present a developmental model for intergenerational ambivalence and an empirical method for exploring it. Part I presents the model and

Intergenerational Ambivalences: New Perspectives on Parent-Child Relations in Later Life
Contemporary Perspectives in Family Research, Volume 4, 313–338
ISSN: 1530-3535/doi:10.1016/S1530-3535(03)04013-5

its theoretical justifications. To summarize, our understanding of social events is shaped by our perceptions, judgments, and culture, as well as by our wishes, fears and feelings; however, it is also influenced, sometimes strongly, by our early experiences, in particular by the ways in which we came to know our parents as young children. This idea has long been advocated by psychoanalysts, psychodynamic theorists and attachment researchers, but when applied to intergenerational relationships, it takes on a new twist. Lüscher (2002) defines ambivalence as "polarized simultaneous emotions, thoughts, social relations and structures that are ... temporarily or even permanently irreconcilable." I propose that the experience of our adult selves with our parents necessarily and simultaneously evokes the early experience of our child selves, a structural and, I will argue, a neural cognitive expression of ambivalence. Part II presents an experimental approach which complements this theoretical model. Using a quantified approach to content analysis, the current experience of a large cohort of young adults, as well as their imagined future lives, are shown to strongly affected by the ways in which they report the earliest memories of their mothers and fathers.

PART I: THEORETICAL MODEL

Several years ago, a young man in psychotherapeutic treatment with me described how he felt having drinks with his father. The patient was in his late 20s pursuing a graduate degree in the humanities, and although he lived several hours away from his parents, he managed to visit them at least once a month. Although he enjoyed seeing them, he freely recalled his difficult childhood with them. "My mother idealized me and always said that I made her happy just by being with her. Of course, she also withdrew when she was depressed. This happened a lot, especially when I seemed to be someone with ideas or feelings different from hers. My father was cold, distant, and at times abusive. I remember times when he would kick me after a morning of fighting. I only have four or five positive memories of him when I was a boy."

By the time he finished college, with a bout of psychotherapy under his belt and a sense of professional direction, he found himself closer to his parents. His mother was more accepting of the ways in which he was different from her, and his father, after suffering a heart attack and bypass surgery, became kinder, more receptive, and appreciative of his son's accomplishments. Still, when the young man would sit down to talk with his father, they seemed at a loss for words. Finally, before going out to dinner with his parents one night, the young man invited the father to have drinks together first. "It was amazing. When we both had a martini or two, my dad gradually began to tell me stories from his life that I had never heard. I found myself telling him ideas and experiences that simply didn't come to mind

when we were sitting around their apartment. It is become a ritual, now, and I'm
always a bit excited before we leave early for the restaurant. And I always have
to coax my father out – he resists a bit – but then we usually have a good time."

I asked him about the most recent meeting. "It was great. He even told me
stories about people he knew in the Kennedy administration, stuff he's always
quiet about. But I have to say, when I was telling him about my dissertation,
I felt . . . flickers of self-doubt. I wondered if he was really interested and I was
afraid he thought I was stupid, even though he was following every word I said.
It was a great relief when he said he liked my project and even went on to suggest
ideas I actually found useful." At that point I wondered aloud if these "flickers"
of self doubt felt like a minor version of the intense anxiety the young man felt
whenever he met with his academic advisor or other persons of authority in his
life. When he agreed, I suggested that the underlying fears with his father were
echoes of his childhood experience of his father, echoes which coexist with the
positive feelings he has when they are together now.

What the clinical vignette shows is that the adult experience of our parents is
layered: Our early experiences of them as all-powerful shapers of our identity,
our expectations, and our self-experience persist within our conscious, adult
understanding of their all-too-human strengths and faults. The young man's
account well captures this phenomenon of the "once and future parents": The
father in his current life is different from the one he knew in his childhood. And yet
the present relationship, compelling because it is a mutual collaboration between
an adult child and an aging parent, does not erase the early relationship that took
place twenty years earlier. That earlier relationship, because it established the
boy's initial experience of himself as unworthy of his father's approval, persists as
an aspect of the present; it informs his feelings and cognitive associations when
out for drinks with his father and may break through if he regresses in the face of
anxiety or perceived rejection. Clinical psychologists are more than familiar with
this phenomenon because transference – the patient's tendency to project earlier
relationship expectations upon the therapist – is a crucial clinical tool.

The Role of the Past

Clinical psychologists have long debated the impact of early childhood experience
on adult functioning. In the 1950s, the pendulum first swung toward psychoanalytic determinism, which assumed that the progression of psycho-sexual
stages and the early development of the ego largely accounts for the personality
and neuroses of adults. According to this model, trauma, anxiety, and the wish
to maintain the love of parents drive the psyche to develop and mobilize defenses
against dangerous thoughts, wishes, fears, and feelings (Brenner, 1974).

The pendulum had begun to swing in the opposite direction by the 1970s, pushed by existentialist claims of freedom and self-determination as well as by the cognitive-behavioral approach developed by Aaron Beck. Beck advocated short-term therapy, focusing exclusively on the ways patients misinterpret their current experience of reality through cognitive distortions. For him, therapy primarily involves helping patients become "scientists" so they may strive to view more objectively the events in their life and the ways they misunderstand them (Beck, 1975). There is no theory of early childhood in the cognitive-behavioral model, except as a time when cognitive distortions somehow come into being.

Today, the pendulum hovers at a comfortable midpoint: Theorists believe that early childhood sets the emotional expectations, the capacity for self-regulation, the sense of agency, and the willingness to depend on others, while as adults we nevertheless have the freedom to become self-aware, to take life-changing risks, and to discover new ways of feeling and thinking through relationships and new experiences. Clinicians integrating psychodynamic and cognitive behavioral therapies can flexibly examine transference, dreams, and early memories while paying attention to the ways their patients interpret their roles in social events (Teyber, 2000).

While psychologists generally accept the idea that early childhood does influence later personality development – it is supported by life events data (Wethington & Kessler, 1986), prospective studies (Schaie, 1983), and attachment theory (Main, Kaplan & Cassidy, 1985) – most are at a loss to say *why* this is so. Psychoanalytic and object-relations descriptions of the developing self are compelling as metaphors, but the "ego" is not a construct one can test or measure. The argument social-cognition theorists make, that attitudes and behaviors are learned and reinforced in early childhood, begs the question as well: Why would early learned behavior have more weight than recently learned behavior? Wouldn't something just observed have more impact than something experienced twenty years ago? Why would adults who were physically abused as children seek partners who hit them when the original abuse was hardly positively reinforcing?

Cognitive developmentalists, who observe the first stirring of infant cognition (e.g. Johnson, 2000) and follow with subtlety the increasingly complex schemata and problem-solving skills, can now explain how thinking develops. However, there is no substantial corresponding research on how the child acquires or internalizes emotional, and interpersonal expectations. This is true primarily for two reasons: First, because the psychoanalytic and social learning theories rely on constructs difficult to test or measure, they have not led to convincing empirical studies; second, unlike cognitive development (which can be inferred by watching how infants pay attention to shapes and other stimuli), experience of the nascent, emerging self cannot be clearly observed. Once children have gained enough command of language to describe their experience, however, researchers suddenly have much to study. This is especially true when children are seven or older, as most developmental models note the sudden leap in abilities at this age. Psychoanalysts call it "latency." Piagetians call it "concrete operations." Sociologists note that children begin to exclude others for the social reasons by the time they are in second grade – a dramatic change from kindergarten where peer rejection is virtually absent. (Most people have "daily" memories from second grade, but have only flashes or images from kindergarten.)

Still, clinicians assume that our experience between infancy and age seven is very important, even if we cannot remember much of it. This crucial time – "pre-latency" for want of a better term – holds the key to understanding our nascent self and its relationship to our parents. I have proposed a model for pre-latency (Segal, 2001) which attempts to integrate developmental, clinical and neurocognitive research and theory. I begin by renaming the span of ages 2–7 the *Projective Phase* of development.

The "Projective Phase"

The most striking and universal quality of these childhood years is the primacy of play (Corrigan, 1982; Fenson, Kagan, Kearsley & Zelazo, 1976). The richness of the child's inner world is one that delights most parents and will "hook" any college student volunteering at HeadStart. What is less obvious to most is that children use play to express feelings, to take symbolic risks, and to resolve conflicts. Child therapists consider this *projection* – children project onto stuffed animals and action figures their feelings, thoughts, wishes and fears – and in doing so, reveal their inner experience which they cannot directly put into words, primarily because they don't yet have the cognitive capacity to do so (Bromfield, 1997).

The Projective Phase ends because children achieve a greater cognitive complexity which allows them to assemble self-schemata strongly influenced by their family's cultural, social, and moral values. The earlier "projective" mode of consciousness is gradually superseded by self-attribution, objective judgment, and the capacity for abstract thought. I call this the Social-Cognitive Phase. But since social-cognitive judgment is powerfully influenced by social and cultural expectations, it necessarily involves censoring some of the wishes, fears, feelings, and thoughts that were so spontaneously projected when the child was young. It may leave people believing things about themselves that are socially acceptable, but which are not true. This accounts for the kinds of biases and distortions found in self-judgment by social psychologists (for a recent example, see (Kruger &

Dunning, 1999) or in the difficulties gay teenagers have recognizing their desires on the way to coming out (Savin-Williams & Cohen, 1996).

Of course, the projective way of thinking is not replaced by social cognition. We are always ready to project. When you "suspend" your disbelief while watching a movie or reading a novel you are, in essence, returning to the projective mode (Harris & Beggan, 1994; Singer, 1998). Similarly, intense emotional states, such as falling in love or feeling intense rage, often compel a return to the projective mode through unavoidable daydreams or fantasies. Finally, severe personality disturbance – such as borderline personality disorder – is often marked by a person's inability to refrain from falling into the projective mode and ascribing implausible and idiosyncratic interpretations to interpersonal events (e.g. Gunderson, 1984). Indeed, psychotherapy may be reconceived as helping patients to regain an adaptive *balance* between these two modes of consciousness, avoiding the flood of projecting on the one hand and over-intellectualizing on the other.

An Evolutionary Model for the Projective Phase

Working our way backward in time, what gives rise to the projective mode? And what evolutionary function does the Projective Phase serve? I propose that infants bring into the world their biologically determined temperament and respond to events with a limited but intense set of emotions: happiness, sorrow, fear, anger, anxiety, and excitement. As soon as they interact with their bodily experience and their caregivers, babies begin to form a neural network of interpersonal events derived from their self and interpersonal experience. This mood-and-body-driven experience is then shaped by the actions and feelings of parents and siblings who, in turn are influenced by social, economic, and cultural forces. This neural network of interpersonal events is likely developed in the same way that babies learn to perceive discrete objects or begin to distinguish separate words – through an innate, biologically driven attention to frequency and probability. Groundbreaking work by Saffran (2001) showed that 8-month-old infants recognize the segmentation of words from fluent speech *solely* on the basis of statistical relationships between neighboring word sounds. That is, simply hearing words grouped together by syntax and content allows the infant to predict word sequences; ultimately these sequences – paired with mood, expression, and gestures – lead to expressed and received meaning. In related work, researchers constructed computational models of this neural network which approximate the learning Saffran describes. One group (Rodriguez et al., 1999) used a backpropagating learning algorithm (Rumelhart, Hinton & Williams, 1986) to show how a neural net could learn to count and to organize linguistic syntax by building hierarchical clusters of event sequences without semantic meaning. Another group has proposed neural network modeling to explain cognitive skill acquisition in babies (Plunkett, Karmiloff-Smith, Bates & Elman, 1997).

Neural network modeling provides explanations for emotional and interpersonal events that are comparable in value to what it tells us about how babies acquire perceptual and linguistic skills. Substituting behavior for words, a baby feeling wet and cold will cry – and that cry may be followed by a diaper change and a hug, or by nothing, or by an angry comment by the caregiver. Later, babbling may lead to positive or negative attention. Still later, toddling around the house may lead to parents' encouragement or dangerous neglect resulting in pain. I am not proposing a classical or operant conditioning model; rather, a grammar of expectations formed by the infant's prewired attention to event frequency and probability. Once the child begins to predict the responses to behaviors and need-states, these predictions inform the child's later responses to stories, cartoon characters, school, and social interactions. These endure because of the statistical power of the initial events. In other words, if a child's early experience of event sequences leads her to predict that crying leads to comfort, laughing leads to affiliation, and curiosity leads to enthusiastic support, she will expect these responses later even if they are not always forthcoming. Her imaginative associations (i.e. projections) will reflect the attention and empathy she received as a young child.

I believe that this neural network of interpersonal events is the bedrock of personality and self-experience, and that it gives rise to the projective mode of early childhood. As soon as infants begin to remember their parents after they leave the room (this takes place at about 9 months) this neural network provides the fabric of the infant's earliest projections. An attentive and loving father results in the baby imagining him tickling her when he is out of the room. Later, the neural network is active by informing the wishes and fears the growing child brings to more complex events – pre-school, picnics, the playground, creative play with toys – even as she understands their objective social or physical meanings. If this neural network reflects an early experience where love and attention were reciprocated, where positive and negative events were predictable (thus resulting in lower levels of anxiety), then the child will: (a) have an easier time making use of the cognitive skills she learns in later childhood; and (b) her projections will convey her early positive experiences by implicit assumptions that she is valued, and that others will treat her with respect and love. If the neural network is shaped by negative early experience, then: (a) the child's cognitive skills will be overwhelmed by anxiety and negative expectations; and (b) her projections will convey implicit assumptions that she is unworthy (given the inconsistent or abusive early experiences) and that others are capable of betrayal or neglect.

To return to the beginning of this chapter, I argued that one important aspect of intergenerational ambivalence is expressed by the way early experiences of our parents persist as an active facet of our current perception of them. The model presented here provides a mechanism for how this situation comes about. Early infant and childhood events lead to the formation of a neural network of interpersonal events; this network in turn generates and informs the projections which mark the Projective Phase; those projections persist even as the capacity for social cognition and, ultimately, abstract reasoning is achieved.

Although the social-cognitive mode of reasoning dominates our consciousness as we engage in the world, the projective mode is always active. It generates the daydreams or fantasies we return to during a boring lecture or a long drive; it accounts for the paranoid suspicions we have when frightened by an anonymous threat or impersonal enemy; it allows us to become absorbed in movies, drama, and literature; it accounts for the transient belief in spirits that many non-religious people acquire for several months after a loved one has died. And because it is readily available, it also can be assessed or measured by means of projective tests.

Projective Tests

The way psychologists first emphasized the impact of childhood on adult personality, then discounted it, and now are discovering it again has its parallel in the way they view projective testing. From the 1940s through the 1970s, tests such as the Thematic Apperception Test (TAT), the Rorschach inkblot test, the Sentence Completion Task, and Draw-A-Person were standard assessment tools for psychologists. All of these tests are based on the same principle: Give patients an ambiguous stimulus to interpret, and they will provide an idiosyncratic response expressing the unique qualities of their inner world (Allison et al., 1968). (The TAT, for example, asks respondents to make up stories about a series of pictures, with attention to what characters are thinking and feeling.) Unfortunately, clinicians have free range to interpret these tests – which means they are vulnerable to *projecting* on the *projections* of their patients. Cognitively-oriented researchers sought to discard the projective tests and replace them with norm-based self-report measures, such as the Minnesota Multiphasic Personality Inventory (MMPI). Some doctoral programs have stopped training students on projectives altogether.

In response, researchers since the 1980s have begun developing empirically based coding schemes demonstrating that projective tests are useful tools for conducting research and assessing psychopathology. Their efforts to apply statistical rigor to projectives have resulted in established norms for the Rorschach (Holtzman & Swartz, 1983), in coding measures for the TAT (McAdams, Hoffman, Mansfield & Day, 1996; Westen, Lohr, Silk, Gold & Kerber, 1990; Woike, 1994), coding measures for early and autobiographical memories (McAdams et al., 1996; Nigg, Lohr, Westen, Gold & Silk, 1992), as well as stories told to the Picture Arrangement subtest of the WAIS-R (Segal, Westen, Lohr & Silk, 1993; Segal, Westen, Lohr, Silk et al., 1992; Westen, Feit & Zittel, 1998). Recently, one group went even further and used projective tests to expose the weaknesses of norm-based self-report measures.

For my purposes, however, the most important finding has been the sensitivity of projective tests to early childhood experience. For example, TAT stories scored for social cognitive qualities (such as range of affect, interpersonal trust, attributions of social causality) by coders unaware of study hypotheses have correctly identified patients suffering from borderline personality disorder, distinguishing them from patients suffering from depression and from normal comparison subjects (Westen et al., 1990). In other words, the way borderline patients compose stories is distinct from other diagnostic groups (and borderline personality disorder has been linked empirically with trauma and chaos in early childhood). Similarly, early memories have correctly distinguished adults who were sexually abused in childhood from those who were not (Nigg et al., 1992). In research my colleagues and I have conducted, results from the Narrative Completion Test, a set of seven story stems completed by participants and coded for interpersonal qualities, showed that early childhood experience and maternal memories predicted positive and negative outcomes in the stories (Segal, Vizueta, Biuckians & Pollak, 2003a).

PART II: EMPIRICAL METHOD

The Anticipated Life History

In 1994, I developed a hybrid measure that draws upon both projective and social-cognitive thinking. Eighteen-year-old respondents are asked to describe the course of their future life, from their 21st birthday until their death, and they are told specifically *not* to imagine an idealized life but one they plausibly expect to live. I named this instrument the Anticipated Life History (ALH), and I was interested in seeing how first year college students would balance the conflicting requirements of the task. Consider it: They must objectively assess their strengths, their economic resources, the likelihood of reaching their goals – all of which requires social cognitive reasoning – while allowing themselves to dream up their future with all of the excitement and anxiety such fantasies evoke. The ALH narratives are scored for social cognitive qualities *and* projective qualities, as well as for future life events such as marriage, children, and professional accomplishments. Finally, to study the personality forces influencing the writing of the ALH, I put together a battery of instruments and structured interviews measuring early life events, early parental memories, socio-economic status, family demographics, psychiatric history, current depression levels, quality of life satisfaction, and an estimate of IQ by 2000, with the help of a NIMH grant, my research team had recruited and tested more than 400 subjects drawn from several sites including a private liberal arts college, a rural community college, a rural high school senior class, and several university and college counseling centers.

My colleagues and I devised a detailed scoring manual for coding ALH narratives for projective and social cognitive qualities (Segal, DeMeis & Wood, 1997) which includes training procedures for establishing scorer reliability and provides coders with detailed rules for scoring on a 4-point scale, from little or no presence of the quality to pervasive presence of the quality. The clinical scales, which measure *projective* qualities, were designed to gauge the integrity and coherence of the participants' thinking (*Narrative Integrity*), their mood and self-esteem (*Depression*), the degree to which they impose fantasies on their future even when asked to write a realistic one (*Fantasy Distortion*), deficits in self-regulation which leads to risky behaviors (*Impulsivity*), and the quality of their interpersonal expectations (*Malevolence*) (Segal, Wood, DeMeis & Smith, 2003). The *social cognitive* scales were designed to gauge participants' awareness of their self-concept as well as the qualities of others (*Psychological Complexity*), their sense of the social demands of adult developmental stages (*Life Role Complexity*), the quality of their imagined future interpersonal relations (*Resolution of Conflicts* and *Mutuality of Relationships*), and their projected commitment to family and community (*Altruism*). See Fig. 1 for a brief synopsis of each of the scales.

Here are two sample ALH narratives, with the social cognitive and clinical scores.

ALH No. 1 – Social Cognitive Scores
My graduation will be June of 1996. I will be twenty-two and feeling happy. My parents and brother will be at my graduation with tears and tissues at hand. I will hope to have matured intellectually and socially at [college name]. My career goals would include medical school at [medical school name] where I would concentrate on anesthesiology in my last two years of medical school.

Scales	Principles
Social-Cognitive	
Psychological Complexity	The degree to which the subject understands him or herself and others, including tolerance of positive and negative qualities; self-awareness and psychological functioning improve over time.
Life Role Complexity	The degree to which the subject understands there are multiple roles at various developmental stages, that social adjustment takes time and effort to make a personal fit between self and social demands.
Mutuality of Relationships	The degree to which relationships are depicted as mutual, where individuals make compromises and where family relations involve reciprocity.
Resolution of Conflicts	The degree to which the subject anticipates conflicts and imagines their resolutions.
Altruism	The degree to which subjects intend to perform selfless acts for their family or for society at large. General intentions and specific plans are scored.
Clinical	
Narrative Integrity	The degree to which the narrative is coherent, progresses logically, and is easily understood, regardless of content.
Depression	The degree to which depression colors the ALH. Sadness, low-self-esteem, hopelessness and early deaths are scored.
Fantasy Distortion	The degree to which the ALH resembles fiction, dreams, or movies, rather than a plausible account of one's future.
Impulsivity	The degree to which impulsive acts are found in the ALH. These include substance abuse, rage attacks, and reckless behavior.
Malevolence	The degree to which the narrator intends, enacts, or expects physical or psychological malevolent actions.

Fig. 1. ALH Scoring Categories.

My prediction to go on to medical school may be delayed due to the need to retake the MCAT's and possibly obtain a "shadowing" program for two years after graduation – age 22–24.

I sense that throughout my determination/pursuance to go on to medical school, I may question my goals. I will continue to love medicine and want to help others, yet I will have met a man whom I will want to marry – my age now is 23–26. I will be torn between a career that I have worked very hard for and a family. I have always wanted above anything else.

I see myself becoming an anesthetist and then having a family. I seem to think that a happy medium will be reached – 8–2:00 p.m. job and then pick the kids up from school and take care of my husband. I am late twenties to early thirties now and I am kept very busy.

I will be missing something though – my art. Art is my love and forever will be. I will always feel that I was never good enough to make a career out of it, yet the desire to create burns inside. I may open a gallery or submit a few pieces of my own – just for me. I now may work part time at a hospital and continue raising my two children with a great husband. I am now mid to late 30's.

The 40's are now here and I want to resume community service. I will be still at the hospital working, yet I feel the need to raise money, to urge research, to go into impoverished neighborhoods and give to the needy. I will be looking to save the world in my own little niche – in my own little ways. I will not be known by many, but will be happy for myself. I have always liked it that way.

In my 50's the children will be in college and it will be time for my husband and I to take time for ourselves. We will be comfortable – not extremely well off, but secure and comfortable financially. Maybe go on a cruise, take long walks, love each other. My mom and dad will be enjoying retirement – going here and there and having the marriage I always knew they could. I am finally happy, peaceful, restful.

My faith will always be with me. God will continue to test me and bring me through trials – illness with me or my family, possibly life threatening. I will overcome the battles, realizing that God never left me, just carried me. I will fully realize that every obstacle is just a challenge that can be overcome and that everything that I or my family encounters has a purpose; that I will learn or better myself from them.

In my 60's, I will be loving my grandchildren, yet saddened by the loss of one of my parents. I am saddened as I write this now – not knowing why I am writing or why I feel this to be true. I'd rather not think about this – yes, I'm scared of death, rather the fear of losing a loved one. I will be fearful of being without my mother.

I will have lived a full life, but will be time to live in heaven by my 80's. I will no longer be fearful of death.

Psychological Complexity: This ALH scores a 4 because throughout the life cycle she considers her feelings, motivations, and how she can achieve her personal, social, and spiritual goals.

Life Role Complexity: This ALH scores a 4 because she anticipates life role complexity throughout her narrative, from balancing career and children in her 30s to being a grandparent with aging parents in her 60s.

Mutuality of Relationships: This ALH scores a 1 because there are no instances of mutual exchanges between characters.

Resolution of Conflicts: This ALH scores a 4 because the subject anticipates conflicts throughout her life cycle and offers specific ways to resolve them.

Altruism: This ALH scores a 3 because she lists specific goals to "feel the need to raise money, urge research, to go into impoverished neighborhoods" which are specific altruistic intentions.

ALH No. 2 – Clinical Scores
21st birthday – I'll be drunk. Soon following I will end my birthday binge and return to life as normal. I will graduate from [college name] in a degree of one of the following, Physics, Natural Resources, or Anthropology. After graduating I may work for awhile, attempting to pay off loans. In the United States our technology is developing rapidly, and if I feel it has put too much power in the hands of the government. I will leave for Canada. If my degree is Anthropology I would like to spend a large portion of my life with natives in Papua New Guinea, or the aborigines of Australia. If I am initiated into a tribe, I may live out the rest of my life in the jungle.

If I stay in the United States, I will marry at a young age, 24 or 25. Children are a venture too taxing on the environment, especially in the U.S. so I would like to have only two or three, depending on my wife's feelings on the matter. I may have a well paying job and lots of money but it is an issue that rarely concerns me.

As I get older I'd like to start writing books, devote much of my time to meditation and physical exercise. If World War III breaks out I will flee to Canada to avoid the Draft.

From 45 – older, I do not see myself particularly interested in working for money. I would be perfectly content aging away with the tribes, but if I remain in the States I'll most likely be a hermit. Hopefully the Mrs. will join me.

I will most likely die of cancer. It runs in my family and I'm a smoker so it'll be curtains for me a fairly young age, not much older than 85. I will probably smoke the rest of my life, not a heavy smoker, but I will have never quit entirely.

Narrative Integrity: This scores a 3 because the narrative is elliptical at points (for example, he skips from age 45 to his death) and doesn't cohere into a well-organized story.

Depression: This scores a 2 because of the general pessimism about the world's future, and his prediction of becoming a "hermit" if he stays in the United States – a statement likely influenced by depressed mood.

Fantasy Distortion: This scores a 2 because of his certainty of being initiated into an aboriginal tribe. Note that he tends to couch his future narrative in the conditional tense, thus avoiding a higher Fantasy Distortion score.

Impulsivity: This scores a 2 for the "birthday binge" and his predicted difficulty quitting smoking.

Malevolence: This scores a 3 because of the well-developed theme that that world is a dangerous place, from his sense that the government has "too much power" to his explicit fear of World War III.

Principal Findings Using the ALH

Before presenting the principal findings from the ALH Project, here is a description of the participants, the protocol, and how it was administered.

Sample Demographics
Participants were 234 women and 155 men recruited from a private liberal arts college ($n = 130$), a rural community college ($n = 100$), a rural high school senior class ($n = 60$) and first- and second-year students seeking psychotherapy at one of three college counseling centers ($n = 99$). Male and female participants did not differ significantly on the WAIS-R subtests, SES, ethnicity, or quality of life satisfaction. As predicted, they differed on depressive symptomotology as determined by the CES-D summary score (see Table 1).

Procedure
Participants from the private college ($n = 130$) responded to the self-report battery in groups of 20 or less. Participants then scheduled an individual session to undergo structured interviews and cognitive tests within 10 days. Fourteen participants who failed to appear for scheduled interviews were excluded from the study. The rest of the sample ($n = 259$) participants completed both the self-report battery and the individual session in one session. Participants signed an informed consent, written in accordance with APA guidelines, giving permission for researchers to contact them in four years.

Measures
For the self-report battery, participants began with the ALH which asks them to imagine their entire future life, beginning with their 21st year and ending with their death. Participants are asked to give a *realistic* account of their entire future life as it is *most likely* to occur, and to spend approximately 25 minutes composing it. They also completed a measure developed for this study: a 45-item Life Events Checklist eliciting significant life events and their impact (LEC; Segal, 1996). From the LEC, a composite variable, *negative early life events* (NEGLIFE), was created by summing the presence of negative events from the LEC: parental strife

Table 1. Sample Characteristics and Word Count by Gender.

	Women	Men
N	226	168
Mean Age	18.3 (2.4)	18.6 (0.8)
SES		
Upper Middle/Upper	58.1%	58.9%
Middle	25.2%	19.9%
Lower Middle/Lower	16.7%	21.2%
CES-D Summary Score[*]	37.9 (9.9)	35.8 (10.0)
QOLI Summary Score	2.42 (1.5)	2.35 (1.5)
ALH Total Word Count[**]	453 (169)	412 (155)
ALH Narrative Integrity	3.63 (0.54)	3.65 (0.54)
ALH Depression	1.46 (0.82)	1.53 (0.80)
ALH Fantasy Distortion	2.21 (1.12)	2.30 (1.10)
ALH Impulsivity[+]	1.21 (0.53)	1.60 (0.92)
ALH Malevolence	1.11 (0.41)	1.15 (0.57)
ALH Psychological Complexity	1.64 (0.83)	1.53 (0.73)
ALH Life Role Complexity[++]	1.74 (0.78)	1.39 (0.62)
ALH Mutuality of Relationships	1.56 (0.69)	1.55 (0.70)
ALH Resolution of Conflicts[&]	1.50 (0.70)	1.36 (0.56)
ALH Altruism[&&]	1.49 (0.80)	1.29 (0.64)

[*] $t = 2.03, p = 0.004$ (2-tailed).
[**] $t = 2.06, p = 0.04$ (2-tailed).
[+] $t = -5.04, p = 0.0001$ (2-tailed).
[++] $t = -4.81, p = 0.0001$ (2-tailed).
[&] $t = -2.2, p = 0.03$ (2-tailed).
[&&] $t = -2.7, p = 0.008$ (2-tailed).

and divorce; parental job loss, substance use or criminal activity; deaths of parents, family members, or close friends; participant serious injury or illness; participant trouble with school or police; participant substance abuse; and participant being shot, wounded, or raped. To assess participants' current mood and satisfaction with their current lives, they completed the Center for Epidemiological Studies Depression Scale (CES-D; Radloff, 1977) and the Quality of Life Inventory (QOLI; Frisch, Cornell, Villaneueva & Retzlaff, 1992). The CES-D is a 20-item instrument measuring depressive symptoms in the past week in non-clinical populations. The QOLI is a 34-item instrument which measures the participant's satisfaction with, and the importance of, four life domains: self, personal fulfillment, relationships and environment.

During the interview session, participants were first administered the Family Demographics & Medical History (FDMH; Segal, 1996), a structured interview developed for this project which collects data on family demographics, composition of family of origin, ethnicity, religious preference, individual medical history, and SES (Hollingshead & Redlich, 1958). Participants were then administered two subtests of the Wechsler Adult Intelligence Scale-Revised (WAIS-R; Wechsler, 1981): Vocabulary and Picture Arrangement. Vocabulary subtest scores have been found to correlate with full scale IQ and thus may be used to control statistically ALH scores for intelligence; Picture Arrangement subtest scores measure the degree to which the subject can place narrative elements in a logical order and were used for discriminant validity, since this capacity should be unrelated to mood and interpersonal expectations (Wechsler, 1981). They also were administered a modified version of the Early Memory Test (Mayman, 1968) which prompted them for their earliest memory, earliest memory of mother, and earliest memory of father.

Early Memory Coding
Participants provided recollections of their earliest memory, earliest memory of mother, and earliest memory of father. Using the Adelphi Early Memories Index (AEMI; Karliner, Westrich, Shedler & Mayman, 1996), each memory was double coded on a 5-point scale (with 1 = not applicable, 3 = somewhat applicable and 5 = highly applicable) along the following dimensions with reliability calculated by using Pearson's r with Rosenthal correction: Affect tone is positive 0.82, affect tone is negative 0.86, others are benevolent 0.86, others are malevolent 0.84, subject is confident 0.85, subject is insecure 0.87, the memory's outcome is positive 0.86, the memory's outcome is negative 0.84, caregivers are abandoning 0.81.

Once this extensive database was scored and analyzed, the results supported the developmental model of the projective and social-cognitive phases. After coding the ALH narratives for social cognitive qualities, we found that the 18-year-old women were more astute about the social aspects of their future lives: They scored higher on Psychological Complexity, Life Role Complexity, and Resolution of Conflicts (Segal, DeMeis, Wood & Smith, 2001). In keeping with this theory that the social cognitive mode supersedes the projective, none of the variables from early childhood – early life events, early memories of father or mother – had any impact on these scores. Even the current mood and quality of life satisfaction scores was divorced from the ways our participants imagined the social and psychological quality of their future lives.

Findings with the clinical scales were nearly mirror images of these. There were no gender differences on any of these measures except for Impulsivity; current mood and quality of life satisfaction correlated with high scores on ALH Depression, Fantasy Distortion, and Malevolence. Most intriguing, though, was the impact of the maternal memories. The participants were asked to describe their earliest memory, earliest of mother, and earliest of father. These memories were then scored for positive and negative qualities (see Methods below). If the participants had a negative early memory of mother, they were likely to write a narrative high on ALH Depression and Malevolence (Segal et al., 2001). This was not true for the earliest memory or earliest memory of father, which suggests that the projective coding of the ALH was tapping into the participants' earliest experiences – in particular, their memories of their mothers. We have since found this to be true with a sample of prison inmates as well as with ALH narratives written by our first cohort of participants five years after their first evaluation (manuscripts in preparation). In other words, as with other projective tests, the ALH was eliciting aspects of the Projective Phase of development.

Intergenerational Ambivalence and the Anticipated Life History

This brings us to the topic of this volume. The ALH can be used to explore the mature, conscious ambivalence that adult children feel towards their parents, as well as the more primitive ambivalence established in early childhood. As an instrument, it is sensitive to the *social cognitive ambivalence* adults express towards their parents as well as to the *projective ambivalence* which dates back to early childhood.

To select for projective ambivalence, we turned to the earliest memory of mother and earliest memory of father provided by our participants. Since the Adelphi Early Memory Index yields separate scales for negative and positive qualities for these memories, we hypothesized that participants scoring high on *both* positive and negative scales had conflicting feelings about their parents when they were children – dating back to the Projective Phase. Conversely, we hypothesized that participants demonstrating social cognitive ambivalence would be aware of their competitive feelings toward their parents as well as their need for dependence and autonomy from them, and so would include the deaths of their parents as events in their ALH narratives. Although it is possible that some participants wished for their parents to die, none openly acknowledged it. Instead, these participants seemed brave enough to face the likely prospect of outliving their parents, and this courage suggests that they have achieved a kind of mature ambivalence. Put another way, unlike the group whose early experiences are highly conflicted, this group may have worked out their dependence issues sufficiently to imagine life after their parents' death.

Results

Table 1 presents the entire ALH database, which includes differences by gender on self-report measures and the ALH Clinical and Social-Cognitive scales.

Table 2. Comparison of Testing Characteristics of Ambivalent Memories with
ALH Parental Death.

	Ambivalent Memories	ALH Parental Death	t	Prob.
N	119	73		
Female	81	53		
Male	48	20		
SES				
Upper Middle/Upper	49.7%	61.6%		
Middle	30.9%	19.2%		
Lower Middle/Lower	19.4%	19.2%		
CES-D Summary Score	37.6 (10.4)	38.12 (9.3)		
QOLI Self-regard	1.82 (3.5)	3.09 (2.9)	3.13	0.002
QOLI Romantic Relationships	80 (4.3)	1.77 (3.8)	1.92	0.056
QOLI Friendships	3.48 (3.2)	4.06 (2.5)		
QOLI Family	2.30 (3.0)	3.29 (2.8)	−2.17	0.031
QOLI Summary Score	2.20 (1.5)	2.57 (1.49)	1.96	0.051
ALH Total Word Count	431 (181)	526 (129)	−2.94	0.014
ALH Clinical Scales				
ALH Narrative Integrity	3.64 (0.61)	3.68 (0.53)		
ALH Depression	1.53 (0.87)	1.75 (1.43)	−1.97	0.05
ALH Fantasy Distortion	2.43 (1.2)	2.79 (1.05)	2.78	0.006
ALH Impulsivity	1.33 (0.69)	1.40 (0.75)		
ALH Malevolence	1.13 (0.51)	1.19 (0.64)		
ALH Social Cognitive Scales				
ALH Psychological Complexity	1.55 (0.79)	1.74 (0.76)	−1.81	0.071
ALH Life Role Complexity	1.60 (0.72)	1.84 (0.83)	−2.03	0.044
ALH Mutuality of Relationships	1.44 (0.66)	1.58 (0.71)		
ALH Resolution of Conflicts	1.36 (0.59)	1.60 (0.74)	−2.49	0.014
ALH Altruism	1.54 (0.81)	1.44 (0.71)		

Note: Eight participants who scored on both variables were removed from these comparisons.

Table 2 compares 119 participants with Ambivalent Memories, those we consider expressing "projective ambivalence." This group includes 73 participants who mention the death of at least one parent in their ALH, which we consider expressing "social-cognitive ambivalence." As predicted, there was little overlap between them with only eight participants being dropped from the analysis. The Parental Death participants wrote ALH narratives which were longer, included more

Table 3. Correlations Among Ambivalent Memories, ALH Parental Death, and Self-Report Measures.

Variables	1	2	3	4	5	6	7
1. Ambivalent Memories	–	0.05	0.07	-0.19^{**}	-0.13^{*}	-0.10	-0.13^{*}
2. ALH Parental Death			0.06	0.01	0.00	0.00	-0.07
3. CESD Summary Score				-0.52^{**}	-0.33^{**}	-0.40^{**}	-0.53^{**}
4. QOLI Self-Regard					0.30^{**}	0.33	0.65^{**}
5. QOLI Romantic Relationships						0.18^{**}	0.50^{**}
6. QOLI Friendships							0.48^{**}
7. QOLI Summary Score							

$^{*}p \leq 0.05.$
$^{**}p \leq 0.01.$

depressive themes and fantasy elements than the Ambivalent Memory group. This may be an effect primarily of ALH length – the more you write, the more opportunities for fantasy and sad events. What confirms our hypotheses, however, is that they score consistently higher on all the social cognitive measures, with significant differences for Life Role Complexity, Psychological Complexity, and Resolution of Conflicts. They also score higher on the nearly all of the Quality of Life Satisfaction subscales.

Table 3 shows that the Ambivalent Memories participants are feeling less satisfied with the quality of their lives. Since higher scores on the QOLI subscales and summary score indicate greater satisfaction, the negative correlations indicate that people in this group have lower self-regard, less satisfaction with romantic relationships, and lower overall satisfaction with the quality of their lives. This is not true of the Parental Death participants, offering further evidence that these are separate groups. Table 4 shows that the Ambivalent Memory group scores high on ALH Fantasy Distortion and ALH Altruism, but lower on ALH Mutuality. Note that the Parental Death group correlates with ALH Life Role Complexity and ALH Resolution of Conflicts.

Finally, Table 5 explores the findings from Table 4 with hierarchical regression model with ALH length, participant SES, sex, IQ, current depression and negative early life experiences (NEGLIFE) as independent variables. Ambivalent Memories remains a significant positive predictor for ALH Depression and ALH Altruism, and a significant negative predictor for ALH Mutuality. Regression analyses were performed using Parental Death as a predictor with all of the ALH scales as dependent variables: There were no significant results.

Table 4. Correlations Among Ambivalent Memories, ALH Parental Death, and ALH Clinical & Social Cognitive Scores.

Variables	1	2	3	4	5	6	7	8	9	10	11	12
1. Ambivalent Memories	—	0.06	0.02	0.09	14*	0.02	-0.02	0.0	0.04	-0.14*	0.05	0.15**
2. ALH Parental Death			0.04	0.18**	24**	-0.02	0.07	0.09	0.15**	0.02	0.13**	0.01
3. ALH Narrative Integrity				-0.02	0.09	-0.27**	-0.02	0.11*	0.27**	0.19**	0.19**	0.12*
4. ALH Depression					0.31**	0.23**	0.43**	0.19**	-0.05	0.01	0.20**	-0.02
5. ALH Fantasy Distortion						11**	0.24*	-0.01	-0.02	-0.05	0.15**	0.13*
6. ALH Impulsivity							0.24**	-0.03	-21**	-0.15**	-0.02	-0.08
7. ALH Malevolence								0.09	-0.02	0.02	0.04	0.02
8. ALH Psychological Complexity									0.17**	0.25**	0.37**	0.06
9. ALH Life Role Complexity										0.32**	0.38**	0.11*
10. ALH Mutuality of Relationships											0.0**	0.17**
11. ALH Resolution of Conflicts												0.09
12. ALH Altruism												—

*$p \leq 0.05$.
**$p \leq 0.01$.

Table 5. Hierarchical Regressions of Ambivalent Memories on ALH Scores.

Dependent Variable	Predictor Variables	R	β	βSE	R^2	Probability
ALH Depression	ALH Count	0.15	0.14	0.00	0.01	ns
	SES	0.27	0.16	0.06	0.04	ns
	IQ	0.26	−0.08	0.01	0.04	ns
	SEX	0.26	0.06	0.14	0.04	ns
	CES-D	0.30	0.13	0.01	0.05	ns
	NEGLIFE	0.30	0.05	0.01	0.05	ns
	Ambivalent Memories	0.35	0.18	0.01	0.07	0.04
ALH Mutuality	ALH Count	0.36	0.00	0.35	0.13	0.000
	SES	0.39	0.05	−0.13	0.13	ns
	IQ	0.39	0.01	0.08	0.13	ns
	SEX	0.39	0.11	−0.01	0.12	ns
	CES-D	0.42	0.01	0.14	0.14	ns
	NEGLIFE	0.42	0.02	0.06	0.14	ns
	Ambivalent Memories	0.49	0.01	−0.25	0.20	0.003
ALH Altruism	ALH Count	0.18	0.17	0.00	0.03	ns
	SES	0.20	−0.09	0.05	0.02	ns
	IQ	0.22	0.08	0.00	0.02	ns
	SEX	0.23	−0.06	0.11	0.02	ns
	CES-D	0.24	−0.09	0.01	0.02	ns
	NEGLIFE	0.24	0.02	0.02	0.01	ns
	Ambivalent Memories	0.35	0.26	0.01	0.07	0.004

Note: Beta refers to the final-step beta weights; *r* values are additive.

Discussion

Before this study, research with the Anticipated Life History instrument had already shown that early memories, and early life events, influence the act of imagining one's future. And since other projectives are similarly sensitive to early experience, including the Narrative Completion Test which explicitly asks participants to make up stories (Segal, Vizueta, Biuckians & Pollak, 2003), it is safe to take the next conceptual leap: that the cognitive act of imagining, of creating a narrative that has not happened, necessarily activates the neural network of early events. This explains why fiction writers, who "dream up" plots and characters, seem to rework the same themes over and over, revisiting what Henry James liked to call the same "scene." (Some famous examples include Shakespeare's fathers who cannot let their daughters, and Mark Twain's characters considered dead by their townsfolk but who are really alive.) This is not to say that early experience dictates the form and content of imaginative work; rather, early experience emits a signal that finds its way into the projected material. At the risk of being whimsical, the act of imagining is much like taking a piece of bread and dragging it through the gravy on your plate; like gravy, the neural network, and the Projective Phase it generates, inevitably seep into the created fiction, giving it flavor and richness.

Of course, the act of imagining is not the only event that evokes feelings and conflicts which formed our projections when we were young. Visiting our parents as adults evokes those early feelings even more strongly. The woman who still feels put down like a child by her mother is not simply "regressing," to use the slang of clinicians. Instead, seeing her mother evokes the neural network of early events which in turn surfaces the projections so troubling when she was a girl.

The findings from this study support the theory that the Projective Phase of development, dominant in early childhood, is followed by a more culturally determined, Social Cognitive Phase. From a database of nearly 400 people, two distinct groups were selected based on their early memories and future life narratives. The people in the first group, whose earliest parental memories were scored high for both negative and positive qualities, were assumed to be individuals whose early experiences of their parents were full of conflict – the Projective Ambivalence group. If so, then their early projections should have been marked by anxiety, depressed mood, and a sense of helplessness; it is these projections, then, which should inform the quality of their Anticipated Life Histories. Furthermore, the turbulence generated by their early experience should make their use of social-cognitive skills less effective. The group of people who mentioned the death of their parents in the ALH narratives, the Social-Cognitive Ambivalence group, were assumed to be those whose imagining of the future was less influenced by their Projective Phase and who were more able to make use of social-cognitive skills.

Our findings met many of these expectations. First, the members of the Projective Ambivalence group are not doing as well as the Social-Cognitive group. They are less satisfied with themselves, with their friendships and romantic relationships, and with the quality of their lives in general. Moreover, they wrote ALH narratives that were lower in social-cognitive qualities, such as Psychological Complexity, Life Role Complexity, and Resolution of Conflicts. Finally, simply belonging to the Projective group predicted elevated scores of ALH Depression in the regression models.

Conversely, people in the Social Cognitive group are feeling better about themselves and their lives, and they are making better use of social-cognitive skills. They do score higher on ALH Depression and Fantasy Distortion, but perhaps this is because they are more willing to imagine the deaths of their parents as well as other more negative events more realistically than their counterparts. When controlling for other variables, their early memories do *not* predict ALH

Depression, suggesting that the source of the depressive themes does not stem from their early childhood.

CONCLUSION

I hope these data offer empirical evidence for something most of us have experienced without being able to explain fully: Being with our parents can be satisfying or boring, joyful or depressing, but there is often a divided quality. It may seem as though psychologically one foot is in the past, the other in the present. For those whose early experiences with their parents reflected a secure loving attachment, that double quality may be a pleasant echo, a subtext or ghost of early trust. For others depending, frankly, on how bad or troubled it was, the echo can be so loud as to drown out the real conversation in the present. So many of us have known friends who cannot do anything but take whatever their parents say as an insult or put-down. For them, the social-cognitive ways of thinking are of no use to them when they go home.

These data also suggest that a retrospective approach to exploring aspects of intergenerational relationships can be fruitful, despite complaints that early memories are hard to verify. This criticism misses the point. Early memories are neither fully true or simply fantasy; rather, they are a dreamlike impression of our first years which follow us from childhood and persist among the other perceptions and filters through which we construct our interpersonal reality. In this study, they provide a window on a key feature of child-parent ambivalence: Early memories exert the pressure on us to be and experience ourselves as adult *children* by virtue of their power to convey the burden of early trauma or the freedom of secure attachment; it is our later capacity for perspective-taking and empathy which gives us the strength to be *adult* children.

Let's now return to the clinical vignette which opened this chapter. The young man's early relationship with his parents was marked by conflict and anxiety. When he grew up and had to face his own wishes to succeed, he suffered from mild depression and a diminished sense of himself, especially when confronted with authority figures in his life, such as his academic advisor. And he felt uneasy and "not himself" when visiting with his parents. To apply our model, the neural network of interpersonal events had been formed in part by his turbulent relationship with his parents, and that turbulence made itself felt in the way he experienced them as an adult. Thankfully, psychotherapy helped to make conscious those early events, and he found a way of making contact with his father – a strategy which seemed to permit them to be close, finally. By understanding his early projections, his *projective ambivalence* gave way to a more mature, *social-cognitive ambivalence*, which allowed him to see his father for who he is, while remembering and experiencing the resonant memories of who he had been.

REFERENCES

Allison, J. B., Blatt, S. J., & Zimet, C. N. (1968). *The interpretation of psychological tests.* New York: Harper & Row.

Beck, A. T. (1975). *Cognitive therapy and the emotional disorders.* New York: International Universities Press.

Brenner, C. (1974). *An elementary textbook of psychoanalysis.* New York: Anchor Books.

Bromfield, R. (1997). *Playing for real: Exploring the world of child therapy and the inner worlds of children.* Northvale, NJ: Aronson.

Corrigan, R. (1982). The control of animate and inanimate components in pretend play and language. *Child Development, 53,* 1342–1353.

Fenson, L., Kagan, J., Kearsley, R. B., & Zelazo, P. R. (1976). The developmental progression of manipulative play in the first two years. *Child Development, 47*(1), 232–236.

Frisch, M. B., Cornell, J., Villaneueva, M., & Retzlaff, P. J. (1992). Clinical validation of the Quality of Life Inventory: A measure of life satisfaction for use in treatment planning and outcome assessment. *Psychological Assessment, 4,* 92–101.

Gunderson, J. (1984). *Borderline personality disorder.* Washington, DC: American Psychiatric Press.

Harris, M. J., & Beggan, J. K. (1994). Making believe: A descriptive study of fantasies in middle childhood. *Imagination, Cognition and Personality, 13,* 125–145.

Hollingshead, A. B., & Redlich, F. (1958). *Social class and mental illness.* New York: Wiley.

Holtzman, W. H., & Swartz, J. D. (1983). The Holtzman Inkblot Technique: A review of 25 years of research. *Zeitschrift für Differentielle und Diagnostische Psychologie, 4*(3), 241–259.

Johnson, S. P. (2000). The development of visual surface perception: Insights into the ontogeny of knowledge. In: C. Rovee-Collier, L. P. Lipsitt & H. Hayne (Eds), *Progress in Infancy Research* (Vol. 1, pp. 113–154). Mahwah, NJ: Erlbaum.

Karliner, R., Westrich, E.-K., Shedler, J., & Mayman, M. (1996). Bridging the gap between psycho-dynamic and scientific psychology: The Adelphi Early Memory Index. In: J. M. Masling & R. F. Bornstein (Eds), *Psychoanalytic Perspectives on Developmental Psychology.* Washington, DC: American Psychological Association.

Kruger, J., & Dunning, D. (1999). Unskilled and unaware of it: How difficulties in recognizing one's own incompetence lead to inflated self-assessments. *Journal of Personality and Social Psychology, 77,* 1121–1134.

Lüscher, K. (2002). Intergenerational ambivalence: Further steps in theory and research. *Journal of Marriage and the Family, 64,* 585–593.

Lüscher, K., & Pillemer, K. (1998). Intergenerational ambivalence: A new approach to the study of parent-child relations in later life. *Journal of Marriage and the Family, 60,* 413–425.

Main, M., Kaplan, N., & Cassidy, J. (1985). Security in infancy, childhood, and adulthood: A move to the level of representation. In: I. Bretherton & E. Walters (Eds), *Monographs of the Society for Research in Child Development: Vol. 50. Growing Points of Attachment, Theory and Research* (pp. 67–104).

Mayman, M. (1968). Early memories and character structure. *Journal of Projective Techniques and Personality Assessment, 32,* 303–316.

McAdams, D. P., Hoffman, B. J., Mansfield, E. D., & Day, R. (1996). Themes of agency and communion in significant autobiographical scenes. *Journal of Personality, 64,* 339–377.

Nigg, J. T., Lohr, N. E., Westen, D., Gold, L., & Silk, K. R. (1992). Malevolent object representations in borderline personality disorder and major depression. *Journal of Abnormal Psychology, 101,* 61–67.

Plunkett, K., Karmiloff-Smith, A., Bates, E., & Elman, J. L. (1997). Connectionism and developmental psychology. *Journal of Child Psychology and Psychiatry and Allied Disciplines, 38,* 53–80.

Radloff, L. S. (1977). The CES-D scale: A self-report depression scale for research in the general population. *Applied Psychological Measurement, 1,* 385–401.

Rodriguez, P., Wiles, J., & Elman, J. (1999). A recurrent neural network that learns to count. *Connection Science: Journal of Neural Computing, Artificial Intelligence and Cognitive Research, 11,* 5–40.

Rumelhart, D. E., Hinton, G. E., & Williams, R. J. (1986). Learning representations by back-propagating errors. *Nature, 323*(6088), 533–536.

Saffran, J. R. (2001). Words in a sea of sounds: The output of infant statistical learning. *Cognition, 81*(2), 149–169.

Savin-Williams, R., & Cohen, K. M. (Eds) (1996). *The lives of lesbians, gays and bisexuals: Children to adults.* Fort Worth, TX: Harcourt Brace.

Schaie, K. W. (1983). Can the longitudinal method be applied to the study of psychological development? In: F. J. Monks, W. W. Hartup & J. de Wit (Eds), *Determinants of Behavioral Development.* New York: Academic Press.

Segal, H. G. (1996). Family demographics and medical history, self-report version (Unpublished instrument).

Segal, H. G. (2001). Projective assessment, recurrent neural networks, and a new look at pre-latency using the Anticipated Life History measure. Paper delivered at Psychology Department, Harvard University (April 4).

Segal, H. G., DeMeis, D. K., & Wood, G. (1997). Anticipated life history qualitative scoring manual (Unpublished manuscript).

Segal, H. G., DeMeis, D. K., Wood, G. A., & Smith, H. L. (2001). Assessing future possible selves by gender and socioeconomic status using the Anticipated Life History measure. *Journal of Personality, 69*(1), 57–87.

Segal, H. G., Vizueta, N., Biuckians, A., & Pollak, K. B. (2003). The impact of early experience on the creative process: Findings from a new story completion task. *Imagination, Cognition and Personality, 21*(2), 91–109.

Segal, H. G., Westen, D., Lohr, N. E., & Silk, K. R. (1993). Clinical assessment of object relations and social cognition using stories told to the Picture Arrangement subtest of the WAIS-R. *Journal of Personality Assessment, 61*(1), 58–80.

Segal, H. G., Westen, D., Lohr, N. E., Silk, K. R. et al. (1992). Assessing object relations and social cognition in borderline personality disorders from stories told to the Picture Arrangement subtest of the WAIS-R. *Journal of Personality Disorders, 6*(4), 458–470.

Segal, H. G., Wood, G., DeMeis, D. K., & Smith, H. L. (2003). Future events, gender, gender & mental health: Clinical assessment using the anticipated life history measure. *Assessment, 10*(1), 1–12.

Singer, J. L. (1998). Imaginative play in early childhood: A foundation for adaptive emotional and cognitive development. *International Medical Journal, 5,* 93–100.

Teyber, E. (2000). *Interpersonal process in psychotherapy* (4th ed.). Belmont, CA: Brooks/Cole.

Wechsler, D. (1981). *WAIS-R manual.* New York: Harcourt Brace Jovanovich.

Westen, D., Feit, A., & Zittel, C. (1998). Methodological issues in research using projective methods. In: P. C. Kendall, J. N. Butcher & G. N. Holmbeck (Eds), *Handbook of Research Methods in Clinical Psychology* (2nd ed., pp. 224–240). New York: Wiley.

Westen, D., Lohr, N. E., Silk, K., Gold, L., & Kerber, K. (1990). Object relations and social cognition in borderlines, major depressives, and normals: A thematic apperception test analysis. *Psychological Assessment: A Journal of Consulting and Clinical Psychology, 2*, 355–364.

Wethington, E., & Kessler, R. C. (1986). Perceived support, received support, and adjustment to stressful life. *Journal of Health and Social Behavior, 27*(1), 78–89.

Woike, B. A. (1994). The use of differentiation and integration processes: Empirical studies of "separate" and "connected" ways of thinking. *Journal of Personality and Social Psychology, 67*, 142–150.

ABOUT THE AUTHORS

Pauline Boss is Professor, Department of Family Social Science, University of Minnesota; and a family therapist in private practice. Her research interests are in the area of family stress, specifically when there is ambiguous loss or boundary ambiguity in families. Her research has included various types of ambiguous loss ranging from loved ones physically missing after war or terrorism, to those psychologically missing due to Alzheimer's disease or other chronic mental illnesses.

Bertram J. Cohler is Professor, the Committee on Human Development, the College, and the Departments of Psychology and Psychiatry at the University of Chicago. His research interests include study of continuity and change across the course of adult lives, the family, narrative and writing the life story, social change and sexual identity, and the study of nostalgia in personal and popular memory.

Frank Fincham is a Distinguished Professor and Director of Clinical Training at University at Buffalo. His interests include forgiveness, cognition in relationships, and the impact of interparental conflict on children.

Karen Fingerman is Associate Professor and Berner Hanley University Scholar at Purdue University. Her research focuses on positive and negative emotions in relationships. Her work has examined mothers and daughters, grandparents and grandchildren, friends, acquaintances, and peripheral social ties.

Elizabeth Hay is a Doctoral Student in Human Development and Family Studies at the Pennsylvania State University. She is interested in intergenerational relationships and how they contribute to health and well-being throughout adulthood.

Lori Kaplan is an Assistant Professor of Neurology at the Rush Alzheimer's Disease Center in Chicago, Illinois. Her research focuses on family systems and relationships across the life cycle. She has published articles on child custody arrangements after divorce, chronic illness and its effects on family relationships, and family caregiving to an elder with Alzheimer's disease.

David M. Klein is Associate Professor of Sociology and Director of Graduate Studies at the University of Notre Dame. His current research interests include intergenerational relations, romantic relationship formation, and the sociology of science with an emphasis on the development of theoretical and methodological perspectives in the family sciences.

Frieder R. Lang is Professor of Human Development at Martin Luther University Halle-Wittenberg, Germany. His research interests are processes and mechanisms of the development of social and family ties over the life course, motivational psychology of human development and successful aging.

Frank Lettke is Assistant Professor in the department of History and Sociology at the Universität Konstanz (Germany), Fachbereich Geschichte und Soziologie and directs the Research Center "Family and Society." He is interested in intergenerational relations and the diversity of family forms. His current research focuses on family relationships in the context of inheritance.

Dagmar Lorenz-Meyer is Assistant Professor of Gender Studies at Charles University, Prague, Czech Republic. Her research interests include institutional and practical arrangements of intergenerational relations, and gender equality in the enlargement process of the European Union.

Kurt Lüscher, Ph.D., held a chair in Sociology at the Universität Konstanz (Germany), Fachbereich Geschichte und Soziologie until 2000, where he was also director of the research center on "Society and Family" (he is now professor emeritus). He has longstanding research interests in the family, the life course, and intergenerational relations. He has also worked extensively in the areas of socialization, child and family policy, and the relationship between family and the legal system.

Greg Maio is a Reader in Psychology at Cardiff University. His research interests include attitudinal ambivalence, attitude change, relationships, and social values.

Francesca Giorgia Paleari is Lecturer at Catholic University of Milano, Italy. Her research interests include family relationships, forgiving, and research methodology.

Karl Pillemer is Professor of Human Development at Cornell University, where he also directs the Cornell Gerontology Research Institute. His research interests include the impact of life course transitions on family relationships, the causes and consequences of parent-child relationship quality, and the interaction between families and community institutions.

Andrejs Plakans is Professor and Chair of the Department of History at Iowa State University, Ames, Iowa; and editor of *The History of the Family: An International Quarterly* (Elsevier). His research interests focus on post-1800 eastern Europe, and include historical demography, rural family structures, and kinship.

Camillo Regalia is Professor of Social Psychology at Catholic University of Milano, Italy. His research interests include family relationships, self-efficacy beliefs and forgiving.

Harry Segal is Senior Lecturer in the Departments of Psychology and Human Development at Cornell University, Ithaca, USA. His research interests include the clinical assessment of narrative, the implicit processes involved in the imagination, computational modeling of early experience, and the cognitive-affective aspects of transition from early to mid-childhood.

AUTHOR INDEX

343

SUBJECT INDEX

communication, as a coping strategy in
close-kin relationships, 246
Contextual Family Stress Model, 220
coresidential patterns, in premodern
Europe, 65

daughters and ambivalence, 164
dementia, and parent-child ambivalence,
207–222
developmental stake. *See* "generational
stake hypothesis"
Draw-a-Person, 320

evaluative cognitive inconsistency, 291

factor analysis, 98, 108, 165, 177
family boundaries, 213, 214
family stress theory, 208, 213
father-child ambivalence, 130, 146, 290,
293, 302, 303, 308
as a predictor of attachment strength,
130, 293, 302, 303, 308
fathers and ambivalence, 164
filial relationship styles, and adult-child
satisfaction, 196, 197, 196t
and parent-child contact, 197, 198, 198f
and the heuristic model of
intergenerational ambivalence, 199,
200
dyadic analysis of, 195, 196, 196t
as a function of gender, 201
statistical analysis of, 193–198
filial task, defined, 183, 184
focus group discussions, 118

"generational stake" hypothesis, 162, 165
Griffin formula, 97, 99t,163n, 163

hierarchical cluster analysis, 193, 194
hierarchical regression model, 333t

indirect ambivalence score, calculating, 96,
97
inheritance, in premodern Europe, 76–79
instrumentality, as a dimension of
parent-child relationships, 187–189
intergenerational ambivalence, survey of
methodological approaches, 85–110

intergenerational relationships, cultural
patterns governing, 51
in premodern Europe, 63–80

Kahn and Antonucci diagram, 139, 140,
190, 191
evaluation of data from, 140, 141
Konstanz model of intergenerational
ambivalence, 47–53, 155, 168, 169,
199, 200, 228, 249
used to analyze the management of
ambivalence, 241–244
visualized as a circumplex model, 51f
Konstanz project, 172

Likert scale, 161, 165

Mannheim's theory of generations, 43
marriage patterns, in premodern Europe, 65
Midlife Development Inventory, 121
Minnesota Multiphasic Personality
Inventory, 320
mother-child ambivalence, 115–130
correlated with other variables,
125–127, 126t
indirect assessment of, 124
statistical analysis of, 122–128

Narrative Completion Test, 321
non-communication, as a coping strategy
in close-kin relationships, 244–246,
249, 250
Norton's Quality of Marriage Index, 301

OASIS study, 101
open-ended measures, 295
operationalization, defined, 39, 40

parent-child ambivalence, 6, 89–110,
153–179
ability to tolerate, 227
and "coming-out" experiences, 255–277
and gender roles, 228
and its effect on ALH test scores,
328–333, 330t, 331t
and other social ties, 147
and perceived need for autonomy, 260
and socialization, 262

romantic relationships, ambivalence and
  attachment in, 300, 301, 308
Rorschach Inkblot Test, 320, 321

sampling, 117, 139, 155–157, 157t,
  229
Sentence Completion Test, 320
social-cognitive ambivalence, 330, 334,
  335
social-cognitive phase, 317, 318, 329, 334
social constructionism, 216
social desirability response sets, 104, 108
socialization, reciprocal, 262
solidarity, intergenerational, 5, 6
sons, and ambivalence, 162, 164, 166
split-half technique of cluster analysis,
  193, 194, 193t
Status Passages and Risk in the Life
  Course (study facility, Bremen
  University), 229

stepfamilies, 109
  in premodern Europe, 70–73
stigma, 261
Survey Center Mannheim. *See* ZUMA

T-transformed scores, 190–192
telephone survey, 155
Thematic Apperception Test, 320, 321
theme-centered analysis, 230
Transcoop Program of the Alexander
  Humboldt Foundation, 3

"uncovering," as a research strategy, 54,
  154, 157, 170, 172
"unfolding of consciousness" (Erdelyi),
  215

Ward algorithm, 193

ZUMA (Survey Center Mannheim), 156

Set up a Continuation Order Today!

Did you know you can set up a continuation order on all JAI series and have each new volume sent directly to you upon publication. For details on how to set up a continuation order contact your nearest regional sales office listed below.

To view related **Sociology** series

visit

www.socscinet.com/sociology

30% Discount for Authors on all Books!

A 30% discount is available to Elsevier book and journal contributors **ON ALL BOOKS** plus standalone **CD-ROMS** except multi-volume reference works. To claim your discount, full payment is required with your order, which must be sent directly to the publisher at the nearest regional sales office listed below.

ELSEVIER REGIONAL SALES OFFICES